THE POWELL EXPEDITION

THE POWELL EXPEDITION

NEW DISCOVERIES
ABOUT JOHN WESLEY POWELL'S
1869 RIVER JOURNEY

DON LAGO

UNIVERSITY OF NEVADA PRESS *Reno & Las Vegas*

University of Nevada Press | Reno, Nevada 89557 USA
www.unpress.nevada.edu
Copyright © 2018 by University of Nevada Press
All rights reserved
Cover photographs courtesy of Grand Canyon National Park Museum Collection
Cover design by Rebecca Lown

LIBRARY OF CONGRESS CATALOGING-IN-PUBLICATION DATA
Names: Lago, Don, 1956– author.
Title: The Powell Expedition : new discoveries about John Wesley Powell's 1869 river journey /
    by Don Lago.
Other titles: New discoveries about John Wesley Powell's 1869 river journey
Description: Reno : University of Nevada Press, [2017] | Includes bibliographical references
    and index. |
Identifiers: LCCN 2017009458 (print) | LCCN 2017014914 (e-book) |
    ISBN 978-1-943859-43-6 (cloth : alk. paper) | ISBN 978-0-87417-599-8 (e-book)
Subjects: LCSH: Colorado River (Colo.-Mexico)—Discovery and exploration. | Colorado River
    (Colo.-Mexico)—Description and travel. | Grand Canyon (Ariz.)—Discovery and explora-
    tion. | Powell, John Wesley, 1834–1902—Travel—Colorado River (Colo.-Mexico) | White,
    James, 1837–1927—Travel—Colorado River (Colo.-Mexico) | Howland, —Travel—Colorado
    River (Colo.-Mexico) | Howland, Oramel—Travel—Colorado River (Colo.-Mexico) |
    Sumner, John Colton—Travel—Colorado River (Colo.-Mexico) | Explorers—Colorado River
    (Colo.-Mexico)—Biography.
Classification: LCC F788 .L3373 2017 (print) | LCC F788 (e-book) | DDC 979.1/3—dc23
LC record available at https://lccn.loc.gov/2017009458

22 21 20 19 18   6 5 4 3 2

Manufactured in the United States of America

Contents

Part III: John Wesley Powell

Part IV: Naming Names

Part V: The End of the Adventure

Part VI: The Fate of the Howland Brothers and William Dunn

Illustrations

Introduction

John Wesley Powell's 1869 expedition down the Green and Colorado Rivers and through the Grand Canyon is one of the few feats of American exploration that ranks with the Lewis and Clark expedition and the Apollo landings on the moon. In terms of sheer life-and-death struggle in a dramatic landscape, the Powell expedition might be the most dramatic story of them all. As America's frontier era has grown smaller in our national rearview mirror, many of our frontier heroes have shrunk, too, mainly because those heroes were agents of Manifest Destiny who viewed the land, wildlife, and Native Americans as obstacles to conquer and resources to exploit. Powell, however, has gained stature over time. Powell was first of all a scientist with a deep curiosity about nature, and this curiosity motivated his explorations. Because Powell viewed the landscape and waterscape as a scientist, he realized that the arid West couldn't fit into America's Manifest Destiny dreams, and thus he became a pioneering conservationist. As one of the founders of the U.S. Bureau of Ethnology in 1879, Powell studied Native American life with much more respect than most of his contemporaries. In recent decades millions of Americans have taken up river running and have appointed Powell one of the patron saints of river runners. For these reasons and more, interest in Powell has been growing, generating some valuable books about him and his expedition.

A century ago Robert Stanton, who led the next expedition down the Colorado River after Powell's, wrote a long book on Colorado River history—in fact, it was so long no publisher wanted it. Stanton's first words in his book were, "Why another book on the Colorado River?"[1] If Stanton already believed he had to justify his Colorado River history book, then it's only fair that readers today, after a century of additional books, should ask if there can be any new discoveries about it, or at least discoveries of any significance.

The answer is "Yes," a surprisingly strong "Yes." There are enough new discoveries to substantially rewrite the story of the Powell expedition.

This book had a simple beginning. Books about the Powell expedition didn't say much about his crewmember William Hawkins except that he was

John Wesley Powell, December 1869, a few months
after his first river expedition. Photo courtesy of Grand
Canyon National Park Museum Collection.

from Missouri. I am also from Missouri, and so was curious to know more
of Hawkins's story. Was he from my own neighborhood? How did he come
to join the Powell expedition? As I looked into Hawkins's story, I was startled
to discover a case of mistaken identity: the guy in the history books was the
wrong guy. Back in the 1940s Powell's first major biographer, William Culp
Darrah, had looked for Hawkins but latched onto the Civil War record of
someone else and put him into the history books, with the wrong birthdate,
wrong birthplace, wrong family, wrong military record, even the wrong name.
All subsequent historians had simply copied Darrah's homework, not looking
into original sources, and perpetuated his mistake. Looking further, I found
that some of Darrah's other statements about Hawkins had no source in the
historical record, and in fact the record contradicted them. Darrah had portrayed Hawkins as a criminal, a fugitive, a liar, a shady character. Again, subsequent historians had simply repeated Darrah's image. Yet when I looked into
the sources, it appeared that Darrah had twisted some evidence and fabricated

other claims. His motives were not hard to guess: In his later years Hawkins had written two strong denunciations of Powell's leadership of the expedition. Darrah greatly admired Powell and wanted to defend his reputation, so he was eager to discredit Hawkins, to the point of dishonesty. I was to discover that this was only one of several times Darrah cooked the books to make Powell look better in his book.

The biographies of most of the other crewmembers were also skimpy, and I became curious about them, too. I soon found that they also had untold stories—important stories. I found documents about them, and also found their living families. Historians had never located, and hardly tried to find, the families of Oramel and Seneca Howland and William Dunn, who left the expedition near the end and left us with two big controversies: why they left and why they disappeared without a trace. All along, for a century and a half, the Howland and Dunn families had passed from one generation to the next letters, photos, family memories, and documents about their ancestors. Such discoveries not only told the stories of the crewmembers, but also began to suggest new explanations for some of the events of the expedition. Powell's crew included two of the most famous names in America in the 1860s: Howland and Sumner. The Howlands were a *Mayflower* family, whose early start in America helped them to become very successful and rich. The Sumners included one of America's most powerful politicians. When I learned more about Howland family history and placed the Powell expedition within its context, I saw new reasons why the Howland brothers might have decided to leave the expedition. When I learned more about Sumner family history, I saw a new reason why Jack Sumner might have decided *not* to leave the expedition. The background stories of William Hawkins and Bill Dunn also offered new hints about their decisions about leaving or not leaving the expedition.

Historians have neglected the crewmembers, and some other important stories, because most were drawn to this subject out of admiration for John Wesley Powell. Like scientists who rely on paradigms to organize data into a coherent story, historians often start out accepting some basic stories, some assumptions about what happened or what events mean. Powell historians assumed that Powell was the whole story, that his crewmembers were peripheral characters: it hardly mattered who they were, where they were from, or what their motives were. Thus, historians' research agendas were centered on Powell. Even historians who were inclined to debunking, such as Otis—better known as Dock—Marston, nevertheless remained Powell-centric in their research agendas. Historians for whom Powell was a personal hero, especially Darrah and Wallace Stegner, were eager to defend Powell from the written criticisms of crewmembers Hawkins and Sumner and the implied criticism of the Howland brothers and Bill Dunn, whose abandonment of the trip could be taken as as a sign of their dissatisfaction with Powell's leadership. Thus Darrah and Stegner were downright eager to ignore Hawkins and Sumner. But at least Hawkins and Sumner got their names on the Powell Memorial on the canyon South Rim in Grand Canyon National Park. Other Powell admirers, especially Frederick Dellenbaugh, who was the chronicler of his second expedition, made sure that the Howland brothers and Bill Dunn were branded as deserters and that their names were left off the memorial.

Another factor in focusing research on Powell was that two of Powell's biographers, Wallace Stegner and Donald Worster, were environmental historians—and very important ones—who were mainly interested in Powell the environmental prophet. Both Stegner and Worster did good jobs of placing Powell within the context of his times. Yet neither was nearly as interested in Powell the river explorer; for them the river expedition was just the prelude to the more important story. Biographical details about Powell's crewmembers were largely irrelevant to their purposes. For information about the crew, Stegner, Worster, and other historians relied heavily on Darrah's research. We do owe Darrah a large debt, for in the 1940s, when people who had personally known Powell and his crew were dying out, Darrah amassed a valuable collection of documents. Yet Darrah had his own agenda. In the course of this book, we will explore some interesting cases in historiography, of how history gets written. For instance, another historian perpetrated a hoax regarding the fate of the Howland brothers and Bill Dunn.

I also dug deeper into Powell's story and came up with several important stories that had gone unnoticed. I visited archives and checked out leads no one had thought to explore, found documents that cast new light on various elements of the expedition, and made new connections between people and events. Some of these connections came from placing the Powell expedition in the context of the social, political, and cultural forces of his time. The Powell expedition did not take place in a vacuum, but was embedded in historical currents often as strong as the river currents that propelled their boats.

This book includes several parts. Part I takes a deep look into one of the longstanding controversies of Colorado River history: Was John Wesley Powell really the first person to go through the Grand Canyon? In 1867 a battered man named James White showed up on a crude raft downriver from the canyon. Ever since, people have debated whether he could or could not, did or did not make it through the canyon. White's own testimony was vague enough that people can make a plausible case either way. Most of this debate has taken place in a vacuum, with insufficient facts for a foundation. In an archive no one else checked, I located a U.S. Army document that gives an authoritative account of one part of White's story to which we can compare White's version of events. I also look deeper into some of the other elements of his story. Powell's fame has always been tangled up with the James White mystery, so it is appropriate that a book on Powell begins with White.

The heart of this book consists of the chapters on the crewmembers. In a symbolic reversal of the usual pattern of Powell books, I have placed these chapters in part II, before the chapters on Powell. Part III covers Powell, and part IV is on the origins of some of the names the expedition gave to one of their boats, and to a canyon. Part V is on the ending of the expedition, which was recorded by two outsiders, and on the fate of one of the boats.

Finally, part VI offers a deeper exploration of another of the longstanding mysteries and controversies about the expedition: the fate of the Howland brothers and Bill Dunn. I examine the two leading theories of what happened to them. Here, too, there are important new documents and facts to consider. When we explore the life of William Hawkins after the expedition, it casts a startling new light on his claim, totally ignored by Powell historians, that he buried the bodies of his crewmembers. The Howland brothers had another brother who conducted a private investigation into the fate of his brothers, and his correspondence with Mormon leaders has remained in Howland family hands, unknown until now. In exploring the political events and contexts of southern Utah in 1869, we find and follow a scenario that has not been imagined before.

This book consists of what's new in the history of the first (1869) Powell expedition: new documents, new background facts and stories, new historical contexts, new connections between facts, new scenarios. I have not pursued the second Powell expedition of 1871–72. This book is neither a biography of John Wesley Powell nor a play-by-play account of the Powell expedition. Readers need not have a deep knowledge of either, although it would be advantageous. For those entirely unfamiliar with the expedition, I will offer a brief summary to end this introduction. For those readers, this book can still serve as a good introduction to the expedition's personalities, events, and controversies. I explore some of those matters thoroughly, though for other matters I focus mainly on what is new. Most of the chapters are self-contained stories, some of which are quite improbable and rather entertaining. In a few chapters

I simply present new documents, with an explanation of their importance. While this book does not offer a thorough retelling of the Powell expedition, it does rewrite that story considerably.

Though this book emphasizes the crewmembers, it does not offer much about three of them, for this book is also about new discoveries and I was not able to find much new material about crewmembers Walter Powell, George Bradley, and Frank Goodman. I tried to find out more about Walter Powell's mental instability, which eventually led to his commitment in St. Elizabeth's Hospital in Washington, DC (then known as the Government Hospital for the Insane), but its medical records disappeared long ago. Historian and veteran river guide Michael Ghiglieri has looked energetically for further biographical information about George Bradley but found more gaps than new details, and I was not able to make further progress. Historian Vince Welch has found more about the life of Frank Goodman both before and after the expedition.

Most of the chapters of this book originally appeared in the quarterly magazines of the Grand Canyon River Guides and the Grand Canyon Historical Society. The Grand Canyon River Guide's *Boatman's Quarterly Review* has a more personal and informal style than academic history journals—to many river guides, a footnote is the sound your sandals make when walking through an echoing slot canyon. Every *Review* issue features a friendly and candid interview with a leading river figure, and this conversational style seems to have rubbed off on the other history articles, giving them the tone of an honest conversation among friends, where "honest" means having enough respect for your friends to sometimes say, "I don't know" or "Let's consider this interesting scenario." In academia such a style is considered bad form. Academic historians are trained to write like Victorian novelists—omnipotent, showing little trace of their thought processes. Yet the truth is that researching and writing history is often more of a Faulknerian exercise, involving multiple viewpoints and outright confusion. Historians might be more honest if they presented their work as an unfolding detective story, and if they were allowed to occasionally say, "Here is an interesting possibility," or "I'm really not sure about this." Thus, while I've tried to uphold academic standards for accuracy, this book occasionally retains some of the tone of an honest conversation among friends.

My research has been led by simple curiosity. I have not done my research or writing with any agenda, any need to promote anyone's reputation or to diminish anyone else's, to prove one theory or debunk another. I have followed questions to new facts, and followed new facts to new ideas, discarding old ideas when they faltered. Historians sometimes need to step beyond the safe catalog of facts and to construct scenarios that make sense of the facts, and I have done so here. At the same time, I've tried to be careful and honest about identifying when I am offering a scenario, and about whether it seems strong, tentative, or dubious. I am aware of the foolishness of starting this book by citing the shortcomings of other historians: no doubt I have made my own misconnections. I don't imagine that I have finally wrapped up some of the longstanding questions about the Powell expedition. There are undoubtedly more documents still undiscovered, more ideas to float, more possibilities around more bends. But this book does open up previously unimagined vistas and might stimulate new inquiries and new debates.

Now, to set the stage:

One of the guiding stories of the American nation is the exploration of a vast continent. Many of our greatest national heroes were explorers: Meriwether Lewis and William Clark, Daniel Boone, John C. Frémont. Many of our literary heroes were also much more adventuresome than the frilly characters of European pages: Huck Finn rafted down the river, and Ishmael sailed the ocean. Exploration became so central to American identity and energy that presidents Teddy Roosevelt and John F. Kennedy worried what would happen to us after the wilderness was gone, so one established national parks and the other aimed us at the moon.

By the 1860s most of the American continent had been mapped, and settlement was spreading outward rapidly from trails, rivers, ocean ports, and railroads. In 1869 the completion of the transcontinental railroad more than symbolized the binding together of the national quilt. Yet on May 24, only two weeks after the driving of the final ceremonial spike, right at the foot of the transcontinental railroad bridge across the Green River in Wyoming, ten men launched four boats into a thousand miles of what their leader, John Wesley Powell, rightly called "the Great Unknown." They were entering the last large unmapped region of the United States. They would encounter very few people, not even Native Americans. Americans knew that this region held a great river system, the Colorado and its tributaries, and great canyons, but they knew few details. A few people still held out hope that the Colorado would prove navigable to steamships and commerce, while others predicted that Powell would perish in waterfalls, whirlpools, boulder dams, and underground cascades. Powell couldn't be sure what he would find, but he was ready to trust his life to science, whose rising power had captivated him in his youth, derailing his father's hopes for him to become a Methodist minister. Powell had studied geology, more on his own than in classrooms, and he now taught geology and other natural sciences at Illinois Wesleyan University in Bloomington. Uniformitarian theory, which many geologists still rejected, convinced him that an ancient and powerful river like the Colorado should have steadily carved away all major obstacles and smoothed out its course, allowing boats to traverse it. The canyons of the Colorado called to him because they offered Earth's greatest cross section of geological strata, time, and processes. Powell's scientific curiosity was matched by his taste for adventure: before the Civil War he'd rowed boats down the Illinois, Ohio, and Mississippi Rivers (though some Powell historians have wondered, in the absence of any documentation, if Powell's early river trips were as extensive as he claimed). In the Battle of Shiloh, Powell had lost his right arm, which would have ended most men's adventuring, but not Powell's. Indeed, we can wonder if Powell now had something to prove. And Powell was an American citizen of the mid-1800s, very aware of the power of the explorer myth, eager to cloak himself in its heroism.

Unlike the Lewis and Clark expedition, which was sponsored by the federal government because it served the cause of national expansion, Powell's was a do-it-yourself expedition. The nation seemed to see little value in impassible rivers and stony canyons. Powell had to cobble together his funding from various sources, and his crew from men he ran into in the Rockies, men with little experience with boats, even on smooth water. In the two summers (1867 and 1868) before his river trip Powell led some of his friends and students from Bloomington to Colorado, whose natural history had barely been studied, where they explored the landscape and collected specimens. Powell began meeting the nine men who would become his river crew, mostly Civil War veterans who had become even hardier from roaming the mountains. There were Oramel Howland, a printer for Denver's *Rocky Mountain News,* and his half-brother Seneca. There were Jack Sumner, the brother-in-law of the publisher of the *Rocky Mountain News,* William Byers. There were William Hawkins and William Dunn, two mountain men who worked with Sumner at Byers's trading post at Hot Sulphur Springs. Powell added his own brother Walter, whose long imprisonment in a Confederate prisoner camp had left him emotionally raw. At Fort Bridger Powell was impressed by soldier George Bradley and got him out of the army to join his crew. At the last minute, Powell saw young Andy Hall messing about in a boat and recruited him. Finally, an English immigrant with a taste for adventure, Frank Goodman, invited himself on the trip. The crew shared Powell's sense of adventure but not his love of geology; they were hoping to make some money from trapping, maybe even from finding gold.

Powell was the first person to go down a major whitewater river for the sheer adventure of it, but he really didn't know what he was doing. His boats, with keels that kept them heading straight ahead, were not well designed for whitewater rivers, and no one on the crew knew techniques for maneuvering through the river's powerful currents, waves, and boulders. They tried to learn fast. Only two weeks into the trip they wrecked one boat in the Canyon of Lodore and lost an alarming portion of their supplies. At that point, Frank Goodman decided to leave the trip, and the psychology of the trip shifted from an adventure to a survival ordeal. To protect their boats, they dragged and lined them (that is, guided them with ropes from the shore) around most rapids, but this required exhausting labor. Onward they went, amazed by the landscapes, frightened by the rapids, damaging and repairing the boats, shredding their clothes, getting sunburned—onward through a series of canyons they named as they went: Flaming Gorge, Split Mountain, Desolation, Cataract, Labyrinth, Glen. On August 5 they entered the Grand Canyon, with some of the worst rapids yet. They were moving faster than planned, for they were not having much luck in hunting for food and were counting their disappearing rations.

We know what the men were seeing and thinking because some of the men wrote letters and diaries (which have been accurately assembled by Michael Ghiglieri in his *First Through Grand Canyon*).[2] Yet even with these sources, we've been left with some lasting uncertainties and controversies about what was happening between the men. Considering the stress they were under, it's not surprising there were tensions, but the exact nature and cause of these tensions have been debated among historians and around river camp-fires. Some argue that Powell was an incredible leader, bravely doing what few men could do, but that some of his crew were unworthy of him, cowardly and disobedient, and finally three of them deserted at what became known as Separation Rapid. Separation Rapid was indeed a difficult rapid, but historians and river runners have debated whether it was scary enough to fully account for the three men leaving. Others take their cues from the criticisms written by Hawkins and Sumner decades later—that Powell was a petty, egomaniacal tyrant whom his men tolerated until the trip was virtually done, until they finally had a chance to leave for known towns in southern Utah. The Howland brothers and Bill Dunn never had a chance to speak for themselves. Powell was gracious in speaking about them and the rest of his crew. The river expedition lifted Powell into an important career in Washington, DC, but left his surviving crew in obscurity.

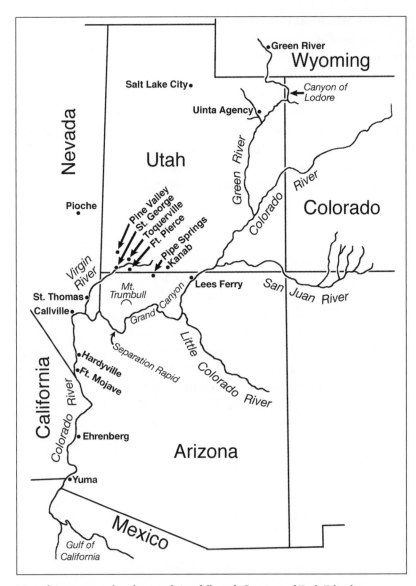

Map of river system that the expedition followed. Courtesy of Zack Zdinak.

For anyone who loves southwestern canyons, river running, American exploration, geology, Native American anthropology, or conservation visions, John Wesley Powell remains a compelling figure. Yet as with most heroes, Powell's gravity has shaped the writing of history in ways that left the story incomplete.

Like old-time mountain men sitting around campfires and entertaining themselves by telling stories, river runners have a long tradition of storytelling, which carries the danger of inflating the facts for the sake of a good story. This has sometimes created problems for historians. Some of this book consists of sorting the facts from the inflation. Yet I have sometimes presented my findings with a bit more storytelling style than might be the case for most academic history books. This is especially true for chapter 11, which uses alternating strands to weave together a surprising intersection of the Powell expedition and the Donner Party.

One procedural note: This book includes extracts from many letters and other documents from 1800s frontier America, where many people received only a limited education. Some of these letters are riddled with misspellings. Even newspaper stories from this time contain spellings that are antiquated today. Rather than loading these pages with hundreds of [*sic*] to indicate that a word is appearing in the way it was originally written, I have let the spellings stand as they were written. Where extracts contain an emphasis, such as italics or underlining, these were in the original unless indicated otherwise.

NOTES

1. Robert Brewster Stanton, *Colorado River Controversies* (New York: Dodd, Mead & Co., 1932; repr. Boulder City, NV: Westwater Books, 1982), xxxiii. Page references to 1982 ed.

2. Michael Ghiglieri (ed.), *First Through Grand Canyon: The Secret Journals and Letters of the 1869 Crew Who Explored the Green and Colorado Rivers* (Flagstaff, AZ: Puma Press, 2nd rev. ed., 2010).

The Powell Expedition

Prologue

Dreams of Rivers

PERHAPS THE MOST enduring phrase and image of the Powell expedition is "the Great Unknown." Among river runners it's become a camp ritual to bring out Powell's book and read these lines: "We are now ready to start on our way down the Great Unknown.... We have an unknown distance yet to run, an unknown river to explore. What falls there are, we know not; what rocks beset the channel, we know not; what walls rise over the river, we know not."[1]

Powell had enough sense of mythos to capitalize the words "Great Unknown." The image of brave explorers venturing into an unknown wilderness still resonates in the American imagination, even in an age when environmental consciousness and sympathy for Native Americans has deflated the sense of Manifest Destiny heroism that drove most American explorers.

For Powell, unsure of his survival, the Colorado River and its canyons were indeed seriously unknown. The geographers and natural historians of Powell's time would agree with his phrase "the Great Unknown." Yet in another sense the Colorado River wasn't such a blank slate. For many decades the American imagination had been projecting powerful images onto the Colorado River and the rest of the West, images that came from the heart of Manifest Destiny, from the conviction that Nature and Nature's God had given a vast, abundant continent to a new people for a special adventure in the history of nations. Americans looked west and saw a treasure chest of farmland, timber, wildlife, minerals, and rivers just waiting to serve American greatness. This sense of destiny generated a powerful fantasy world about western rivers, a fantasy world that drew in men as serious and smart as Thomas Jefferson, a fantasy world that remained alive right up to the time of the Powell expedition and that helped to launch it. Powell's boats were tossed not only by strong currents and waves, but also by the equally powerful clash of national dreams and natural realities. By 1869 reality had been seeping into this fantasy for decades,

Engraving from *Scribner's Monthly*, Feb. 1875. Photo courtesy of Grand Canyon National Park Museum Collection.

prompting it into a reluctant retreat. The Powell expedition would give this fantasy its *sockdolager,* a nineteenth-century slang word for *knockout punch,* a name Powell gave to one Grand Canyon rapid.

This fantasy began as not much more than a whim among early French explorers of America, but it soon grew into an obsession that would control the hands of mapmakers and the plans of presidents. The whim was that all the great rivers of western North America originated at the same source, somewhere up in "the shining mountains," an early American name for the Rocky Mountains. This source was conceived in various ways: as a gigantic lake, or as a high plateau, or as a modest mountain range. The important thing was that all these rivers were navigable—not just for canoes with expert paddlers but also for freight boats—and that river traffic could switch from one headwaters into another with little effort, making it readily possible to cross the continent by boat. The location of this common source gradually shifted, retreating as geographical knowledge advanced. In 1778 Jonathan Carver, a mapmaker who traveled no farther west than Minnesota, proposed that this common source lay just west of Minnesota; from it flowed the St. Lawrence to the Atlantic, the Mississippi to the Gulf of Mexico, the Columbia to the Pacific, and the Bourbon to Hudson Bay. As Americans got to know the upper Midwest, the common source fled westward, and the St. Lawrence was detached from it, but other rivers got attached, including the Colorado and Rio Grande and the wholly imaginary Buenaventura, which supposedly flowed across the Great Basin and all the way to San Francisco. Lewis and Clark also invented an imaginary river, the Multnomah: it started out honestly enough as the Willamette but soon reached far eastward and nearly touched the headwaters of the Rio Grande. The Multnomah endured on the map for decades. Thomas Jefferson expected Lewis and Clark to have an easy portage between the Missouri and the Columbia. Even after this portage proved to be a major ordeal, Zebulon Pike insisted that the Yellowstone, Colorado, Rio Grande, Platte, Arkansas, and Red Rivers originated in a single "grand reservoir of snows and fountains.... I have no hesitation in asserting that I can take a position in the mountains from whence I can visit the source of any of these rivers in one day." Pike was equally sure that the Colorado was the key to western access: "By the route of the Arkansas and the Rio Colorado of California, I am confident in asserting, there can be established the best communication...between the Atlantic and Pacific oceans.... The Rio Colorado is to the Gulf of California what the Mississippi is to the Gulf of Mexico."[2] William Clark himself, in his post–Lewis and Clark expedition mapmaking, still seemed enthralled by the dream of the common source, and he drew the Missouri and Yellowstone well south of their actual sources and the Rio Grande well north. Even as the "grand reservoir" got moved over the decades, mapmakers continued squeezing river headwaters close together and minimizing the mountain barriers between them. This was the way it was supposed to be. In the *Missouri Herald and St. Louis Advertiser* on March 11, 1826, William Ashley, the leading sponsor of the fur-trapping mountain men, declared that the Platte and the Buenaventura were laid out by "the Great Author of nature, in His wisdom," to provide Americans with an easy route from Missouri to California. As Americans explored the Great Basin, the Buenaventura River started to vanish, and some of Frémont's men decided that this river must exist underground, formed by some whirlpool in the center of the Great Salt Lake. Decades later, on May 20, 1869, only days before John Wesley Powell launched his expedition, the *Milwaukee Sentinel* announced, though with some skepticism, that explorer-artist George Catlin had determined that a river as mighty as the Mississippi flowed underground beneath the Rocky Mountains.

This dream of rivers was inspired by more than just a rich national fantasy life. This was still the age of rivers, before the age of railroads, when rivers dictated the location and size of cities and the success of commerce. The generation of Lewis and Clark was still in awe over what Americans had discovered in the center of their continent: a river system unlike any in the world. East Coast rivers fit the images of rivers Americans had brought from Europe, where the Thames was only two hundred miles long. But even before Lewis and Clark left St. Louis it was clear that the Ohio-Mississippi-Missouri system offered thousands of miles of navigable, barge-carrying waters, in a river system as massive as the Nile or Amazon—except that while the Nile ran through deserts and the Amazon through jungles, the Ohio-Mississippi-Missouri ran through rich agricultural plains. By 1800 Americans knew there were powerful rivers, the Columbia and Colorado, pouring off the west side of their continent, perhaps rivers as powerful as the Mississippi. Americans could not yet imagine that their continent was so vast and their mountains so extensive that even the mightiest rivers could be swallowed up, reduced to mountain creeks.

William Ashley's dream of rivers was encouraged because he was based in St. Louis at the junction of the Mississippi and the Missouri, with the wealth of a continent flowing past his window. For his mountain men trapping in the upper reaches of the Missouri River, the Colorado River took on a special fascination. They were a long way from East Coast fur shops, but it was supposed to be a much shorter distance to the Spanish Southwest. When the United

States was still an upstart frontier nation, Spain was a wealthy world empire. If there was an easy transportation route from the upper Missouri to Santa Fe, it would open up a major new market for furs. In querying Native Americans about the distance to Santa Fe, John Colter and George Drouillard, veterans of the Lewis and Clark expedition, apparently misunderstood their answers, and thus William Clark included on his 1814 map of the West a notation that it was only a few days' ride from the Bighorn Basin to the Spanish settlements—when in fact it was more than five hundred miles.

William Ashley grasped early and correctly that the beaver-rich Green River was the same river that emptied into the Gulf of California, and mountain men sometimes referred to the Green simply as the Colorado. (Later, Americans defined the Colorado as beginning at the junction of the Green and Grand Rivers, and in 1921 the Grand was rebranded as the Colorado, placing the Colorado's headwaters in the Rocky Mountains, though by some geographical standards, such as length and drainage area, the Green could be considered the main river.) In 1825 Ashley and seven men set off down the Green River in two boats. While this trip served an immediate purpose of setting up the rendezvous system that became central to the fur-trapping business, it's quite likely that Ashley was also interested in proving that the Green was a viable route to the Spanish Southwest. For several weeks Ashley worked his way downriver. Though his crew included skilled river men, they soon faced a river like none they'd ever seen—a river locked inside deep, twisting canyons, a powerful, erratic river that raced through boulder-choked rapids. Ashley's bad experiences made little impression on the nation. Nearly half a century later, when John Wesley Powell found the inscription "Ashley 1825" beside a rapid Ashley had portaged, Powell knew little about him.

The national dream of a West of river superhighways endured right up to 1869, but it went out with a flourish because of Samuel Adams. Powell historians have ridiculed Adams as a lunatic, a con artist, and a megalomaniac, and in his personal qualities Adams was certainly eccentric and brash, but you can call him crazy only if you are also willing to use the same brush on Thomas Jefferson, Lewis and Clark, Zebulon Pike, and William Ashley. Adams was merely the latest prophet of an old and still-powerful idea. In January 1867, six months before Powell first showed up in Colorado, some of Colorado's most serious leaders, including its most influential newspaper publisher, William Byers of the *Rocky Mountain News,* were listening seriously to Adams. On January 10, 1867, the *News* launched sympathetic coverage of Adams that would echo through Colorado newspapers for the next two and a half years. One of the typographers at the *News* was Oramel Howland, who would later join (and ultimately walk off) the Powell expedition, so it's possible that Howland set the type for this story and that this story helped set his expectations of what sort of river he was getting into.

> We received a call, to-day, from Hon. S. Adams, who accompanied Captain Trueworthy in his recent trip up the Colorado River [from its mouth]. From this exploration, and other facts obtained from Mormons...together with accounts given by various parties of trappers and miners who have visited the river at points above, there is abundant reason to believe that the stream is navigable into our own Territory, and most probably clear up to the mouth of Green River....
>
> Lieutenant Ives reported the navigation of the river as difficult and dangerous, encountering "roaring rapids" and almost impassible canons. Captain Trueworthy, who steamed one hundred and fifty miles further up the river than Ives' expedition, and who made the trip both at high and low stages of water, did not find any such difficulty. In the canons, rapids were encountered for a short distance in places, while between them are deep, quiet lakes, with the current running only at the rate of three to five miles per hour....
>
> The benefits that must accrue to our Territory should the river prove navigable to a point within our boundaries, which is undoubtedly the case, are incalculable. With water navigation to the Pacific on the west of our mountains, and a railway to the Atlantic, it will be an easy matter to improve our mines so that the poorest of them may be worked with immense profits....
>
> Mr. Adams goes to Golden City to-day to lay the matter of exploring the upper Colorado before our Legislature, and hopes to enlist their aid, and that of our citizens in the project. It is one of the greatest importance, and we sincerely hope our people will be alive to the fact.

On January 16, after Adams had lectured in Denver, the *News* reported it a success and added, "It is probable that the upper Colorado, like other western rivers, presents less impediment to navigation than the lower portion of the same stream. The commercial interests of the country demand that this question be brought to a satisfactory conclusion the present year." What "other western rivers" was Byers thinking of? This was another indulgence in both ignorance and fantasy. The day before, on January 15, the Central City *Weekly Miner Register* had gotten on the bandwagon: "It is now a demonstrated fact that the Colorado River is navigable for a much greater distance than the mind of man anticipated, without extensive improvements being made in the channel in the way of removing boulders, sand-bars, etc." A week later, on January 22, the *Register* reported that local citizens had formed a committee to urge the U.S. Congress to fund the exploration of the Colorado River.

Belief in a navigable Colorado River was also receiving strong support at the other end of the line, in California, which hoped that the river would enhance its reach into the continent. One guidebook published in San Francisco in 1865 declared it to be a "fact that the Colorado River is navigable to steamers, in all seasons, for six hundred miles from its mouth…. The importance of this hitherto misrepresented stream has been fully proven." The guidebook predicted that great cities would arise along "this great thoroughfare," and also great mining enterprises, and that the river would funnel the wealth of the whole West toward California.[3]

Yet Coloradans were getting to know their immediate neighborhood fairly well and weren't ready to believe things that contradicted their own experience. A few months after beating the drum for Samuel Adams, the *Register*, on August 8, 1867, rebuked Adams for going too far:

> Mr. Samuel Adams, who was here a year ago trying to enlist capital and influence to procure an exploration of the Colorado river, has written a letter which is published in the San Francisco *Times,* in which he says that the Colorado river is navigable to the point where the Union Pacific Railroad [UPRR, or U.P.R.R.] will cross it, which he says is six hundred and eighty miles from its mouth. Whether or not it is navigable for the number of miles he claims, we do not know, but we certainly do know that it is not navigable to the point where the U.P.R.R. crosses it. The railroad does not cross the Colorado at all. It only crosses the Green river, one of its branches, and that too at a distance of more than a thousand miles from the mouth of the Colorado, following the course of that stream. We further know that the Green river is not navigable, nor is the Colorado navigable for fifty miles below the junction of the Grand and Green, which forms it. This shows Mr. Adams statement entirely unreliable. We should be glad to learn that the Colorado is navigable to the point to which it has been explored from this side, but the proof of it must be better authority than the letter of Mr. Adams.

When Adams failed to win congressional support, he organized a private expedition that launched in July 1869 on the Blue River in Colorado, a branch of the Grand River, even as Powell was heading down the Green River. On July 1, 1869, the *Weekly Miner Register* reported, "Wild excitement prevails about Breckenridge over the action of Sam Adams.... Mr. A is a well known frontiersman of great experience, and it is predicted by those who know him that his undertaking will prove a success." Actually, Adams quickly wrecked his boats and abandoned his effort.

Adams had arrived in Colorado at a good moment for getting the attention of Colorado boosters. The Pike's Peak gold rush of 1859 had generated wild optimism about Colorado's golden future, but by 1867 Colorado was badly stuck. Its placer gold, easily panned by solo amateurs, was largely gone, and it was now in the hard-rock mining business, requiring enormous infrastructure, manpower, and capital. Without any railroads, transporting equipment and supplies into the mountains was very expensive. Colorado depended on East Coast investors, but after years of low profits, speculative bubbles, and outright hoaxes, many investors had called it quits. The easiest and richest mineral veins had already been tapped and the remaining lower-grade ores required a new smelting process. Throughout 1867 Colorado newspapers anxiously watched the efforts of Professor Nathaniel Hill to bring the Swansea smelting process to Colorado. In the meantime, many mining towns were idle and impoverished. Colorado still lacked statehood, limiting its power to control its own destiny. The transcontinental railroad was bypassing Colorado. Amid such frustrations, the possibility of a liquid railroad to California sounded like salvation.

William Byers was one of Colorado's leading boosters. With Colorado so dependent on outside investors and Washington politicians, he was eager to make it look good and constantly bragged about new mineral finds, booming towns, and splendid new Denver hotels. Yet Byers's local readers depended on him to give accurate accounts of rapidly changing mining, economic, and settlement trends. When Byers started his newspaper, he published a statement of principles pledging never to publish misinformation that served private interests. Before settling in Denver, Byers had been a surveyor who ranged from Omaha to Oregon; surveying was a scientific discipline all about geographical facts, not economic wishes. As a newspaperman, Byers felt conflicted between hopes and facts, between being a Colorado super-booster and being an explorer and journalist. Some of his readers, who might have lit out for a new but distant mining camp because of Byers's glowing reports about it, had decided that Byers was a humbug. Byers had enough experience of the real West that he should have suspected that Samuel Adams was a humbug. Byers was no fool about western rivers. His Hot Sulphur Springs trading post was right on the Grand River, not far below its headwaters, and it served hunters and trappers who came in from the west, who relied on horses and not boats, and who told their tales of rivers cascading through deep canyons to anyone who would listen, including trading post manager Jack Sumner, Byers's brother-in-law, who would become another of Powell's boatmen. Yet in the absence of a scientific survey of the Colorado River and its tributaries, Byers was left with decades of national myths about western rivers; when those myths coincided with Colorado's urgent economic needs, Byers was ready to be seduced by myth.

Then again, Byers *could* be a big fool about western rivers, allowing his boosterism to prevail over his geographical common sense. When he arrived in Colorado in 1859, two towns, Auraria and Denver City, were booming on either side of Cherry Creek, competing to become the dominant town. Native Americans with long memories watched with amazement as foolish whites built buildings not only in the creek's flood plain but also in the dry streambed itself. Byers needed support from both towns, so to emphasize his neutrality he built his newspaper office right in the creek bed, and he avoided using either town's name in his newspaper's name, listing his location as "Cherry Creek." In 1864 a spring flood swept away Byers's office. One of his printing presses wouldn't be found for a third of a century, buried in twelve feet of sand. We don't know if Oramel Howland was working for Byers at the time, or if he learned any lessons about the power of rivers versus the power of human desires.

Even before Byers set foot in Colorado he was already spellbound by the idea that rivers existed to serve Colorado's destiny. When the Pike's Peak gold rush started, Byers was a newspaper publisher in Omaha, where he printed a guidebook for people heading for Colorado. His was one of about thirty such guidebooks, many of them written by people who had not made the trip themselves but who cobbled together their information from travelers' tales and newspaper accounts—often wildly erroneous to begin with—and then further warped the truth by boosting their own jumping-off town and the route from it. The guidebooks often exaggerated the ease of finding gold and underestimated the time, supplies, and trouble required to get there, leading to terrible hardships. Travelers ran out of food and water in the middle of nowhere. The guidebooks often boosted routes that followed rivers like the Smoky Hill and the Republican, on which travelers depended for direction, water, food, wood, tree shade, game, and forage grasses for livestock. In his book *The Contested Plains,* historian Elliot West noted, "A few guidebooks were guilty of appalling incompetence or outright fraud. A guide by William Byers featured a map with the Smoky Hill originating about sixty miles east of the Rockies, at least fifty miles closer to the mountains than was actually the case. The Republican was shown rising even closer to Denver. It flowed from the large (but nonexistent) Lake Kansas."[4]

The Smoky Hill route was already the driest route to Colorado, so when the river disappeared fifty miles before people expected, they faced a life-and-death crisis. The Smoky Hill route became notorious for its suffering and death toll. Still, the phrase "appalling incompetence or outright fraud," which is also typical of the scorn Powell historians heaped on Samuel Adams underestimates the hypnotic power of national myth. Like everything else about the American continent, rivers were supposed to serve Manifest Destiny, and they were presumed to be patriotic unless proven otherwise.

The Pike's Peak guidebooks soon became notorious, and many were burned in the campfires of disappointed people returning east, who cursed William Byers and hung him in effigy. Yet Colorado had an urgent need for boosterism, and there Byers was amply encouraged and rewarded for his boosting, even as frustrated miners started calling him and his newspaper "The Rocky Mountain Liar," a name repeated by eastern newspapers.

Even after the derision heaped on him for his Pike's Peak guidebook, Byers fell for another dream of rivers. Back in Omaha and other Midwestern river cities, newspapers had often included reports about steamboat arrivals and departures. In an attempt to gain respectability for his newspaper and his new town, Byers began printing the shipping news for Denver's Platte River and Cherry Creek, which were navigable only by raft or canoe. According to Robert L. Perkins in *The First Hundred Years,* his generally sympathetic history of the *Rocky Mountain News,* Byers "sought to remedy this situation by sheer force of language.... Nature refused to co-operate with Byers' determination to convert the Platte into a navigable stream and Denver into a river port. He began the campaign by starting to print 'shipping news,' surely one of the most cheerful anomalies in American journalism.... A month later...Byers was still hammering away—and the Platte hadn't deepened by an inch.... Byers at last bowed to hydrology and shifted his promotional energies elsewhere."[5] Yet Byers didn't seem to learn from this experience either, and he would soon be seduced by Samuel Adams and the dream of a navigable Colorado.

It was in this fog of myth and ignorance, hope and boosterism, that John Wesley Powell arrived in the summer of 1867. Powell had the kind of scientific credentials Byers could respect, and Powell offered a real chance to get to the bottom of the river mystery. Byers became Powell's most important supporter, giving him lots of good publicity; providing him a home base, guides, and supplies for his mountain explorations; accompanying him on his first ascent of Longs Peak; providing half of his river crew; and providing more money than any other source. And it seems that for a while Byers was planning to go down the river with Powell.

Powell owed a lot to Byers, and more than he might like to admit to Samuel Adams, but most of all he was indebted to the old national dream of generous rivers. Without these dreams, the Powell expedition might not have happened. Many thought of his expedition as being a test of the Colorado's navigability. When Powell obtained some supplies from a vote of Congress in 1868, the July 17 *Montana Post* in Virginia City, Montana Territory, explained it: "Navigable or not navigable, has been the question in regard to the Upper Colorado. It is to be settled. An act of Congress authorizes the Secretary of War to issue rations to a party not to exceed 23 men, who in return are to furnish the United States government with full topographical information of the upper waters of the Colorado." It's likely that some members of Congress voted for these rations only out of hopes that the river might prove a practical highway.

What did Powell think of the idea of a navigable Colorado River? He never made this clear, and Powell historians have treated the whole idea as so silly that they did not need to ask what Powell thought of it. After the expedition, Powell was quite ready to take credit for being a daring leader through ferocious obstacles other men would not have faced or triumphed over. But as Powell was preparing for his trip, part of him, his biological survival instincts, must have hoped that the river would offer a manageable journey. If he was not already aware of the idea of an easy Colorado River before he arrived in Colorado in 1867, Byers and others surely would have soon made him aware of it. Yet Powell was a geologist, and he had a better scientific basis for judging this idea than most people. There was an opposite idea about the Colorado River that held that the river was impassible to any craft, full of waterfalls, monster whirlpools, boulder jungles, and stretches where the river ran underground. As a geologist who accepted the still-controversial idea of uniformitarianism, of an ancient Earth with steady forces at work, Powell reasoned that since the Colorado River was very old and very powerful, it should have carved away serious obstacles and smoothed out its path, at least enough to be passable. But geology also told Powell that a river that dropped thousands of feet was not going to hold placid currents, that canyons of sedimentary rock a mile deep should hold plenty of debris, some of it in the river, and that it was extremely unlikely that steamboats would ever chug through the Grand Canyon. Powell

was far less under the spell of Manifest Destiny than most of his contemporaries, as he proved when he later tried to warn the nation that the arid West
would not allow the settlement juggernaut that had triumphed farther east.
But Powell hadn't yet figured this out when he was planning his river trip, and
he was a man of his times, for whom the idea of exploring the Great Unknown
rang with national heroism. It's never been clear exactly when and why Powell
decided to go down the Green and Colorado Rivers. Yet long before Powell was
born, national mythology had decided that someone would do it. When Powell
came under the influence of William Byers, a vague mythic imperative soon
turned into an immediate possibility and necessity.

Powell met genuine mountain men in his two summers in the Rockies,
and it's not likely they endorsed Byers's hopes for the Colorado River. For all
their tall and wildly exaggerated tales, sometimes the mountain men did know
exactly what they were talking about. When Powell visited Byers's Hot Sulphur
Springs in 1867, one of his companions was George Platt, an artist from Rock
Island, Illinois, whom Powell hired to record his summer's natural history
work. Platt wrote a series of letters to the Rock Island newspaper, *The Evening
Argus,* including the following from a letter on August 28, 1867:

> While here I met with several trappers and hunters who had roved
> long and far over these western wilds, and, while we were gathered
> around our fires at night listening to their several stories, I was re-
> minded of the wild tales of Cooper and other compilers of romantic
> and thrilling adventures. Many strange stories were told about the
> river which ran before us—of deep-cut canyons, roaring torrents,
> and of the wild, mythical land...[and] of those who had attempted to
> pass its great canyon of two hundred miles in length and hundreds
> or thousands of feet in perpendicular depth, and never more been
> heard from.

Two decades previously, mountain man knowledge of the Colorado River
had been showing up in print. In 1846 Rufus Sage, who explored the West as
a journalist and later became a mountain man, published *Scenes in the Rocky
Mountains.* Though he endorsed the idea that the Colorado River's headwaters were "interlocking" with four other major rivers, he reported, "Owing to
the rapidity of its currents and its frequent falls and cascades, the navigation
is entirely destroyed till within about one hundred miles of its mouth."[6] The
Colorado also appeared in David Coyner's 1847 *The Lost Trappers,* which he
presented as the history of the first band of trappers to ascend the Missouri

River after Lewis and Clark, led by Ezekiel Williams.[7] For decades *The Lost Trappers* was accepted as an important document of western history; as late as 1889 historian Hubert Howe Bancroft expressed high confidence in it. Yet as historians looked into Ezekiel Williams they found little resemblance between his real life and the adventures he recounted in the book. When Hiram Martin Chittenden published his classic *History of the American Fur Trade of the Far West* in 1902, he dismissed *The Lost Trappers* as "one of the completest fabrications that was ever published under the guise of history," and Coyner as "chiefly a coiner of lies."[8] *The Lost Trappers* fell into complete disrepute. Yet when it came to the Colorado River, Coyner stated, "Its length is about twelve hundred miles, eight hundred of which are broken into falls and rapids, so numerous and dangerous as to defy navigation in any way whatever. From one to two hundred miles of its lower part is in all practicality navigable for vessels of the larger class."[9] Not bad for 1847, especially for a Presbyterian minister who spent most of his life in Virginia and Ohio and apparently never got west of Missouri.

Coyner did have a good chance to soak up the lore of mountain men. For several years he lived in the same Missouri county where William Ashley lay buried on a bluff overlooking the Missouri River. Mountain men from the now-defunct fur trapping era had become farmers in the area, an area that was now the route to the nearby starting points of both the Oregon and Santa Fe Trails. As a steady stream of wagons headed west, a steady stream of guides and information flowed back to Missouri. Coyner combined this lore with published histories, such as Washington Irving's *Astoria* (which was packed with mountain man adventures and horrible disasters from John Jacob Astor's attempt to set up an Oregon colony around 1812), from which Coyner lifted whole episodes and passages.[10] Coyner stirred it up with his own fertile imagination.

Coyner has his band of twenty trappers roaming through misadventures until only three are left. Two of them, James Workman and Samuel Spencer, want to reach Santa Fe by following the Rio Grande but mistakenly latch onto the Colorado River (which for Coyner includes the Green River). Coyner's river has fanciful elements, such as forty-foot waterfalls, yet his descriptions of river running capture its genuine looks and sounds, and even the fear. Here the trappers are scouting a great rapid:

> Through this narrow defile the river flowed almost with the velocity of an arrow. Beyond these rapids there were evidently falls, as their tumultuous roar could be distinctly heard, and clouds of spray could be seen suspended in the air....

At one time the roaring of the distant cataract would rise and fall with the breeze that bore the lulling sound to their ears. Again, as the gentle gale would sink, the tumult of angry waters would for a while die away in the distance. The feeling of disappointment, for a time, was lost in those of wonder and awe, and the trappers seemed to forget their situation, as they mused upon the picturesqueness and romance of this exhibition of nature.[11]

Coyner has the Colorado River start out as "a delightful spring of water" in the mountains and become a small stream the trappers follow until it is wide enough for them to build a canoe. "They glided along in fine style for the first fifty miles," through a wide-open prairie. But then "a frowning mountain enclosed their prospect, and seemed to hem in the river." They took to land. "When they had passed the narrow passage, the Colorado expanded again to its usual breadth, and poured over falls about forty feet high. The river in the falls was full of large rocks, many of which projected above the surface of the water. Against these the waters of this great river dashed, and rebounded, and boiled up until the whole surface seemed to be in a perfect rage." They followed the river as closely as possible for several hundred miles, hoping to use a canoe again, but the river "was filled with rapids, and rocks, and other obstructions, that not only rendered the navigation unsafe, but utterly impossible.... They frequently passed places where for several miles the banks rose up into precipices of an awful height, from the tops of which they sometimes took a view of the river below, as it whirled, and dashed about, and foamed, and struck the basaltic rock, impatient, furious and wild."[12]

Another set of images that ring true to today's river runners are found in the diaries of Warren Ferris, a mountain man who roamed the Rockies in the early 1830s. Ferris published his adventures in the journal *Western Literary Messenger,* edited by his brother in Buffalo, New York, in the early 1840s, but the journal's obscurity meant that Ferris's writings were forgotten for a century. When historians rediscovered them in the 1940s they were amazed by the map Ferris had produced in 1836, showing the Rocky Mountains and its river system with more detail and accuracy than any map of its time. At the bottom of this map Ferris encased the Colorado River inside two long thin boxes he labeled "great chanion of the Colorado." Since this "chanion" begins right below the junction of the Green and Grand Rivers, he must be talking about Cataract Canyon. On July 20, 1842, Ferris published an article titled "Chanion of the Colorado":

The Colorado a short distance below the junction of Green and Grand rivers, enters the great chanion, which is a canal in many places more than a thousand feet deep, and bounded on either side by perpendicular walls of rock, that bid defiance to horsemen, who would descend to the river; in fact, they are seldom accessible to footmen…. This chanion confines the river between two and three hundred miles; and even to those, who have seen and for years been familiar with the mightiest productions of nature, presents a scene from which they recoil with terror.[13]

Ferris tells us that from the canyon rims you could imagine yourself to be looking down on a pleasant little creek lined with bushes:

You will certainly attempt to descend to the lovely scene beneath, and perhaps may resolve to step over the brook, and recline yourself in the shade of a cluster of willows; alas,! if you succeed, how sadly you will be disappointed. The little brook will gradually enlarge itself as you descend, until it becomes a mighty river, three hundred yards wide; the bushes will increase in size, and stature, until they become giant cotton woods; the narrow strip of meadow land between the walls, will expand into broad fields of verdure; and you will see, kind reader, in imagination, what many a half-starved trapper, has seen in reality, on the Colorado. These walls approach each other so closely, in some places, that the bottoms disappear; and the river being compressed to one fourth of its ordinary width, dashes through with inconceivable fury, like the Niagara…which renders its navigation impracticable. Its tributaries are likewise confined by walls.[14]

Confronted by a continent that defied even the most sublime visions of European romanticism, the American imagination was working feverishly to come to terms with its home. Americans were confused between their belief that their continent was a promised land for God's new chosen people, and the evidence that some of their land was made for giants, not people. Somewhere between the visions of David Coyner and those of Samuel Adams lay the real Colorado River and the real West. Even a man like John Wesley Powell, in whom mingled the latest geographical knowledge, the romantic pull of sublime landscapes, and the lure of national destiny, couldn't be sure what was real.

There was only one way to find out.

NOTES

1. John Wesley Powell, *The Exploration of the Colorado River and Its Canyons* (New York: Viking Penguin, 1987), 247. First published as *The Canyons of the Colorado* (Meadville, PA: Flood and Vincent, 1895).

2. Zebulon Pike, *The Journals of Zebulon Montgomery Pike,* ed. Donald Jackson (Norman: University of Oklahoma Press, 1966), Vol. 2, 26–27, 25–26.

3. S. M. Holdredge, *State, Territorial, and Ocean Guidebook of the Pacific* (San Francisco: S. M. Holdredge, 1865), no page nos.

4. Elliot West, *Contested Plains: Indians, Goldseekers, and the Rush to Colorado* (Lawrence: University Press of Kansas, 1998), 128.

5. Robert L. Perkins, *The First Hundred Years: An Informal History of Denver and the Rocky Mountain News* (Denver: Denver Publishing, 1959), 18, 156–57.

6. Rufus B. Sage, *Scenes in the Rocky Mountains* (Philadelphia: Carey and Hart, 1846), 188.

7. David Coyner, *The Lost Trappers*, ed. David J. Weber (1847; repr. Albuquerque: University of New Mexico Press, 1970), 108. Page references to 1970 ed.

8. Hiram Martin Chittenden, *History of the American Fur Trade of the Far West* (1902; repr. Palo Alto: Stanford University Press, 1954), Vol. 2, 651–56. Page references to 1954 ed.

9. Coyner, *The Lost Trappers,* 108.

10. Washington Irving, *Astoria* (Philadelphia, PA: Carey, Lea, and Blanchard, 1836).

11. Coyner, *The Lost Trappers*, 111–12.

12. Ibid., 110, 110, 112–13, 113.

13. Warren Ferris, *Western Literary Messenger,* July 20, 1842, reproduced in *Life in the Rocky Mountains: A Diary of Wanderings on the Sources of the Rivers Missouri, Columbia, and Colorado, 1830–1835* (Denver: Old West Publishing, 1983), 397.

14. Ibid., 398.

PART I

The James White Mystery

· 1 ·

Introduction to the James White Mystery

AMONG THE MANY VAGUE, confusing, and disputed claims about the James White story, there's one thing about which everyone agrees: on September 7, 1867, a crude raft floated down the Colorado River, dozens of miles downstream from the Grand Canyon, toward the small Mormon town of Callville. The raft held a man in terrible condition: starved, nearly naked, sunburned, bruised, semiconscious, confused. The people of Callville pulled him ashore and nursed him back toward health. They were eager to hear his story, and not just from simple curiosity. Callville had been founded, less than three years previously, to serve as a port that connected the Mormons in Utah with the outside world via the Colorado River and the Gulf of California. But the Colorado River had proven tricky for steamboats, often allowing only small barges to get through to Callville. The roads linking Callville with the rest of Utah were terrible, and the transcontinental railroad was fast approaching northern Utah, so Callville was already failing economically and being abandoned. But Callville would benefit if the Colorado River upstream proved to be more navigable. Five months before White arrived, Mormon explorer Jacob Hamblin and two other men had dragged a sixteen-foot skiff overland to the base of the Grand Wash Cliffs, where the Colorado River emerged from the Grand Canyon, and floated down the river sixty-five miles to Callville. Most of the rapids they encountered were manageable, but one had a six- or eight-foot fall and required them to portage; they judged this rapid to be the limit of navigation upstream from Callville, at least for commercial vessels. But this could be argued, since the river fluctuated greatly in volume and might fluctuate in navigability also. Like Coloradans and Californians, the Mormons, too, had been tempted by the idea that the Colorado River might be navigable much farther upstream. Maybe this stranger on his raft had come downriver a long way, even through the "Big Canyon."

James White told his hosts that he had been on his raft for fourteen days. His ordeal had started far upstream, along the San Juan River, where he and two other men were prospecting. Their leader was a Captain Baker, originally from St. Louis, and the other man's name was Strode—or at least that's how it was first recorded; later it was Strole. Ute Indians attacked them and killed Baker, and White and Strole fled down a canyon to the Colorado River, where they built a raft out of cottonwood logs and headed downriver. After three days, a rapid washed Strole overboard and he drowned. White continued alone, with little to eat, roping himself to the raft to survive the rapids.

White's story spread quickly downriver, first to the town of El Dorado Canyon, which had been a booming silver mining town but now was temporarily shut down, with only three residents for most of 1867. E. B. Grandin was the caretaker of a closed mill and heard about White when Captain L. C. Wilburn, taking his barge downriver from Callville, stopped there. Grandin wrote a letter about it to El Dorado postmaster Frank Alling, who presumably was not then in town; Alling occasionally visited San Francisco and served as a correspondent for San Francisco's newspaper *Alta California,* and there Grandin's letter got published on September 24. A few weeks later, on November 12, Grandin's letter was reprinted in the *Daily Register* of Central City, Colorado, only twelve days after John Wesley Powell had left that city.

Central City was the center of mining activity in Colorado, its Gilpin County producing two thirds of the state's mineral wealth. Thus local leaders were keenly interested in geology, and they had established a Miners and Mechanics Institute that seemed to pull in every prominent scientist passing through Colorado to give public lectures on things geological and geographical. John Wesley Powell was wrapping up his first summer of exploring the natural history of the Rockies, and he came to town on October 31. The Institute advertised Powell too generously as the "state geologist of Illinois" and charged people fifty cents to hear him lecture on how Colorado's landscapes evolved. The next day, November 1, 1867, the *Daily Register* gave a long glowing account of Powell's talk. "Our report," the article concluded, "does no sort of justice to the beauty of the lecture or the pleasing style of its delivery."

If the newspaper editor had already seen the *Alta California* with Grandin's letter about James White, it would have made a natural topic of conversation with Powell, who was so obviously interested in western geography and rivers. If Powell didn't hear about White right then, it might soon have been called to his attention by the men with whom he had roamed the mountains that summer, such as Oramel Howland, who had worked as a printer for the Central

City newspaper, or Jack Sumner, who years later said that he and Powell had earlier in 1867 discussed going down the Colorado River. Or maybe Powell heard about it through William Byers, Sumner's brother-in-law, the Denver newspaper publisher who was still hoping the Colorado River was navigable all the way to Colorado. However he heard, it's likely Powell quickly became aware of the James White story. Whether he believed it or not, whether it encouraged his own plans or not, has never been clear. George Bradley, one of Powell's 1869 crew, was under the impression that Powell had met White, which would have been logical since Powell was investigating sources—very skimpy sources—of information about the river. Yet Powell and his other crewmembers never said that Powell had met White, and White himself said they never met.

But Powell's crew was aware of White's story, and they seemed to be testing it against reality as they descended the river. Reality had gotten really tough by August 13, when they camped atop Hance Rapid, one of the rockiest and trickiest in the Grand Canyon. It appears that the crew held a discussion of White's story that evening, for two of them commented on it in their river journals. George Bradley: "I am convinced that no man had ever run such rappids on a raft.... I pay little heed to the whole story."[1] And Jack Sumner: "How anyone can ride that on a raft is more than I can see. Mr. White may have done so but I don't believe it."[2]

Twenty years later, Robert Stanton led the next expedition down the river (after Powell's two,) and within twenty-five miles of leaving Lees Ferry and entering the Grand Canyon Stanton had suffered two accidents that drowned three men. Stanton, too, decided that White couldn't possibly have done it, and he became one of the fiercest critics of White's story. Over the next half century there were few river runners in the canyon, and fewer still got through without mishaps, so not many experts were willing to endorse White's story. River running has grown into a mass activity, and today most river runners have judged White's feat as highly improbable. Boat designs have improved a great deal, and experience and skill levels have risen with them, yet river runners still have to summon all their abilities to get through the toughest rapids, and even professional guides sometimes get into trouble. A clueless guy on a crude raft would have far too many obstacles and far too little power and control to get through intact. Even most advocates of White's story admit he made it against heavy odds.

On the other hand, as river experience has accumulated, so have stories of the improbable. Beginners have made it through Lava Falls while the best guides have flipped. Rafts have gotten untied and drifted unmanned through many miles and many rapids, with loose items riding merrily on the deck all the way. People have deliberately swum the whole canyon, and lived. This accumulation of freak events has left a more relaxed attitude about White's story: even most skeptics admit it is possible.

This debate has taken place more on theoretical grounds than on the specific facts of White's story, and the debate drifted even farther from the facts when it moved onto ego grounds. Most of this debate has been conducted by river runners, some of whom became important river historians; river runners, even as they are awed and humbled by great rivers and canyons, also tend to be proud of themselves. Pride is not the best ink for writing history. Some river runners have felt diminished by the James White story: If White could make it through the canyon without any skill, then it must not take any skill to make it through the canyon. If White could make it while Robert Stanton's expedition killed three people, then Stanton must have been criminally incompetent. Stanton's effort to diminish White did not have the style of a disinterested historian. Yet those on the other side of the debate, too, have been guilty of pride—family pride in the case of White's granddaughter, Eilean Adams, and Colorado pride in the case of Thomas Dawson, a Colorado historian who claimed priority for the Coloradan White. Some of the debate has consisted of accusing the other side of having ulterior motives—which was often true. Perhaps, unfortunately, I am going to contribute more to this tendency by examining further the motives of two of the debaters. Yet James White himself can't be accused of pride or self-promotion, for he remained pretty quiet about the whole thing.

It also seems that some people take sides in the debate simply because they like the idea of James White or the idea of John Wesley Powell, the idea of a common-man frontier hero, a Davy Crockett, blundering his way down the river, or the idea of a heroic scientific explorer and skillful boatman.

With all these factors steering the James White debate, it would have been helpful if the evidence had exerted more gravity, but unfortunately the evidence has been vague and confusing. Even worse, when the facts have gotten in the way, both sides have been ready to argue that, obviously, James White was delirious so he can't be held literally to what he was saying.

One of the movable "facts" about James White was his statement that he was on the river for fourteen days, and only by day, tying up his raft at night. He went from somewhere far above the Grand Canyon to sixty miles below it. Today's rowing trips take about fourteen days to go less than half White's distance. Eilean Adams tried to escape this problem by adding more days to the trip. Skeptics have declared that the fourteen-day timeline disproves the whole story, or they've proposed other entry points that fit. Robert Stanton reduced it to sixty miles, with a starting point below the Grand Wash Cliffs, but then he had the opposite problem of explaining how White could take two weeks to go only sixty miles, or just four miles per day. Yet this argument has taken place in a factual void, without anyone knowing how high the river was in September 1867. Now we have a previously unknown source: on July 10, 1867, a San Francisco newspaper quoted William Hardy, the founder of Hardyville, a river crossing below Callville, saying that the Colorado River was flowing as high as American settlers had ever seen it, with very full banks, covered with driftwood and still rising. Two other sources point to the same conclusion: tree ring data from Navajo Mountain, near Glen Canyon, suggest that 1867 was an unusually wet year, and 1867 was one of the few years when the Colorado flooded high enough to overflow into the Salton Sea.

Before it was dammed, the Colorado River used to peak in late spring or early summer, then drop significantly. By September it was a much milder river, although still subject to brief spikes from annual monsoon thunderstorms. Yet the abnormally high flows of the summer of 1867, which probably translated into higher September flows, make it much more plausible that White could have covered the distance he claimed. It could also lend more plausibility to White's claim that at the mouth of the Little Colorado River he was caught in a powerful whirlpool. Today's river runners don't see any whirlpools there. Skeptics have ridiculed White over his imaginary whirlpool, while supporters have said that he must have gotten the location wrong. But when the river is flooding, all sorts of whirlpools and other hydraulic phenomena break out, often in unlikely places. And a high river would have covered many boulders and smoothed out many rapids. On the other hand, a high river full of powerful currents, eddies, and whirlpools would have made a raft without oars even more helpless, and far more likely to get trapped.

The Little Colorado whirlpool is only one of the vague, moveable "facts" that have muddied the James White debate. White said that the Little Colorado flowed into the main river from the right, when it really comes in from the left. On the other hand, he described a waterfall that is a good fit for Deer Creek Falls. But White's accounts held outright contradictions. The Grandin letter offered a statement that sounds pretty accurate: "He describes the Big Cañon of the Colorado as terrific, a succession of rapids and falls. Some of the falls, he thinks, are fully ten feet perpendicular. His raft would plunge over such places, rolling over and over.... He says there are rocky cliffs overhanging the river that he believes to be a mile and a half high."[3] Yet in interviews with Charles

Parry, Robert Stanton, and Ellsworth Kolb, White significantly reduced the
height of the canyon walls and the presence and difficulty of the rapids, and
said that most of the canyon consisted of a white sandstone. Some of White's
descriptions don't fit the real canyon and river very well. Ellsworth Kolb commented, "I would like to know the truth about White. I talked with him a few
years before he died, but he was so childish it was impossible to make head or
tail of his story. He told me he…did not think it was so very bad except for a
couple of falls."[4] And according to Stanton (although his statement has been
disputed), White said, "In all the journey there was only one big rapid, the one
with the twenty-foot fall. All the other rapids were small ones."[5]

Speaking of ulterior motives, Grandin and the other residents of the dying
towns of Callville and El Dorado Canyon should have been economically motivated to claim that White had an easy voyage, proving that the Colorado was
navigable far upstream, and in fact Frank Alling, who placed Grandin's letter
in the San Francisco newspaper, had often written booster letters to the paper
urging its readers to invest in El Dorado Canyon. But clearly Grandin has not
fallen to this temptation, and his report shuts down hope for the river's commercial value.

Since White's adventure took place in the most solitary of places, with no
witnesses, it has seemed we would never be able to get beyond the vagueness of
his account and make reliable comparisons with reality. And yet, all along there
was one eyewitness to White's adventure, at least the beginning of it, and that
eyewitness casts White's credibility and story in a considerably different light.

NOTES

1. Bradley quoted in Ghiglieri, *First Through Grand Canyon*, 205.

2. Jack Sumner, quoted in ibid., 206.

3. E. B. Grandin, *Alta California*, Sept. 24, 1867.

4. Ellsworth Kolb to Lewis Freeman, December 27, 1922, in Robert Brewster Stanton,
Colorado River Controversies (1932; repr. Boulder City, NV: Westwater Books, 1982), 243.
Page references to 1982 ed.

5. Quoted in Stanton, *Controversies*, 51.

·2·

WANTED—James White

THE JAMES WHITE DEBATE has involved rivers of speculation in a canyon-like void of facts, since White's adventure took place without any witnesses, except for its ending at Callville. Yet there was one part of White's story that was indeed witnessed. White's story began when he and some companions stole some horses from Indians near Fort Dodge, an army post in southwestern Kansas, and headed for the Rockies. Like most army posts, Fort Dodge kept extensive records of area events, but no historian has thought to check them. It turns out that White's departure from Fort Dodge was especially well documented. It turns out that the real events were substantially different from White's story, and far more serious. The events near Fort Dodge cast a long shadow on White's credibility and on the rest of his story.

Fort Dodge was founded in 1865 to protect migrants, stagecoaches, and commercial and military freight wagons on the Santa Fe Trail, as well as local settlers. The fort was located on the Arkansas River, which the trail followed through Kansas as long as possible; twenty-five miles west of Fort Dodge the trail crossed the river at a ford called Cimarron Crossing, then headed across sixty miles of dry land to where it picked up the Cimarron River. The Atchison, Topeka and Santa Fe Railway would not arrive for another six years, when it would spawn Dodge City a few miles from Fort Dodge.

In 1867 the commander of Fort Dodge was Major Henry Douglas (in some sources, his name is spelled Douglass). Though the fort was meant to subdue the region's Indians, Douglas was unusually sympathetic to Indians, at least for his time, and at least for an army post commander. Two years later—to flash forward for a moment—Douglas became superintendent of Indian Affairs for Nevada. In that role he cracked down on corruption and abuse at the Pyramid Lake Reservation, where the Indian agents had opened the Paiute's reservation to American cattle grazing in exchange for $15,000 in payoffs, and allowed so many white fishermen to string nets across the Truckee River that the Indians were forced to fish from boats in the lake. Some whites were calling for the reservation to be abolished and opened to settlement. Seeking the Paiute point of view, Douglas wrote to the commander of the nearby army post, and the commander had his young Paiute interpreter, Sarah Winnemucca, write a response. Douglas was so impressed by her letter, both its despair and its pride, that he sent it to the commissioner of Indian Affairs. The letter began circulating in Washington and got published in *Harper's Weekly* magazine, making a big impression nationally—few Americans had ever read a piece by an articulate Indian protesting against American mistreatment. A decade later Helen Hunt Jackson reprinted Winnemucca's letter in her famous critique of American Indian policy, *A Century of Dishonor.*[1]

In the winter of 1866–67 Major Douglas was very worried. Many in the U.S. Army favored a policy of Indian expulsion or extermination, and the railroad, with its big political clout, was aiming straight for Fort Dodge and wanted the Indians out of its way. Yet after the Sand Creek Massacre of 1864 and the national dismay it triggered, white Americans were supporting more-conciliatory policies, at least for the moment. Native Americans, too, were deeply divided between those who accepted accommodation with whites and those who insisted that armed resistance was their only hope. The U.S. government had pushed a treaty for Kansas tribes in October 1865 but many Indians didn't agree to it; near Fort Dodge some Indians continued raiding wagon trains, stealing horses, killing whites, and taking hostages. But on the whole the peace was holding, at least for the moment. With the passage of the Homestead Act and the end of the Civil War, settlement on the Great Plains was expanding rapidly, placing much greater pressure on Indian lands. Over the winter of 1866–67 it was becoming clear to Douglas that area tribes were getting ready for war, waiting only for spring rains to provide forage grasses that would allow unlimited mobility for large forces. For two years, in an attempt to reward the Indians for accepting the presence of whites, Fort Dodge had been a major distribution center for food and other supplies, which had attracted a large concentration of Indians to the area, from several tribes—Comanche, Kiowa, Apache, Cheyenne, Sioux, and Arapaho. With the peace looking increasingly fragile, Douglas worried that even a small incident could trigger an explosion, which he would not have the forces to control.

Over the winter, Douglas repeatedly wrote to his commanding officers to convince them of the danger and to ask for reinforcements for Fort Dodge. He reported that his scout and interpreter Fred Jones was bringing in ominous warnings, including that the Indians were obtaining an arsenal of guns and ammunition from white traders who were legally prohibited from selling weapons to Indians but who were breaking the rules to enrich themselves. In February the Indians began giving Douglas ultimatums: whites should cease all settlement activities, stop hunting buffalo, stop cutting trees, stop traffic on the Santa Fe Trail, stop railroad construction, close Fort Dodge, and leave the region. On March 14, 1867, Douglas wrote that Chief Santana of the Kiowas "gave me ten days to move from this post, that he wanted the mules and cavalry horses fattened, as he would have use for them, for he intended to appropriate them."[2] Spring was arriving, the grasses growing fast. Douglas succeeded in convincing General Winfield Hancock of the threat, and Hancock organized a force of 1,400 men at Fort Riley. By April 7 they'd gotten as far as Fort Larned, some fifty miles from Fort Dodge, but they had to pause there because they were having trouble finding enough forage for so many horses.

On February 24 Douglas received his first report of a band of eight white trappers operating in the area. While they were trapping wolves for bounty money on the upper Cimarron River, six of their mules and horses had been stolen by Cheyennes. Two weeks later Douglas heard about trappers, presumably the same group, camped on Mulberry Creek some thirty miles south of Fort Dodge: it seemed they were heading in his direction. A few days later the trappers showed up at Fort Dodge, and Douglas, eager for reports of Indian activities, conducted a long interview with their leader, "Captain" Baker.

James White didn't tell us much about Baker, except that he was an old Colorado frontiersman who had prospected in the San Juan Mountains in 1860 but been driven out by Indians. When Baker and White arrived in the San Juans later that summer of 1867, Baker showed White his old diggings. This makes it plausible that Baker was Charles Baker, one of the leaders of the San Juan gold rush of 1860. Baker had gotten a reputation as a swindler for hyping mining claims. At Fort Dodge, Baker did sign his name "Charles," though James White would always call him "Jim." White also said that Baker was from St. Louis, although Charles Baker is not known to have had any St. Louis connection.

Baker gave Major Douglas a detailed report of tribal numbers and movements and reported that the Indians were extremely well armed. Baker had camped near the Cheyennes and watched them target shooting. On March 19, 1867, Douglas wrote to his commanding officer:

> Mr. Baker stated to me that after 23 years experience in dealing with Indians, his opinion derived from the present aspect of affairs and the conduct of Indians was that they will break out into open hostility in

the spring. He also stated that the Cheyennes are splendidly armed with rifles and revolvers, with an almost inexhaustible supply of ammunition, that he encamped for some time near a party of them. They practiced continually at target-firing, and were for the most part very good shots, that this party had about 1300 rounds of ammunition per man, and used it more lavishly than he had ever seen Indians use it before. On his expressing his surprise at their prodigal use of it, they said they had plenty more of it at home.

When Baker showed up in the area, James White was driving the Barlow and Sanderson stagecoach on the twenty-five-mile run between Fort Dodge and Cimarron Crossing, a risky route: troopers often escorted stages from Fort Dodge. Along the entirety of the Santa Fe Trail, Cimarron Crossing was the Indian's favorite place for stealing horses from whites. In the 1820s and 1830s, before the Mexican–American War (1846–48), Cimarron Crossing was on the border between the United States and Mexico and became a rendezvous spot for fur trappers and traders. Indians started coming there to trade, and decades later they continued coming to trade with the wagon trains that camped there for a day or two to rest and prepare for the next sixty miles without water. Sometimes the Indians didn't trade but raided, especially wagons in the process of fording the river. The Arkansas River here was shallow but the current was swift, and wagons often wobbled or sank into quicksand and were powerless to escape an attack. A lone stagecoach in this area was even more vulnerable, and White must have understood that in the event of an Indian uprising he was in the most dangerous place and job of all. It was a prudent time to leave. Cimarron Crossing held a ranch or station called Cimarron Ranch, built by two former Barlow and Sanderson stagecoach drivers, and it was actually a stronger fortress than Fort Dodge itself, complete with stockade, guard towers, and rifle portals. When Baker's party left Fort Dodge, they went to Cimarron Ranch, and perhaps it was here that James White fell in with them.

Baker didn't tell Major Douglas that he was observing the Cheyennes so closely because he intended to take back his livestock. Upon seeing how heavily armed these Cheyennes were, Baker must have decided there were easier Indian camps from which to obtain livestock, such as the village of about five hundred Sioux and Cheyennes on the Pawnee Fork River. Soon, Major Douglas received an urgent letter, dated March 29, from the owner of Cimarron Ranch: "It has come to our knowledge that a man calling himself Capt. Baker and a party of men with him have the intention of making a raid upon a party of

Indians camped on the South branch of Pawnee Fork about 25 miles north East from here for the purpose of obtaining <u>Horses</u> and <u>mules</u>. As some of the Indians have visited the Ranch and seen the above named party at the Ranch should they lose stock they would natualy vent their rage towards the ranch and occupants thereby exposing innocent men and women to their <u>tender mercies</u>." Douglas saw a much greater danger than the threat to Cimarron Ranch. The whole prairie was a powder keg, and a band of whites attacking an Indian camp was just the spark to set it off. On March 30 Douglas sent a courier to Cimarron Ranch with a letter to Baker:

> It has been reported to me that it is your intention to make a raid on the Indians camped in the Pawnee Fork for the purpose of capturing horses and mules.
>
> Proper steps for the recovery of <u>animals</u> stolen from you by Indians cannot be objected to, but a raid to make <u>reprisals</u> will not be countenanced. It is contrary to the present Military and Civil policy of the Government; and it is my duty to prevent it, and if such a raid is intended by you, to protect the Indians concerned. Please make me aware of what you intend to do by the return of bearer.
>
> I have this morning sent my guide to the Indians camped in the Pawnee Fork to put the Indians on their guard against any raids that may be made by white men.

Baker immediately wrote back:

> Your information is not correct. I entertain no such intentions. But I do intend to go south for the purpose of recovering from the Indians the stock stolen and if we fail to recover the stolen stock to make reprisal upon the Indians that stole our stock and no others. As I know the Indians that stole our stock & know near where they are camping I expect to recover it. I understand fully the responsibility attaching to those who are instrumental in bringing on Indian difficulty. I have neither the wish or intention of violating the military or civil policy of the Government.

Baker had the gall to sign his letter, "I have the honor to be very respect-fully yours, Chas. Baker."

Now that the Pawnee Fork village was on alert, Baker had to find another target. He had already sized up the Arapaho camp on Mulberry Creek. The Arapaho's Chief Little Raven was one of the few chiefs who had remained on good terms with whites and was trying to prevent a war, yet even within his own tribe there were many angry young braves asserting that whites were treacherous thieves whom they needed to fight.

On April 17 Douglas received word that Baker and eight other men (notice the addition of another man—presumably James White) had raided Little Raven's camp and stolen twelve horses. Douglas was enraged. On discovering that Baker was heading up the Arkansas River, Douglas dispatched orders to Fort Lyon in Colorado to intercept Baker:

> A white man by the name of Baker with eight others has made a raid on the stock of Little Raven's band of Arrapahoes and stolen 12 horses. They drove the horses to the cimarron crossing and up the roads and were last heard from near Fort Aubrey. It is believed they will pass your post on the way to the Mountains. If they do please hold on to Baker and seize the horses.
>
> This man declared to persons here that he would steal horses from the Indians, and run them off to the Mountains, and he did not care whether it brought on war in these parts or not....
>
> Upon being warned by me he disclaimed any intention of stealing from any other bands than the one who stole his Stock (4 mules & 2 horses) his object was to get his own Stock. But he has made his raid on a friendly band not connected in any manner with the stealing of his stock.
>
> If you can capture Baker and get back the stock you would confer a favor.

Colorado legend says that Charles Baker was a Virginian and that at the start of the Civil War he returned to Virginia to join the Confederate army, so he could have had a political grudge that left him downright hostile to the orders of a U.S. Army major (some of whose Fort Dodge troops were blacks), and maybe even eager to stir up trouble. James White, too, could have held a grudge against the army, for at the end of his three years of service he had been court-martialed on a charge of stealing two hundred pounds of coffee, though in the end he got an honorable discharge.

Unfortunately, we can't trace further Douglas's orders to Fort Lyon, because the records at Fort Lyon were extremely skimpy for this period.

The U.S. Cavalry would soon be quite preoccupied with matters much bigger than Captain Baker. Within days, fighting exploded all around Fort Dodge, and it soon spread across the prairie; the uprisings of 1867–68 became one of the major events of the Indian wars. Only two weeks after Major Douglas had tried to protect the Pawnee Fork village from Baker, the U.S. Cavalry burned it to the ground, and Lieutenant Colonel George A. Custer was chasing down its fleeing residents. The Indians attacked wagon trains, stagecoaches, stage stations, and settlers. On June 12 about two hundred Kiowas attacked Fort Dodge and captured most of its cavalry horses. The army struck back hard and sometimes as indiscriminately as had Baker. The fighting continued into late 1868, and on September 3 the Indians again attacked Fort Dodge, with General Phil Sheridan inside it, and killed or wounded twenty-one soldiers. In November 1868 Custer waged one of the most famous battles of the uprising at Washita, killing Black Kettle, who had advocated for peace with Americans and who had survived the Sand Creek Massacre. Among whites, too, peace advocates were soon drowned out by the drums of war. The uprising occupied much space in American newspapers, partly because Henry Stanley, who later would presume to find Dr. Livingstone in Africa, was working as a reporter for a St. Louis paper and arrived at Fort Dodge soon after hostilities began. Newspaper coverage was especially heavy and indignant in Colorado, where the uprising had cut off the flow of new emigrants and supplies at a time when Colorado's mining industry was already badly depressed. On April 26, 1867, the Central City *Daily Register* declared, "If the government has at last awakened to the idea that these murderous Indians must be overawed and suppressed, there is certainly cause for thanks. If however the government means peace, they will soon be made cognizant of the fact the Indians mean war." In his *Rocky Mountain News,* William Byers's impatience turned into mockery of the army; he complained that the government was spending $24,000 per Indian killed, when Colorado militiamen could have done the same job for $20 per Indian, provided they were allowed to keep Indian scalps for sale as souvenirs. But the army proved effective enough, and they soon brought a permanent end to the ancient way of life of the southern plains tribes.

The 1867–68 uprising disrupted travel across the Great Plains, including John Wesley Powell's plans to explore the Black Hills in the summer of 1867; instead, he followed the safer Oregon Trail route across Nebraska and headed for the Colorado Rockies, but along the way he saw enough wreckage from the conflict to make him nervous.

Now that we finally have a documented version of part of James White's story, what can we say about White's veracity?

White told us some of the truth, but left out the most important part, and falsified other parts. White claimed that his band included only four men, when it included nine. White told us the raided Indian camp was one hundred miles east of Cimarron Ranch, when it was more like forty miles south-southeast, an unlikely mistake for the stage driver who knew the road east from Cimarron Ranch better than anyone. White claimed that on the night after their raid the Indians retaliated by seizing a dozen horses from inside Cimarron Ranch, when in fact no such raid occurred. According to Louise Barry, a staffer for the Kansas State Historical Society who researched Cimarron Ranch for an article in the *Kansas Historical Quarterly,* the first Indian attack near the Crossing in 1867 did not take place until June 7.[3] The well-fortified Cimarron Ranch was the last place Indians would try to get horses. White's implication that the Indians traveled a hundred miles in twenty-four hours is dubious on its own terms. In one version, White implies that Baker was recovering horses from the same Indians who had stolen his. In another version, Baker is just a fellow stagecoach driver.

White had a clear motive for lying. As he and Baker headed for the hills, they heard reports that a major Indian uprising was breaking out behind them, and they feared they would get the blame and be hunted down and punished. It might be a good idea to disappear into a remote wilderness a long way from Kansas. When White was "caught" in Callville, the only way left to distance himself from the crime was with lies: White wasn't at the Arapaho camp, he was a hundred miles east. White didn't know anything about those other five men. White was justified in helping Baker recover his stolen horses. (But decades later, when White prepared a statement for historian Thomas Dawson, White admitted, if a bit obliquely, that the horses they stole were not Baker's.) Don't feel sorry for the Indians because the next night they got an equal number of horses back from Cimarron Ranch and they were thieves, too, anyway. Then again, Baker was just a stage driver who deserves the blame for prompting White to run away from his job. White didn't profit from selling the stolen horses because when Baker and White got to Utah, Indians stole the horses back. Most importantly, because Baker was killed by Indians in Utah and George Strole was drowned in the Colorado River, they'd received their punishment and the case was closed. There was no need to interrogate White about Baker's whereabouts. By applying to the Colorado River story the same two deceptions he had used in the Kansas story—blame it on the Indians and greatly distort the geography—White could avoid admitting where he and Baker might have traveled overland until they split up. They could have traveled overland a long way, to get as far away from Kansas as possible, a long way into western Arizona.

It is true that James White never sought fame for his Colorado River journey, and some have interpreted this as proof that he was a modest man, with no motive for making up his heroic story. But White had a good reason to keep quiet: He probably would have been dismayed that he had gotten himself mixed up with a man like Baker, who had turned White into a fugitive, and he might have wanted to not be associated with a serious crime against the U.S. Army. And possibly he knew that somewhere out there Baker and Strole were still alive, that they knew that the story White told about his river journey was not entirely true, and that at any moment they could step forward and discredit his story.

On the other hand, while the Fort Dodge documents lower White's credibility significantly, they do not prove that he was lying about his river trip. Even if he was lying about Baker, including his death, the possibility remains open that White's trip occurred much as he described it. During the week that Baker and White were stealing their horses in Kansas, at least four Kansas newspapers published Samuel Adams's claims that the Colorado River was easily navigable. Perhaps Baker and White imagined that the river offered an easier escape route than would a route on land, and that it would easily carry them to California.

NOTES

1. Helen Hunt Jackson, *A Century of Dishonor* (New York: Harper and Brothers, 1881).

2. All Douglas letters are from Records of Fort Dodge, Kansas State Historical Society, letters sent 1866–82, microfilm boxes 147–53.

3. Louise Barry, "The Ranch at Cimarron Crossing," *Kansas Historical Quarterly* 29 (Autumn 1973): 345–66.

·3·

An Old Story

To the people of Callville who rescued him from his raft, James White told an adventure story that must have sounded fantastic. Or, at least, some of it did. Some of it might have sounded rather familiar. Even decades earlier, the ever-growing lore of the American frontier included a significant body of stories in which Americans were attacked by Indians, fled to a river, and made their escape on a raft or boat. One of these stories, almost entirely forgotten today, holds some startling similarities to the story James White told.

The Americans who were pioneering the wilderness were living a life never imagined in the culture and folklore they'd brought with them from Europe, and they needed new folklore, new heroes, new cautionary tales that illustrated and supported their lives, including ones about dealing with Indians. Americans developed a rich lore about being attacked by and sometimes captured by Indians. By the time Hollywood took over this lore it was almost always triumphant, with the U.S. Cavalry charging to the rescue or a brave cowboy shooting down hordes of Indians. But in the early 1800s much of the lore about Indian attacks was decidedly less optimistic. For the trappers roaming alone or in small bands through Indian country, or for families in the outermost cabins in the forest or on the plains, there was little possibility of rescue and little chance of outmatching the Indians. Often, the best you could hope for was to run away or hide. The lore of Indian attacks focused on the speed, cleverness, or strength with which whites evaded them. Sometimes they failed to get away and were captured. Americans developed a special, grim fascination with stories about white women being captured by Indians. When Daniel Boone's daughter was abducted by Indians and Boone rescued her, it struck a mythic chord with Americans and was celebrated in painting and sculpture. Since the main form of frontier transportation was on rivers, it's not surprising that stories about escaping from Indians often featured rivers.

Perhaps the most famous of all river escape stories involved John Colter, a veteran of the Lewis and Clark expedition. After the expedition, Colter became a mountain man and roamed so widely that historians are still not sure where he went, but he does get credit for being the first white man to see Yellowstone. In 1808 Colter was jumped by a band of Blackfeet, who killed his companion and stripped Colter naked. The Blackfeet decided to have some sport with killing Colter and asked him if he was a good runner, and he answered no. They set him running, with braves in pursuit, but it turned out Colter was a very strong runner and was soon outdistancing his pursuers. He headed for the Madison River five miles away, with his feet being cut by rocks and thorns. Colter jumped into the cold river and swam to a raft of driftwood lodged against an island, dove under it, and found a spot where he could keep his head above water. The Blackfeet searched the shore and the driftwood but didn't see Colter, and at night he emerged. He had to walk for two hundred miles over eleven days to reach safety at Fort Raymond.

Another famous river escape story also involved veterans of the Lewis and Clark expedition. Lewis and Clark brought the chief of the Mandan tribe, Sheheke, to meet President Thomas Jefferson; after that meeting Nathaniel Pryor was assigned to take Sheheke home, up the Missouri River. When Pryor's keelboat stopped at a large village of the Arikara tribe, who were at war with the Mandans, the Arikaras attacked. Pryor's men pushed their boat from shore and tried to flee downriver but got stuck on sandbars, forcing the crew to get out and drag the boat as arrows flew around them, hitting some of them. When they got the boat free and headed downstream, hundreds of warriors followed on both shores, not giving up until sunset. A few years later Pryor was running a trading post at Galena, Illinois, near the Mississippi River, when Indians attacked and set the place on fire, but Pryor ran onto the frozen river and escaped.

In 1823 William Ashley was keelboating up the Missouri River and stopped at the Arikara village to parlay for horses. In the night, with some of Ashley's men asleep on shore, the Arikaras attacked. The men still on the boats panicked and refused to bring the boats back to shore. Jedediah Smith, already becoming a legendary mountain man, made a brave stand on shore, but as men fell steadily, Smith and others dove into the river, swam ninety feet to the boats, and fled downriver.

On the taller side of tales, Mike Fink was taking a flatboat down the Mississippi River when Indians jumped on board at night; Fink cut the rope so the boat drifted downriver, and fought them off. And one time Davy Crockett was walking through the woods when Indians gave chase, and he escaped by hiding inside a hollow log that he launched onto a river. Perhaps this tradition of river escape stories left a cultural trace that Mark Twain followed when he created the greatest of all river raft escape stories, *The Adventures of Huckleberry Finn*.

A third of a century before James White and John Wesley Powell, the Colorado River already had its own lore about Indian attacks and raft escapes.

In 1827 Jedediah Smith and his trapping party, heading for California, followed the Virgin River to the Colorado, then the Colorado to a Mohave Indian village on the river. Smith built rafts of cane to ferry his men and supplies across the river, but when Smith was halfway across, the Mohaves attacked and killed the ten whites still on shore. As with much of mountain man lore, the original sources are vague enough that the details come out differently in the accounts of different historians. Here is William H. Goetzmann's telling: "Smith and eight men were left stranded on a raft in mid-river with only five guns, few supplies, and very little ammunition. Miraculously, they made their escape by drifting downstream and constructing a fort on the opposite riverbank, where they were able to hold off the Indians until nightfall and then made their escape westward into the desert."[1]

The story that most interests me is that of a trapper named Jim Baker, who hailed from St. Louis and was often called "Captain." Baker was leading a small party of trappers through southwestern Colorado when they ran into hostile Utes. Baker retreated down the San Juan River to the Colorado River. Presumably he built a raft, for he did cross the Colorado, and made his escape into the desert. This story has all the central elements of the story James White told. To the end of his life White always referred to Baker as "Jim," not as Charles, even though the Fort Dodge records reveal that Baker was calling himself Charles and being called by that name there. White called him "Captain," and said he was from St. Louis. White's story has hostile Utes, a retreat down the San Juan to the Colorado, and the building of a raft to navigate the Colorado.

We can now say that James White's story definitely did happen—in 1842.

The Captain Jim Baker in the 1842 tale was, in his time, a famous mountain man in the same league as John Colter, Jim Bridger, and Jedediah Smith. Baker was one of the first white settlers in Colorado and sometimes served as a scout for the army, Governor Gilpin, and John C. Frémont. Baker has faded from the pantheon of American frontier heroes, partly because he didn't publicize himself in the way other frontiersmen did. Today Baker is remembered mostly in Wyoming, where his fort-like cabin is a historic site and where the sixteen-foot canoe he carved from a cottonwood tree for use on the Snake River was for years on display in the state museum; and in Colorado, where in 1900 he was one of only sixteen Colorado pioneers selected to have their portraits placed in the Colorado Capitol building (another portrait was that of William Byers). Baker was the subject of only one major biography, back in 1931, a third of a century after he died. Historian Nolie Mumey interviewed old-timers and Baker's relatives and combined these with letters and newspaper accounts, but the resulting biography contained major gaps and vagueness, along with rumors Mumey could not verify in any source. One tall tale has Baker showing up at Mountain Meadows in Utah soon after the 1857 massacre, inspecting the carnage, and declaring that the Indians didn't do it, whereupon Brigham Young, president of the Church of Jesus Christ of Latter-day Saints (LDS Church) at the time, offered $2,000 for Baker's scalp. Jim Baker still resides in the realm of mountain man campfires, where the facts might not be as important as a good story.

We do know that Jim Baker was born in 1818 in Belleville, Illinois, across the Mississippi River from St. Louis. With all the tales he heard about the West, he found it hard to settle for the life of an Illinois farmer, and at age twenty, in St. Louis, he let Jim Bridger talk him into signing up with the American Fur Company, for a life of adventure. Baker was soon trekking across the prairie and into the Wind River Range and Green River country, and he got hooked on mountain life. For years he continued wandering and trapping and getting into fights with Indians, wildlife, blizzards, horse thieves, and Mexicans who tried to stop Baker from stealing their horses. Like many mountain men Baker earned the honorary title of "Captain" for guiding various army expeditions, though he was never officially in the military. Baker hung out at traditional mountain man rendezvous spots like Brown's Hole on the Green River, but he had gotten into the fur-trapping business rather late and watched it dying slowly, so he adapted to other pursuits. During the California gold rush, Baker opened a ferry across the Green River in Wyoming, where twenty years later John Wesley Powell launched his river expedition. In his book Powell mentioned, "From our point of view we can see his lodge, three or four miles up the river." In 1859 Baker opened a ferry and toll bridge across Clear Creek in Denver, though he usually let his family—including his two Indian wives—operate it while he continued roaming the mountains. Sometimes he got to Hot Sulphur Springs in Middle Park and eventually he got to know its trading post manager, Jack Sumner, who would join Powell's crew. At some point Baker and Powell met, and it sounds as if Powell asked him about the rivers he was thinking of exploring, for in his book Powell wrote, "James Baker, an old-time mountaineer, once told me about a party of men starting down the river, and

Ashley was named as one. The story runs that the boat was swamped, and some of the party drowned in one of the canyons below."[2] When Walt Disney made his movie about the Powell expedition, *Ten Who Dared,* in 1960, he has Jim Baker walk into Powell's river camp one night and tell Powell that after their discussion the previous winter he had inquired of the Indians and they reported that the river was unrunnable, with falls as large as Niagara waiting to kill them.

When they met in real life, did Baker tell Powell about his encounter with the Colorado River in 1842? Baker had more experience with western rivers than almost anyone at that time. On one of Baker's trips, according to Nolie Mumey,

> They constructed a raft of cottonwood logs fastened with thongs of elk hides. This was to be used in crossing the Yellowstone River. Their furs, camp equipment, and firearms were placed aboard, then the raft was towed upstream by four men and was pushed into the current and rowed to the opposite shore. The rest of the party followed on horse-back, plunging recklessly into the water through the swift stream. They all succeeded in reaching the opposite bank except one man and two horses. They were entangled in driftwood and carried below the mouth of the Big Horn. The man, however, succeeded in swimming close to shore and was rescued by means of a rope which was thrown out from the raft. The two horses were drowned.[3]

In the winter of 1842 Baker trapped his way through the Southwest and was heading back into Colorado. Mumey: "After reaching their cache on the Puerco, they moved to the San Juan and crossed the river, where they met a large band of hostile Ute Indians. They were prevented from continuing their journey by the red men, who held council with Baker, Whitney, and the chief of the Ute tribe. The Indians demanded that the trappers keep out of the White River country. They finally had to agree to these terms, and turned west down the valley of the San Juan to the west bank of the Colorado. They continued westward."[4] Baker made a huge detour around Ute country and headed north, and got into a long ordeal in the desert, requiring him to kill one of his horses for food.

Like much mountain man lore, this story is frustratingly vague. We aren't told how closely Baker followed the San Juan River or where he crossed the Colorado or where he found an exit in the west-side cliffs. There are very few places where humans on foot or even on horses can cross the Colorado, so it's likely Baker built a raft, probably of cottonwood, as he had for the Yellowstone River. This would have made Baker, as far as we know, the first white person to raft across or down the Colorado River in the five hundred–mile stretch that includes Glen Canyon and Grand Canyon.

Given the vagueness of this story, you could make a lot out of it, or nothing at all. You could say that when James White was asked to explain his arrival on a raft at Callville, he simply pulled out Jim Baker's old tale of twenty-five years before, even retaining the name "Jim," and threw in some new elements. On the other hand, you could protest that such an accusation is very unfair. The name "Baker," after all, is very common, and White really was with a trapper named Baker in Kansas. (However, it was not the real Jim Baker: newspaper reports indicate that Jim Baker was in Denver at this time, and when I compared the handwriting in the letter White's Baker wrote to Major Douglas with the handwriting in Jim Baker's ledgers, it does not match.) St. Louis was the center of the fur trade and produced lots of fur trappers, so it would not be surprising if both Jim Baker and Charles Baker were connected with St. Louis. There might be some similarities in the two stories, but there are also big differences.

It's also fair to ask whether James White would have known about Jim Baker's river story of twenty-five years before. Colorado River historians have never noticed Baker's story. But there is a reasonable chance White had heard it. In these years Jim Baker was a national figure. In September 1866 *Harper's Weekly* magazine featured an illustration of Baker in hand-to-paw combat with a bear—a true story, more or less.[5] James White, after giving up working for his two older brothers as a carpenter's apprentice in Kenosha, Wisconsin, spent six years in the West before 1867, and he was in some of the best places to hear river lore and mountain man tales. While serving in the army, White was stationed at Fort Yuma on the Colorado River near the Mexican border, and he must have heard tales and speculations about the river upstream. On his way west, White had gone through Denver, and he returned to Denver right after leaving the army in 1865 and stayed there a few months. He also returned to Colorado after leaving Kansas in 1867. Denver was still a small town and Jim Baker was one of its most prominent characters. In early October 1867, shortly after James White arrived in Callville, Baker and William Byers were waging a public duel of words. In his *Rocky Mountain News* on October 7, Byers denounced the "highway robbing process carried out at Baker's bridge." Baker did indeed have a profitable business; according to his own ledgers, in the six months between April and September 1867 he made $1,477.87. In a letter dated October 8 or 9, 1867, in a rival Denver newspaper, the *Gazette,* Baker struck back at Byers: "I brand him an infamous liar. The 'News' has always been in on the 'robbing process' itself, so I presume it thinks everyone is in the same boat. Its proprietor took my money in 1859 for advertising which he never inserted in his sheet, and I think there is not a bigger thief in the country than he, and if he is desirous of a little personal matter he can have it to all intents and purposes."

If White needed any reminders about Jim Baker, he could have received one from a story widely covered in Colorado newspapers. On June 4, 1867, just about the time White should have returned to Colorado from Kansas, the *Rocky Mountain News* reported, "Our citizens were startled, yesterday, by the sight of a wounded man being carried into the office of Drs. Strode and McClellan. It was no other than Jim Baker, the celebrated mountaineer and trapper, who, it was soon ascertained, had been severely injured by the accidental explosion of a gun in the Ute camp, about twenty-five miles up Cherry Creek." When the Central City *Daily Register* echoed this story two days later, it said that Baker was "severely if not fatally injured." Baker was holding a shooting match with the Utes and testing out a new repeating rifle when it blew up against his cheek, badly lacerating him. He later grew a beard to hide the scars.

Does this newspaper article ring any bells? Here again are some of the basic elements of the story James White told at Callville: Utes, Captain Baker shot, a guy named Strode. "Strode" was the name White gave for the other man with Baker and White himself. Or to be more accurate: the first written account of White's adventure, the letter from E. B. Grandin that was published on September 24, 1867, in the *California Alta,* used the name "George Strode." But Grandin was hearing this tale secondhand, and so was J. B. Kipp, who in his letter published in the *Los Angeles News* on September 20 changed one letter, making the name "George Strobe." When James White wrote to his brother on September 26, in a letter full of misspellings, he used the name "gorge Strole." (White's poor writing skills were typical for his time, when public education, especially on the frontier, might last only a few years, but his terrible spelling might have encouraged some historians to treat White as a dummy, and thus unreliable.) Ever since, the name in the history books has been "Strole." Still, it is curious that the name of "Strode" popped up three months apart, five hundred miles apart, in connection with Utes and a Captain Baker who gets shot. Strode is a very rare name. Doctor Strode's first name was Edward; after serving as a surgeon in the Union army he moved to Denver, where he soon became highly respected.

Given the extraordinary nature of White's adventure, it was inevitable that right from the start some people would doubt its veracity. Some have accused him of being a glory-seeker, but this was unfair since White remained quiet and modest about his trek, even among his family and friends. Others have suggested that White was too exhausted and delirious to know what he had done. Others have suggested that White's story was designed to hide something ominous: Robert Stanton told White, to his face, that maybe he and not the Utes had killed Captain Baker and Strole. White objected strongly to this, and Stanton retreated.

Yet White did have a strong motive for "killing off" Captain Baker in another sense, for covering his tracks along with the tracks of Baker and Strole, and for disconnecting himself from the people and events of Fort Dodge. If White needed raw materials for a good cover story, they were not hard to find. There were decades of mountain man lore about the Colorado River, such as that published by David Coyner in *The Lost Trappers*. There were decades of Indian attack and river escape stories. There was Jim Baker's story about running into hostile Utes and heading down the San Juan River to the Colorado. There were the recent newspaper headlines about Utes, Baker getting shot, and a guy named Strode. And there were two previous claims about solo raft trips down the Colorado River.

On October 30, 1866, the San Francisco *Daily Evening Bulletin* published a report from Richard Sneath, the chairman of the San Francisco Chamber of Commerce, offering proof that the Colorado River was navigable all the way to Utah.

> Mr. Sneath informs us that a Mr. Nugent (son of a contractor of this city) from Southern Utah, called on him and stated that on his way hither he embarked in a dug-out, at a point where the Colorado river crosses the southern boundary of Utah Territory. From that place he voyaged safely down the Colorado, through the Big Canon, to Callville. Mr. Nugent reported from personal inspection that no great difficulty would be experienced in steamers passing through the canon, and it is well known that the river is perfectly navigable for good sized boats from above it to the confluence of Grand and Green rivers in Utah territory, some 300 miles further in a northeasterly direction. Should the report of this gentleman prove to be correct, a vast extent of territory in the interior of the "Great Basin," between the Sierra Nevadas and the Rocky Mountains, and reaching to Colorado Territory will be of comparatively easy access from this city.

This sounds like the national dream of river superhighways, plus the wishful thinking of California businessmen, stoked by one big teller of tales.

Another claimant was John Moss, a prospector who really got around and made good mineral strikes in California, Arizona, and Colorado. Moss was one of the discoverers of silver in El Dorado Canyon on the Colorado River in the early 1860s. He was also notorious for exaggerating the value of his claims and selling them to wealthy speculators, including George Hearst. Moss claimed that in 1861, at Lees Ferry, some soldiers helped him build a raft fourteen feet long and five feet wide. The Indians warned him that he could not make it through the canyon, but he pushed off anyway, with only a pole for steering. In a whirlpool he soon lost his pole, all his provisions, and his gun. He was tossed by endless rapids and whirlpools and clung to the raft in terror, unable to reach shore. He did not sleep for three and a half days, which is the time it took him to go all the way through the Grand Canyon and well beyond. That's more than a hundred miles per day, and this was at low water. Finally, some Indians spotted him and pulled him out. Like James White, he was starving, naked, bruised, and sunburned.

If Colorado River historians even knew about the claims of Nugent and Moss, they chose to dismiss them due to their blatant impossibility. And Moss may not have made his claim until 1877, when it was published in a San Francisco newspaper. Moss might have simply stolen James White's story. White was taken more seriously because he was actually seen on the river.

Did White steal anyone else's story? Perhaps. But on the other hand, plenty of events, even very unlikely events, happen to coincide with past events, stories, and names. Coincidences happen all the time. Nothing in this chapter proves that White lied about his adventure; even if he did lie about some things, it still does not prove he didn't really raft down the Colorado River.

NOTES

1. William H. Goetzmann, *Exploration and Empire: The Explorer and the Scientists in the Winning of the American West* (New York: W. W. Norton, 1966), 136.

2. Powell, *Exploration*, 131, 142–43.

3. Nolie Mumey, *The Life and Legend of Jim Baker, 1818–1898, Trapper, Scout, Guide, and Indian Fighter* (Denver: World Press, 1931), 70.

4. Ibid., 45.

5. *Harper's*, September 1866.

· 4 ·

Rivals and Rails

IN THE ABSENCE of enough solid facts, much of the James White debate has consisted of casting doubts on the motives of the opposing side, usually motives of pride. Yet one of the major players in the debate, Charles Parry, who was the first man to conduct an inquiry into White's story and to champion his cause, has received little examination regarding his personal background and his possible motives for promoting White. Parry's motives might have involved personal pride, but also went deeper. A case could be made that Parry was using White's story as a political weapon. But I should begin by admitting that this chapter is an exercise in speculation, offering a strong circumstantial case that has some gaps and one big flaw, and no convincing proof.

This story begins with two men whose lives ran so parallel it seems they were destined to end up in an angry competition for the job of America's top botanist. They were Charles Parry and George Vasey. Parry and Vasey were both born in England, within a year of one another, in 1823 and 1822. Their parents soon moved them to New York state, where they grew up a few dozen miles apart. Both obtained medical degrees from Columbia University in 1846. There they connected with one of America's foremost botanists, John Torrey. Both soon moved to the Midwest, where they lived about a hundred miles apart. Both earned their living as physicians but devoted their free time and energy to botany. Yet as their botanical work took root, their tracks seemed to diverge. While Vasey was stuck in Illinois studying prairie grasses, Parry turned his medical training into a ticket for traveling the West with government and railroad surveys. In his three years with the Mexican Boundary Survey, starting in 1849, he became the first botanist to extensively study southwestern plants. Parry's favorite realm was the Colorado Rockies, then still mostly unexplored by botanists. Parry's Colorado collections won him great respect from fellow botanists; Sir Joseph Hooker, director of the Kew Gardens in London, would call Parry "the king of Colorado botany"; this would be the title of a 1997 biography of Parry. Parry's work also won him respect and friends in Colorado. In 1863, in his *Rocky Mountain News,* William Byers published an article Parry had written on mountains; the next year Parry and Byers teamed up to attempt the first ascent of Longs Peak, although they failed to reach the summit. When Parry was appointed America's government botanist, Byers declared in his newspaper, on March 23, 1869, that it was "an excellent appointment."

In the 1860s the world of American professional botany was very small, with few botany professorships, so Parry and Vasey pursued their work as amateurs, while constantly keeping an eye out for the rare opportunities to do botanical travel and research work that paid. Parry was disadvantaged by his lack of a scholarly bent; his publications were mostly popular articles in newspapers. Vasey was more scholarly, and by 1870 he was editing a botanical journal and publishing scientific papers. Soon he was serving as the curator of the natural history collection at Illinois State Normal University. It would have been human nature for Parry and Vasey to keep an eye on one another jealously. It probably rankled Parry, who had financed all his Rockies trips out of his own pocket, when Vasey attached himself to an upstart but resourceful professor named Powell, himself a capable botanist, who got sponsorship from the federal government, two Illinois colleges, the Illinois Natural History Society, and the Union Pacific Railroad to go explore the Rockies in the summer of 1867. Powell was poaching on the turf of "the king." Powell invited Vasey to go with him to take charge of the botanical studies. Personal priorities forced Vasey to drop out of the 1867 trip, but he would join Powell for his second summer in the Rockies the next year. By the time Powell and Vasey arrived at Cheyenne, Vasey had already collected 150 specimens. At this point William Byers was giving Powell great publicity and assigning his brother-in-law Jack Sumner to guide Powell. In 1868 Powell and Byers became the first team to scale Longs Peak. Powell had stolen Parry's mountain-climbing glory. Powell had no doubt benefited from the lessons learned from Parry's failure. And now Powell was planning to make the first descent of the Colorado River.

The rivalry between Parry and Vasey exploded in 1871 when Parry was fired from his job as the first official botanist for the Smithsonian Institution and the U.S. Department of Agriculture. He was replaced by George Vasey. The events behind this replacement remain obscure, but the battle over the job involved the scientific giants of the day and left the job unfilled for half a year. At first, Parry's scientific friends, including Asa Gray and Smithsonian director Joseph Henry, rallied around him and demanded his reinstatement.

They strongly opposed Vasey's nomination, and John Torrey even vowed to sabotage Vasey's career if he got the job. It didn't hurt Parry that he had named mountains for Gray and Torrey. Yet Gray's biographer, A. Hunter Dupree, saw evidence that Parry, after his years of independence, "proved unsuited to the life of a civilized botanist. When Gray and others tried to domesticate him by securing his appointment as botanist of the Department of Agriculture, he found the political necessities of government service intolerable."[1] Vasey's advocates asserted that the unscholarly Parry had mismanaged the botanical collection. Gray refused to concede this point, but slowly opinion swung to Vasey, and Gray and Henry ended up supporting him.

It's likely that behind the scenes John Wesley Powell was using his new stature as an American scientific hero to push for Vasey. Their friendship had begun at least a decade previously when they helped found the Illinois Natural History Society, of which Vasey was elected president. In 1865 George Vasey's brother Richard moved from the Chicago area, near George, to Bloomington, Illinois, to give his children a better location for acquiring a college education. George's nephew Lucius attended Illinois Wesleyan University, where Powell began teaching that same year, and Lucius was in Powell's class. George Vasey prepared a complete flora of the state of Illinois and presented it to Illinois Wesleyan. When Powell went through the Grand Canyon in 1869 he named a magnificent, cliff-draped, wildflower-loaded spring as Vasey's Paradise. When Powell went back to the river two years later and so could not fulfill his duties as curator of the Illinois State Normal University natural history collection, he got Vasey to fill in for him. On February 15, 1871, Vasey wrote to Powell asking for his help in securing a job:

> It has occurred to me that in your intercourse with public men and public affairs you might see an opportunity when some appointment was to be made of persons possessing my special qualifications, in which appointment you might use an influence for my advantage. For instance if any surveys are ordered on the lines of the Pacific RRs, like King's survey of 1869, when a botanist is wanted.... Again, if it shall prove that...there will be a vacancy of Dr. Parry's place in the Agricultural Department, a place which I could certainly fill, and for which abundant recommendation could be procured.[2]

Vasey and Powell both soon started long Washington careers, and in 1888, after Powell had warned the nation that the settlement practices that had worked in the Midwest would not work in the more arid lands beyond the

100th meridian, George Vasey set up a botanical research station in Garden City, Kansas, just west of the 100th meridian, to study and breed forage grasses that would work best in the West.

Long after Parry lost his job to Vasey, Parry still despised Vasey, writing to George Engelmann, for whom Parry had named a spruce, that Vasey was so slow and incompetent that he needed to send out his specimens to others to get them identified, and that at this rate he'd take a whole generation to produce one botanical catalogue.[3]

Yet all of this was in the future in September of 1867, when Parry was the doctor/naturalist for the Kansas Pacific Railway, which was surveying the lower Colorado River region to find a 35th parallel route to the Pacific coast.

Parry was involved at the tail end of a long, intense, bitter competition to select a route for building the transcontinental railroad across the West. The competition had pitted city against city, state against state, senator against senator, cabinet member against cabinet member. Most seriously, it was fueled by the same rivalry between North and South that in the 1850s was leading the country toward civil war. Cities were motivated by economic self-interest, and thus Omaha and San Francisco wanted a northern route of which they would be the termini, while San Diego wanted to anchor a southern route following the 32nd parallel; William Byers and other Denver leaders were campaigning for a middle route that, of course, would go through Denver and across Colorado and thus access America's richest mining region. But for the nation the competition would decide whether the North or the South would reap not just the economic but also the political rewards of the railroad era to come. Jefferson Davis, who as Secretary of War in the 1850s was in charge of western surveys, was pushing for a 32nd parallel route that would unavoidably pass through his native Mississippi and benefit the whole South, helping to enhance the slavery economy and expand it across the West. Northerners were determined to build a northern route that would starve slavery. Both sides pleaded their cases passionately. Southerners argued that a northern route would be crippled by blizzards and impossibly steep mountains. Northerners argued that a southern route would be blocked by deep canyons, heat, and lack of water, and that deserts could not support the agriculture or timber industry needed to make a railroad profitable. Both sides agreed that a middle route, if it went through the worst of Colorado's mountains, would be ridiculous. To prepare the way for his 32nd parallel plan, Jefferson Davis made the Gadsden Purchase, acquiring from Mexico nearly 30,000 square miles that offered the easiest railroad route. Missouri senator Thomas Hart Benton ridiculed Davis's efforts, for Benton wanted a middle route that would serve Missouri and, besides, his son-in-law John C. Frémont was one of the founders of the Kansas Pacific Railway. Davis feared an alternative middle route that would take away the advantages of a southern route by following the 35th parallel through northern Arizona and New Mexico, avoiding Colorado's mountains, but then veering north through Kansas and toward Missouri and Illinois, avoiding the South and benefiting the North. Davis was so determined to discredit a 35th parallel route that in his report on it to Congress he fudged the data. This debate generated several route surveys that were also of questionable honesty, touting the advantages of one route and exaggerating the difficulties of rival routes. Only when the South seceded from the Union was the North free to build its northern railroad.

But Northerners continued debating which northern route was best—the Union Pacific Railroad's route across Nebraska and Wyoming or the Kansas Pacific Railway's two possible routes, either straight through Colorado or across northern New Mexico and Arizona. Though the Union Pacific was the heavy favorite, for a while Congress left it an open contest, with the two railroads' construction crews racing each other across the plains. With less financial support, the Kansas Pacific had to go deep into debt to keep up with the Union Pacific, gambling everything on winning congressional designation and funding as the national railroad. To claim some of the credibility and investor support of its rival, the Kansas Pacific disguised itself under the name "Union Pacific Railroad, Eastern Division." But when the real Union Pacific reached the 100th meridian first, Congress backed the Union Pacific. The Kansas Pacific was facing bankruptcy. Its only hope was to convince Congress that the nation needed a secondary route to the Pacific. To make its case, the Kansas Pacific had to quickly identify a viable route and win federal funding for it. It decided that getting through Colorado's mountains was too expensive and no longer necessary, since its line would only end up linking with the Union Pacific line farther west. The 35th parallel route was the better option. But after years in which the Union Pacific and Jefferson Davis had agreed completely that the 35th parallel route was stupid, the Kansas Pacific faced deep skepticism. In June 1867 the Kansas Pacific tried a public relations blitz to win congressional support, but Congress, well bribed by the Union Pacific, wasn't impressed. Soon the Indian uprising in Kansas shut down construction on the Kansas Pacific. By September 1867 the Kansas Pacific was facing a deep crisis.

In the context of the long rivalries over railroad routes, it is interesting to take a new look at one of the most famous statements ever made about the

Grand Canyon. In 1858 Joseph C. Ives led a federal survey of the lower Colorado River, using a primitive steamboat to move up the river as far as Black Canyon (later the site of Hoover Dam), then heading overland as far as Havasu Canyon, the most beautiful tributary of the Grand Canyon. In his final report, Ives declared, "The region last explored is, of course, altogether valueless. It can be approached only from the south, and after entering it there is nothing to do but to leave. Ours has been the first, and will doubtless be the last, party of whites to visit this profitless locality. It seems intended by nature that the Colorado river, along the greater portion of its lonely and majestic way, shall be forever unvisited and undisturbed."[4]

Historians and park rangers have long made fun of Ives for his naïveté in not recognizing the canyon's tourism potential. Yet his comment was rather typical of the geographical slanders associated with the railroad debate. Ives did have a good motive for slandering northern Arizona. He was a protégé of Jefferson Davis. When Davis became president of the Confederacy, Ives quit the U.S. Army and joined him as his aide-de-camp for most of the Civil War. Ives's home in Richmond became one of the hubs of Confederate high society. When Ives wrote his words about the Grand Canyon region, Davis was at the peak of his campaign to slander northern Arizona as a railroad route and economic resource. Though in 1857 Davis had been replaced as Secretary of War by John B. Floyd, Floyd was a Virginian who continued serving the interests of the South, and Ives had married Floyd's niece.

Just when the Kansas Pacific Railway needed a way to discredit Ives, Davis, and the whole idea that Colorado River country was impassible and worthless, fate dropped an unlikely gift into its hands. Ives had insisted that the Colorado River upstream from Callville was unnavigable. But now Callville was reporting that a man had just come down the whole Colorado on a simple raft. The Kansas Pacific's chief surveyor and builder was General William Palmer, the perfect man for launching an attack on the credibility of Ives and Davis. Palmer had commanded a Pennsylvania cavalry unit that, at the end of the Civil War, had helped capture Davis. Palmer sent his survey scientist, Charles Parry, to see White.

Parry might have had a shock of recognition when he heard White's story. The first published newspaper letters and articles about White hadn't said anything about his trek starting at Fort Dodge; perhaps White was trying to keep this a secret. Charles Parry had been doing survey work in Kansas during the spring of 1867, when the Indian uprising was breaking out and shutting down construction on the Kansas Pacific. According to Parry's notebooks, at the end of May, only six weeks after Baker and White had fled Fort Dodge, Parry was at Salina, Kansas, the end of the Kansas Pacific line at that moment. He left there on June 7, worked his way along the planned line, and arrived at Fort Wallace, a U.S. Army post in western Kansas, on June 24, staying there two weeks. By July 13 he was at Fort Lyon in Colorado and remained there about ten days. Fort Lyon was where Major Henry Douglas had sent his orders to intercept Captain Baker and seize his horses. For nearly two months Parry had been in Kansas and at two army posts as Indian chaos was breaking out around them. Parry had a good chance to hear lots of stories about what was happening, including the story of Captain Baker and his gang of horse thieves who, against the best efforts of the U.S. Army to keep the peace and protect the interests of the Kansas Pacific Railway, had helped trigger a war.

When telling his story to his Callville rescuers, White said he had begun in Colorado, and he had mentioned a Captain Baker. Baker had gotten into the newspaper accounts, so Parry might have asked White about Baker. Parry would have been shocked to realize that White's Captain Baker was the same Baker who had stirred up that trouble in Kansas and helped shut down Parry's railroad, and that James White was one of Baker's gang. Parry should have looked on White with considerable animosity, seeing him as a thief, a liar, a scoundrel, a traitor against the U.S. Army, a fugitive from the law, and totally untrustworthy. Parry should have been skeptical about White's story about his river trip. Even if Parry hadn't known anything about White's Fort Dodge connection, Parry, as a scientist, could be allowed a bit of caution. Instead, in the report he wrote for the Kansas Pacific, Parry went all out to proclaim White's reliability: "Now, at last, we have a perfectly authentic account from an individual who actually traversed its formidable depths, and who, fortunately for science, still lives to detail his trustworthy observations." And, "His narrative throughout bears all the evidences of entire reliability, and is sustained by collateral evidence, so that there is not the least reason to doubt that he actually accomplished the journey in the manner and time mentioned by him."[5]

Parry's report was soon published by the St. Louis Academy of Science and then in newspapers around the country. Parry made several points that made Ives look incompetent. First, with all his steam technology and navigational skills, Ives had hit a rock and wrecked his boat in Black Canyon and declared that the Colorado was unnavigable beyond that, while the hapless James White had passed hundreds of miles of rocks and rapids. Second, "the estimated average elevation of the Canon at 3,000 feet, is less than that given on the authority of Ives and Newberry, but may be nearer the actual truth, as the result of more continuous observation." Third, Parry endorsed White's description of the canyon cliffs as consisting of "white sandstone," which was not what Ives and his geologist Newberry had reported. Fourth, though Parry mentioned the rapids that had plagued White and drowned Strole, in his report summary Parry barely acknowledged rapids, saying that if the river was unnavigable it was because of "the long distance and the inaccessible character of the river margin for the greater part of its course."[6]

In her book defending her grandfather James White, Eilean Adams rebuked Charles Parry for his recklessness: "Concluding that White's estimates of elevation might be nearer the actual truth than those of Ives and Newberry is, of course, nonsense; the latter gentlemen were on an official scientific exploration. White was at every moment in danger of losing his life and in no condition to be accurate about anything within the canyon."[7] Then she rebuked Parry for proclaiming that the canyon consisted of white sandstone. Adams was worried about these claims because they had been used by James White skeptics to argue that White didn't know what he was talking about or was never in the Grand Canyon at all. Yet one of the leading skeptics, Robert Stanton, joined Adams in being baffled by Parry's claims:

> I have always been puzzled to understand why the "geologist" of Gen. Palmer's expedition should thus attempt to discredit the geological reports of Dr. Newberry, or question Ives's measurement of the height of the Canyon. What was Dr. Parry's duty, under all these circumstances? Plainly, it was to examine all existing records and prove or disprove White's story by such evidence and testimony as was then accessible.... He knew of this work, as is seen in the fact that in his letter to Gen. Palmer he quotes from it twice in his prologue and once in his conclusions. The truth is that both Ives and Newberry had published positive refutation of the whole case which Dr. Parry was so earnestly making out for James White.... Had Dr. Parry carefully and conscientiously reread Lieut. Ives's report, with Newberry's accurate geological descriptions, he would not have been led into the further ridiculous error of concluding that a half-starved, half-mad miner afloat on a raft could come "nearer the actual truth as to the height of the Canyon," as the result of "more continuous observation" than could Ives by instrumental measurement.[8]

Stanton decided that Parry had been swept away by reckless enthusiasm for a dramatic story, so swept away that it was actually Parry and not White

himself who launched the claim that White went down the whole Colorado—
Parry had coached White to believe this. It didn't occur to Adams and Stanton
that Parry's main goal was not to promote James White but to tear down
Joseph C. Ives and, by association, Jefferson Davis. As a big bonus, Parry could
also diminish John Wesley Powell.

By establishing James White as the first man down the Colorado River,
Charles Parry could steal the glory from the upstart professor Powell, the tres-
passer on Parry's Colorado kingdom, the thief of his Longs Peak glory, the
friend and mentor of his bitter rival George Vasey. It meant that even a coma-
tose dummy could blunder his way down the river and that Powell needed
no skill or courage to do it. And it meant that the evil Union Pacific Railroad,
which had become Powell's patron (it would ship Powell and his boats for free
to the put-in beside its bridge over the Green River in Wyoming), would get
less glory.

But when it comes to Parry and Powell, we need to give more careful scrutiny to the timeline. Remember, White's journey was in September 1867. That
summer Powell had arrived in Colorado and was doing botany in a realm that
Parry had considered his own, so Parry could have felt some rivalry. But Powell
would not bring George Vasey with him to Colorado until 1868. Powell would
not climb Longs Peak until 1868. Powell had taken wagons to Colorado in the
summer of 1867 and would not make use of his Union Pacific patronage until
he and his men returned home that fall, so how would Parry have heard about
it? The year 1867 was a few years before Parry and Vasey would duel over the
same job. Most important, Powell was still two years away from making his
river trip. It's never been clear when Powell made up his mind to go down the
Colorado River. The first public indication that he was planning any kind of
river trip came on November 6, 1867, in the *Rocky Mountain News*: "Major J. W.
Powell left for the east this morning. He will return to the territory next spring
to prosecute his scientific labors, and will go down the Grand to its junction
with the Colorado river." This was the kind of news that would have interested
surveyors like Parry, but it was still a big step short of going down the whole
Colorado River. (Later Powell would switch his starting tributary to the Green
River.) So how would Parry have known about Powell's plans and been scheming to discredit him?

There are, however, two small windows of possibility. Powell first publicly
announced his hopes of exploring the whole Colorado River at a meeting of
the Illinois Natural History Society in Bloomington on December 18, 1867. He

also acknowledged that the Union Pacific Railroad had signed on as his patron. Charles Parry did not meet with James White until at least two weeks after December 18. Some historians have listed their meeting date as January 6, 1868, but in fact that was the date Parry put on his report to the Kansas Pacific, and it seems unlikely that Parry wrote up his whole report on the same day he met White. They met in Hardyville; from a letter that town founder William H. Hardy wrote to the Prescott *Arizona Miner*, printed on January 11, 1868, we know that Parry arrived in Hardyville on the evening of December 31. This gives him six days to meet White and prepare his report. Even if the meeting was on January 6, there was less than three weeks' time in which Parry might have heard about Powell's plans. This was even more of a long shot since Charles Parry was a long way from Illinois. After leaving Fort Lyon in July, Parry had followed the proposed line of the Kansas Pacific. In September, as James White's story was spreading, Parry was in Santa Fe. By December 18 he had left Prescott, Arizona, for the mines in the Mojave Desert near the Arizona-California border, one of the most remote areas in America. How would Parry have heard news from a meeting of the Illinois Natural History Society? Powell's announcement of his Colorado River plans was still rather vague and didn't even make it into the Bloomington newspaper. On the other hand, Parry was from Davenport, Iowa, just across the Illinois border, and he was active in Iowa scientific circles that overlapped heavily with Illinois scientific circles. Did a friend write him a letter? It's still a long shot.

The other window of possibility is William Byers. Byers and Parry must have hit it off enough to try to climb a mountain together, and Byers appreciated that Parry, in a series of 1864 letters to a Chicago newspaper, had strongly endorsed Denver, not rival Cheyenne, as the best hub for a railroad through the Rockies, and had generously praised Byers's newspaper and the beauty and medicinal value of Byers's tentative resort at Hot Sulphur Springs. In 1864 Parry was proposing to run the Kansas Pacific line, via tunnels, from Denver into Middle Park, the location of Hot Sulphur Springs, and then onward to Salt Lake City; Byers would have struck it rich. Parry and Byers had stayed in touch. Parry saved a couple of letters from Byers—one from 1866, the other from 1868—and in the 1868 letter Byers is keeping Parry informed about Powell's activities and plans to run the Colorado River the next year. (I'll examine this letter more closely in a later chapter.) Parry soon relayed this news to George Engelmann, who had facilitated the publication of Parry's survey report by the St. Louis Academy of Science, in a letter conspicuously ungenerous to Powell:

Long's Peak has been <u>successfully ascended</u> and <u>barometrically measured!</u> By the Powell exploring expedition. The guide of the party was one of our unsuccessful companions, Mr. Byers of Denver and profiting by our experience…. But the result given by them does not differ <u>materially</u> from my estimate…. They expect to winter on Green River and continue…next season down the Colorado perhaps through the Big Cañon. A short time ago I received from an acquaintance in Wisconsin in answer to some enquiries, the original letter written by <u>James White</u> the…hero to his brother describing his voyage written 18 days after his accomplishment. It agrees in every respect with the information given me and it completes the reliability of his testimony.[9]

It had now been nearly a year since Parry had met White and filed his report, but he was still working to prove his case, and in this letter it is more obvious who he is working against. Five months later Parry reported to Engelmann, "Powell's party wintering on Green River is mostly broken up. Vasey was with him last year but did not accomplish much as they did not get on any new ground."[10]

William Byers must have known Powell's thinking in late 1867, for Byers had published that brief article about Powell's plans to explore the Grand River to its junction with the Colorado. Had Powell told Byers anything further, such as his hopes of exploring the whole Colorado? Had Byers shared this information with Parry in a letter in late 1867? No such letter survives. Once again, we are wandering around on thin ice.

Byers published Parry's report on James White in February 1869, even as John Wesley Powell was getting ready for his river trip. Byers was a former railroad surveyor and a key backer of the Kansas Pacific Railway. He kept up a drumbeat of articles about the railroad rivalry, slanting everything in favor of the Kansas Pacific. A few days after publishing Parry's report, Byers was ridiculing the Union Pacific because its train was stuck in Wyoming snow drifts. Later in 1869, with its tracks still stuck in Kansas, the Kansas Pacific pleaded with Byers to raise $2 million to complete the tracks to Denver. One of Byers's printers was Oramel Howland, Powell's future crewmember, and if Parry's article about James White inclined Howland to believe that boating the Colorado should be easy, he was in for a shock.

General William Palmer was soon handing out Parry's report on James White to U.S. senators. When Powell's request for funds for his river expedition came up before the Senate in 1868, one senator opposed Powell on the grounds that this river and region had already been explored by James White and "a very competent man, General Palmer." [11]

After the Kansas Pacific abandoned its Pacific dreams and settled for being a Kansas and Colorado route, William Palmer became the president of a Denver railroad company. He always defended the James White story, and perhaps he was taken too seriously by two other Denver railroad men, Frank Brown and Robert Stanton, for when they rode Palmer's railroad to begin their own Colorado River expedition, they seriously underestimated the Colorado. Frank Brown drowned. Stanton became the fiercest critic of the James White legend.

John Wesley Powell was politically astute enough to realize the motives behind the James White legend. Perhaps when Powell helped drive Parry out of Washington, Powell was getting even.

NOTES

1. A. Hunter Dupree, *Asa Gray* (Cambridge, MA: Harvard University Press, 1959), 389.

2. George Vasey to J. W. Powell, February 15, 1871, *Letters Received by John Wesley Powell, Director of the Geographical and Geological Survey of the Rocky Mountain Region, 1869–79* (microfilm), National Archives, Washington, DC.

3. Parry to George Engelmann, Dec. 19, 1872, Charles Parry Papers, Special Collections, Parks Library, Iowa State University (hereafter Parry Papers).

4. Joseph C. Ives, part 1, "General Report," in *Report upon the Colorado River of the West, Explored in 1857 and 1858 by Lieutenant Joseph C. Ives* (Washington, DC: Government Printing Office, 1861), 71.

5. Quoted in Eilean Adams, *Hell or High Water: James White's Disputed Passage through Grand Canyon, 1867* (Logan: Utah State University Press, 2001), 60, 64.

6. Ibid., 65, 65.

7. Ibid., 66.

8. Stanton, *Controversies*, 27, 28, 29.

9. Charles Parry to George Engelmann, Nov. 17, 1868, Parry Papers.

10. Parry to Engelmann, April 10, 1869, Parry Papers.

11. Senator John Sherman, May 25, 1868, *The Congressional Globe,* 40th Cong., 2nd Sess., pt. 3, p. 2563.

· 5 ·

Dawson and Teller

ONE OF THE MOST important historians of the James White story was Thomas F. Dawson, who did his research while serving as the executive clerk of the U.S. Senate. In 1917 Dawson published his findings as an official U.S. Senate document, giving it extra prestige. Dawson was a former newspaper reporter and editor, and a serious historian: after his career in the Senate, he returned home to Colorado and became the Colorado state historian and curator of the Colorado Historical Society. While in Washington, he had written a biography of Colorado senator Edward Wolcott. Back in Colorado he was at work on a biography of his mentor, Colorado senator Henry Teller, when Dawson was killed in a car accident while taking part in President Warren Harding's 1923 car tour of Denver. Dawson's research into the James White story was conscientious: he wrote to White's arch critic Robert Stanton, and to the civic leaders of the town where White had been living for four decades, Trinidad, Colorado, asking them if White was an honest character. In his document, Dawson sorted through the evidence, found White to be a reputable and modest man, found testimony that supported him, and implied that White's denouncers might have been motivated by pride in their own river running feats.

Of course, given the acrimony of the James White debate, Thomas Dawson, too, would be accused of having ulterior motives, of Colorado pride that tempted him to inflate a Coloradoan, James White, into a major hero. White had settled in Colorado in the 1870s, which by 1917 defined him as a pioneer, practically a native. Dawson's attention was drawn to the White story when in 1915 the U.S. Congress funded the Powell Memorial for the Grand Canyon's South Rim. That memorial set some people and historians murmuring that perhaps Powell hadn't really been the first through the canyon, and that anyway it was unjust that the names of the Howlands and Dunn had been left off the list of crewmembers on the memorial plaque, which implied they were cowards unworthy of Powell. The Howlands and Dunn, too, were Coloradoans, making the memorial a double snub to Colorado pride.

Thomas Dawson's motives might have gone deeper than pride. For four decades Dawson's career was thoroughly enmeshed with the career of Senator Henry M. Teller. Teller was a political enemy of John Wesley Powell.

On the surface, Powell and Teller had similar biographies. Both were Methodists, abolitionists, and early supporters of the Republican Party. Both started out as small-town schoolteachers. For the adventure of it, Teller boated down the Ohio River in 1852, Powell in 1857. Teller was born in upstate New York in 1830, Powell in the next-door county in 1834. Powell settled in Illinois in 1853, Teller in 1858. Teller arrived in Colorado in 1861, Powell in 1867. Powell began a long Washington, DC, career in 1872, Teller in 1876. Their big difference was that Powell saw the West as a scientist, Teller as a pioneer. Powell campaigned for humbler use of land and water, enforced by the federal government, and for more respect for Indians, and Teller was a champion of Manifest Destiny.

Teller's values and career can be summarized by the words on an interpretative panel that for many years was in the museum of the Colorado Historical Society:

> He was an outspoken opponent of conservation legislation and attacked any bill prohibiting the full exploitation of western forestlands. "Why did the Almighty clothe those hills in timber," he railed, "if it was not that they might be beneficial to mankind? Are not homes better than forests?" Teller also spoke for most westerners on the Indian question. After the Meeker Massacre in 1875, he led the fight for the swift and total removal of the Utes from Colorado. For those who agreed with him, Teller was hailed as the "Defender of the West."[1]

Teller was also an enemy of William Byers, the editor of Denver's *Rocky Mountain News* and an important patron of Powell's explorations of the Colorado mountains in 1867 and 1868. Byers's brother-in-law, Jack Sumner, and longtime printer, Oramel Howland, went down the Colorado River with Powell in 1869. On March 14, 1868, in between his favorable coverage of Powell's activities in 1867 and 1868, Byers blasted Teller in the most savage, personal terms: "The brand of Cain is upon him.... [Teller] has reviled Colorado, let Colorado revile him. Let the curse of every citizen be upon him. Let him be a dead man among us, so vile, so corrupt, so offensive, that the very mention of his name will excite loathing. Let the guilt of his own base acts be made to weigh so heavily upon him that he will only be too glad to escape [to] where he cannot even hear the name of the territory he has so abused."

William Byers and Henry Teller had a lot in common: both came from the Midwest to Colorado in the Pike's Peak gold frenzy and became leading boosters of Colorado—Byers as a newspaper editor, Teller as a lawyer and businessman. Yet they landed on the opposite sides of a bitter rivalry that would dominate Colorado for years. Byers settled in Denver, still a small town in the early 1860s. Teller settled in the leading mountain mining town, Central City, where today one of the most prominent buildings is the Teller House Hotel, built by Henry Teller in 1872. During territorial days, when Colorado's population and fortunes were in rapid flux, Denver and Central City competed to become the state capital and economic center of Colorado. At its peak Central City was larger than Denver and was generating Colorado's wealth, and it looked down on Denver as a mere staging area for the mining activities in the mountains. Denver considered itself to be the geographically obvious and socially stable and respectable hub for Colorado's political and economic life, in contrast with mountain towns full of transients, ruffians, and foreigners, and saddled with boom-and-bust economies.

The rivalry between Byers and Teller was heightened because both men were politically ambitious. When Colorado became a state in 1876 Teller was elected U.S. senator, becoming Colorado's longest-serving senator. In 1896 Teller was the front runner for president—not in his own Republican party, but as a Democrat, since Teller had led a walkout of Republicans at their convention over the issue of silver versus gold. Then William Jennings Bryan's famous "Cross of Gold" speech snatched the Democratic nomination from Teller. Byers had a good chance of being elected Colorado's first governor in 1876, but a romantic scandal, widely publicized by his enemies, left him humiliated and discredited.

Byers's 1868 tirade against Teller was sparked by the issue of statehood. During the Civil War years, statehood was being pushed by outsiders who wanted Colorado's electoral and congressional votes for Lincoln, and wanted Colorado draftees and taxes for the war effort. Some Colorado leaders, including Byers, wanted statehood as a matter of pride and political power; Teller originally supported statehood with the understanding that he would be nominated for the U.S. Senate. Yet Teller soon realized that a majority of Coloradoans, especially in the mining towns, were opposed to statehood, since they didn't want to pay taxes or be drafted into the army or add to Lincoln's political base. Teller switched sides, and Byers branded him a traitor to Colorado.

In early 1868 the Denver faction again went to Washington, DC, to campaign for statehood. Against the objection that Colorado didn't have enough population to warrant statehood, Byers and his colleagues claimed that the population was more than 75,000 and that a good majority favored statehood. Teller went to Washington and insisted that the population was more like 30,000 (the 1870 census proved him correct) and largely opposed to statehood.

Amid Byers's attacks on Teller that continued through 1868, Teller probably noticed Byers's October 14 story headlined, "The Powell Party: Latest Items from the Expedition," that began, "Our Mr. Howland writes us as follows from the Powell Expedition in camp on Bear river."

Byers sold the *Rocky Mountain News* in 1878, but the paper continued blasting away at Senator Teller. According to Teller biographer Duane A. Smith, "The *News* railed against Teller in the no-holds barred partisan political reporting of his generation.... The paper accused him of being...a 'very ordinary statesman,' and said it would be a 'novelty' if his speeches contained even a 'slight infusion of law, reason, or intelligence.' The *News*...said his speeches fell flat, spoke of the 'growing opinion of your incompetency,' and finally, accused Teller of 'hopeless mediocrity.'"[2]

Henry Teller did find one strong journalistic supporter: Thomas F. Dawson. Born in Kentucky in 1853, Dawson began his journalism career there; in 1876 he was hired as the state news editor of the Denver *Tribune,* at a time of intense rivalry between the *Tribune* and Byers's *Rocky Mountain News.* In 1882 Dawson bought a one-third interest in the *Denver Times* and became managing editor; he gave major support to Teller, who was then serving as secretary of the Interior under President Chester A. Arthur, and thus had far more authority—and generated more controversy—over western land policies and Indian policies. According to Teller's other biographer, Elmer Ellis, "Teller's need of Republican journalistic support in Denver was supplied by Thomas F. Dawson of the *Denver Times.* To him Teller confided his own case, and Dawson defended him against the attacks in the *Republican.* This intensified a friendship that was to last for the rest of their lives."[3] When Teller finished his term as secretary of the Interior, he returned to the Senate and hired Dawson as his private secretary, an association that lasted until Teller's retirement in 1909. As a reward for his loyalty, Teller got Dawson appointed the executive clerk of the Senate.

Henry Teller's public career began in the heyday of the Wild West, and he retired on the same day as President Teddy Roosevelt, who had brought the conservation movement into power. Teller didn't change nearly as much as America did: his political values remained rooted in the Wild West, with its faith in rugged individualism and an endless frontier. Teller was offended by the concepts of public lands, national forests, national parks, and federal management of water, timber, minerals, and wildlife. Speaking out against an 1880 bill to expand federal authority over the Arkansas springs that later became Hot Springs National Park, Teller declared it a matter of principle: "The entire principle is wrong…[and] the people of that section would have been infinitely better off, if the Government had allowed the first man that got there to take it. That ought to be the rule in reference to valuable springs or valuable lands. The man who has the enterprise to go and put his claim on the land in accordance with law ought to take it."[4] Teller biographer Duane A. Smith wrote: "Henry Teller has been sharply criticized by Yellowstone Park historians for his role involving the park during his term as secretary of the interior. He has been described as 'the weakest secretary' in terms of the park's interests, a 'negative force,' and 'antipark.'"[5]

As the conservation movement gained momentum and then the White House, Teller was exasperated by its portrayal of the pioneers as agents of greed and destruction. He and President Roosevelt feuded in bitter personal terms. At the end of his career Teller vented, "Forest rangers now move prospectors off reserves. My friends, if that had happened when I first came to this state there would have been one less ranger…. I haven't heard that the government claims the air yet, but I expect that some of these gentlemen who favor conservation will claim it and try to get revenue from this air for the government…. We could not have settled Colorado if we had this new-fangled notion of conservation."[6]

Like a majority of Americans in his time, Teller regarded the Caucasian race as inherently superior, giving whites rights over Indians and setting limits to what they should do for Indians: "We insist on treating him as if he were a civilized man, when he ought to be treated as a savage, full of superstitions and weaknesses that belong to savage life."[7] When the Sand Creek Massacre shocked the nation and cast a shadow on Colorado, Teller denied that it had been a massacre and defended the perpetrators. Teller opposed citizenship for Indians and favored opening unused reservation lands to white settlement. Indians shouldn't be given private land rights because they couldn't be good capitalists and, besides, this would make it harder to displace them. Indian schools should concentrate on teaching agriculture, not reading and writing.

By contrast, John Wesley Powell, true to the human rights passion that had led him to join the Union army and that would forever ache in the Shiloh-lost stump of his arm, regarded Indians as fellow humans, with legitimate rights.

From his youth, he had been fascinated by their cultures, although like many scientists in the early decades of evolutionary thought, Powell viewed Indian societies through an evolutionary framework and regarded their societies as "primitive." The prospect that Indian societies would soon disappear encouraged Powell to found the U.S. Bureau of Ethnology in 1879 and to launch the most comprehensive study of Indian life, languages, and cultures yet done in the United States. Powell did support Senator Teller's efforts to remove the Utes from Colorado to Utah, but whereas Teller was motivated by punishment, Powell believed it would serve assimilation, supposedly advancing the Indians' cause.

Two years later Powell became the second director of the U.S. Geological Survey and organized an equally ambitious study of the American land, its geography, soils, agriculture, rivers, groundwater, flood problems, irrigation possibilities, minerals, metallurgy, paleontology, and general geology. It was science for the sake of science, which brought hostility from senators who wanted only practical economic benefits (especially mineral wealth), who saw no use for paleontology (which smacked of Darwinism), and who didn't welcome Powell drawing conservation lessons. In his 1878 report on the arid lands of the West, Powell warned that the West did not have enough water to support Manifest Destiny, the settlement habits that had worked in the East and Midwest. Powell was picking a fight he could not win, a fight against the guiding myth of the American nation, a fight that in years to come would lead to his downfall.

When Powell began his efforts to study arid lands and Indian ethnology in 1878 and 1879, he was supported by a secretary of the Interior, Carl Schurz, who sympathized with his values and goals. Schurz had been a young firebrand in Germany's 1849 democratic revolution, and its failure forced him to flee to America. Schurz joined the abolitionist movement and in the Civil War was a Union general. After the war he became a St. Louis newspaper editor (his cub reporter was Joseph Pulitzer) and Missouri's U.S. senator, a seat from which he opposed Gilded Age capitalism, Grant administration corruption, and American imperialism. When Rutherford Hayes became president in 1877 he appointed Schurz Secretary of the Interior. Schurz was ahead of his time as a conservationist and sympathizer with Indian rights. Wallace Stegner wrote, "There is no evidence of intimacy between Schurz and Powell, but there is every evidence of essential agreement."[8] When Schurz referred Powell's report on the arid lands to the Senate, he wrote, "I have the honor to commend the views set forth by Major Powell."[9] Among other measures, Schurz pushed to stop timber poaching on federal lands, a taken-for-granted practice in the West, and this enraged westerners, especially Senator Teller.

Schurz and Teller also clashed over removal of the Utes. According to Teller biographer Duane A. Smith, "His longstanding disagreements with the policies of Secretary of the Interior Carl Schurz led to open warfare.... Relentlessly, he unmercifully censured Schurz's 'liberal' policy."[10] Powell expected to have a friend in President Hayes's successor in the White House, James A. Garfield, but Garfield was assassinated the same year he was sworn in, and replaced by his vice president, Chester Arthur, who appointed Teller as Secretary of the Interior. Arthur was open to trends for conservation and better treatment of Indians, but Teller resisted. "Secretary Teller," wrote Arthur's biographer Thomas C. Reeves, "being a westerner, held a less kindly attitude toward Indians than did the president."[11]

For Powell, the transition from Schurz to Teller must have been wrenching. Secretary Teller did arrange to triple the budget of the Geological Survey to more than half a million dollars in 1885–86, and he publicly bragged about all the mapping and mineral discoveries Powell was accomplishing, but for Teller that was the Survey's entire purpose, not science, and definitely not conservation. While Teller saw the land through the eyes of a mining lawyer, Powell saw it as the son of a prairie farmer and as a geologist.

The stage was set for more than two decades of conflict and contempt between Teller and Powell, and for Teller and his protégé Thomas Dawson to take pleasure in taking down Powell's reputation a few notches by claiming that the honor of being the first to descend the Colorado River belonged not to a bleeding-heart, tree-hugging Washington bureaucrat, but to a genuine, gold-seeking Colorado pioneer.

Yet as plausible as this scenario might seem, like much else about the James White story it soon fades into vagueness. When it comes to documenting or proving this scenario, we come up empty. Powell and Teller left relatively little documentation about their Washington careers and nothing about their dealings with one another over the issues that divided them. In the Teller papers that Dawson collected for the Colorado Historical Society there are few exchanges between Teller and Powell. (One of them concerns an 1887 letter that Colorado surveyor Edward Berthoud wrote to Teller supporting the idea of a Grand Canyon National Park, a letter Teller sent to Powell for his opinion.) In two Teller biographies, there is no mention of Powell, and in Powell biographies there are few mentions of Teller, while Nevada senator William M. Stewart gets the starring role as Powell's nemesis—although in Wallace Stegner's biography *Beyond the Hundredth Meridian,* all six times he mentions Teller it is always "Stewart and Teller." Another leading Powell nemesis was Colorado's other senator, Edward Wolcott—about whom Dawson wrote an admiring biography.

One can make a good case against this scenario. Powell died in 1902 and had been rendered politically powerless nearly a decade previously. Dawson did not do his James White research until 1916–17, a quarter of a century after Powell had been a political rival to Teller. Was there really much to be gained by taking down Powell's reputation? Teller had died in 1914, so he had nothing to gain. Dawson's promotion of James White fit logically with his coming role as a Colorado state historian, his role of boosting Colorado pride. Dawson was more of a gentleman than some in the James White debate; he was willing to credit Powell as the first real explorer of the canyon, with plenty of skill and courage, although Dawson did insist that Powell embarked on his trip only when reassured by White's story that safe passage was possible.

Yet Dawson, like many historians then and later, regarded Henry Teller, not Senator Stewart or anyone else, as the primary "Defender of the West" against interference by people like John Wesley Powell. Political grudges tend to endure. It probably crossed Dawson's mind that Henry Teller would have enjoyed seeing Powell diminished as a hero.

NOTES

1. History Colorado Center, Denver, 2012. Copied by hand by author.
2. Duane A. Smith, *Henry M. Teller: Colorado's Grand Old Man* (Boulder, CO: University Press of Chicago, 2002), 108.
3. Elmer Ellis, *Henry Moore Teller: Defender of the West* (Caldwell, ID: Caxton, 1941), 150.
4. *Congressional Record,* 46th Cong., 3rd Sess., 754–61.
5. Smith, *Henry M. Teller,* 240.
6. Quoted in Smith, *Henry M. Teller,* 236.
7. Quoted in Ellis, *Henry Moore Teller,* 106.
8. Wallace Stegner, *Beyond the Hundredth Meridian: John Wesley Powell and the Second Opening of the West* (Boston: Houghton Mifflin, 1953), 211.
9. John Wesley Powell, *The Arid Lands,* ed. Wallace Stegner (Lincoln: University of Nebraska Press, 2004), 4.
10. Smith, *Henry M. Teller,* 102.
11. Thomas C. Reeves, *Gentleman Boss: The Life of Chester Alan Arthur* (New York: Alfred A. Knopf, 1975), 362.

·6·

Conclusion?

D O THE NEW FACTS and scenarios presented in this book offer grounds for finally settling the James White debate? Not really.

The debate might have been settled if James White's account of his river trip had included some unmistakable descriptions of famous rapids or archaeology sites, but White's account was too vague. In the absence of compelling facts, the debate has been carried out primarily on theoretical grounds: Was it technically possible for someone on such a craft to survive such obstacles? On these grounds James White has always been at a big disadvantage: even his advocates admit that his voyage was very unlikely. But very unlikely things do happen, occasionally. This book has not added anything new to the facts about his river voyage. At this point, it's highly unlikely that any such new facts will appear.

Much of the James White debate has been fueled by ulterior motives. The pride of some river runners, such as historian Robert Stanton, has motivated them to try to discredit White. But two of White's most important advocates, Charles Parry and Thomas Dawson, also had ulterior motives which were not so conspicuous. In sketching out their backgrounds and motives, this book has better balanced the scales of ulterior motives, but—unfortunately—perhaps further lowered our image of the integrity and quality of the entire debate. But even if Parry and Dawson had dubious motives, does this prove that White didn't make his journey? No.

The James White debate has often centered on whether White was an honest person, and here this book offers some major new evidence. We can now document that White was lying about the beginning of his adventure, and that he had very good motives for lying about further portions of it, such as the fate and whereabouts of Captain Baker. If Baker and White were running from the law, they might have traveled a long way overland, perhaps heading for California, and White did not want to reveal his motives or his route or his continued association with Baker. Perhaps White was already in terrible physical condition before he entered the Colorado River toward the end of the Grand Canyon. Then again, the events at Fort Dodge and White's dishonesty about them do not prove that White did not make his river trip. Indeed, perhaps in their haste to flee the law and head west, Baker and White decided that the Colorado River provided the fastest route. It was even the safest route— they would not run into any U.S. Cavalry troops on the river. They had heard years of claims that the river was navigable all the way to California. And just because the story that White told at Callville echoed previous stories, such as that of Jim Baker, does not prove his story didn't happen.

On the whole, this book has lowered the credibility of James White and two of his most important advocates, and has redrawn the parameters of the debate. But it doesn't really settle the debate. The James White mystery has actually thrived on ambiguity, and there is plenty of that left. A century from now, river runners will probably still be sitting around their dinner circles, debating whether or not James White really ran the river.

PART II

The Crew

·7·

The Howland Connection

OUR LONG-ACCEPTED STORY of the Powell expedition was built on an assumption, an assumption fully encouraged by Powell himself and by the historians who admired him: the assumption that Powell was the whole story, deserving all the credit for the expedition. Powell did it all: he conceived the expedition, got the funding, found the crew, led the journey, and endured the ineptitude of some of his crew. Powell's crewmembers were peripheral characters: it hardly mattered who they were, where they came from, how they got onto the expedition, or what they thought of it. This assumption has guided historical research into the expedition, guided it onto Powell and away from the crewmembers. Historians who admired Powell were downright eager to ignore Jack Sumner and William Hawkins, who later criticized Powell's leadership, and to portray them as ungrateful losers. Powell's admirers arranged for the names of three other crewmembers—Oramel Howland, Seneca Howland, and William H. Dunn—to be left off the Powell Memorial in Grand Canyon National Park, on the premise that they were cowards and deserters, unworthy of Powell. Even historians who were inclined to be critical of Powell, such as Dock Marston, nevertheless remained very Powell-centric in their research agendas.

Yet when a wider circle of sources is examined, they suggest a scenario in which Powell was not quite so central to the story. From various people who worked with Powell—Sumner and Hawkins, some of his second expedition members, even his own brother-in-law Almon Thompson—we have repeatedly heard the complaint that Powell was not good at giving credit to those who helped him. But it appears that he owed some large debts, unrecognized before. In this scenario, some of the group dynamics and events of the Powell expedition become much more logical than they have seemed before.

Before John Wesley Powell went down the Colorado River in 1869 he spent two summers exploring the Colorado Rockies. In the first summer, 1867,

Powell Memorial at Grand Canyon National Park (with Stephen Mather, first director of the National Park Service). Powell admirers made sure that the names of the Howland brothers and William Dunn were left off the plaque. Photo courtesy of Grand Canyon National Park Museum Collection.

Powell began making connections with five men who would be the core of his river crew. The only thing these five men had in common was their connection with William Byers, the editor of the *Rocky Mountain News*. Oramel Howland was a printer for Byers, and through Oramel came his half-brother Seneca. Jack Sumner was Byers's brother-in-law, who ran Byers's trading post at Hot Sulphur Springs in Middle Park in the Colorado Rockies, and through Sumner came Bill Dunn and William Hawkins, trappers and hunters who used the trading post. It's interesting to note that all five of these men became resentful of Powell's leadership of the river expedition. Three of them walked off the trip—although Powell admirers have usually denied they were motivated by dissatisfaction with Powell, and of course they left no written explanation of their motives. The other two, Sumner and Hawkins, later wrote strong complaints against Powell. Meanwhile, the other four crewmembers seemed much less resentful of Powell. Does this pattern mean anything? And here's another question: Why was it Oramel Howland who instigated the walkout? In the absence of other reasons, historians have assumed it was because Oramel Howland was in charge of one of the boats, the *No Name,* when it wrecked early in the expedition, losing precious supplies, making the remainder of the journey much grimmer, and leaving Powell resentful of Oramel.

When Powell went to the Rockies in 1867 he was leading a group of men, most of whom were from Bloomington, where Powell taught at Illinois Wesleyan University. Yet this was not the first time that a group of men from Bloomington had explored the Colorado Rockies. Back in 1860 sixteen Bloomington men had spent six months exploring the Rockies and had done many of the things Powell would do: they collected natural history specimens, sent reports back to the Bloomington newspaper, built a boat and went down a river, and were even guided by a relative of Oramel and Seneca Howland.[1] This 1860 trip wasn't about natural history but about the Pike's Peak gold rush. The previous year, at the start of the gold rush, a Bloomington man named Linus Graves had gone to the Rockies, prospected, built a cabin, then returned home to Bloomington and helped spread gold fever there. Graves's cabin (a dozen miles from the goldfields at Central City, where Oramel Howland would later live and work as a printer) would serve as the headquarters for the 1860 expedition, which was rather disorganized, with separate bands wandering this way and that, working at mining here and there, occasionally regrouping at Graves's cabin. At one point some of the men headed for the headwaters of the Arkansas River, eagerly because, as Edward J. Lewis reported to the Bloomington newspaper, the *Pantagraph,* "the Arkansas region is near to the Blue and Grand river country on the western slope, which *everybody* here anticipates will be found exceedingly rich as soon as the snow melts off enough to allow of prospecting it thoroughly."[2] At the end of the summer some of the men built a boat and tried to head home on the South Platte River, but the river proved so shallow and braided that "even a fish could hardly find its way down it without a bird to soar above and look out the channel."[3]

The men on this expedition would soon be civic leaders of Bloomington. Linus Graves became a founder and trustee of Illinois Wesleyan University, which hired Powell. Two men belonged to the Fell family; their relative Jesse Fell was that summer helping to run Abraham Lincoln's national presidential campaign; later he helped establish Illinois State Normal University, where Powell would also teach. The man who was sending reports to the Bloomington newspaper, Edward J. Lewis, was the newspaper's editor, and soon he would be captain of a Bloomington regiment in the Union army. As Lewis wandered through Colorado he stopped at two newspaper offices and introduced himself to their editors, but if he was planning to introduce himself to William Byers at the *Rocky Mountain News* when he camped in Denver on July 30, he was no doubt discouraged by the event he recorded in his diary: "Great excitement in town today about noon, a party having attacked the News office and one of them fired a shot through it; the latter then fled on a horse, crossed and re-crossed the river and came back into town, and was shot down at Bradford's corner with a gun loaded with buckshot. He died during the P.M.... Threats were said to be uttered, that the gamblers would burn the town tonight, and numerous guards were set; among the rest a kind of one at our camp."[4] These Bloomington men were among the civic leaders who sponsored Powell's expeditions to the West; it was as if through him they were reliving the great adventure of their youth. Though disappointed they had not found any gold, they retained golden memories of their adventure. After returning home and resuming his editorship of the Bloomington newspaper, Edward J. Lewis mused,

> The bee wanders far in search of honey, but, whether successful or not, the homeward instinct is pretty sure, sooner or later, to draw him back to his old work-shop in the hive; and he feels none the less at home there for all his erratic excursions among foreign flowers.
>
> Dear readers, since I last talked with you from the editorial chair, I too have wandered far, and looked upon new scenes and new aspects of nature and of men. I have seen the buffalo and the Indian ranging the vast deserts of the central continent, the snowy ramparts of the great mountains heaving their stupendously beautiful forms into the sky...[,] the springs of the Colorado gushing forth on their way to the far Pacific, and the colossal energies of young civilization rearing the foundation walls of a mighty State in regions which nature seems to have dedicated to savage solitude since the world began.[5]

When Powell went to Bloomington a few years later, after his service in the Civil War, his friends there included men who still enthused about "the springs of the Colorado gushing forth on their way to the far Pacific." Powell absorbed their fond memories, and offered them a second chance to pursue those gushing springs westward.

The main thing that interests us here is that Linus Graves was a distant cousin of Oramel and Seneca Howland. When Oramel Howland's mother died, his father married a woman named Elvira Graves, who became the mother of Seneca Howland; thus, the Howland brothers were actually half-brothers. Elvira Graves and Linus Graves belonged to the same Vermont Graves clan.[6] They were not very close on the Graves family tree: their connection lay with their great-grandfathers, Abraham and David, who were brothers. But Elvira and Linus were close geographically. They were born about twenty miles and six years apart, and they had many siblings closer in age. There is a good chance these two Graves families knew one another. Seven young members of these two families migrated to the richer farmlands of central Illinois. Elvira Graves's brother Thomas moved to Tonica, Illinois, and one record suggests he was accompanied by his sister Caroline. They were forty-five miles from Bloomington, where Linus Graves eventually settled. Linus went to Illinois in 1835 and taught school in two towns, then married a schoolteacher in Waynesville, and they lived there for two years. Linus opened a general store, but soon saw better prospects in Bloomington fifteen miles away, and they moved there.

All four of Linus's brothers moved to Illinois, two of them to Waynesville. It seems that three of Linus's brothers couldn't stop hearing the call of the West, for they soon moved onward: Oliver Graves, who for a while was a partner in Linus's store, had settled in Colorado by 1869. Elvira Graves's sons Oramel and Seneca also heard the call of the West. We know that as of 1870 Linus Graves was very aware of the Howland brothers, for it was Linus Graves's son, Walter Graves, who accompanied John Wesley Powell to Mount Trumbull to ask the Indians what had happened to the Howland brothers, as if Walter Graves was representing the Graves family. Walter was a student at Illinois Wesleyan and served Powell as a topographer in his land surveys in southern Utah. It's likely that Linus Graves had known about the Howland brothers three years earlier. It was probably not a coincidence that seven years after Linus Graves guided an expedition of Bloomington men through the Colorado Rockies, John Wesley Powell showed up in the Rockies and, out of the tens of thousands of men he could have run into, quickly linked up with the sons of Elvira Graves. It's likely that Linus Graves told Powell that he had two cousins in Colorado who would be good guides or at least good contacts, especially since Oramel Howland worked for William Byers, the most important booster of Colorado exploration.

There is some provocative evidence that Oramel Howland was indeed Powell's contact in Colorado. In the winter and spring of 1867 Oramel was living just outside Denver in the town of Bellville. Occasionally he went into Denver and checked into the Planter's House Hotel. We know this because in its early years the *Rocky Mountain News* included a list of who was staying at Denver hotels, so we can track Oramel Howland's comings and goings.

According to the report Powell prepared for his Illinois sponsors, Powell arrived in Denver on July 1. Also on July 1 the *Rocky Mountain News* reported that Oramel Howland arrived in Denver the night before. He stayed two days. The newspaper's hotel listings included the origin of guests, and Howland was listed as "News."

The Planter's House Hotel was also a popular spot for newspaper staffers to have dinners and parties. There seems to be some confusion over exactly when the Powell expedition arrived in Denver, for on July 8 the *Rocky Mountain News* reported that the expedition had arrived the evening before. Powell's biographer William Culp Darrah interpreted this discrepancy to mean that Powell rode ahead of the rest of the expedition. In any case, on July 8 the *Rocky Mountain News* reported that Oramel Howland again checked into the Planter's House Hotel. On the next page of the same edition the *News* reported of Powell's arrival, "They came for a tour of exploration among the mountains, and we trust will have every facility afforded them." Doesn't the *News* sound confident that the Powell expedition will have "every facility afforded them"? "Every facility" might have included a welcoming committee named Oramel Howland. After July 8 news of the Powell expedition disappeared for sixteen days, until on July 24 the *News* ran a brief article: "We were pleased to meet, yesterday, Mr. Platt, the artist connected with the scientific expedition now in the territory." And guess what: after July 8 Oramel Howland disappeared for sixteen days, and checked back into the Planter's House Hotel just in time to have been the one who met Mr. Platt and wrote this article.

Was this all a coincidence?

Historians have simply assumed that when Powell got to Denver he looked up William Byers, and thus it was through Byers that Powell met the five men at the core of his river crew. But according to Byers's diaries, Byers wasn't in Denver when Powell arrived; he was in the mountains, though he soon returned for three days, then headed off into the mountains again.[7] So it couldn't have been Byers who wrote those articles welcoming Powell to Colorado.

This scenario begins to suggest a different group dynamic, a different psychology, for Powell's river expedition. If it was Oramel Howland who welcomed Powell and introduced him to Byers, then it was Oramel who deserved the credit for connecting Powell with his river crew.

This was only the beginning of Powell's debt to Oramel Howland. It appears that Byers became the largest bankroller of the Powell expedition, at least for its two summers in Colorado, 1867 and 1868. The job of hosting and guiding Powell in the Rockies was passed to Jack Sumner. At the end of their

Oramel Howland. Photo courtesy of Kenneth Barrows.

1867 season Powell left Denver for Illinois on November 6, and a few days later Byers gave Jack Sumner a check for $200.25 for a bill at M. L. Rood, a Denver gun and supply store.[8] A week later Byers gave Sumner a check for $456.37 for a bill at Salomon, a Denver grocer. I've looked through seven years of Byers's financial records and this is the only time Byers gave Sumner checks for such large sums. When Byers was purchasing supplies for his own household, the checks were much smaller. Over the whole of the previous year, 1866, Byers made a total of $170.60 in outlays. A good explanation for these sums is that when Byers sent Powell to Hot Sulphur Springs he directed Jack Sumner not only to serve as Powell's host and guide, but also to support Powell with supplies. If this evidence is too ambiguous, then there's something more definite: In 1868 the highlight of Powell's efforts was the first ascent of Longs Peak on August 23, for which Byers joined Powell, his brother Walter Powell, Jack Sumner, Bloomington students Lewis Keplinger and Samuel Garman, and Byers's colleague Ned Farrell. The climb seemed to mean a lot to Byers: his diary entry for it was far longer than for anything else in years, including for his son's birth, his newspaper office getting swept away by a flood, or the assassination of President Lincoln. On the same diary page where Byers records that he and Powell are leaving Denver to head for Longs Peak, Byers writes, "J. W. Powell: in cash loaned $100."[9] Right below this, Byers records that he's spent $37 for Powell at two Denver stores. In the week before Byers and Powell left for Longs Peak there was a flurry of outfitting expenditures, including $185 for two mules, and more than $40 for items like horse feed, a pack saddle, tent cloth, ropes, axes, and fishing hooks. Along the way to Hot Sulphur Springs Byers spent $48 on things like hotels, tolls, and blacksmithing. On the day they reached Hot Sulphur Springs, Byers gave Jack Sumner $100. In only two weeks Byers had spent more than $500 to support Powell's explorations. And there's still more: $50 for a saddle on the way to Longs Peak, and, five days after Byers got home to Denver, $295 for a bill at Salomon the grocer.[10] On top of these expenses, there's an unexplained entry in Byers's ledger for his business at Hot Sulphur Springs. For August, the month they'd climbed Longs Peak, he paid $383.30 for "Loss by J. C. Sumner." Was this more money Sumner had spent on Powell? Or was it financial losses because Sumner was not there to manage the business? Historians have thought that Powell's largest financial backer was the Illinois Board of Education, which gave him $500 for 1867 and $600 for 1868. But Byers provided much more. On November 2, 1902, Jack Sumner wrote to the *Denver Post* to protest statements in their obituary of John Wesley Powell and claimed, "I paid out of my own pocket more than $1,000, and gave nearly two years' time, but I have received neither money nor credit to this day for it." Five years later, in his statement to Robert Stanton, Sumner repeated this "more than $1,000" figure.[11] According to Jack's son Ed, this money came from Jack selling his pack animals and furs. Once again, Powell-friendly historians chose to ignore or dismiss this claim as another wild Sumner brag, but it appears that his "more than $1,000" was quite true—even if he really paid it out of William Byers's pocket. As sometimes happened, Sumner was telling us something important but got a bit carried away.

These financial outlays further change the social dynamic of Powell's river trip. Powell was indebted to Oramel Howland not only for his river crew, but also for his largest source of money.

Most importantly, we have two sources that say that Byers was planning to go down the Colorado River with Powell. The first source is a letter Byers wrote to botanist Charles Parry on September 12, 1868. Unfortunately the letter is partly torn away, so we miss a few words at the beginning of this paragraph: "...about my again joining the Powell expedition this fall. It moves too slow and business requires my attention so much that I can hardly stand the sacrifice of so much time. It will probably winter between Middle Park and Green—possibly at Green—the mouth of White. I will try to join it next year in time to go through the canyon."[12] Was this just a fleeting fantasy that Byers never thought of before and never told anyone again? On the other hand, Parry wasn't a close friend of Byers, so if Byers was mentioning this possibility to him, it's likely he was mentioning it to others, especially his brother-in-law and his employee who were going on the expedition.

The second source is an article in the *Rocky Mountain News* on June 26, 1868: "A letter was received here yesterday from a gentleman connected with Prof. Powell's expedition, which says it was to leave Chicago to-day; would probably go via the Union Pacific Railroad to Green River; down that to the Colorado; and so on through the great canon…. Prof. Powell himself will come to Denver, where at least one gentleman, Wm. N. Byers of THE ROCKY MOUNTAINS NEWS, will join him." By the normal rules of English sentence construction, when this article says that Byers "will join him," it should refer to the previously mentioned action: going down the Colorado River. One problem here is that this article is from 1868, and Powell wasn't going down the river in 1868. The rest of this article, which quotes an also-garbled Chicago newspaper account of Powell's plans, makes it clear that the *News* reporter doesn't really know what's going on. But it does appear that he's picked up the idea that when it comes to Powell going down the Colorado River, Byers is supposed to join him.

We can wish we had a more compelling context for these two statements. Nevertheless, we've got two indications that Byers was planning to go with Powell. When we take this idea seriously, the events of the Powell expedition click into a more logical shape.

William Byers had far more wilderness experience than John Wesley Powell. In the 1850s Byers was a railroad surveyor and got all the way to the Oregon coast, and by 1869 he'd spent a decade roaming all over the Colorado Rockies. When it came to leading a wilderness expedition, Byers far outranked Powell. Then add the personal element: Would Jack Sumner have been taking orders from Powell when his own brother-in-law was on the trip? Would Oramel Howland have been taking orders from Powell when his longtime boss was on the trip? Would Seneca Howland have been taking orders from Powell when his own brother was more obedient to someone else? No, if Byers had gone on the river trip, we might not today be talking about "the Powell expedition," but "the William Byers expedition," or perhaps "the Byers and Powell expedition," and Powell would be the secondary figure, the guy who supplied the boats and much of the money, while Byers supplied the crew, the experience, and the leadership. It could be that right from the start Byers's five friends expected to be going on the Byers expedition. When Byers didn't go, they were left resenting Powell's leadership, even more so when Powell started bullying them. Why was Powell bullying his crew, and why, by all accounts, did he aim the greatest bullying at Oramel Howland? Because Powell recognized that he had a credibility problem and he was trying to assert his authority over the crew, especially over the man he owed the most, who now had the most cause to resent him.

Why didn't Byers go on the river trip? We don't know. We can't be sure that Byers was really serious about this possibility or ever mentioned it to Powell. Byers was indeed a very busy man, so he might have decided that he couldn't get away from his newspaper for the half year that Powell's expedition might require. On the other hand, over the previous decade Byers had repeatedly left Denver for long periods to pursue other interests, including exploring and prospecting, and he seemed confident about letting his partners manage the newspaper. But Byers and Powell would have had different motives for the river trip. Byers might have wanted to prove that the Colorado River was navigable, an idea Powell likely found ridiculous; Powell was motivated mainly by his deep geological curiosity. Or perhaps Byers was hearing too many warnings that the Colorado was not a navigable river after all, and he decided not to risk his life. Or, since both Powell and Byers were very strong personalities, both men probably recognized they were destined to clash. Powell might have recognized that if Byers went on the river trip, Powell could end up going along for the ride on the Byers expedition.

There are four sources of evidence that suggest that Powell and Byers had a falling out. First, after the Longs Peak ascent, Byers never gave Powell another dime. Second, a year after Longs Peak, even as Powell was on the river, Byers wrote to Bloomington demanding to be paid back for his $100 loan to Powell and for that $37 at two Denver stores. When this repayment came up $7 short, Byers wrote directly to Powell in December 1869, demanding his $7.[13] Considering that Byers was one of the wealthiest men in Colorado and that he'd gone to great lengths to cultivate friendships with the leaders of Western exploration and development, of which Powell was now one, this is odd. Third, over the winter of 1868–69, Byers began publishing articles about how James White had already conquered the Colorado River. Fourth, when Jack Sumner finally made it back to Denver, Byers published a scathing attack against Powell in the *Rocky Mountain News*, August 9, 1870, declaring that Powell was an imposter, that Powell wasn't the real leader of the Colorado River trip, and that the real leader was Jack Sumner: "Brave by nature, inured to hardship, and fearless in the face of all danger, he was during all that terrible voyage its leading and ruling spirit, the commander of the signal boat which led the way through cañon and rapid and torrent, down the unexplored river and through the mysterious chasm. The expedition was a success, thanks to the dauntless man who *led* it, as much to him who has clothed a portion of its history in the elegant diction of the lecture room."

This became the Sumner family version of events: Jack was the real leader and Powell was "an infernal natural born liar," as Jack's nephew Chauncey Thomas told Wallace Stegner in 1948. Thomas said that decades after the expedition, Powell "lectured on the Cañon in Fort Collins. My father was prof. of History there then, the Agric. College. He said Powell stood on that platform and told such a mess of lies, all becoming Powell, that my father said he was sorely tempted to get up in the audience and tell them there was barely a word of truth in what Powell was saying."[14]

At the same time that Powell's crew felt they'd gotten stuck with Powell, Powell had a good reason to resent these five crewmembers. Historians have sometimes wondered why Powell chose these men: surely out of all the tens of thousands of hardy men in Colorado, Powell could have found somebody who actually knew how to row a boat. The answer could be that Powell chose them for their money—or actually for Byers's money—plus the enormous publicity Byers could provide. When Byers cut Powell off, Powell felt he was stuck with worthless men. The mutual resentments spiraled downward.

But after all it was Powell who gave the lectures and wrote the history articles and books. And who was going to contradict him? The Howlands and Bill Dunn were dead, and they never had a chance to tell their version of events. Byers spent the rest of his life being a super-booster for Colorado, and once Powell held major power over western development, was Byers going to publicly attack him? No. After his 1870 outburst, Byers dropped into total silence about the Powell expedition. Byers and Jack Sumner had a nasty falling out, probably exacerbated by Byers's betrayal of his wife (Jack's sister Elizabeth) in an affair that became a major public scandal. Byers and Sumner didn't even see one another for fifteen years. Sumner wasn't going to speak up for Byers's important role.

But too often this is the way that history gets written.

Powell got a monument on the canyon rim, and Oramel Howland didn't even get his name on it, even though without Oramel, the Powell expedition probably wouldn't have happened at all.

NOTES

1. The 1860 trip was recorded in the diaries of Edward J. Lewis, McLean County Historical Society, Bloomington, IL. His diary was also published as "Diary of a Pike's Peak Gold Seeker in 1860," *Colorado Magazine* 14, no. 6 (Nov. 1937): 201–19, and concluded in the next issue, pp. 20–33.

2. Edward J. Lewis, *Weekly Pantagraph,* June 6, 1860. Lewis was the editor of the *Pantagraph,* and would be captain of a Bloomington regiment in the Union army.

3. Edward J. Lewis, "Across the Plains to the Rocky Mountains in 1860," *Daily Pantagraph,* August 2, 1902.

4. Edward J. Lewis, "Diary of a Pike's Peak Gold Seeker of 1860," *Colorado Magazine,* 14, no. 7 (1937): 28.

5. Edward J. Lewis, *Weekly Pantagraph*, April 3, 1861.

6. Graves genealogical details from John Card Graves, *Genealogy of the Graves Family in America,* Vol. 1 (Buffalo, NY: Baker, Jones, and Co., 1896).

7. William N. Byers, Diaries, Byers Collection, Western History Collection, Denver Public Library (hereafter Byers Collection), July 1–10, 1867.

8. Byers recorded his financial transactions in two places, in nearly identical detail. One is in his diaries, Byers Collection. The other is in his financial ledgers, Stephen N. Hart Research Library, Colorado Historical Society, Denver.

9. Byers, Diaries, July 29, 1868, Byers Collection.

10. Byers, Diaries, Sept. 4, 1868, Byers Collection.

11. Stanton, *Controversies,* 211.

12. Byers to Parry, Sept. 12, 1868, Parry Papers.

13. William N. Byers letter to John Wesley Powell, December 18, 1869, from Powell Collection, National Archives, Washington, DC, as copied for William Culp Darrah, Darrah Collection, Utah State Historical Society, Salt Lake City (hereafter Darrah Collection). This letter makes reference the previous attempt to collect debt and the August 15, 1869, partial repayment of debt.

14. Chauncey Thomas memoir provided to Wallace Stegner, 1948, Darrah Collection.

·8·

Seneca Howland

The Unsung Hero

WHEN SENECA HOWLAND, Oramel Howland, and Bill Dunn left the Powell expedition at Separation Rapid, the seeds were planted for a lasting controversy about the reasons for their departure. Two of the crewmembers who continued the trip, Jack Sumner and William Hawkins, later wrote indictments of Powell's personality and leadership, outlining the bad feelings between Powell and his crew that led to the separation. The Howlands and Dunn, of course, never had a chance to explain their action, but their abandonment of the expedition could easily be interpreted as an indictment of Powell too. Historians who admired Powell have felt obligated to defend him by portraying the Howlands and Dunn as cowards and deserters, which seemed plausible since Separation Rapid was one of the most formidable rapids they had encountered. This verdict was cast in bronze when the names of the Howlands and Dunn were omitted from the Powell Memorial.

An even greater sin of omission was committed by Powell's most important biographer, William Culp Darrah.

We owe Darrah a large debt, for in the 1940s, when people who had personally known Powell and his crew were dying out and crucial documents were being scattered or lost, Darrah sleuthed out many sources and amassed an archive of Powell materials. Darrah devoted years to Powell because Powell had been Darrah's hero since his youth. As a boy, Darrah fell in love with geology, and he went on to become a Harvard paleobotanist, writing important textbooks, so he admired Powell the explorer of geological time. At age fifteen Darrah developed respiratory problems that often left him severely weakened and housebound, so he admired Powell for overcoming a serious disability. In 1947 Darrah developed severe eye troubles that left him blind in one eye and confined to a darkened room, in which he dictated his Powell biography. Darrah was very aware of the accusations that Powell was a petty tyrant who bullied his men until they quit, but Darrah deflected all blame from Powell. Darrah said bluntly of the Separation three, "The simple fact is they were afraid to go farther and deserted."[1] But even as Darrah helped create an enduring image of the three as cowards, Darrah possessed—and suppressed—one important fact that might have altered our perception of what happened at Separation Rapid.

William Culp Darrah seemed to be proud of his middle name, for he used it regularly. The Culps, to whom he was related through his mother, were one of the most famous families of Gettysburg, Pennsylvania. Two years after the publication of his Powell biography, William Culp Darrah moved to Gettysburg, where he taught biology at Gettysburg College for more than twenty years. The Culp family had settled in the Gettysburg area in 1787 and, during the Civil War battle in 1863, owned the town blacksmith shop. There were Culp graves on Cemetery Ridge, where the armies collided and where President Lincoln delivered his Gettysburg Address. Near Cemetery Ridge was Culp's Hill, which played a major role in the battle, anchoring the Union's right flank, just as Little Round Top and Big Round Top anchored the left flank. Culp's Hill was the farm of Henry Culp, the grand-uncle of William Culp Darrah. As a child, Darrah visited and played on this Culp farm. A famous story of the Battle of Gettysburg is that of Gettysburg-born John Wesley Culp, who had moved to Virginia a few years previously and who had returned as a Confederate soldier. The night before the battle he ventured away from his regiment to visit his Culp sisters, and the next day he died fighting to capture Culp's Hill, which was owned by his own family. John Wesley Culp's brother William fought for the Union.

In Gettysburg William Culp Darrah became curator of the county historical society and oversaw a great deal of material about the battle. Yet it's likely that even before he moved to Gettysburg, as he was working on his Powell biography, Darrah knew enough about the battle to recognize a problem with his desire to dismiss Seneca Howland as a coward. Darrah would have realized that Seneca took part in one of the bravest actions of the battle. If Darrah reported honestly what Seneca had done, his readers would be far less likely to believe that at Separation Rapid Seneca had suddenly turned chicken.

Seneca Howland joined the Union army in response to President Lincoln's call in August 1862 for another 300,000 soldiers. To make recruitment easier, men were paid a bounty and enlisted for only nine months. Vermont responded by organizing the 2nd Vermont Brigade, five regiments with a total of about five thousand troops. Colonel Wheelock Veazey organized the 16th

Seneca Howland. Photo courtesy of Kenneth Barrows.

Vermont Regiment in southeastern Vermont, the homeland of Oramel and Seneca Howland. Seneca Howland was twenty years old and working as a farmer when he enlisted in Company G of the 16th Regiment on September 4, 1862, though he would not be mustered in until October 23, which meant that his nine months of duty would end on July 23, 1863, three weeks after the Battle of Gettysburg. His enlistment form offers us almost the only physical description we have of him: five feet, nine and one-half inches tall; light complexion; gray eyes; light hair. The new recruits were sent to a training camp in Brattleboro, Vermont, then sent to Washington, DC, where they spent almost all of their career doing guard duty—first in the city and then at a series of camps in northern Virginia. More-seasoned regiments and officers distrusted the "nine-months" soldiers for their lack of experience and questionable commitment, and didn't want to give them much responsibility.

At Camp Vermont (near Mount Vernon), from which Seneca wrote a letter to his family, the Vermonters helped construct Fort Lyon to better defend Washington, DC. The winter turned into one of the hardest in Virginia history, with more snow than in Vermont, including drifts of eighteen inches in early November. Lieutenant George G. Benedict of the 12th Vermont Regiment, whose father published the Burlington newspaper, sent a stream of letters to the paper, and on November 24 he reported, "We have had four days of almost incessant rain.... I have the facts...for an essay on Virginia and *mud*...and I assure you it is a *deep* subject."[2] The bad weather worsened illness in camp. When the Union army marched to disaster at Fredericksburg in mid-December it weakened Union defenses, so the Vermonters were sent to Fairfax Courthouse to fill the gap. The 16th was sent to patrol nearby Bull Run, still desolate from the two major battles there, with rotting corpses protruding from shallow graves. Some of the Vermonters—by some accounts, including Seneca's regiment—finally saw action when J. E. B. Stuart launched the Dumfries Raid to test the Union lines. The Vermonters achieved national embarrassment when Confederate raider John Singleton Mosby grabbed the 2nd Vermont Brigade's Brigadier General Edwin Stoughton right out of his bed and carried him off to prison; Stoughton was replaced by George Stannard. Stannard's brigade was large compared with many; Seneca's 16th regiment had 735 men. In late March the 16th moved to Union Mills, upstream on Bull Run River. In June, as Robert E. Lee marched north, Stannard's troops were attached to the Army of the Potomac, also marching north. For the Vermonters their very first battle would be one of the greatest battles in world history, bringing them literally face to face with Lee's most seasoned troops.

They marched for a week. Since the Vermonters were close to the end of their service they had not been given new boots, and many worn-out boots disintegrated and many feet were blistered and bloody, with some men going shoeless. Men collapsed from exhaustion and the heat. Bringing up the rear, the Vermonters missed the first day of fighting at Gettysburg, but they could hear it from far away. That night they camped on Cemetery Ridge.

On July 2 Lee attacked the flanks of the Union army, including at Culp's Hill. Union commanders still distrusted the untested Vermonters, so while other brigades were rushed to reinforce the Union lines, some Vermonters were assigned to guard ammunitions wagons in the rear, and others, including the 16th, remained to hold Cemetery Ridge, filling a serious gap in the Union line. George Benedict wrote, "With the darkness the firing ceased, and we heard then from our front that sound which, once heard, will not be forgotten by anyone—a low, steady indescribable moan—the groans of the wounded, lying by the hundreds on the battlefield."[3]

The next day Lee sent General Pickett and some 12,000 soldiers marching up a field toward Cemetery Ridge, a sight that awed the soldiers on both sides. The top of the ridge held a stone wall, behind which the Union troops waited and fired. At one point the wall jutted outward and folded back, giving the troops there a more forward position, and Stannard stationed his regiments even more forward, beyond the wall, taking advantage of a modest dip in the land that was further reinforced with piles of dirt and fence rails. Stannard's troops were farther out front of the Union lines than any others, giving them a long view of the front line, which soon turned into a long view of the attacking Confederate line just to Stannard's right. Though they took heavy fire and casualties, the Confederates managed to reach the stone wall and began breaching it, a massed column against a line often only two men deep, and it seemed possible that Lee might break through, scatter the Union forces, and win the war right then. But from his vantage point General Stannard was looking into the unprotected right flank of the Confederate line, and he saw his opportunity. He ordered three of his regiments, including the 16th, to leave their shelters, climb over their entrenchments, rush into the open field, line up at right angles to the main Union line, and begin firing into Pickett's flank. The 16th lined up farthest out from the Union line, making them most vulnerable to Confederate attack. Just as Union troops had admired Pickett's charge, one Confederate captain, Henry T. Owen of the 18th Virginia Regiment, found time to admire the Vermonters' maneuver: "There off to our right was the grandest sight I have ever seen. A body of Yankees…coming at double quick…[with] uniforms looking black in the distance, muskets glittering in the sunlight and battle flags fluttering in the breeze created by their quickened motion."[4] Some thousand Vermonters opened fire, advancing as they continued firing, with devastating effect. George Benedict described it: "This was more than the rebels had counted on. Their column began to break and scatter from the rear, in less than three minutes, and in three more it was an utter rout. A portion made their way back to their own side, but fully two thirds, I should think, of their column, dropped their arms and came in as prisoners. Of course they suffered terribly in killed and wounded."[5] The main Union line was thrilled by the sudden, unexpected crumbling of the Confederate attack. Major General Abner Doubleday waved his hat and shouted, "Glory to God, glory to God! See the Vermonters go it!"[6]

Then another Confederate column appeared and advanced to the left of the Vermonters. Colonel Veazey talked a reluctant Stannard into ordering his 16th Regiment to wheel and rush out to meet the new threat, though it would leave the 16th alone and far beyond the Union line. Veazey wrote, "Upon receiving the order to charge the men cheered and rushed forward at a run without firing a shot. They quickly struck the rebel flank and followed it until the whole line had disappeared. The movement was so sudden and rapid that the enemy could not change front to oppose us."[7] Benedict observed, "The 16th hurrying down on the double quick took them on the flank, and bagged about the whole brigade of them.... With these repulses of the enemy the big fight in effect closed."[8]

Civil War historians have ratified the importance of the Vermonters with praise of the grandest sort. In his classic study *Pickett's Charge,* George R. Stewart says, "These raw troops from the far-northern hills were to be granted, and were to seize, a military opportunity such as a professional soldier might dream about during a lifetime of fighting and never realize." And, "Stannard suddenly realized that his Vermonters might become agents of the destiny of a nation." And, "The Union soldiers fighting desperately to hold the wall...all sensed that the battle had turned. Some of their own troops...had come in upon the enemy's flank and were tearing at it." It was "the pivotal movement of the pivotal battle of the war."[9]

It's likely that as Powell and his crew sat around their campfires, they swapped Civil War experiences. Powell's role at the Battle of Shiloh was impressive, his sacrifice and suffering severe. But both Union veterans and today's historians could make a case that the 16th Vermont played an even larger role in deciding the war. When it came to Civil War heroism, Powell might be outranked by Seneca Howland. This would make it even more inappropriate for Powell to assume the airs of a general and to treat Seneca Howland badly.

William Culp Darrah must have recognized Seneca Howland's role at Gettysburg. Casual tourists to the battleground see the prominent monuments to Stannard's Vermonters. You might think that any biographer would be delighted to have such a famous, dramatic, and courageous feat to enhance his story. But in his *Powell of the Colorado* almost the only thing Darrah says about Seneca Howland is, "He had fought in the war and had been wounded at Gettysburg."[10] As if Seneca didn't accomplish anything but getting wounded. In his compilation of his Powell research material in the 1947 *Utah Historical Quarterly,* Darrah was more specific about Seneca's day at Gettysburg: "He suffered a minor wound at the battle of Gettysburg and was temporarily incapacitated for further action."[11]

Yet Darrah's claim that Seneca Howland was wounded and incapacitated at Gettysburg is impossible to verify. There is no record of such a wound in any source—not in Seneca's U.S. military records, not in Vermont military records, and not in Gettysburg National Military Park records. As long ago as 1878, the Office of the Surgeon General in Washington, DC, reported that the medical records for the 16th Vermont did not extend beyond June 19, 1863, two weeks before Gettysburg. The Howland family discovered this when Seneca's brother John, who served with him, applied for a disability pension for lung problems that started a few days after the battle and soon became chronic; the lack of medical records made it hard for John to receive benefits. Because of John's voluminous pension file we do get some glimpses of Seneca's activities around the time of the battle. We hear of Seneca nursing his brother, Seneca talking a general out of sending John to a hospital, Seneca later accompanying his brother back to Vermont. There is no mention of Seneca being wounded. There is no mention of Seneca's wound in the diaries, letters, or post-trip writings of members of the Powell expedition. There is no mention of Seneca's wound in the accounts published in *The Rocky Mountain News,* where Oramel worked. The Howland family today knows nothing of such a wound. The 2nd Vermont Brigade recorded 248 wounded out of about 2,000 men in the battle, and Seneca's 16th Regiment recorded 89 wounded out of 735 men, so if such statistics count for anything, there was only about a 12 percent chance that Seneca was wounded. Finally, Darrah's own research notes, which he deposited at the Utah State Historical Society, contain no mention of Seneca being wounded. Sadly, the easiest explanation is that Darrah realized that anyone familiar with the Battle of Gettysburg would recognize the heroism of Seneca's regiment; to create an escape clause by which Seneca might be dismissed from the action, Darrah simply fabricated Seneca's wound. Subsequent historians have taken Darrah's word for it and never checked for sources.

It's obvious why Darrah didn't want Seneca Howland to be known as a courageous hero. If Darrah revealed that Seneca charged straight into Robert E. Lee's toughest troops, making him as big a hero as John Wesley Powell, if not bigger, his readers would have had a hard time believing that at Separation Rapid Seneca suddenly became terrified by some gnarly waves and fled. If it wasn't cowardice that made Seneca leave, it must have been something else, perhaps something about Powell's leadership. Darrah wanted Powell to be the hero, so Seneca had to be sacrificed. Indeed, while the Separation Rapid controversy has filled hundreds of pages elsewhere, Darrah hid the whole issue away in two curt footnotes.

In the middle of one of the greatest tests of leadership in American history, Seneca proved he was ready to die for the right leader; perhaps Powell was not the right leader.

The fight atop Cemetery Ridge was not quite the end of the battle for Seneca Howland. A few days later the 16th Vermont, presumably including Seneca, was sent in pursuit of Lee's retreating army. But Lee had already crossed the Potomac River, now swollen by rains, and escaped into Virginia. The war would continue, but not for Seneca.

With their nine-month enlistments ending, the Vermont troops boarded trains and headed home, some of them charged with guarding Confederate prisoners on their way to Baltimore. When the Vermonters reached New York, the city had been wracked by several days of riots over the military draft, with more than a hundred deaths. Pressed to remain in the city as a militia, the men of the 14th Vermont, whose enlistments had already expired, voted not to remain, but the 15th and 16th still had a bit of time left in their enlistments and their commanders did not put it to a vote, so the 16th was stationed at the Battery and patrolled the streets for two days. They finally made it home on July 23. They were welcomed as heroes, with speeches and parades. Indeed, on their train ride through Maryland and Pennsylvania, heading for New York, they were, as one 16th Regiment soldier wrote home, "greeted with unexpected cheers from the people who thronged the roadside in every village we passed and waved flags and handkerchiefs."[12] Yet in spite of their new identities as heroes, most of the Vermont troops believed they had done their duty and few reenlisted.

Seneca Howland was officially mustered out on August 10, 1863. Perhaps he went back to his life as a farmer. The next apparent sign we have of him is on January 4, 1867, when the *Rocky Mountain News* listed "S. B. Howland" as a guest at Denver's Tremount House Hotel for several days. He is listed as a resident of the nearby town of Platte Cañon. Platte Cañon is long gone and has not left much trace in the historical record, so we can only guess what Seneca was doing there. William Culp Darrah was not aware that Seneca had been in Colorado in early 1867 and once again he engaged in a bit of invention and said Seneca "had come west, at his elder brother's insistence, to join the expedition."[13]

Walt Whitman would have agreed that the town of Platte Cañon's namesake canyon was a good place to be inspired for a wilderness adventure. In 1879 Whitman wrote a poem there, "Spirit That Form'd This Scene," which included these lines:

These tumbled rock-piles grim and red,
These reckless heaven-ambitious peaks,
These gorges, turbulent clear streams, this naked freshness,
These formless wild arrays.[14]

NOTES

1. William Culp Darrah, *Powell of the Colorado* (Princeton, NJ: Princeton University Press, 1951), 141.

2. George G. Benedict, *Army Life in Virginia: The Civil War Letters of George G. Benedict,* ed. Eric Ward (Mechanicsburg, PA: Stackpole Books, 2002), 85.

3. Ibid., 192.

4. Henry T. Owen letter to H. A. Carpenter, January 27, 1878, John W. Daniel Papers, Special Collections, Alderman Library, University of Virginia, Charlottesville.

5. Benedict, *Army Life,* 195–96.

6. Quoted in George R. Stewart, *Pickett's Charge: A Microhistory of the Final Attack at Gettysburg, July 3, 1863* (Boston: Houghton Mifflin, 1959), 233.

7. Quoted, without further source, in Howard Coffin, *Nine Months to Gettysburg: Stannard's Vermonters and the Repulse of Pickett's Charge* (Woodstock, VT: Countryman Press, 1997), 238.

8. Benedict, *Army Life,* 196.

9. Stewart, *Pickett's Charge,* 62, 210, 232.

10. Darrah, *Powell of the Colorado,* 114.

11. William Culp Darrah, *Utah Historical Quarterly* 15 (1947): 93.

12. Quoted, without further source, in Coffin, *Nine Months to Gettysburg,* 270.

13. Darrah, *Powell of the Colorado,* 114.

14. Walt Whitman, *Leaves of Grass* (1879; repr. New York: New American Library, 1958), 371. Page references to 1958 ed.

.9.

Call Me *No Name*

The transition is a keen one, I assure you,
from a schoolmaster to a sailor, and requires a strong decoction
of Seneca and the Stoics to enable you to grin and bear it.

—Herman Melville, *Moby Dick,* Chapter 1[1]

THIS WAS GOOD ADVICE for a schoolmaster named Powell, although the Seneca he took wasn't the Roman philosopher Melville had in mind.

Ishmael, the protagonist of *Moby Dick* and a man of the mid-1800s, might have understood why Seneca and Oramel Howland named their boat the *No Name*. The Howlands and the rest of the crew might have assumed that they didn't need to explain this already famous name, but Jack Sumner, when listing the boats in his diary, did give us a clue when he added in parentheses after the *No Name* "(piratic craft)."[2] But this clue has been lost on historians, who have taken the name *No Name* to mean that the Howlands were too unimaginative to think up a name for their boat.

Ishmael spends the first dozen chapters of *Moby Dick* introducing the world of whaling by wandering the streets of New Bedford, Massachusetts, then the world capital of whaling. At its peak, New Bedford was the home port for over one third of the world's whaling ships. Ishmael could not avoid noticing that one of the leading whaling firms belonged to the Howland brothers, George and Matthew Howland. This was most evident at the Howland wharf, where the Howland fleet docked. In 1867 the Howland brothers astonished the whaling world with their new ship *Concordia,* the most expensive and magnificent whaling ship New Bedford had ever seen. Nearby was the Howland counting house, where the Howland brothers managed their businesses. The Howland candle factory processed whale oil. If Ishmael walked along New

Bedford's wealthier streets, he would have seen Howland mansions. Ishmael might have lodged on Howland Street, homes to sailors' boarding houses and saloons, and might have seen the Howland School, the Howland Fire Station, and the Howland Mission Chapel. Years later, when whaling was in decline, Ishmael could have worked at one of the Howland textile mills. But for now Ishmael signed on with Captain Ahab, who, considering the propensity of the Howland brothers for associating with obsessive, one-limbed captains, could have been a Howland captain.

Both sets of Howland brothers were descended from an even more famous set of Howland brothers, *Mayflower* pilgrim John Howland (who nearly died when he fell overboard) and his brother Henry, who came to America a few years after the *Mayflower*. Henry was a Quaker, and the Puritans of the Plymouth Colony, being too puritanical, made his descendants uncomfortable, so they left in the late 1600s and founded what became New Bedford. At about the same time, one of John Howland's sons, Isaac, settled in Middleboro, a dozen miles from New Bedford, and here the line of Oramel and Seneca remained for five generations. The Middleboro Howlands could have been among the many Howlands who got involved in whaling. Various branches of the Howland family owned over 10 percent of the New Bedford fleet, and many more served as captains or crew. I checked crew rosters for the name Howland and found many, but there's no Oramel or Seneca. It's likely that John Wesley Powell recognized the association of the name Howland with ships, and we have to wonder if he liked the idea of having Howlands manning his ships.

The Howland family's connection with ships might also be why Powell sometimes referred to Oramel Howland as "Captain Howland." Unlike almost all of Powell's crew, Oramel did not serve in the Civil War, so he did not acquire such a title in the military. Oramel spent the war years working in Colorado, which did have its own small pro–Union army, but Oramel's name does not appear on any of its rosters. There were also local volunteer militias, which didn't always leave thorough rosters, so it's not out of the question Oramel served in one. The term *captain* was also sometimes used on the frontier as an honorary title, especially for men who had served as army scouts; even some Indian chiefs noticed this usage and began calling themselves captain. Yet we don't know that Oramel served in any such role. Perhaps Powell called Oramel captain simply because he was essentially the captain of the *No Name*. Yet it's plausible Powell was thinking of the fame of the Howland family as owners and captains of great ships.

We also have to wonder if Powell, who was continually struggling to cobble together funds for his expeditions, also liked associating with Howlands because the Howlands were one of the richest families in America. The Howlands who founded the New Bedford whaling industry had great timing, for whaling was ready to boom, and its old center, Nantucket, did not have a port deep enough for the larger ships that soon dominated the business. By 1839 nearly half of American whaling ships were based out of New Bedford. One Howland in-law and company owner, Edward Robinson, also had the good timing to get out of the whaling business around 1860 and put his money into other, rising industries, for he realized that the discovery of petroleum in Pennsylvania might eliminate the need for whale oil. Other Howlands clung to the family business through the later 1800s and "went down with the ship." In 1865 Robinson died and left his fortune to his daughter, Hetty Howland Robinson, but this sparked a lengthy legal battle that filled the national newspapers and became, in the words of Hetty's biographer Charles Slack, "one of the most watched civil cases of the century."[3] Hetty was accused of forging her aunt's signature on portions of the will. To help settle the matter, Harvard's Louis Agassiz, the most respected scientist in America, was enlisted to examine the signatures with both his microscope and his judgment, and he cleared Hetty of forgery accusations. Hetty became the richest woman in America and would prove to be a shrewd Gilded Age financial dealer: at her death in 1916 she owned 1/500th of America's gross national product. Agassiz was enlisted in the Howland case in the spring of 1867, only weeks before Powell met Oramel Howland. Yet the Howland fortunes didn't do Powell any good, for Oramel and Seneca came from a much humbler branch of the family. Still, Powell probably didn't mind the status that the name "Howland" conferred in 1867.

Oramel and Seneca weren't the only pair of Howlands pioneering in western waters in the summer of 1869, and with tragic results. On the shores of Lake Tahoe, Captain David Howland was building a forty-foot wooden steamer, the *Truckee,* that would haul lumber, freight, and sometimes tourists around the lake. Apparently he was being assisted by Edward Howland, the son of one of the New Bedford Howlands, who had been crewing aboard a ship that had docked in San Francisco. "He [Edward] had become somewhat irregular in his habits," wrote the *San Francisco Examiner* on August 23, 1869, "and appears to have left his ship and became a boatman, attending on the pleasure parties on the lake." On August 18, two weeks before Oramel and Seneca died, Edward Howland put a gun to his head and "a portion of his head was blown off."

The Civil War brought a serious threat to the Howlands' whaling business, for the Confederates launched several ships to attack Northern merchant and fishing fleets on seas all over the world. The prominence of New Bedford ships made them leading targets. The most successful Confederate pirate ship, the CSS *Alabama,* sometimes sought out regions frequented by whaling ships. In total, twenty-five New Bedford ships were sunk. In a sense, all of them were Howland ships. Throughout the Civil War, George Howland Jr. was the mayor of New Bedford, and he had to deal with the economic disaster inflicted on his town. Even for firms that didn't lose ships, the rise of insurance rates was staggering. By 1862 one hundred whaling ships were removed from operation, and over the course of the war New Bedford's revenues dropped by 50 percent. One Confederate raider continued operating for three months after the war ended, sinking more whalers. Many docked whalers would never sail again, for the whaling business never fully recovered.

Confederate pirates took special pleasure in sinking New Bedford ships, for New Bedford had become famous as a center of the abolitionist movement. This was partly because Quakers had long been among the staunchest leaders of abolitionism, and New Bedford was led by Quakers, including the Howlands. When the Fugitive Slave Law was passed in 1850, Mayor Abraham Howland convened a public meeting to organize local resistance to it, and a few years later city funds were donated to pay for the funeral of an impoverished fugitive slave. New Bedford became one of the major destinations of the Underground Railroad and hosted the largest percentage of blacks in New England, many of whom worked in maritime jobs, including on Howland ships. Its public schools were integrated. It was in New Bedford that Frederick Douglass settled when he escaped from slavery, and he praised it as one of the best examples of human equality he had seen. New Bedford contributed three dozen soldiers to the all-black 54th Massachusetts Infantry, and some of its sea-experienced blacks joined the navy. New Bedford also provided far more than its share of whites to the war, including one infantry company headed by Captain Cornelius Howland Jr. The Howlands set aside their Quaker disapproval of warfare and became strong supporters of the war as a way to abolish slavery. Howlands helped organize "the stone fleet": two dozen obsolete whalers loaded with granite and sunk in the Charleston, South Carolina, harbor in an attempt to block it. Throughout the war Mayor George Howland Jr. led local pro-war efforts, including fortifying the harbor with artillery against Confederate pirates.

One of the most daring Confederate raids was done by the CSS *Tallahassee,* a London-built steamer faster than anything in the Union navy. The

Tallahassee was captained by John Taylor Wood, whose middle name came from his grandfather, President Zachary Taylor. In 1850 Wood had stayed at the White House and, on July 4, accompanied his grandfather as he laid the cornerstone of the Washington Monument. Wood was also the nephew of Jefferson Davis, future president of the Confederacy, and in 1861 this relationship helped swing Wood's conflicted loyalties toward the South. Wood's service as a gunnery instructor at the U.S. Naval Academy at Annapolis led to him becoming the artillery commander of the CSS *Virginia*, better known as the *Merrimac*, in its famous ironclad duel with the *Monitor* in 1862.

In seven days in August 1864, Wood led a raid that destroyed thirty-three Northern ships. After removing the crew and any passengers, Wood burned or sank most of the ships. He wrote, "As night came on the burning ship illuminated the waters for miles, making a picture of rare beauty." He first stationed himself outside New York City and used a captured pilot boat to lure incoming ships to him. He had planned to steam right into New York harbor and fire on the city and navy yard, but he needed the help of a pilot who would guide him safely into the harbor and he was unable to capture one. Instead he continued all the way up the New England coast, causing great alarm throughout the North. When he reached harbor in Halifax, Nova Scotia, he read New York City newspapers. Wood wrote, "The published reports of most of the prisoners were highly colored and sensational.... A more blood-thirsty and piratical-looking crew never sailed, according to some narratives. Individually I plead guilty, [after] three years of rough work, with no chance of replenishing my wardrobe."[4] The crew also read that the U.S. Navy had sent thirteen ships to pursue them, which never caught up. (After the war, the *Tallahassee* was sold to the Japanese, and it sank in 1869, only nine days after the Howland brothers wrecked their *No Name* on the Green River on June 8.)

John Taylor Wood's triumphant pirate raid contrasted with his chaotic flight at the end of the Civil War, but here, too, Wood proved resourceful and courageous. Wood spent the rest of the war as aide-de-camp to his uncle Jefferson Davis, and he was present when Davis received word from Robert E. Lee that Lee had surrendered. Wood accompanied Davis and other Confederate leaders as they fled Richmond and tried to avoid capture. When Davis was captured in Georgia, Wood escaped and continued southward. In Florida, Wood met up with another Confederate leader in flight, Secretary of War John C. Breckinridge. Only five years before, under President Buchanan, Breckinridge had been vice president of the United States, and in 1860 he ran for president

Wood and Breckinridge capture the *No Name*. Courtesy of *Century Magazine*.

against Lincoln and carried the South, but now he was hiding in shadows and anonymity. Wood decided that their best hope for escape was to find a boat and sail for the Bahamas, and Breckinridge trusted Wood's expertise as a sailor.

Wood learned where a lifeboat had been stashed on Florida's St. John's River, yet when Wood loaded Breckinridge, four other men, and their supplies into the lifeboat, he was dismayed at how low it rode, making it "a very frail thing" for open seas. They rowed on the river a while, then got an oxcart to portage their boat thirty miles to the East Coast. They struggled south on the swampy inland waterway, then portaged to the ocean, where they were spotted and stopped by a Union cruiser. Wood used all his pirate's wiles to bluff his way out. When they tried to sail east, the headwind forced them to retreat, and they decided to continue south and aim for Cuba. After a less-than-friendly encounter with Indians on land, they spotted a sail coming toward them and feared another Union patrol, but when this sail suddenly turned to avoid them, Wood decided they were Union deserters fearful of capture. Wood recognized that this sloop, though not much larger than his own lifeboat, was a much sturdier ship, well-decked and well-rigged, and he decided to seize it. With the advantage of oars on a calm sea Wood pursued the sloop, and upon reaching it he and Breckinridge pulled their revolvers and forced a trade of boats. The sloop bore no name. "After our experience in a boat the gunwale of which was not more than eighteen inches out of the water, we felt that we had a craft able to cross the Atlantic."[5]

Wood tried to obtain supplies at a trading post operated by pirates, with the result that the pirates jumped into five canoes and attacked the sloop, but the Confederates fought them off. Near Key Biscayne a schooner started pursuing Wood, and Wood tried to escape into the shallows, but they soon ran aground and had to get out and push. Just as the schooner opened fire, Wood found a break in the coral reefs and darted away. Provisioning themselves with coconuts, they sailed for Cuba. Their course paralleled the Florida Keys for a while and gradually veered in a more southerly direction, so they did not get as far as No Name Key, which had been named in the 1840s. Florida historians have been unable to discover why No Name Key got its name, if, indeed, it can be said to have a name.

Soon a fierce storm hit, and Wood needed all his sailor's skills:

> I thought we were swamped as I clung desperately to the tiller, though thrown violently against the boom. But after the shock, our brave little boat, though half filled, rose and shook herself like a spaniel. The mast bent like a whip-stick, and I expected to see it blown out of her, but, gathering way, we flew with the wind. The surface was lashed into foam as white as the driven snow. The lightning and artillery of the heavens were incessant, blinding, and deafening; involuntarily we bowed our heads, utterly helpless. Soon the heavens were opened, and the floods came down like a waterspout.[6]

Two days after the storm they were nearly out of food and water and tried to approach an American brig for supplies, but the wary captain warned them to stay away; they bartered at a distance and the brig's crew tossed supplies into the water. "We cannot wonder at the captain's precautions, for a more piratical-looking party than we never sailed the Spanish Main. General Breckinridge, bronzed the color of mahogany, unshaven, with long mustache, wearing a blue flannel shirt open at the neck, exposing his broad chest, with an old slouch hat, was a typical buccaneer.... Doubtless the captain reported on his arrival home a blood-curdling story of his encounter with pirates off the coast of Cuba."[7]

Hungry, thirsty, sunburned, exhausted, and feverish, they finally reached Cuba. "Their astonishment was great at the size of our boat, and they could hardly believe we had crossed in it."[8] Required by Cuban customs officers to register their boat, Wood gave the name *No Name*. Wood soon sold the *No Name* to the president of the local railroad.

American reporters in Cuba recognized a sensational story—a recent American vice president fleeing the United States through storms and pirates—and they swarmed Wood for details. Soon the *No Name's* story was famous. On June 27, 1865, even the *New York Herald* hailed the sheer adventure of it: "The manner of his escape from the coast of Florida savors of the romantic, and may yet form the groundwork of an exciting novel or thrilling drama." Southerners loved the tale because their leaders had escaped Yankee clutches. Yankees liked the symbolism that a once haughty Confederacy had been humiliated into piracy and flight. There were three men in Massachusetts who must have felt a special glee. For the New Bedford Howland brothers, one of the pirates who had threatened their whaling empire had been reduced to the captain of a tiny sloop. For Senator Charles Sumner, the ardent abolitionist who had developed a bitter personal hatred for the former vice president, Breckinridge had been reduced to a pathetic, ragged pirate. It's possible that for three other men named Howland and Sumner, the story of the *No Name* also won special attention.

In the spring of 1869 all of America was talking about Confederate pirates, and it's quite likely that Powell's future crewmembers were among those talking. In 1869 the United States filed claims against Great Britain for its role in building Confederate pirate ships, especially the CSS *Alabama,* which roamed the high seas, never even docked at a Confederate harbor, and became the most deadly of the Confederate pirates. The Confederates had secretly commissioned the building of the *Alabama* in a private British shipyard, but both the American and British governments noticed its design and figured out its likely purpose; the American ambassador protested, but the British government released it anyway. The British allowed the *Alabama* and other Confederate warships to use British ports, while British merchant fleets benefited considerably from the drying up of business for American fleets. Americans were outraged, with some regarding it as an act of war. In 1868 the Johnson administration began negotiating with Britain for redress, but as usual the Radical Republicans who had impeached Johnson thought that he was being far too lenient. On April 13, 1869, only six weeks before the launch of the Powell expedition, Senator Sumner took the floor of the U.S. Senate and delivered a long and indignant speech opposing Johnson's proposed agreement with Britain. As the chairman of the Senate Foreign Relations Committee, Sumner had jurisdiction over foreign affairs and treaties. He also considered himself to be representing the New England shipping interests—like the Howlands—who had suffered major losses from Confederate pirates. Sumner talked the Senate into voting down Johnson's agreement by fifty-four votes to one. Sumner demanded that Britain pay $2 billion or cede all of Canada to the United States. Sumner's speech came only weeks after Ulysses S. Grant had become president, and Grant was more willing to take a hard line. Throughout 1869 newspapers carried frequent reports of the latest developments in "the *Alabama* case," one of the hottest political topics of the year. Many of the newspaper stories about the Powell expedition shared the same pages as the *Alabama* case. Negotiations between the United States and Britain went on until 1872 and involved international arbitration in Geneva, Switzerland, becoming a landmark in the forging of international law. The arbitrators agreed with the American position, and Britain apologized and paid the United States $15.5 million, including for damages done by John Taylor Wood; some of that money went to the Howlands of New Bedford.

Senator Sumner's suggestion that Britain turn over Canada as payment must have made John Taylor Wood nervous, for Wood had left Cuba and settled in Halifax, Nova Scotia. After the American Revolution Halifax had become a major destination for Americans so loyal to the British crown that they refused to remain in the United States, and having retained its anti-American sentiments into the Civil War years, it was happy to give harbor to Confederate ships, including Wood's *Tallahassee* right after his pirate raid. Now Halifax drew die-hard Confederates. Wood never gave up his Confederate sympathies, refused offers of clemency, and attended the dedication of a statue to Robert E. Lee in Richmond, Virginia, in 1890. In Halifax he went into the shipping business.

All the 1869 newspaper coverage of the *Alabama* case reminded Americans of the whole subject of Confederate piracy, including Wood and his *No Name*. Oramel Howland, Seneca Howland, and Jack Sumner might have been paying extra attention. For them the name "*No Name*" might now ring with triumph in a new way, and might seem a good omen. The name invoked a brave little boat that had defied all the odds and obstacles, especially walls of whitewater. It invoked a dare for Yankees to be as bold as their foes. The name turned out to be a truer omen than Seneca and Oramel would have wished, for like the crew of the original *No Name*, they, too, nearly starved.

NOTES

1. Herman Melville, *Moby Dick* (1902; repr. New York: New American Library, 1961), 24. Page references to 1961 ed.

2. Quoted in Ghiglieri, *First Through Grand Canyon,* 84.

3. Charles Slack, *Hetty: The Genius and Madness of America's First Female Tycoon* (New York: Ecco Press, 2004), 56.

4. John Taylor Wood, "The Tallahassee's Dash into New York Waters," *The Century Illustrated Monthly Magazine* (July 1898).

5. John Taylor Wood, "Escape of the Confederate Secretary of War," *The Century Illustrated Monthly Magazine* (November 1893).

6. Ibid.

7. Ibid.

8. Ibid.

·10·

The Howland Brothers Write Home

ORAMEL AND SENECA HOWLAND have been defined largely by one event: their leaving the Powell expedition. For some historians, this defined them negatively. Historians also have negated the Howlands by doing little research into them. We have been left with little sense of their personalities. Little of Oramel's personality comes through in the two letters he sent from the first leg of the expedition, for these were journalistic reports to the *Rocky Mountain News,* his longtime employer. Yet back in 1862 each brother wrote a letter to their family in Vermont, letters that open a window into their lives. Seneca wrote from a Civil War camp, and Oramel from Colorado during its mining golden age. Kenneth Barrows, the great grandson of Nathan Howland, another Howland brother, has kindly shared these letters with us. It is worthwhile publishing these letters in full, because they might be the only chance we'll have to get to know Oramel and Seneca as individuals.

Even a casual glance at the letters reveals two distinct personalities. Seneca's handwriting is oversized, his letter brief; Oramel's handwriting is pinched, his letter long. Seneca is an atrocious speller. Oramel's letter is full of intelligence, humor, and caring—just what the comments of his fellow boatmen suggested about him.

Seneca's letter seems to have been prompted by Oramel's letter a month earlier. Seneca was writing from Camp Vermont, a Virginia base for several Vermont regiments, including the 16th Vermont Regiment in which Seneca and his brother John were serving. Camp Vermont was eight miles from George Washington's Mount Vernon, to which off-duty soldiers would walk for inspiration. The Vermonters provided the outermost protection for Washington, DC. The Confederate lines were perhaps thirty miles away, but occasionally someone took a shot at Vermont troops on picket duty. Camp Vermont was

William Henry Jackson's drawing of a winter storm in Seneca Howland's Civil War camp in Virginia, 1862. Jackson later became a famous photographer of the West. Courtesy of Scotts Bluff National Monument.

built on the plantation of George Mason, the grandson of the George Mason who signed the Declaration of Independence; though their Mason hung out a white flag and declared himself to be neutral, the Vermonters had little doubt that he was a loyal Confederate, especially since his brother was the Confederate ambassador to Great Britain. In early November the weather turned unusually cold and snowy for Virginia, and even Vermonters struggled to keep warm; on December 5 another snowstorm hit. The next day, the Vermonters celebrated Thanksgiving, not yet a national holiday but a Vermont state holiday; people back home shipped them huge supplies of food. Life at Camp Vermont was portrayed in sketches by Private William Henry Jackson of the 12th Regiment, who went on to become a famous photographer of the American West. It's possible that the little figures in Jackson's drawings included Seneca Howland, but we'll never be able to tell.

Three days after their Thanksgiving feast, Seneca wrote a letter describing daily camp life and his opinions about the army. He reveals a lack of respect for military authority, a trait Major Powell might later have experienced. I have left Seneca's grammar intact, because this, too, reveals something about him.

> Camp Vermont
> Dec. 9th 1862
> Dear Brother & Sister,
> Perhaps you think it strang that I have not wrot you before this but better lat than never. we have been tough and well most of the time. I have not been sick a day since I came out here. John has been unwell for the last four days but he is better now. we have not lost but one man from our Reg. yet he died with the thypoid fever. The is but one from our comp. in the Hospital now. you asked how we liked camp life and wahat we had for grub. I like camp life well and have enough to eat. we fare a great deal bter here than we did at Brattleboro. the is some things in the millitary line that I do not like so well as some, that is when we are out on picket if some of the boys draws a chicken or millks a cow he is put in the guard house about two days although they have not ketched me yet. we have had some snow here and the ground has been froze as hard as I ever see it in Vermont. we have very cold nights here and [The next section is partly illegible, but he talks about their tents, camp fires, and staying warm.] the is in camp we have got some good Officers. our Colonel's name is Veazey. the men like him first rate. he is a smart man. our Brigadeer Gen. has not been here but a few days. his name is Stotons [Edwin Stoughton]. we are in Gen. Casey's division. I have seene him once he is an old man his head is as grey as an old rat he dosn't lok as if he knew any thing and I do not believe he does. But I guesse I have scribbed about enough so I will come to a close. Pleas writ again,
>
> S. B. Howland

At the time he wrote his letter home Oramel Howland had been in Colorado for two and a half years, and it seems he had not been a good correspondent, for he uses this letter to describe some of the details of his life there. Oramel was one of many thousands of men who were drawn to the Rockies by the Pike's Peak gold rush but who ended up earning a living through more-mundane jobs, in his case as a printer. His letter shows us many childhood memories and feelings about his family, feelings strong enough that he was ready to return east and join the army as a replacement for his married

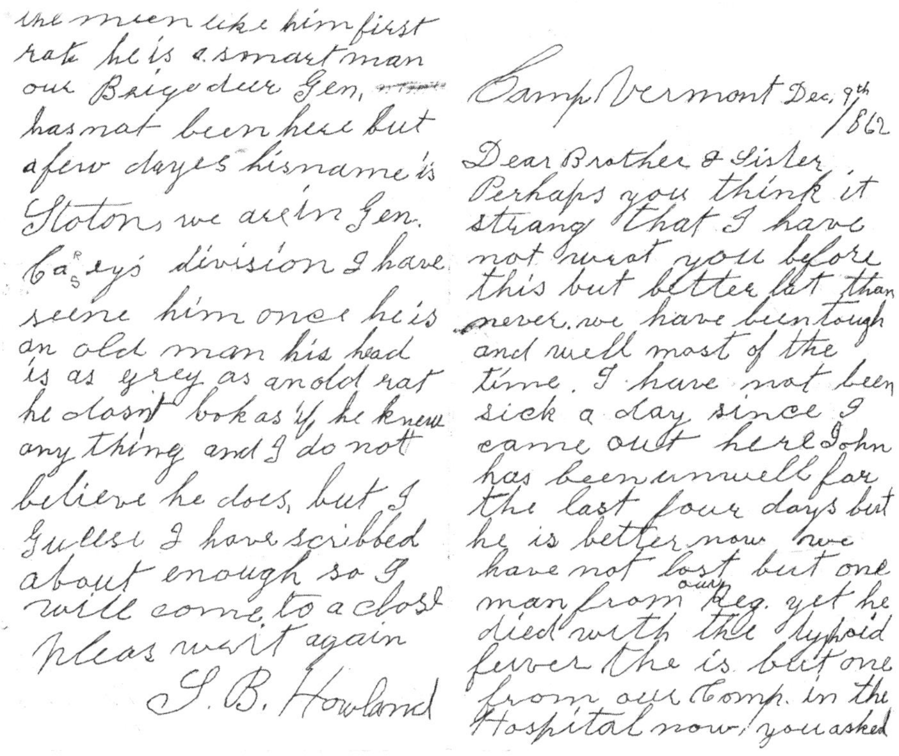

[Handwritten letter, left column:]

the men like him first
rate he is a smart man
our Brigadeer Gen,
has not been here but
a few dayes his name is
Stoton, we are in Gen.
Casey's division I have
seene him once he is
an old man his head
is as grey as an old rat
he dosn't look as if he knew
any thing and I do not
believe he does, but I
Guess I have scribbed
about enough so I
will come to a close
pleas writ again
      S. B. Howland

[Handwritten letter, right column:]

Camp Vermont Dec. 9th
                    /862
Dear Brother & Sister,
Perhaps you think it
strang that I have
not writ you before
this but better lat than
never, we have been tough
and well most of the
time. I have not been
sick a day, since I
came out here John
has been unwell for
the last four days but
he is better now we
have not lost but one
man from our Reg. yet he
died with the typhoid
fever (he is but one
from our Comp. in the
Hospital now) you asked

Beginning and end of Seneca Howland letter to his brother and sister during the Civil War, 1862. Courtesy of Kenneth Barrows.

brothers if they were drafted—a practice the Union army allowed. (The close-ness of the Howland family could have encouraged Seneca to join Oramel in going down the river.) Oramel was passionately pro-Union, but not because he had any sympathy for slaves; on the contrary, he felt that blacks belonged to an inferior race, an attitude so widespread among Northern whites that Oramel assumes that President Lincoln shares it. Oramel never did join the army. We have to wonder if Oramel's racial prejudices added a bit more to his conflict with John Wesley Powell, who came from a family of staunch abolitionists. Yet Powell surely appreciated Oramel's keen interest in geology. Powell historians have tended to portray his crew as rough frontiersmen motivated mainly by a hope for riches, but this letter shows that Oramel Howland, who had spent more years in the Rockies than anyone else on the expedition, shared Powell's fascination with rocks.

here today than it has been for two years past. The troubles and disturbances in Missouri has driven a great many here, who would have otherwise staid, to find homes under the protecting crags of the Rocky Mountains, consequently, business is made better by the emigration. To be sure there are some with rebellious proclivities who escape here; but as the loyal sentiment preponderates, they keep very quiet and make very good citizens, letting their sympathies remain unrevealed, unless some extraordinary circumstances occurs to throw off the mask. But such circumstances do not so often happen as in the States—this seeming to be a sort of neutral ground—isolated so far from the States. We expect that times will be still better in the Spring when the Mint is established and we get a coin currency in circulation, and the emigrants get settled on their ranches and in their mines. The mines are yielding steadier and more certain profits to miners and millmen than at any time heretofore since the country has been settled. Quartz mining is, with a few exceptions, the only mining done here now, the gulches being, as far as discovered, worked out, generally; still there are "diggings" which will pay at some future time, when produce becomes cheaper, and more advantages are acquired in the way of water and fixtures for working. The "Lodes" are, as you may say, inexhaustible, and almost numberless, and are almost all paying well at the present prices of current expenditures.

But I am afraid, that in my endeavors to get you up a letter, I am growing tedious and will wind up directly; hope you will excuse me if it is uninteresting; and I know that it is so, for I have puzzled myself trying to rake up this batch of stuff and still I find it a mess of rubbish after all. But I will try and do better next time, before which something may turn up that I may recount which will be better worth the while of writing.

Do not fail to write me a good old-fashioned letter, full of old associations, news etc, I find that myself very often gossipping of bygones and it gives me a great deal of satisfaction and enjoyment. When you write to Frank, Nell, George, Carrie, Sereno or John, or to those at home, do not fail to urge my request that they write me as often and as much as they can, of this and you will have the gratitude of your ever obedient servant and brother

O. Howland.

P.S.— I had intended to have sent you some specimens of minerals; but have not been able to gather many as yet. There are some rare curiosities in the way of petrifactions here:— fish impressed in the sand as plump and perfect, with all the various colored scales, as when they were in their native element; wood of almost every description is clearly defined in the grain, and so perfectly that, until you have lifted it, you will not be satisfied that it is solid rock. There are petrifactions of almost every other substance such as leaves of trees, shells, plants of various kinds, fruits etc. etc. But among the most curious which I have ever seen is one perfectly resembling a play-ball covered with four pieces of leather, with all the stitches distinct and perfect. This specimen was blasted out of solid rock at the depth of seventy-five feet from the surface and is turned into sandstone. Now who the devil ever played ball among the Rocky Mountains! perhaps millions of years ago? There has also been discovered bones of mastodons, one supposed to be a tusk, nine feet in length, and eight inches in diameter at the butt and four at the tip! What a tooth the must have had for cold victuals! There are also all kinds of precious stones here: Ruby, emerald, topaz, carnelian, garnet, opal, and some inferior quality of diamond besides a host of crystal of all shapes and kinds. I shall gather some of them before I leave here as curiosities

One page of Oramel Howland letter to his brother and sister from Colorado, 1862. Courtesy of Kenneth Barrows.

Denver

Nov 9th 1862

Dear Brother and Sister,

I received yours of the 28th of September two weeks after being mailed; much obliged—such favors are always very acceptable. My correspondence being limited makes them more so on that account. I feel that I have been very remiss in my duty to you and also to those at home, since I found where you and they were in writing but will try and atone for it in future, although I find it hard work to scrape together enough of interest to write a letter worthy in response to yours; but I will try and fill a sheet of something. And I could make it up much easier but that you have already stolen as much on me by reading some of my scribbling to others, of my trip out here and some account of how I passed my time since my arrival up to about six months ago. Since then, my time has been spent in the usual routine of labor appertaining to a job printing establishment (Eliza can understand what a dull place that is).

First of all, permit me to offer you, although rather late, "an old bach's" congratulations upon your marriage, and also add the wish that your marital relations may never be ruffled by any disturbing element to upset your connubial felicity; that you may live to a good old age, and be surrounded by happy group of children and grandchildren to make it pleasant and free from care.

Elizabeth, receive a thousand thanks, from your most obedient servant, for your very thoughtful lines. You could not have written anything more interesting. I had almost lost sight of Warren Whitcomb—they had escaped me altogether—the last time I heard from them was in the fall of '59 in Peoria, Ill. Although a portion of the news is sad yet there is satisfaction in it. And Warren, my dearest and best friend, is among the things that were. His short but brilliant career among us is ended. His jovial and manly voice and friendly, kindly beaming face will be heard and seen no more among us. But his many virtues will live in the memories of those who knew him well and truly, long after his body shall be lost, and his untimely death will be sincerely regretted and cast a deep shade of sorrow over the feelings of his many friends, who will drop a tear of sadness to his memory, when they hear of his death.

So Seneca and John have enlisted. I am glad to hear it. I was afraid there would be none of the family who would take up arms in defense of the flag and government under which they were reared—the only government in the world which I care about living under and which I am determined to help sustain if need be in the Spring if there is no change for the better before. And if it is broken up, why down I go with it. I cannot think for a moment of living under any other, and I think there are a great many more in the same fix. The "niggers" may be the cause of this war; if they are I hope they may be blotted out of existence before the Union should be broken. I have no sympathy with them. They are an idle and insolent sort of people. You will not find them, if free, engaged in a really laborious pursuit to gain a livelihood as white people do; the reaction puffs them up too much, when freed; they throw themselves back on their dignity, and instead of cultivating the land and raising produce to live on they flock into the large cities, set up a barber pole and shave the white people out of their living, or loaf around the corners to pick up a stray job, which when finished they sit down until hunger again forces them to do some other petty job to make a raise. The fact of the matter is, I never knew of one who engaged in any legitimate calling by which to sustain life. The Devil take 'em, say I, at least as far off as possible. I wish the country was never cursed with them either as slaves or freemen. They are a nuisance in either capacity; but if we are obliged to have them as slaves, leave them among the chivalrous (?) Southerners who like them so well; if free, for God's sake take them away from among the honest, hard-working people of the North, where they can only be dispised, and if possible, place them in a position where their own efforts must make them support themselves—then, and only then, can they make themselves respectable. Therefore, if this war proves to be a war of extermination of the slaveholder as traitors, and their slaves are confiscated and then freed, I hope the government will not let them over-run the North, but find some place to put them away from amongst whites. And I think "Old Abe" will do it too, as far as lies in his power.

By the way, I hear that drafting has commenced in Massachusetts. Now, Ned, if you or George are drafted, I claim it as my right and duty as a single man, and a brother to "sub" for you, and I shall take it as a very great oversight in you if you do not let me know in time to offer myself in your place; this is one reason among others why I have not enlisted before. I do not know how you may feel about running the risk of losing your lives, but I consider it little better than suicide in a married man to leave his family, especially when there is a chance offered him to escape such a dilemma. We do not anticipate a draft in the Territories, so I am free to make this offer with a certainty of being able to fulfill it. And, Ned, if Seneca and John are mustered into the service—actual service—and you know of their whereabouts, or if not, write and tell them (or if you don't I know "Liza" will; now say you will, "Liza," for an old "craftsman's" sake. That's right! do) to write to me of their camp life, how they like it, their treatment, officers, etc. etc. Tell them that "Orm" will try and write them something of a little interest which may suffice, in camp, to while away a few moments of its usual dulness and give them food to chat about, which, I know they will, for "I have been there" to all intents and purposes. I want to know of Seneca if he has ever been, since we moved away, to the old Robinson farm, and whether he has tasted the fruit from any of those apple scions which I incorporated into those old trees in the orchard there. Whether the new orchard back of the old school house which he will remember I help set out has borne any of the rich fruit which we saw in the prospective then, and if the plum trees have recovered from the "black-knot" sufficiently to furnish him with a taste of their fruit? All these and a hundred other queries which I could fill half a dozen pages like this with—I would like to hear of through him and John.

Why, Ned, it rather surprised me to hear that John and Seneca were old enough to enlist: they were small boys when I saw them last. They cannot be much over the required age. Corydon, I suppose, is the only one left at home with the exception of the girls—that is with the exception of Carrie—she, you said was at Lowell.

I should like much to be back in Worcester and East Brookfield for a short time to see my old acquaintances; but I am afraid I shall have to deny myself that privilege for some time yet. There are some pleasant associations connected with my stay in E. B. which as I now recall them, become very vivid. The place I remember perfectly—the old mill, foundry, depot, Aiken's hotel—the "lake house"—church, not forgetting the lake over which I remember of skating with my axe on my shoulder, accompanied by Solon Aikens, to cut cord-wood, and as I think of it now I remember that I came very near slipping into one of the air holes on one of these trips. Where are all our cousins? Do you know anything about them? Is the old mill still running? but hold! I think that was burned before I left Worcester. Where is your "shoe-Rat" shop located? How do you thrive in the "Biz"? etc.

Oh! that "fifty"—it came to hand. I had like to have forgotten much obliged—it was just the thing—helped me a good deal. Do you want it—I'll send it if you need to use, soon.

Since I wrote to George, we (that is, myself and three other "old Bach's") have changed our style of living. Instead of wielding the broomstick and rolling pin and wading elbow deep in the bread-tray as formerly we did we have delivered up those important weapons of housewifery, along with a supply of pots, kettles, pans, knives and forks, dishes, etc. into the hands of an old stoger in the business—a

Mrs. Noteware—who is now serving up for us, the raw material, in palatable lots, three times a day, besides washing, ironing, and doing little jobs of mending: and the only remuneration she receives is what herself and three children consume in the way of "grub", and our thanks, of course. This is a great luxury! We are the envy of a host of "baching outfits," who are not blessed with such good fortune. We now instead of washing dishes after supper, throw ourselves back on our stools, light our pipes and puff complacently, while our housekeeper goes through the very interesting ceremony of "setting things to rights", and making everything in readiness to get breakfast the next morning. But there is one thing that puzzles me in housekeeping, and that is, how a person can spend so much time about it? Now, I can get up a meal of "grub" for five or six in less than half an hour—to be sure I do not wash the dishes for what's the use—they'll be dirty immediately after meals. Kind of clean up things once a week or when visitors appear, I think answers as well as spending an hour or so in scrubbing up every day. So I tell our housewife, but she only laughs at me for the well intended advice, and still keeps wasting her time; but her time is her own and if she will fool it away it is her lookout, not mine. But how long this pleasant state of things will last is hard to tell; for Noteware has gone to the States to bring another load of freight this season, and will be back in about six weeks, when he may knock all our domestic arrangements in the head by withdrawing his family from us, and leave us to adopt our old system again. But I shall try to prevail on him to go "shucks" with us and keep the present-order of things intact, so long as he and his family make this their home. And I think I can pour a strong flood of argument into his ears in favor of perpetuating our present system. If we can do this, with the exception of rolling ourselves into our blankets and sleeping on the soft side of a pine board, instead of in clean sheets and on soft pillows and mattresses, we shall feel that we are living more like civilized beings, than in the old way. So mite it be—as much like "Home sweet, sweet home", as possible.

You ask me how the war affects us out here. Not so badly I presume as it does you situated so near as you are, to the real seat of it; but still it does affect us indirectly in the way of taxes and stamp duties; but that's not much. Business is better here today than it has been for two years past. The troubles and disturbances in Missouri has driven a great many here, who would have otherwise staid, to find homes under the prospecting crags of the Rocky Mountains, consequently, business is made better by the migration. To be sure there are some with rebellious proclivities who escape here; but as the loyal sentiment predonderates, they keep very quiet and make very good citizens, letting their sympathies remain unrevealed, unless some extraordinary circumstances occur to throw off the mask. But such circumstances do not so often happen as in the States. We expect that times will be still better in the Spring when the Mint is established and we get a coin currency in circulation, and the emigrants get settled on their ranches and in their mines. The mines are yielding steadier and more certain profits to mines and millmen than at any time heretofore since the country has been settled. Quartz mining is, with a few exceptions, the only mining done here now, the gulches being, as far as discovered, worked out generally; still there are "diggings" which will pay at some future time, when produse becomes cheaper and more advantages are acquired in the way of water and fixtures for working. The "lodes" are, as you may say, inexhaustible, and almost numberless, and are almost all paying well at the present prices of current expenditures.

But I am afraid that in my endeavors to get you up a letter I am growing tedious and will wind up directly; hope you will excuse me if uninteresting; and I know it is so, for I have pushed myself trying to rake up this batch of stuff and still I find it a mess of rubbish after all. But I will try and do better next time, before which, something may turn up that I may recount which will be better worth while writing.

Do not fail to write me a good old-fashioned letter full of old associations, news, etc. I find myself very often gossiping of by-gones and it gives me a great deal of satisfaction and enjoyment. When you write Frank, Nell, George, Carrie, Seneca, or John, or to those at home do not fail to urge my request that they write me as often and as much as they can find time to. Do this and you will have the gratitude of your ever obedient servant and brother.

O. G. Howland

P.S. I had intended to have sent you some specimens of minerals, but have not been able to gather many as yet. There are some rare curiosities in the way of petrifactions here: fish impeded in the sand as plump and perfect, with all the various colored scales, as when they were in their native element;—wood of almost every description is clearly defined in the grain and so perfectly that until you have lifted it you will not be satisfied that it is solid rock. There are petrifactions of almost every other substance such as leaves of trees, shells, plants of various kinds, fruits etc. etc. But among the most curious which I have ever seen is one perfectly resembling a play-ball covered with four pieces of leather, with all the stitches distinct and perfect. This specimen was blasted out of solid rock at the depth of seventy-five feet from the surface and is turned into sandstone. Now who the devil ever played ball among the Rocky Mountains!? perhaps millions of years ago? There has also been discovered bones of mastadons, one, supposed to be a tusk, nine feet in length and eight inches in diameter at the but and four at the tip! What a tooth he must have had for cold victuals! There are also all kinds of precious stones here:—Ruby, emeralds, topass, cornelians, garnets, opals, and some inferior quality of diamonds, besides a host of crystal of all shapes and kinds. I shall gather some of them before I leave here, as curiosities.

Oramel would indeed gather more rocks.

·II·

What's Eating the Howland Brothers?

EVERYONE IN AMERICA knew the story. It was one of the most dramatic stories in the American national saga of conquering the wilderness and building a great nation. It was dramatic partly because it was not supposed to happen; it was a miscarriage of national mythology. Yet it seemed to hold some sort of moral lesson, even a message from God to the nation. It was shocking, gruesome, unspeakable, and utterly fascinating. For Oramel and Seneca Howland, the story of the Donner Party held more personal meaning than for most Americans. Some of the most famous figures in this story were their cousins.

▰   ▰   ▰

John Wesley Powell blamed Oramel and Seneca Howland for everyone else going hungry.

As usual Powell and Jack Sumner were in the lead boat, scouting out the way, when Powell saw a rapid he judged too dangerous to run and raised his signal flag to warn the other three boats to pull ashore. The first boat behind him stopped readily enough. But in the second boat Oramel Howland wasn't paying attention. The *No Name* was swept into the rapid (soon to be called Disaster Falls). Oramel and his brother Seneca lost control and the boat crashed into one boulder, then another, and was smashed to pieces. Oramel and Seneca were lucky to make it to shore.

Powell couldn't get to sleep that night. All the men knew they were in trouble. The *No Name* had held a third of their provisions. Now lost, all lost. They were only two weeks into a trip that was planned to last for months. They would spend the rest of the expedition worrying about running out of food and desperately hunting for food in desert canyons. A few days later, on June 13, George Bradley, reflecting their gloomy mood, wrote in his journal,

Our rations are getting very sour from consistent wetting and exposure to a hot sun. I imagine we shall be sorry before the trip is up that
we took no better care of them. It is none of my business, yet if we fail
it will be want of judgment that will defeat it, and if we succeed, it will
be *dumb luck,* not good judgment that will do it.

The men have all come in from hunting as ever without game. We
frequently see mountain sheep as we pass along, and if we kept *still,*
we might kill them. But as soon as we land, the men begin to shoot
and make a great noise and the game for miles around is allarmed
and takes back from the river. This makes me think that these are not
hunters.... They seem more like school boys on a holiday than men
accustomed to live by the chase.[1]

The hapless hunters included Oramel and Seneca Howland, who might have
been trying to make amends for losing their boat's grub but clearly were not
getting any respect from George Bradley.

◼ ◼ ◼

The Howland connection to the Donner Party story was back in Vermont, and
back in their family tree. The Howland brothers were actually half-brothers,
Seneca being the son of Nathan Howland's second wife, Elvira Graves, and
nearly a decade younger than Oramel. Elvira belonged to an old New England
Graves clan that started when Thomas Graves emigrated from England to
America in the early 1600s. The Graves family proliferated and spread to Vermont. Elvira was born in Barnard, Vermont, in 1808, which was just down the
road from Pomfret, where she married Nathan Howland and raised Oramel
and Seneca. About forty miles away was the home of Zenas Graves, who had
served as a fifer for the Minutemen in the American Revolution; his son Franklin Ward Graves was born near Wells, Vermont, in 1789. Elvira and Franklin
were third cousins once removed. Their lines had branched off three generations into the Graves family tree. Franklin's great-grandfather (Daniel) and
Elvira's great-great-grandfather (Samuel) had been brothers.

Like many New Englanders in the 1800s, Zenas Graves saw little reason
to continue struggling with New England's stony soil and cold climate when
he was hearing about much more generous farmlands to the west. Zenas took
his family to Indiana, where his son Franklin married Elizabeth Cooper and
they began raising a family. Franklin continued following the national dream
of better lands to the west and moved his family to Illinois in 1831, to rich

farmlands on the Illinois River in Marshall County. His oldest child, Sarah, married a young man named Jay Fosdick, who, like the Howlands, traced his ancestry to the *Mayflower*. The Fosdicks, too, had become heavily involved in the New England whaling business, some serving as captains, perhaps captains on Howland-owned whaling ships. Franklin had a bad case of westering fever, for after years of working to build a successful farm he decided to head for the new promised land, California.

᠁   ᠁   ᠁

Oramel Howland did not entirely accept Powell's blame for the wreck of the *No Name.* In a June 19 letter he wrote for publication in the *Rocky Mountain News* he defended himself by saying that while he had not immediately recognized Powell's warning flag, he still would have had time to get to shore if his boat was not already swamped with water from the last rapid. He had tried his best to get to shore. But Oramel knew the wreck meant serious trouble: "With this boat we lost 2,000 pounds of provisions."[2]

A few days later a campfire turned into a wildfire, forcing the men to flee in their boats and leave behind much of their cooking gear. The cargo compartments Powell had designed turned out to be far from watertight, and the remaining food continued to get soaked and to spoil. Powell was acutely aware of their deteriorating food supply. In the book he wrote years later, he described their situation a month after the wreck of the *No Name*: "The day is spent in … spreading our rations, which we find are badly injured. The flour has been wet and dried so many times that it is all musty and full of hard lumps. We make a sieve of mosquito netting and run our flour through it, losing more than 200 pounds by the process. Our losses, by the wrecking of the 'No Name,' and by various mishaps since, together with the amount thrown away to-day, leave us little more than two months' supplies, and to make them last thus long we must be fortunate enough to lose no more."[3]

The men looked to the river for food, but had little success. On June 12 Bradley wrote, "I am fishing while I write, but the fish in this cañon are scarce for the water is too swift for whitefish and too muddy for trout." On June 18, at the mouth of the Bear River: "The fish were so large they broke four hooks and three lines for me in a few moments. I could haul them to the top of the water, great fellows, some of them quite a yard long. But the moment they saw me they were off and the hook or line must break." On August 15, at Bright Angel Creek: "There are fish in it. But Howland had tried in vain to catch them."[4]

᠁   ᠁   ᠁

John Wesley Powell knew all about Franklin Ward Graves and his wife Elizabeth. For three years starting in 1858 Powell had taught school in the town of Hennepin, Illinois, on the Illinois River, less than twenty miles upstream from the former Graves farm. Powell arrived in Hennepin only a dozen years after the Graveses left. They were well remembered in the area, and now that they had become national legends, Powell must have heard plenty of talk about them. Powell had boated the Illinois River right past the Graves farm.

Andy Hall, one of Powell's crewmembers, also knew all about Franklin Ward Graves and his wife Elizabeth. Hall grew up in the town of Toulon, Illinois, about twenty miles from the Graves farm. He must have heard plenty of talk about them.

It's plausible that after the Howland brothers wrecked the *No Name* and lost a third of the expedition's food, Powell and Hall thought to themselves, "Damn, we've gotten mixed up in a wilderness expedition with cousins of Franklin Ward Graves, with people who are incapable of obeying instructions and finding their way, and now we are going to starve."

※   ※   ※

Almost every day in their journals the men noted their food situation. They continually tried to hunt and caught little but frustration. On June 13 Jack Sumner wrote, "There is nothing in this part of the country but a few mountain sheep, and they stay where a squirrel could hardly climb." On June 28: "Saw four antelope, but failed to get any." On July 15: "Saw several beaver but got only one. Got one goose out of a flock that we have driven before us for 3 days." On July 27: "Killed 2 mountain sheep today—a Godsend to us, as sour bread and rotten bacon is poor diet for a hard work as we have to do." On July 30 they settled for "a half-starved coyote." The crew did have brief feasts when they caught a batch of trout, a deer, and two bighorn sheep. But they continually lowered their hopes, with Bradley writing, "I have found a lot of currants and have picked about four quarts which will make a fine mess for all hands."[5]

※   ※   ※

George Bradley knew all about Tamsen Donner. Bradley was born in 1836 in Newbury, Massachusetts, which had originally included what became the town of Newburyport. We don't know much about Bradley's youth, but he was still living there as a young man, working as an apprentice shoemaker. Tamsen Eustis was born in Newburyport in 1801. At age twenty-three she journeyed alone to North Carolina and became a school teacher, and then moved to Illinois to help take care of her widowed brother's children. There she met George Donner and married him in 1839. When Donner got the fever for California in 1846, Tamsen wrote to her sister Betsey back in Newburyport: "It is a four months trip. We have three wagons furnished with food.... We take cows along & milk them & have some butter though not as much as we would like."[6] When Betsey received this letter, George Bradley was ten years old and possibly walking down the street in front of her house. The next year, George probably heard Tamsen's friends and family talking about what had happened to her.

It's plausible that after the Howland brothers wrecked the *No Name* and lost a third of the expedition's food, George Bradley thought to himself, "Damn, I've gotten mixed up in a wilderness expedition with cousins of Franklin Ward Graves, with people who are incapable of obeying instructions and finding their way, and now we are going to starve."

▰   ▰   ▰

Bradley's mood was darkening. On July 17, 1867, he wrote, "We have only about 600 lbs. left and shall be obliged to go on soon for we cannot think of being caught in a bad cañon short of provisions." Actually, it is likely they were all thinking of what might happen if they were caught in a bad canyon without food. When Powell stayed two nights in the same camp to make scientific observations, Bradley showed his impatience on August 2: "He ought to get the Latitude & Longitude of every mouth of a river not before known and we are willing to face starvation if necessary to do it but further than that he should not ask us to waite and he must go on soon or the consequences will be different from what he anticipates. If we could get game or fish we should be all right but we have not caught a single mess of fish since we left the junction." Nine days later, on August 11: "The men are uneasy and discontented and anxious to move on. If Major does not do something soon I fear the consequences. But he is contented and seems to think that biscuit made of sour and musty flour and a few dried apples is ample to sustain a laboring man. If he can only do geology he will be happy without food or shelter, but the rest of us are not afflicted with it to such an alarming extent." A week later, on August 18, after a camp accident had dumped their box of baking soda into the river: "Our rations are not sufficient to anything more than just to sustain life. Coffee and *heavy* bread cannot be called *light* rations, but one feels quite light about the stomache after living on it awhile." Three days later, on August 21: "I feel more unwell tonight than I have felt on the trip. I have been wet so much lately that I am ripe for any disease, and our scanty food has reduced me to poor condition."[7]

▃   ▃   ▃

Four months after setting out from Illinois in April 1846, Franklin and Elizabeth Graves and their nine children and son-in-law Jay Fosdick in their three wagons caught up with the Donner wagon train, which had started from Springfield, Illinois. The Graveses had made their own way across Illinois and Missouri to St. Joseph, where they purchased supplies, joined with other emigrants, and headed across Nebraska on the Oregon Trail. But at Fort Bridger in western Wyoming, Franklin Graves made the same decision the Donners had made shortly before them: They would take a new route across the deserts and mountains of Utah and eastern Nevada, a shortcut being promoted by California booster Lansford Hastings—who had not actually traveled his shortcut and had no idea how difficult it was. It was longer than he promised; its mountains held only the sketchiest trail; its forests were almost impenetrable; and its deserts were brutally hot and dry in summer. When the Graves family joined the Donners and their partner families as they struggled through the Wasatch Mountains, the party added up to twenty-three wagons and eighty-seven people, half of them children. Their painfully slow progress meant they got to the eastern wall of the Sierra Nevada in mid-October, which was seriously late in the season. Looking ahead, they saw dark clouds over mountains already covered with snow. They started up anyway. At the top they were caught in a blizzard that dumped many feet of snow and closed the passes ahead of them and behind them. There would be eight more blizzards that winter.

Fearing they were trapped for the winter, Franklin Graves built a sturdy cabin at Truckee Lake. They slaughtered their oxen, but their food supply dwindled far too fast. Drawing on his Vermont boyhood and winter survival skills, Franklin began making snowshoes for an attempt to escape and bring rescue to the dozens who had to stay behind, including his wife and most of his children. Franklin led fourteen of the ablest, including his two oldest daughters and his son-in-law, Jay. But in the snow they lost the trail, made a disastrous wrong turn, and headed into a dead-end. A new blizzard caught them; they ran out of food; they starved; they began freezing; they began dying. As Franklin Graves lay dying, he told his daughters that they should save themselves and the rest of the family by eating his flesh.

▃   ▃   ▃

"We have but a month's rations remaining," wrote Powell in 1875, recalling how on August 13 they had more than two hundred miles to go in the Grand Canyon. "The flour has been resifted through the mosquito-net sieve; the spoiled bacon has been dried and the worst of it boiled; the few pounds of dried apples have been spread in the sun and reshrunken to their original bulk. The sugar has all melted and gone on its way down the river. But we have a large sack of coffee." Four days later, on August 17: "How precious that little flour has become! We divide it among the boats and carefully store it away, so that it can be lost only by the loss of the boat itself." [8] A few days later, on August 25, George Bradley wrote, "We have commenced our last sack of flour tonight." And a few days later, on August 27: "We have only subsistence for about five days." [9]

Powell and his men must have started thinking about the Donner Party. Everyone in America knew the story. It had become a part of the national mythology. America's creation story held that Americans were destined to spread west, carry God's blessings, conquer the wilderness, find abundance, build a great nation, and become heroes. Those who took larger chances would win larger rewards and become larger heroes. Yet twice within a few years this myth had gone seriously wrong, first with the Donners in the Sierra, then with the 49ers in Death Valley. Both stories deeply fascinated Americans and would retain cult followings nearly two centuries later, with monuments, museums, organizations, books, movies, and pilgrimages. The Donners and Death Valley 49ers were treated as heroes who had suffered, almost Christ-like, for the sake of America. Yet why had they been punished? Was it for personal foolishness, or was it for national hubris, the arrogance of Americans lusting for wealth or imagining they were more powerful than nature? Did their punishment come from God, or from being men without God? Preachers and historians drew moral lessons. The Graves family had carried a small horde of silver coins, but what good had it done them? Whatever the moral of the story, it was a riveting tale, scarier than any ghost story.

As Powell's food ran lower and his men got hungrier, the possibility of running out of food became increasingly real. What were they going to do then? They looked at one another with resentment and fear. They looked at one another and saw the cousins of Franklin and Elizabeth Graves.

▬ ▬ ▬

The survivors cut off Franklin's head to make the whole matter less personal, and buried it in the snow. Then, just as they would with a pig, they slit open his body and extracted the kidneys, liver, and heart, then carved into his thighs and arms. Since he had already lost a lot of weight, he might have had only thirty pounds of meat left on him. They stuck the meat on sticks and held it over a fire to roast it, and in spite of their horror, the odor of cooking meat was exciting to them.

Jay Fosdick, too, died and was eaten.

Back at the Graves cabin, the rest of the family was starving and freezing. Franklin and his promised rescue party were long overdue. The Graveses were losing hope. Finally, Elizabeth died. The survivors cut out her liver, kidneys, and heart. They cut off her breasts. They stripped the flesh off her legs and arms. They threw it all into a pot, added snow, and boiled it into a soup. Her youngest child, five-year-old Franklin Graves Jr., also died. He was also eaten. Nine-year-old Nancy Graves would be haunted for the rest of her life by the idea that she had eaten her mother.

Five miles away the Donner family, which had fallen behind the rest of the group, had built their own shelter. They ran out of supplies sooner than the Graves family and died sooner and in larger numbers. Seven Donners died. They, too, resorted to cannibalism. George Donner's skull was split open and his brains removed. Tamsen Donner disappeared; her body was never found. Some people, including later historians, speculated that she was murdered by a nonrelative, and eaten.

■   ■   ■

The crucial question was: Who was going to get eaten?

The Howland brothers had caused everyone's misery by wrecking their boat and losing their food, so rightfully they deserved to bear the burden. There was Graves family karma at work. The Howlands had repeated the Graves's incompetence at navigating a wilderness and now they would repeat the Graves's punishment. When Powell reached civilization, and had to explain that they had committed cannibalism to survive, it would be a scandal if they had eaten someone innocent, but if they explained that they had merely eaten the cousins of Franklin and Elizabeth Graves, the country would say, Of course. It was merely those Graveses again. This was their old way of doing things.

Then again, this whole trip had been John Wesley Powell's idea. He had promised everyone it would be manageable. He had helped design the leaky boats. He had called the shots on the river. He had kept everyone waiting and let them starve so he could make silly scientific observations. He had never gone hunting or shot any game. He was the Lansford Hastings of this trip. In the 1850s Hastings would settle in Yuma, Arizona, and become a booster for the idea that the Colorado River was navigable all the way through the Grand Canyon and beyond. The Colorado was "destined to become the Mississippi of the Pacific," Hastings wrote to Brigham Young in 1861. "I learn from persons well acquainted with that country, that [the Colorado River] is certainly navigable…to the mouth of the Green river."[10] Powell was the hustler who had gotten them into all this trouble, so he deserved to take the punishment. On the other hand, Powell didn't have any other hand: he had only one arm. This limited his value as meat. If anyone shopping for a Thanksgiving turkey had to choose between a turkey with two drumsticks and a turkey with only one, would anyone choose the turkey with the missing drumstick?

Another problem was that both the Howlands and the Powells came in pairs, as brothers. What brother would want to eat his own brother? And if they tried to sacrifice a Howland or a Powell, the brother might help fight back, making the whole matter far more complicated. It would be easier to pick on someone without allies.

Better forget about Hawkins—he was the cook, and you might need him to cook the meal. Besides, he wasn't very tall. If you went by a line-up and body size, then one guy stood out, at five feet, ten inches: Bill Dunn. And he had already fallen out of favor with Powell.

But seriously, it is plausible that as the Powell expedition revealed its poor planning, ran low on food, and got trapped within cliffs as formidable as cliffs of snow, the fate of Franklin and Elizabeth Graves was running through the minds of Oramel and Seneca Howland. They had ignored the advice of Mary Ann Graves, who had watched her father Franklin die but escaped the mountains and written to her family, "I will now give you some good and friendly advice. Stay at home—you are in a good place, where, if sick, you are not in danger of starving to death."[11] Oramel and Seneca had left a good place. It is plausible that the Donner story played at least a small role in the Howlands' decision to leave the expedition. Their decision was a complicated equation with many factors, and other factors loomed larger than a historical event of two decades earlier, but even historical memories, when they were such bad memories, would have magnified their hunger and their doubt.

NOTES

1. All crew quotes from Ghiglieri, *First Through Grand Canyon,* 121–22.
2. Ibid., 113.
3. Powell, *Exploration,* 211.
4. Ghiglieri, *First Through Grand Canyon,* 120, 129, 208.

5. Ibid., 122, 145, 169, 181, 186, 138.

6. Quoted in Gabrielle Burton, *Searching for Tamsen Donner* (Lincoln: University of Nebraska Press, 2009), 63.

7. Ghiglieri, *First Through Grand Canyon*, 173, 188, 204, 211, 215.

8. Powell, *Exploration*, 247, 263.

9. Ghiglieri, *First Through Grand Canyon*, 219, 222.

10. Lansford W. Hastings to Brigham Young, June 30, 1861, Brigham Young Collection, Library-Archives, Church of Jesus Christ of Latter-day Saints, Salt Lake City.

11. Quoted in Daniel James Brown, *The Indifferent Stars Above: The Harrowing Saga of a Donner Party Bride* (New York: William Morrow, 2009), 251.

·12·

The Curse of Howland Island

THOSE WHO DO not remember history, said a philosopher, are condemned to repeat it. Grand Canyon river guides prove their philosophical mettle all the time by telling river stories going back to the Powell expedition. Though cynics have implied that guides occasionally stretch the truth, and though it's true that Mark Twain's years as a river guide turned him into a mighty fiction writer, this living body of river lore has kept many guides out of trouble by reminding them of all the mishaps of the past. The importance of knowing your Grand Canyon river stories is underscored by the case of Amelia Earhart. If only Earhart had been more familiar with river history, she might not have vanished without a trace on her 1937 attempt to fly around the world.

≡   ≡   ≡

Amelia Earhart's fame as an aviator began in 1928, the year after Charles Lindbergh's trans-Atlantic flight, when she became the first woman to fly across the Atlantic. But this flight also introduced a tension into her flying career that would last the rest of her life and that might have helped end her life. As Earhart always pointed out, she was simply a passenger on that flight, but her husband, the book publisher G. P. Putnam, was determined to turn her into a legend, and he publicized her flight as if she had flown the plane. She would spend the next decade trying to keep up with her own legend. She did repeatedly prove her abilities. She became the first woman to make a solo flight across the Atlantic; the first woman to fly solo across the United States; the first woman to fly non-stop across the United States; and the first pilot to solo from Hawaii to California. In addition, she set several new distance and speed records.

Earhart's next goal was an around-the-world flight. Many other aviators declared this to be impossible due to the long, landless distances of the Pacific Ocean, especially between Hawaii and the islands of the South Pacific. No one could fly that far without running out of fuel or without sleep. Then the federal director of Air Commerce, Gene Vidal, pointed out that in the most critical gap, in a thousand miles of ocean, there was a tiny island. It was an uninhabited coral island, less than two miles long and a half-mile wide, rising less than twenty feet above the ocean. It would be tricky to find with the limited navigational tools of the time. Yet Earhart decided to bet her life on finding it. It might be a bad omen that this island bore the name of two brothers who, in another great American feat of exploration, had vanished without a trace.

Howland Island was named in 1828 for one of America's great maritime families, which would soon produce Oramel and Seneca Howland, who would walk off the Powell expedition and vanish without a trace. All the Howlands had nearly vanished without a trace when *Mayflower* pilgrim John Howland fell overboard. His rescue allowed the Howlands—especially the descendants of John's brother Henry—to create America's greatest whaling fleet. Dozens of Captain Howlands sailed Howland whalers all over the world. Inevitably, some Howlands crashed ships, such as Captain Edward Howland, who crashed his *Lyra* on an Oahu reef in 1828. Inevitably, some Howlands vanished without a trace. In 1864 Peleg Nye, the great-great-great grandson of *Mayflower* pilgrim John Howland, nearly vanished into a whale he had just harpooned: the whale pulled him overboard and into its mouth and dove five fathoms, but it soon died from its wound and Peleg was able to wiggle free. Peleg became known as "the Jonah of Cape Cod."[1] When "Captain" Oramel Howland wrecked his boat in Disaster Falls on the Powell expedition, he was just carrying on an old family tradition.

Howland ships were roaming the Pacific Ocean at a time when many islands and coral reefs were uncharted: islands that could turn into crucial sources of food, water, timber, and shelter during storms, and reefs that were often so low-lying they were hard to spot and could turn deadly, especially at night. The Howlands charted and named such islands and reefs, and it was inevitable they would name an island for themselves. In December 1828 Captain Daniel McKenzie, commanding a Howland ship, came upon an unknown island just off the equator, with trees blown down by a hurricane, and recorded his reactions: "Supposing myself to be the first discoverer of this island, as it is not laid down in any charts or books with which I am acquainted, I have, in honor of my owners, called it *Howland's Island*. Found good landing on the West side, but no anchorage. Navigators visiting this part of the world, can easily supply themselves with wood from this island. No appearance of inhabitants, or of its ever having been visited by a human being."[2]

In a Pacific Ocean filled with islands that would come to fascinate the American imagination as metaphors for paradise, Howland Island was far from the best possible tribute to the Howlands. It was not only small and scruffy, but also smelled of some 30,000 tons of guano piled up by the seabirds living there. Sometime in the 1830s a ship must have wrecked on Howland Island, for when a Howland ship came through in 1841 they found the island infested with rats. The grim warfare between the birds and the rats only added to what one Howland captain called the "lonely and forlorn" feel of Howland Island in 1853.[3]

It was the very loneliness of Howland Island that made it essential for Amelia Earhart, but in its forlornness it could not be used as a runway. Fortunately, she had become good friends with the other feminist hero of the age, First Lady Eleanor Roosevelt, who admired Earhart enormously. President Franklin Roosevelt happened to be the first Howland descendant to become president, and he was also a former assistant secretary of the navy with a deep love of sea adventure and knowledge of sea lore. To everyone else, the name Howland Island might have been meaningless, and no Earhart biographer has commented on it, but for Franklin Roosevelt the prospect of Howland Island starring in an epochal American adventure would have been pleasing. Amelia appealed to the Roosevelts to turn Howland Island into a landing strip. Officially, the runway would be developed as an emergency airstrip to encourage commercial aviation in the Pacific, but Earhart biographers have little doubt it was one of many personal favors that the Roosevelts did for Earhart. President Roosevelt arranged for the Works Progress Administration (or WPA), which normally built post offices and schools on the streets where the Great Depression unemployed lived, to build the Howland Island airstrip as a WPA project. Some World War I bulldozers, graders, and rollers, along with a small construction crew, were rounded up and loaded on a navy ship. When the time came for Earhart's flight, President Roosevelt stationed a Coast Guard cutter at Howland Island to broadcast radio signals, as well as a searchlight at night and a smokestack plume by day.

Earhart first attempted to circle the world in a westward direction, starting in California. She made it to Hawaii just fine, but when she tried to take off for Howland Island, her plane, heavily loaded with fuel, suddenly veered to the right; she tried to correct, but the plane swung too far left and smashed the landing gear against the runway. The plane skidded on its belly, sending out a shower of sparks, breaking the gas tank, and sending gas spilling out. Some said it was a miracle there wasn't an explosion. The crash happened on Oahu, where 109 years previously Captain Edward Howland had wrecked his ship *Lyra*.

After shipping her plane back to California for repairs, Earhart restarted her world flight in the other direction, from California east across the United States, then over Africa and Asia. She and her navigator Fred Noonan made it almost around the world, from California to Australia, in good shape, and all that remained was the Pacific crossing. She made it to New Guinea just fine. On July 2 Earhart took off on the twenty-hour flight to Howland Island. She got close to Howland Island, for the radio operators there heard her voice clearly and repeatedly, saying she had started a back-and-forth flight pattern to find the island, but they never saw her plane, and she never saw the island. She and the ground were never able to hold a conversation, due to bad planning, bad training, and bad equipment for communications.

When Earhart disappeared, President Roosevelt ordered a huge naval and air search for her, covering a quarter million miles and involving ten ships, one hundred planes, and thousands of personnel—the largest search-and-rescue mission in American history. It found no trace of her. In the decades since, people have continued searching for Earhart and reported finding airplane parts, shoes, and skeletons, and to have heard stories from native residents about her crash or her survival, but none of these reports has held up. There have been persistent rumors, fueled by a 1943 movie starring Rosalind Russell and Fred MacMurray, that Earhart was really on a secret, heroic spying mission against the Japanese, and that she survived her crash and was taken prisoner and executed. These rumors were a lot like the rumors that Oramel and Seneca Howland were taken prisoner by Mormons and executed.

All we know for sure is that Amelia Earhart twice tried to reach Howland Island, twice crashed on her way there, and vanished without a trace.

Perhaps Amelia should have asked her father about the Howlands. Her father Edwin was a lawyer in Kansas City, Kansas, with a downtown office on Minnesota Avenue, almost right next door to the law office of Lewis Keplinger, who had accompanied John Wesley Powell in his 1868 explorations of the Colorado Rockies. Edwin Earhart and Lewis Keplinger undoubtedly knew one another and passed on the street often. Edwin could have been nearby on the day in 1906 when Keplinger received a letter from Jack Sumner talking about the fate of the Howland brothers. If we indulge in a bit of imagination, we can picture Edwin Earhart running into Keplinger that day on the street corner or in a cafe, asking what was new, and hearing about the unfortunate Howlands. Or maybe Keplinger asked Earhart what was new and heard about how Earhart's nine-year-old daughter was turning into an adventuresome tomboy.

All we know for sure is that to gamble your entire adventure and your life on finding a tiny island named for a family full of adventurers who have crashed vessels and vanished without a trace was an act of hubris that no self-respecting Greek god could possibly have ignored. I do not know much about Polynesian gods, but I doubt they felt any obligations to an American feminist hero flying a loud machine and failing to propitiate the vastness of the sea.

NOTES

1. Judy McAlister, "New Howland House Exhibit: Whaling," *Howland Quarterly* 80, no. 2 (June 2015): 11.

2. Daniel McKenzie journal quoted in *Howland Quarterly* 80, no. 2 (June 2015): 17.

3. Quoted by Llewellyn Howland in *So'west by West of Cape Cod* (Cambridge, MA: Harvard University Press, 1947), 72.

·13·

Introducing William H. Dunn

WILLIAM H. DUNN has long remained the most mysterious of Powell's crewmembers, with both his fate and his origin unknown. Almost the only image we had of him came from Powell's book: "Dunn was a hunter, trapper, and mule-packer in Colorado for many years. He dresses in buckskin with a dark oleaginous luster, doubtless due to the fact that he has lived on fat venison and killed many beavers since he first donned his uniform years ago. His raven hair falls down to his back, for he has a sublime contempt of shears and razors."[1] Dunn seemed to be a long-time mountain man.

All other sources gave only two hints about the geography of Dunn's life before the Powell expedition. A *Rocky Mountain News* article on June 5, 1869, mentioned that Dunn lived in Georgetown, Colorado. In the 1950s historian Dock Marston pursued this lead, contacting a Georgetown historian he called "Mr. Georgetown," but this led nowhere, which was not surprising since Georgetown was a busy mining camp in which thousands of men came and went without leaving any traces in public records. William Hawkins, in the account he gave to William W. Bass in 1919, mentioned that Jack Sumner defended Dunn's abilities to Powell by saying, "Dunn had been wounded four times by Comanches."[2] This meant Dunn must have spent some time in Comanche country—the lower Great Plains, most likely Texas. I looked for Dunns in Texas, especially in jobs that might place a man in harm's way, such as soldier, Texas Ranger, or stagecoach driver, and I came up with a few interesting Dunns. I heard from Texan David E. Dunn, who had once hiked up Separation Canyon to follow in the footsteps of William H. Dunn. But David Dunn was there only as treasurer of the Geological Society of America, which was celebrating its hundredth anniversary in 1988 by taking a trip down the Colorado River—he was not related to William H. Dunn.

I tried searching for William H. Dunn through Civil War records, though it wasn't clear that Dunn had even served in the army. I was also assuming that an ardent Unionist like Powell wouldn't approve of Confederates, so I confined my search to Union army records. Without knowing Dunn's home state, I had to investigate every William H. Dunn in the Union army, hoping he'd used his middle initial. It turned out that an implausibly large portion of the William Dunns in the Union army had the middle initial of "H," a total of more than thirty. The culprit seemed to be President William Henry Harrison, whose death in office in 1841 caused his name to be attached to a large crop of babies in a short time. I went ahead and searched through all the records, assuming that some William H. Dunns had been killed in the war and that others were collecting pensions years later, leaving only a few possibilities. I ended up holding the record of the correct William H. Dunn, but I decided it couldn't be the right one and set it aside for years. Why? Because I trusted John Wesley Powell when he said that his Dunn had spent "many years" in the Rockies. My Dunn was only twenty years old in 1865 and still in the army in late December of that year, leaving him insufficient time to get to Colorado and become the veteran mountain man Powell met in the summer of 1867.

Then historian Michael Ghiglieri mentioned to me that when William Hawkins gave Robert Stanton his other account of the Powell expedition, Hawkins made a comment that had not gotten into print: "The state of Ohio never turned out a man that had more nerve than William Dunn."[3] There were Civil War records for only two William H. Dunns from Ohio. They included the county of origin, allowing me to zero in on local records. It turned out I had found the right William H. Dunn long before. He had indeed gone from the army to being a veteran mountain man in less than two years. On further thought, this agreed with Jack Sumner's comment to Stanton: "I had trained Dunn for two years in how to avoid a surprise" by Indians.[4] The *Rocky Mountain News* even gave us a glimpse of Dunn's apprenticeship on November 12, 1867: "Wm. Dunn has gone over to spend the winter with Sumner in trapping." Perhaps to the greenhorn Professor Powell, Dunn had seemed a master of his realm. In the Wild West, Americans could achieve new identities rather quickly. Intriguingly, this William H. Dunn had ended his army career in San Antonio, Texas, in Comanche country.

William H. Dunn's great-grandfather Thomas Dunn was born in Ireland in 1744 and immigrated to America in 1772, just in time for him to serve as a soldier in the American Revolution. He settled in Fayette County in southwestern Pennsylvania, living in a stable for the first year while he started a farm. He was also a wheelwright and operated a wagon shop. He had twelve children, and on his death in 1804 he deeded his farm to his son John. Thomas's other sons sought land of their own in Ohio, the Western frontier of the time.

Son William Dunn (our William's grandfather) stopped on the eastern edge of Ohio, in the hamlet of Lafferty in Belmont County, about fifty miles from his father's Pennsylvania home. He built a five-room cabin, with foot-thick log beams, that would be the home to five generations of Dunns and the birthplace of 110 Dunns, including his grandson William H. Dunn. Many of those 110 would be buried in the nearby Dunn Cemetery. William (the grandfather) became a leading citizen of Belmont County, getting elected to the state legislature for fifteen years and serving as a justice of the peace, a county auditor, and a general in the Ohio militia.

Ray Sumner, the descendant of Powell boatman Jack Sumner, pointed out an unlikely coincidence. In the 1820s, while grandfather William Dunn was serving as a general in the Ohio militia, another general in the militia was Robert Lucas, the grandfather of Jack Sumner. Dunn and Lucas also served in the state legislature together, though in different political parties, and in 1832, when Lucas got elected governor of Ohio, Dunn got elected to the state senate. Could this coincidence have helped bring their grandsons together in the Colorado Rockies in the 1860s? Then again, Robert Lucas left Ohio in 1838 and left a three-decades gap in which the two families had no obvious chance for further association. William H. Dunn and Jack Sumner were born after their grandfathers had parted ways. But at least it is plausible that when Jack Sumner and William H. Dunn met one another in Colorado, they compared their family histories and discovered some common ground, which helped bond them together before joining Powell's expedition. (We'll explore Robert Lucas's history in two chapters on Jack Sumner, chapters 17 and 18.)

Grandfather William had five sons, including Caldwell, who was born in 1817, built a house a few houses down from his father's house and, on his father's death, took over the family home and farm. Caldwell's first son was William Henry Dunn, born on May 19, 1845, which means he was only twenty-two when Powell met him and had just celebrated his twenty-fourth birthday when the Powell expedition launched. One Dunn family member told me that the Dunns have always aged fast and looked older than they really were.

With ancestors who had fought in the American Revolution and the War of 1812, and one who served as a general in the Ohio militia, it wasn't surprising that when the Civil War broke out and Belmont County organized its own unit, Company K, as part of the 15th Ohio Volunteer Infantry, a Thomas Dunn, who was the right age to be William's son Thomas, joined it. But only three weeks later, at Camp Nevin in Kentucky, Thomas died in a tragic accident. He was on guard duty at night but apparently got confused and wandered beyond the picket line. He was coming back toward the line when another guard shot him. According to Alexis Cope, an officer in the 15th Ohio and later its historian: "The shot struck him in the right breast and passed through his body.... We opened his shirt and saw the ghastly wound the bullet had made and knew that it was mortal.... Towards morning he died. In memory, that night remains one of the most awful in the writer's more than four years of service."[5]

If this tragedy left the Dunns disillusioned with the U.S. Army, it did not stop Thomas's nephew William H. Dunn from enlisting in Company K two years and three months later, at age nineteen. By then the 15th Ohio had distinguished itself in some of the major battles of the Western war. It fought at Shiloh, though not on the first day, when John Wesley Powell lost his arm. It arrived the night of April 6, 1862, and helped force back the Confederate army the next day, but seventy-five men were killed and wounded, five of them from Company K. The 15th fought at Stones River and Missionary Ridge and lost one third of its strength at Chickamauga. With such heavy losses, the regiment needed new recruits, especially since the original soldiers had enlisted for three years; their time would be up in April 1864. In February the men were asked to reenlist and three hundred of them did; as a reward they were given thirty days of furlough and sent home to Ohio, where they were treated as heroes.

One of the new recruits was William H. Dunn, who on February 27, 1864, signed up to serve for three years or the rest of the war, whichever came first. He might have been encouraged to enlist in Company K because only a few weeks previously his brother-in-law, Eber T. Fort, had been promoted to corporal. (Foot was married to Dunn's sister, Hannah.) Dunn was paid a routine enlistment bounty of $300, though he only got $60 of it to start. He enlisted in the town of Flushing, about three miles from the Dunn family home. William H. Dunn was listed as a farmer, probably on the family farm. He was described as five feet, ten inches tall, with hazel eyes, dark hair, and light complexion. After Dunn and the 15th paraded to the state capitol and were hailed by the governor, the parade turned into a hard march toward some of the bloodiest fighting of the war, in General Sherman's campaign to capture Atlanta. From the account of regimental officer and historian Alexis Cope, it sounds like Dunn got a bad start: "As we passed out of the city the rain began to pour. The prospect was not at all pleasant and was quite depressing to our new recruits."[6] In Tennessee they boarded a train, but,

> The train was made up of box cars and, as the weather was mild, many
> of the men preferred to ride on top rather than on the inside of the

cars. Those who were compelled to ride inside were the more fortunate as it afterwards proved, for as the train was nearing Athens [Tennessee] a number of the cars left the track and some of them turned completely over. It was a frightful spectacle as seen from the rear car, and when the train was brought to a stop wounded men were scattered along the railroad on both sides of the track. About thirty were severely wounded.... News of the accident was sent to Athens and a relief party came out from the village, among whom was Governor Andrew Johnson of Tenn.[7]

At one of Dunn's first battles, officer-historian Alexis Cope described what might have been Dunn's feelings at the sight of masses of soldiers advancing to beating drums: "The men moved with such spirit and precision as to provoke a cheer. The scene was wonderfully imposing and those who witnessed it can never forget it. The day was fine and seldom in all our experience was it possible to behold the 'pomp and panoply of glorious war' to better advantage." But other battles were brutal or bungled enough to cure new soldiers of their romantic illusions about war. Even one death could strike a blow, such as the death of the regimental bugler, whose upbeat personality had made him a favorite: "His arm had been amputated and although suffering from pain he was as cheerful as ever, said he would soon be back, and added, 'Adjutant, a bugler only needs one arm.' Poor fellow, he died of that terrible gangrene."[8] The 15th slogged its way toward Atlanta, losing dozens of men at a time. In the battle for Kenesaw Mountain, the wounded included Dunn's brother-in-law Eber T. Fort.

After the capture of Atlanta most of Sherman's army headed for the sea and into South Carolina, but the 15th Ohio was among the troops sent west to head off Confederate general John Bell Hood, who was trying to slam the door behind Sherman. At the battle of Nashville the Union army routed Hood, then pursued him westward across Tennessee. The 15th was still in Tennessee when the news came that Lee had surrendered, and they hoped they would soon be able to return home. But since they were now among the westernmost units of the Union army, they got an unwelcome assignment that would keep them in the army for half a year after most other Ohio units had gone home.

In Texas, Confederate general Kirby Smith was determined to hold out, and across the South die-hard Confederates were talking about fleeing across the Mexican border and establishing a government in exile. Union leaders decided to send troops to Texas to subdue Smith and to block key routes into Mexico. Another worry was that a would-be Mexican monarch, Maximillian, was trying to overthrow Mexico's republican government, with help from French and Austrian armed forces; it seemed possible he might try to take advantage of the chaos in the United States to seize Texas, with help from exiled Confederates and maybe the French and Austrians. An American force on the Mexican border might block an invasion, or allow the United States to invade Mexico. But this political situation was highly sensitive; the American people were exhausted by war and didn't want to begin a new one. Union leaders decided they wouldn't even tell their troops why they were being sent to Texas. After General Smith's troops had melted away through mass desertions and Smith had surrendered, it was even more baffling that Union troops were being sent to Texas.

"When it became known," wrote Alexis Cope, "that orders sending us south had been received, a mutinous spirit developed." The men had signed up only for the duration of the war: "Many thought that the war was now practically over and that they were entitled to be at once discharged and return to their homes. Some of the more reckless, it was said, were secretly signing papers pledging themselves to disobey orders to move to Texas."[9] Nighttime meetings were held away from camp, and the men vented their frustration. Soon their new commander, General Willich, gave a speech that mollified most of his troops, though he also had one mutiny ringleader arrested.

On June 17 the 15th Ohio boarded the *Peytona,* one of a small fleet of steamboats, in western Tennessee and headed down the Tennessee River, then down the Ohio River, then down the Mississippi. To minimize desertions, General Willich gave orders that the boats could stop only to cook meals and could never stop in towns. "Many of the men," wrote Alexis Cope, "were in ugly temper because they were being taken to the far south in midsummer, and every additional regulation looking to their closer confinement to the boats was resented. The boats were crowded and men slept on the floors of the decks."[10] One boat sank, losing its armaments and horses, drowning two men, and leaving the remaining boats even more overcrowded.

Reaching New Orleans, they set up camp in the battlefield where Andrew Jackson had defeated the British half a century before. But, according to Cope,

> The discomforts of the camp, placed, as it was, on the flat bottom land in the hot sun, with no shade, did not improve the temper of the men, which had been sorely tried by the long hot voyage, and there was a good deal of insubordination. Strong guards were placed about all the camps with strict orders to permit no one to go outside the

lines without a pass, but many men broke guard, probably in some instances with the guards' connivance, and went into the city. The city military authorities had orders to arrest all men found there without passes.... The number of arrests of the corps became so great that June 28, General Stanley issued an order absolutely prohibiting enlisted men from going into the city.[11]

On the 4th of July the men had to watch the city's fireworks from a distance. William Dunn had plenty of time on his hands, and he used some of it to write a letter to his father on June 27, 1865. This letter, saved by the Dunn family, is the only Dunn letter we have. It shows that he was not a good speller, and that if he was disgruntled by his assignment, he did not reveal it to his father.

> June 27, 1865
> Camp Near
> Neworleans, Louisanna
> Dear father.
> Its with much pleasure that I seat my self to to answer your leter that came to hand yesterday. I am well at present and hoping those fue lines may reach you the same way. We left Nashvile on the 16 and got hear on the 24. The boy ar all well. We are Campt righ along the river five miles below the sity where the level of the water is two foot higher than where lay wel [we?]. General Wellich told us that would be hear about ten days or two weeks. Well I am glad to hear that Eber Foot has got his discharge but I ges that his brother is not very tired of the service yet. Wel their r. good many of the men going in the regular army the first infantry and first cavalry regular are both hear
>
> The report is that when we move that we wil go back up the river. general Sheridan landed hear yesterday from Texas. So we wil now where we wil have to firing Soon. There is a good many steam ships coming and going out.
>
> Now I cant think of any thing more to write this time so nothing more at presant.
>
> Well I got one from Nancy. That wel do for her to.
>
> Robert Humphrey has not come up. he is wagon master at brigade head quarters.
>
> William H. Dunn[12]

At some future time a Dunn family member wrote Dunn's life data below his signature: "Born May 19th, 1845, Died – – 1866, Twenty one years old, Killed by Indians in Grand Canyon." This year and age were off by three years, and of course because William disappeared, no one knew his death date.

First page of William Dunn letter to his father from Civil War, 1865. Courtesy of Dunn family.

Instead of heading back up the Mississippi and homeward, Dunn was soon aboard a steamship in the Gulf of Mexico. "Most of us," wrote Cope, "were landsmen and had never seen the sea, and the prospect, as we looked out over the broad choppy waters of the gulf, was novel and inspiring."[13] In addition to inspiring patriotic thoughts, it also inspired a lot of seasickness.

When they landed, they began a long, grueling march across the plains without water or shade but with intense heat and mosquitoes. The men were carrying too much weight but too little water and food. Without any explanation for their hardships, the men became rebellious again. "The water in the canteens," wrote Cope, "had become heated in the evening sun, that carried in the wagons was equally hot, and many of the men became sullen and mad

and began firing off their guns. Scores of men in the brigade, broke their guns
and threw them by the road side. Many were exhausted by heat and thirst
and began to straggle and fall out…. It was proposed to replace the guns and
accouterments when we reached Victoria, charging their cost to the men who
had broken or thrown them away."[14] It was probably on this march that Dunn
earned the remarks on his muster roll and payroll for that month: "Stoppage for
Ord. thrown away on march. $2.50 charged by Co. Comdr." When Dunn was
mustered out a few months later, he also owed the army $39.20 for clothing.

On August 21 they reached San Antonio, where they would remain for
three months, until the political situation in Mexico had become more stable
and favorable. Here the men were able to relax, go fishing, gather pecans, and
be tourists, especially at the Alamo. "But amid all these opportunities for enjoyment," wrote Cope, "there was an under current of discontent among the
men, who felt that they had been unfairly dealt with by their government.
Their discontent showed itself at times in disrespect to their officers."[15]

William Dunn's discontent with the army, perhaps starting with his uncle
Thomas being killed by mistake, could have been a major source of his friction
with Major John Wesley Powell. Dunn believed that he had been "unfairly dealt
with" by Powell, too. While the other former privates on the Powell expedition
might have been more inclined to submit to an officer, Dunn had spent months
in a unit that had become openly rebellious and that had developed its own
culture of disrespect for officers, even openly insulting General Willich to his
face, which, as Cope put it, "almost broke his heart."[16] Dunn's officers tolerated
this behavior to an unusual degree; after the war they changed all the "deserter"
designations on their rolls into honorable discharges. A few years later Dunn
might have thought that leaving a poorly organized river expedition was an
honorable discharge, and not an act of desertion.

Finally, the 15th Ohio received orders to muster out—William Dunn was
mustered out on November 21. But they would take another month to get
home—by marching, by railroad, by steamboat on a Mississippi River full of
icebergs, and by an Illinois train so underpowered that on hills the men had
to get off and push. They arrived in Columbus, Ohio, on Christmas, and were
disappointed they received no public welcome.

Alexis Cope's eight-hundred-page regimental history never mentions that
they fought Comanches, and William Dunn's military record makes no mention of his being wounded at any time (although in July 1864 he was briefly
hospitalized for an unnamed sickness). If Jack Sumner was correct about Dunn
being wounded by Comanches, it must have happened after the war. Did Dunn

all my children & their heirs.

Item 7th My son William Henry should he ever return it is my will each of the Heirs shall pay him one hundred dollars apiece $100 in Y & P rail road bond each to Caldwell Marion and Logan.

Item 8th In case any of my daughters should die without heirs before the decease of my wife then her share of Legacy unpaid to her shall be paid to the survivors of the girls now unmarried (viz Emily, Alverty & Irene or the survivors of them equally. My wife is to have the privilege of selling and buying stock the same as I could have done if living I desire that she shall give my minor children a good education.

At my death the wagons Harness and farming utensils to be divided equally among my three younger boys.

Whatever Moneys may be advanced by me in my life time or by my wife or paid by my executors to my daughters shall be credited for or deducted from the $1300 thirteen hundred dollars to be paid to each of my daughters.

I do hereby nominate and appoint Nathan B Nichols and my son John executors of this my last will and testament and hereby authorize them to do whatever may be necessary to carry this will into effect,

In testimony hereof I have hereunto set my hand and seal this 25th day of January A.D. 1881

Signed sealed and acknowledged
by said Caldwell Dunn as his last
will and testament in our presence
& signed by us in his presence

                    Caldwell Dunn (seal)

Thomas D. Ritter
J. Wilbur Nichols

Probate of Will

Be it remembered That heretofore to-wit on the 3rd day of December A.D. 1881 the following proceedings concerning the foregoing Will were had in the Probate Court of Belmont county Ohio and entered on the journal thereof in the words and figures following to-wit;

In the matter of the Will of   Will Produced
Caldwell Dunn Deceased   December 3rd A.D. 1881

This day an instrument of writing purporting to be the last Will and Testament of Caldwell Dunn late of Union town

1881 will of William Dunn's father, with line "for my son William Henry, should he ever return." Courtesy of Dunn family.

actually enjoy Texas and return there after the war? Or did he remain in Texas? There is nothing in Dunn's military records that says he went home to Ohio with his regiment. After nearly two years of wandering America's mountains and rivers and the Gulf of Mexico, of seeing eight states, of seeing French-accented cities like New Orleans and Mexican-accented cities like San Antonio, of adventure and comradery, Dunn might have been one of the many soldiers who could not settle back into a life of farming in a quiet little town. Most discharged Union soldiers returned home in the late spring of 1865, which was good timing for going to work on the farm. If Dunn returned to Ohio it was in the middle of winter, with little to do, so he could have felt free to wander farther. Unlike most Union soldiers, Dunn had gotten a look at the West as it was becoming the Wild West, full of space and opportunity and adventure, the West of Davy Crockett and cowboys. When Dunn headed west he could have taken a job that placed him in conflict with Comanches. In any case, he had only a year and a half to turn himself into the experienced old mountain man Powell hired for his river expedition.

During the expedition the leading newspaper in Belmont County, the *Belmont Chronicle,* published, on July 29 and August 26, letters that Walter Powell and John Wesley Powell wrote to Chicago newspapers from the expedition, but it made no mention that a county native was on the trip.

The Dunn family didn't forget William, even long after he disappeared. They retained his Civil War letter, his birth record in their family Bible, and stories about him. But no one had any photos of him. His father Caldwell Dunn never gave up hoping William would return. When Caldwell drafted his will in 1881, a dozen years after William had disappeared, Caldwell remembered William: "My son William Henry, should he ever return, it is my will each of the Heirs shall pay him one hundred dollars apiece."

The Dunn family cabin, in which William and 109 other Dunns were born, stood for nearly two centuries, and sometime around 2000 it was demolished—according to one local historian. But another local historian said it had been moved and might be restored. As ever, William H. Dunn generates varying stories.

NOTES

1. Powell, *Exploration,* 120.

2. William Wallace Bass, *Adventures in the Canyons of the Colorado* (Grand Canyon, AZ: Self-published, 1920), 23–24.

3. Stanton, manuscript, Archives of New York Public Library.

4. Quoted in Ghiglieri, *First Through the Grand Canyon,* 258–59.

5. Alexis Cope, *The Fifteenth Ohio Volunteers and Its Campaigns* (Columbus, OH: Edward T. Miller, 1916), 45. Cope calls the victim John Dunn, but other sources list the victim as Thomas.

6. Ibid., 417.

7. Ibid., 421–22. Within a year, Andrew Johnson would be president.

8. Ibid., 444, 476.

9. Ibid., 729–30.

10. Ibid., 746.

11. Ibid., 750–51.

12. Provided by the Dunn family, and reprinted here with their permission.

13. Ibid., 754.

14. Ibid., 763–64.

15. Ibid., 786.

16. Ibid., 779.

·14·

Last Words Before the Launch

WILLIAM H. DUNN has remained the most silent of Powell's crew-members. While most of the other boatmen left journals, letters, and memoirs about the expedition, no word from Dunn has been found. Yet it turns out that the day before the Powell expedition launched, Dunn wrote a letter to a friend, James Oliver of Black Hawk, Colorado. Oliver had been the newspaper publisher in Fair Play, Colorado, and he would later publish a newspaper in Black Hawk, so he recognized the newsworthiness of Dunn's letter. Oliver contacted the newspaper in nearby Central City about Dunn's letter, and they published a brief account of it. Unfortunately, they didn't publish the text of the letter, so we receive only a glimpse of Dunn.

From the Central City *Weekly Register,* May 28, 1869:

> Last evening Col. J. R. Oliver received a letter from W. H. Dunn of the Powell Expedition, dated at Green River City, May 23rd, in which he says that the party was to embark the next day on their perilous voyage down the Colorado River. They have 20-foot boats, calculated to carry 4000 pounds burden each on lakes, and they load them with 1800 pounds each. Their next stopping place will be at Fort Mojave, on the Colorado, below the mouth of the Green. He does not state how many persons are now connected with the expedition, how many and what kind of boats they have, nor whether Mrs. Powell is still with the party.

Not much of Dunn's personality comes through here, except perhaps for a very vague sense of geography; Dunn would soon receive a thorough education in just how far Fort Mohave was from the mouth of the Green River.

Dunn might have gotten to know James Oliver at William Byers's Hot Sulphur Springs outpost in the Colorado Rockies, which was the home base

138

Launch of second Powell expedition, Green River City, Wyoming, May 1871. (No photos exist of first expedition.) Photo courtesy of Grand Canyon National Park Museum Collection.

for the trapping activities of Dunn and Jack Sumner. From a brief mention in Byers's *Rocky Mountain News* we know that Oliver spent the winter of 1868–69 at Hot Sulphur Springs. The previous winter, Sumner and Dunn had wintered there and safeguarded the property, but this winter Sumner and Dunn were camped with Powell farther west, so it's possible that Oliver was replacing them as caretaker. Like Byers and Sumner, Oliver grew up in southeastern Iowa and immigrated to Colorado around 1860—although Sumner's stay was apparently brief and he soon returned to Iowa. Oliver might have been working for Byers in the spring of 1864, for when Cherry Creek flooded and swept away the office of the *Rocky Mountain News,* Oliver was mentioned as one of several men who barely escaped.

Oliver had further reasons for thinking that the Central City *Weekly Register* would be interested in a report from the Powell expedition: Oramel Howland had worked as a printer for the *Register* (which originally was the *Daily Miner's Register,* and by 1869 was the *Daily Register* and its weekly version, the *Weekly Register*). So had Ned Farrell, who in 1868 had climbed Longs Peak with Powell and Sumner. That same summer Powell had stopped in Central City and met with the editors of the *Register.* Powell had also come through Central City on October 31, 1867, at the close of his first year in the Rockies, and delivered a lecture called "The Peaks, the Parks, and the Plains" at the

Congregational Church, sponsored by the Miners and Mechanics Institute, with tickets going for fifty cents.

Oliver wasn't the only person who thought the *Register* would be interested in the Powell expedition, for it appears that on the same day Dunn was writing to Oliver, Oramel Howland wrote a letter to the *Register*. Unfortunately, the only mention of this letter is one sentence in the July 8 *Register*: "We have before us a letter from O. G. Howland dated the 23rd of May, the day before they were to start down the river." Yet we need to wonder if this Howland letter might have been sent to some other party and later passed along to the *Register*. It would be a bit odd for the *Register* to report on Dunn's letter to Oliver and not mention a Howland letter to the *Register*, and odder that a week later, on June 3, the *Register* reprinted a *Rocky Mountain News* article about the start of the Powell expedition but still made no mention of a Howland letter.

It's likely that Oramel Howland wrote another letter on the day before the launch. In the first weeks of the trip, Howland wrote two letters to the *Rocky Mountain News*, which were mailed out at the Uinta Indian Agency; he began the first letter with the phrase, "As I wrote you, we started the twenty-fourth ultimo from Green River City." This previous letter has never been found, but it was the most likely source for the unattributed report that the *Rocky Mountain News* published on May 29, which is the article the *Register* would reprint a few days later, on June 3: "The Powell party were all ready for starting, and doubtless got off from Green River city on the twenty-fifth instant. The boats they take are built of wood, twenty feet long, with sharp keel, drawing nine inches of water, and are loaded with from 1800 to 2000 pounds. Two men are assigned to the management of each. The party numbers about ten. Mrs. Powell is in the States. A lot of their stock is on the way back through the White River Valley and Middle Park."

Both this article and the Dunn letter state that Powell's boats are twenty feet long. In his book, Powell stated the boats were twenty-one feet long. Since Powell helped design the boats, his number is probably more accurate.

We have to censure the editors of both newspapers for not having enough sense of history to publish the full texts of the Dunn letter and these two Howland letters. Yet the *Register*'s July 8 article makes it clear they did not expect Powell to make history, but thought he was doomed from the start. It was "our belief that it is impossible for anyone to pass down the river alive, and we so stated to Maj. Powell when here a year ago." The *Register* explained:

We have some experience in this matter. In 1860, we attempted to navigate the Grand forty or fifty miles, as nearly as we could estimate it, above its junction with the Green. Our party was some eighteen strong.… We had built a boat…with which to ferry our baggage and provisions across the river.… We found it impossible to cross where we launched our boat, and so Rice, Pierson, and Hunt, excellent watermen, volunteered to run the boat down seven miles, to a point where the current was less rapid. Mr. Hughes and ourself attempted to run a race with them to camp, but in less than ten minutes they were two or three miles in advance of us, and a minute or two later the boat was hurled end over end, stove up, and it was with great difficulty that they saved their lives. This occurred where the river runs through an open valley, several miles in width. We should not have attempted to navigate the canyon above or below, as it was voted an impossibility by our entire party. The Green river must necessarily descend as rapidly as the Grand where we attempted to navigate it, and it has the reputation of flowing even more rapidly. If the party has not already been lost, we shall expect it will be if it attempts to navigate either the Green or Colorado rivers.

Since the *Register* article is using an editorial "we," it is difficult to know exactly who is speaking here, but for the record, the editors and publishers were Frank Hall, J. Alden Smith, and D. C. Collier.

This account, previously unknown, raises a new possibility about the Powell expedition. Powell originally planned to start down the Grand River, but then switched to the Green River. Historians have supposed that Powell switched plans because he recognized that the Green was the main source of the Colorado, and because the completion of the Union Pacific Railroad meant that Powell could easily ship his boats to the Green River. This is plausible, and might be a sufficient explanation. But Powell could find very few sources of personal experience with either river, and if, when Powell visited Central City in both 1867 and 1868, the newspaper editors related the story of their Grand River disaster and warned Powell about attempting the Grand, they could have made an impression on him and influenced his plans.

On September 23, 1869, the Central City editors admitted that they had been wrong. Reporting that Powell had made it through the Grand Canyon, they added, "accomplishing what we believed never could be done." In noting the deaths of Bill Dunn and the Howland brothers, the paper was just as brief and inadequate to history as it was when it failed to print the Dunn and

Howland letters, saying only, "The men reported killed were Coloradans, and good citizens. O. G. Howland, at one time worked in this office as job printer."

This was the only time anyone mentioned that Oramel Howland had lived and worked in Central City. In his coverage of the Powell expedition in the *Rocky Mountain News,* William Byers didn't offer much background about Howland. When the Denver Typographical Union issued a resolution honoring Howland in early 1870, the *News* on January 18, 1870, offered only a few facts: "Mr. Howland, we believe, was a native of Vermont.... He came to Colorado in the spring of 1860, and from that time until the starting of the Powell expedition, with the exception of about two years, was employed in this office." These two years likely included some time in Central City. We can locate Howland there in early 1864, thanks to five mining-claim certificates that surfaced on the antiques market around the year 2000 and that belonged to and were signed by "O. G. Howland." All five certificates were for claims in the Central City area and two bore dates: March 14, 1864, and April 2, 1864. Both of the dated certificates bore the signature of a witness, D. C. Collier, who was one of the editors of the Central City newspaper and who became Central City's first superintendent of schools. All five certificates also bore the small print, "Register Print, Central City." This was likely the *Register*'s printing shop, where Howland worked as a job printer.

If Oramel Howland arrived in Colorado in the spring of 1860, he likely was one of the thousands of men who had caught gold-rush dreams, though many of these dreams soon collided with reality and the men had to take more practical employment, such as being a printer for a Denver newspaper. Yet many Denver residents made occasional prospecting forays into the mountains, including William Byers. In May 1859 Byers and some fellow newspapermen and printers were prospecting not far from the future Central City when he heard that someone had struck gold there. Byers rushed to investigate and found that it was indeed a major strike—not just placer gold in streams but solid veins of gold. He gave the bonanza major publicity in his newspaper, publicity that flashed across the country, including to Vermont: Howland ended up working for the very man who had summoned him west. Byers remained keenly interested in developments in and around Central City, and he sent his newspapers there via his own "pony express" rather than on the stagecoach. Howland could have gone there to have a safe base as a printer while he tried his hand at prospecting. His mining claims didn't necessarily mean he had found anything; many prospectors just claimed a patch of ground and hoped for the best. Yet the Central City area was swarming with gold-seekers. The prospect of going down the Green and Colorado Rivers, through hundreds of miles of exposed rock few if any prospectors had ever seen, might have rekindled the slumbering prospector within Oramel Howland.

History buffs are fortunate that the two Colorado mining towns where Powell crewmembers are known to have lived in the 1860s, Central City and (for Bill Dunn) Georgetown, are still largely intact, thanks to strong local historic preservation efforts. You can walk through downtown and see much of what Howland or Dunn would have seen. In Central City you can see the 1860 home of D. C. Collier, who signed Howland's mining certificates. You can also see the three-story, 1864 building that once housed the newspaper.

In 2014 I arranged to see the newspaper office, on the second floor, abandoned for maybe half a century. Now that the *Rocky Mountain News* had finally expired, the *Register* was the oldest newspaper in Colorado, but it was produced elsewhere. Someone gave occasional tours of the third floor, which held the oldest Masonic Temple in Colorado, with walls displaying 1860s Colorado landscape paintings and the framed lodge charter, signed by Masonic grand priest William Byers. Another prominent lodge member was Henry Teller, future U.S. senator. My guide said she almost never showed anyone the second floor, which was a mess, but she found a key and took me inside. It was very dark and dusty and full of ancient printing presses and typesetting machines and other hardware. She couldn't get the lights to work, so in the dimness it all looked like a historic black-and-white photograph. Some of the hardware and junk could have survived from the 1860s, perhaps even the metal letters that in 1869 spelled out "Howland."

·15·

William Hawkins

Abducted by Alias!

WHEN WILLIAM CULP DARRAH published the first important biography of John Wesley Powell, *Powell of the Colorado,* in 1951, he introduced a new and lasting image of Powell's boatman William Hawkins. Darrah declared, "Hawkins was a fugitive from justice."[1] Darrah's image was soon taken up by Wallace Stegner in his *Beyond the Hundredth Meridian,* where he states that Hawkins "was wanted by the law in Missouri."[2] Subsequent historians have routinely repeated that Hawkins was a fugitive from the law, though more-cautious historians say he was "rumored" to be a fugitive from the law. In his compilation of his Powell research in the 1947 *Utah Historical Quarterly,* Darrah also introduced a more specific image of Hawkins: "He was uneasy at the approach of a sheriff and otherwise acted suspiciously."[3] Historians have repeated this image, too. Darrah also introduced the idea that Hawkins was trying to hide his identity by going by the alias "Missouri."

Yet where did these images originate? Powell and his boatmen never said anything about Hawkins being a fugitive from the law, or about seeing Hawkins acting nervously at the approach of a sheriff. Nor did they ever refer to Hawkins as Missouri or say that Hawkins was calling himself Missouri.

The claim about the nickname Missouri seems to derive from Lewis Keplinger, one of Powell's Illinois Wesleyan University students who accompanied Powell on his 1868 expedition in the Rockies, during which Powell met Hawkins. In 1919 Keplinger wrote an account of their adventures for *The Trail* magazine, in which he commented, "Missouri—that was what we called our second mountaineer."[4] Notice he says "what *we* called," not what Hawkins called himself. It seems that Missouri was simply a nickname Keplinger was applying to Hawkins, referring to his home state. At a time when virtually every white person in the West was a transplant, it was not unusual for people to get nicknames that reflected their origins, such as "the Virginian." Numerous Western towns and mines also bore names from states of origin. We still make use of this habit, as in "Indiana Jones." Darrah, while not quite explicit about it, invited the impression that Missouri was actually an alias; Wallace Stegner took this idea a bit further, and subsequent historians have repeated it as fact.

Keplinger's article also seems to be the source of the claim about the sheriff. Keplinger said of Hawkins and his fellow mountain man Gus Lanken, "We knew nothing of the antecedents of these men except what might be inferred from these two incidents: One morning Missouri said, 'I had a dream last night. I dreampt I was back in Missouri and the sheriff was after me.' Of course we 'joshed' him and told him that was a dead give-away, and asked what devilment he had been up to in Missouri. But he was not communicative." Darrah seems to have taken Hawkins's dream and transformed it into a literal event, an eyewitness report. Keplinger continued, "On another occasion, when some of us were passing the night in an abandoned miner's cabin, the sound of horses' hoofs were heard approaching. We listened with unconcern, but they both sprang to their feet, got their revolvers and peered anxiously out of the crevices between the logs until the horsemen had passed by."[5]

Keplinger doesn't say that the approaching horsemen were lawmen. These were some of the wildest of Colorado's Wild West years, with some areas having far more outlaws than lawmen. Respectable citizens did not usually ride through mountainous areas in the night. Hawkins's reaction could have been the appropriate one for a seasoned mountain man; Keplinger's "unconcern" might have been the questionable reaction.

Keplinger's is the only account in which Hawkins could be said to have reacted with nervousness to someone approaching. Darrah seems to have combined this event and Hawkins's dream into his statement that Hawkins was nervous about the approach of a sheriff. Darrah did have a motive in trying to portray Hawkins as an outlaw: Darrah was a great admirer of John Wesley Powell, and Hawkins was severely critical of Powell in statements he provided to Robert Stanton in 1907 and William W. Bass in 1919. By portraying Hawkins as a criminal, a fugitive, and a deceiver, Darrah could brand him as unreliable and defuse his complaints against Powell. Darrah tipped his hand at the end of his 1947 *Utah Historical Quarterly* article about Hawkins, where he was a bit too eager to dismiss Hawkins: "Inasmuch as neither of these accounts has much standing as source material, having been written nearly fifty years after the time of the expedition, neither is here printed.... It is not possible to disentangle the errors of fact and colored opinion after such a long period."[6] Darrah's eagerness to discredit Hawkins was part of his larger pattern of playing with the facts to protect and enhance Powell.

It is also worth noting that Darrah insisted on referring to Hawkins as "Billy." None of Powell's crew ever called him Billy. Hawkins was never observed referring to himself as Billy. In the newspaper and local historical accounts of his subsequent life in Utah and Arizona, no one ever called him Billy. Powell did introduce him as Billy in his book *The Exploration of the Colorado River and Its Canyons,* but mainly called him "Hawkins." In his river journals Powell mentioned Hawkins by name three times, and only one of those times was it Billy. In the account Hawkins wrote for Robert Stanton in 1907, Hawkins does depict Powell addressing him as Billy. This isn't much of a mandate, but when Darrah first introduces Hawkins in his *Powell of the Colorado,* he gives us Billy Hawkins. Wallace Stegner soon ratified this name, and ever since historians have called him Billy. Perhaps we should not read too much into this, since after all Darrah's own name was William and he might have had some personal preferences about it. Yet precisely because Darrah had plenty of insight into social perceptions of the name "William," he would have understood that William carries much more dignity than Billy, which is often perceived as the name of a kid or a hick and might even invoke a southwestern outlaw—such as Billy the Kid. By calling Hawkins Billy, Darrah could diminish him further.

Yet there were good reasons for Keplinger and the rest of Powell's 1868 group to be suspicious of Hawkins. He had shown up with his buddy Gus Lanken, who soon stole two of Powell's pack animals laden with supplies and ran off. When a squad of Powell's men tried to track Lanken, he opened fire on them, and the pursuers decided to give up. Hawkins remained with them, but now was suspected of being in league with Lanken. "That night," wrote Keplinger, "I made my bed close to Missouri, with a double-barreled loaded gun by my side, and I did not sleep much. Our plan and my instructions were to shoot to kill at the first unmistakable sign of treachery. We could afford to take no chances.... But Missouri stayed with us, and proved to be a capital good fellow."[7] In these circumstances it is not surprising that Keplinger wondered about Hawkins's past.

Darrah also recorded that Hawkins was going by the alias "Bill Rhodes," and in this he was correct. But it is not clear that Powell's men even realized this was an alias. Throughout the river trip they always referred to Hawkins as Rhodes, never as Hawkins. It might be that as far as they knew Rhodes was his real name, so his use of it would not have stimulated any suspicion. Eventually Powell got the idea that the name "Rhodes" was Hawkins's middle name, and this idea was perpetuated by historians Frederick Dellenbaugh and Robert Stanton. When William Culp Darrah tried to research Hawkins's background he pursued the name "William Rhodes Hawkins," and this threw him off track, leading to a case of mistaken identity that lasted for decades.

With the help of a professional researcher in Washington, DC, Darrah searched Missouri Civil War records for a William Rhodes Hawkins, but came up empty. Then Darrah tried the name "William Rhodes" and came up with a soldier named William H. Rhodes. Rhodes's muster roll for November–December 1863 listed him as "absent under civilian arrest." By January he was back serving in the army. But there were a few problems fitting this Rhodes into Hawkins's story. First, if the name "Rhodes" was an alias, Hawkins was obviously already using his alias when he joined the army, meaning that his arrest while in the army could not have been the crime he was trying to hide from. Second, in his enlistment form Rhodes listed himself as married, but Hawkins had never said anything about being married or leaving a wife behind in Missouri, and official records show that Hawkins did not get married until 1873 in Utah.

Darrah decided to enter this Rhodes into the historical record as Billy Hawkins, and suggested that his arrest in the army accounted for why Hawkins was going by an alias. Darrah never mentioned he was looking at the military record of a guy named Rhodes, who was already using the name "Rhodes" when he entered the army. Darrah could not really account for why an arrest that seemed minor, that was soon resolved, and that did not prevent Hawkins from going back into the army, was also serious enough that Hawkins would be trying to hide from it many years later. Darrah never mentioned that his supposed Hawkins was already married. Darrah went ahead and entered into the record some guy who never had anything to do with the Powell expedition. Darrah listed Hawkins as being born in 1841, making him twenty-eight years old on the expedition. Darrah listed Hawkins as enlisting in the 9th Regiment of Union cavalry on June 20, 1863, in the town of Boonville, and being discharged in St. Louis, with a disability, on May 29, 1865. Of Hawkins's unknown crime, Darrah said, "It is perhaps just as well that no additional facts are included."[8] Atop his shaky case about the arrest, Darrah tossed in the bogus claim that Hawkins was frightened by an approaching sheriff, and asserted, "Hawkins was a fugitive from justice, the result of a minor brush with the law which had even disrupted his service in the Union army."[9]

Walter Powell and William Hawkins, probably photographed
before expedition, but location unknown. Photo discovered by
Ray Sumner. Photo courtesy of Hawkins family.

Billy Hawkins's real name was William Robert Wesley Hawkins, and his
real service record was hiding under the name William W. Hawkins. This record agrees with the Hawkins family records, including their family Bible, and
with public and LDS Church records. (Hawkins joined the LDS Church in the
early 1870s.)

William Hawkins was born on July 15, 1848, the same year as Andy Hall,
which means Hawkins was twenty at the start of the Powell expedition.
Hawkins passed his twenty-first birthday just above the junction of the Green
and Colorado Rivers, though no one made note of it. Hawkins could have
been named for his great-grandfather William Hawkins and his uncle Wesley
Hawkins.

In England the Hawkins family was famous for sailing and exploring. Sir Richard Hawkins was the sixth captain to sail around the world; Admiral John Hawkins designed the ships that defeated the Spanish armada, and he explored South America and sailed up a Florida river; William Hawkins explored Brazil three times around 1530. In America the Hawkins family followed the classic American story of a multigenerational migration westward. William Hawkins's family tree mentions one ancestor as being born in Boston in 1632, and another being buried in Rhode Island in 1656. By 1763, when William's great-grandfather William was born, the Hawkins line was in North Carolina. Great-grandfather William's son Augustine was born in Tennessee in 1814; Augustine moved his family to Missouri in the early 1830s; and Augustine's son, our William, continued westward in a big way. In Missouri the Hawkins family first settled in Gasconade County along the Missouri River, then moved to Gentry County in the northwest corner of the state, which on the whole was better farming country—less hilly, less rocky, and less forested than Gasconade County. It was here that William was born. William's father died in 1856, and by 1860 his widow, Sarah Hutton Hawkins, had moved to be near her Hutton relatives in St. Clair County on the western edge of the Ozark Mountains. The county seat, Osceola, was a river town, the head of navigation of the Osage River, down which eleven counties sent their freight toward the Missouri River. Trees from the Ozarks were rafted to Osceola lumber mills.

St. Clair County was about thirty miles from the Kansas border, which was not a safe place to be around 1860: Missouri was a slave state, Kansas a free state and abolitionist hotbed. Missourians were raiding Kansas and attacking abolitionist towns. Kansans—like John Brown—were fighting back and making the whole nation more militant against slave owners. When the Civil War broke out, Missourians fought one another over whether their state should remain in the Union (which it did), generating an ugly guerilla war with neighbors burning down one another's houses. Missouri Confederates continued attacking Kansas. Confederate general Sterling Price pitched his army's winter camp in St. Clair County and issued a call for new recruits to rally there. James Lane, a Union general who was also Kansas's U.S. senator, looted and burned down the county seat, Osceola. When Confederate guerrilla leader William Quantrill burned down Lawrence, Kansas, and massacred its citizens in 1863, he said it was in retaliation for Osceola. In response to the Lawrence raid and the aid that border Missourians were giving to the raiders, Union commander Thomas Ewing ordered that Missouri's border counties be emptied of residents to create a buffer zone, an action highly controversial even among Union supporters. The refugees flooded into St. Clair County.

Considering the Southern roots of the Hawkins family, and considering that most Southern-rooted Missouri families sympathized with the Confederacy, it was against the odds that the Hawkins family would fight for the Union. St. Clair County was strongly pro-Confederate, which is why General Lane burned down Osceola. But perhaps the Hawkins family still had some Boston in them. William's oldest brother, John, enlisted in the Union cavalry in 1861, in a state militia unit that eventually turned into the 15th cavalry. St. Clair County wasn't the safest place to be a Union supporter, which might be why in November 1863 William slipped across the Polk County line to enlist in the Union army. Crossing this line also placed him outside the jurisdiction of the controversial General Ewing and meant he was able to join his brother's regiment. He enlisted in the town of Humansville, where he had some Hutton cousins. A few months previously William's mother, originally a Hutton, had died, freeing him of filial obligations, but perhaps he waited until the crops were in before enlisting.

Hawkins was fifteen years old, below the legal age for joining the army, but he claimed he was eighteen. It was common for kids to lie to get into the army, and officers, eager for recruits, often looked the other way. Hawkins's enlistment form lists him as five feet five inches tall, gray eyes, light hair, fair complexion. He took with him a horse the Union army valued at $110, and horse equipment worth $20. He signed up for twenty months of service.

Hawkins's regiment performed patrol and scouting duties in southwestern Missouri and engaged in minor skirmishes. It lost seven men in combat, and thirty-six to disease. The main threat they faced, in the autumn of 1864, was the Confederacy's last attempt to seize Missouri. From Arkansas, General Sterling Price marched 12,000 troops (including a Union spy named Wild Bill Hickok) toward the state capital, Jefferson City, but Price decided it was too well defended and headed farther west, where he was joined by William Quantrill's guerrillas, including Frank and Jesse James, fresh from a massacre and dangling the scalps of Union soldiers on their bridles. Hawkins's regiment went in pursuit, chasing Price for 150 miles and engaging him several times. In his 1890 military pension application, William's brother John said that the "excessive hard riding & exposure during Said Price raid" had permanently ruined his health, giving him a heart condition that left him unable to work fully. According to one regimental service list, Hawkins's regiment took part in the final showdown of the Price raid, at Mine Creek, Kansas, where 2,600 Union troops charged a Confederate force twice that size and smashed it, ending the Confederate threat to Missouri. However, the most thorough study of the battle, Lumir F. Buresh's *October 25th and The Battle of Mine Creek,* which contains a list of all the regiments involved in the battle, makes no mention of Hawkins's 15th cavalry.[10]

It turns out that, just like the false William Hawkins, the real William Hawkins got into some trouble with the law while in the military. Hawkins was accused of stealing the gun of a civilian, and he was arrested, imprisoned, and court-martialed.

On Hawkins's muster roll for February 1865, he is listed as "absent," with the note, "absent in arrest." Hawkins was confined in the military prison in Springfield, Missouri, and on its daily report for March 2, under the heading "confined without orders," the prison listed Hawkins as "confined for mutiny." The next day's report also notes mutiny. On the next available daily report, for March 8, there is no mention of mutiny. At Hawkins's court-martial there was no mention of mutiny, nor was there in his subsequent muster forms or pension files. It's possible that the note about mutiny was a clerk's mistake or misunderstanding. Perhaps Hawkins got so annoyed about his arrest that the arresting officer treated it as an act of disobedience, but no actual mutiny charges were filed.

Compared with some of the crimes committed by soldiers, including desertion and murder, Hawkins's crime was relatively mild. Yet, for the army, courts-martial served as an important disciplinary tool, for the army had to regulate the behavior of hundreds of thousands of young men who were away from home for the first time and feeling enormous discomforts, pressures, fear, and boredom, who were prone to drinking and gambling and sometimes fighting, and who were all carrying guns.

The army was especially vigilant about acts of disobeying officers, even when the act itself might be trivial. A small offense might be punished with a loss of pay, but falling asleep while on guard duty could lead to a court-martial and months of hard labor in camp, or even a death penalty. Courts-martial were fairly common and usually fair-minded, more concerned with enforcing discipline than with removing soldiers from the army, for officers knew how hard it was to recruit and train new soldiers. The judge advocate who presided over a court-martial and served as prosecutor was also responsible for helping the defendant prepare his defense, for example by locating witnesses. The one factor that made Hawkins's case potentially more serious was that he had committed a crime against a civilian, and the army had to worry about its reputation in the larger society and thus might be more inclined to impose the sort of penalties that would be imposed by a civilian court.

After Hawkins had stayed in jail for eighteen days, his court-martial trial began on March 11, 1865, with nine officers serving as a jury, three of them from Hawkins's own regiment. He was assigned an attorney. The court read the charges that Hawkins did "feloniously steal, take and carry away with intent to convert to his own use one revolver pistol of the value of twenty-five dollars."[11] In 1865, twenty-five dollars was not a small amount of money. Hawkins pleaded: Not guilty.

The victim, J. J. Wolf, took the stand and testified about the circumstances of the theft, including the presence of two men named Hutton, who were Hawkins's cousins. The younger Hutton, Ben, was serving in the same cavalry company:

> I was working at the mill, and the pistol was in my way and I took it off and laid it upon some plank in the mill.... Old man Hutton, his son, and Hawkins, the accused here came to the mill, and Old man Hutton wanted some flour and I sent a hand to the house.... During the time the hand was gone for the flour, the revolver I suppose was taken, and the accused also left at that time. When the flour came I looked up to get the board that I had laid the revolver on, to make a Calculation of the weight of the flour, and the pistol was gone, I had laid the pistol on this board.... Both of the Mr. Huttons plead innocent and insisted that I should search them. I objected I hated to search a neighbor. I looked around and discovered that Hawkins the accused was missing.

After searching everyone present, Wolf concluded that Hawkins was guilty and went to Hawkins's company officer, Captain Sutherland, to complain. Hawkins was at the home of one of the Huttons in Humansville, some miles from Wolf's mill. The Huttons warned Hawkins that Wolf was mad at him, and in the evening Hawkins went back and tried to return the pistol. He did not find Wolf since Wolf was away seeing Captain Sutherland, so Hawkins did not leave the gun. But, Wolf testified, "Mr. Hawkins, the accused, brought it back to me about Sun rise the next morning." Hawkins said it was just a joke. "He said that Ben Hutton persuaded Him to take it, to pays a joke on me."

The judge advocate, as the prosecution, then swore in William's brother, Sargent John J. Hawkins. When asked William's age, John replied, "I think He was Sixteen years old last July, as well as I recollect." This was a loaded question, for John was admitting that his brother had lied about his age to get into the army. John reported that Captain Sutherland, upon receiving Wolf's complaint about his stolen gun, sent John to find his brother at the Huttons and retrieve the gun. William said that he did not have the gun but it was somewhere in between there and the house of the other Hutton. "As we went back," reported John, "he rode out to the side of the road. But I did not see Him get the pistol. I did not see the pistol until we got to Milton Hutton's." Through a series of questions the judge advocate explored whether William had really hidden the gun along the road or merely pretended he had done so, and whether William told John that hiding the gun was part of the supposed joke; the implication was that William really had intended to steal the gun. John said that the next morning he accompanied William to see Wolf and return the gun.

The defense swore in Ben Hutton, who largely repeated Wolf's testimony about the circumstances of the theft, but emphasized that it was just a joke. The judge advocate tried to undermine Hutton's reliability, asking, "Are you not in arrest awaiting trial for Helping steal this pistol?"

HUTTON: Yes, that is what they have me here for.

The judge advocate then repeatedly tried to catch Ben Hutton in a contradiction, since he had told Wolf he didn't know anything about Hawkins taking the pistol.

JUDGE ADVOCATE: Why did you not tell Wolf that Hawkins had his pistol?
HUTTON: Because it was taken through a joke, and we wanted to see a little sport over it.
JUDGE ADVOCATE: Did you not tell Hawkins for him to take the pistol, and that you and him would go partners?
HUTTON: No, sir.
JUDGE ADVOCATE: When you saw that Wolf was angry about his pistol, and that the affair was about to create a difficulty, why did you not tell Wolf all about where his pistol was?
HUTTON: Because I did not think about him reporting it.

The defense brought in the elder Hutton, John, and asked, "How long have you been acquainted with him [Hawkins]?"

HUTTON: All of his life.
DEFENSE: Are you acquainted with his general character for honesty?
HUTTON: Yes. As far as I know any thing about him.
DEFENSE: What is that reputation, good or bad?
HUTTON: As far as I know he has a good character.

The questioning went through more loops, more examinations and cross-examinations. The prosecution had succeeded in undermining Hawkins's credibility, for he had claimed Ben Hutton was in on the joke but Hutton denied it. But the judge advocate never insisted that Hawkins had really intended to steal the pistol, or that hiding it along the road was part of this plan. The nineteen-page trial proceedings wrapped up:

> The accused offered no further testimony. The case was submitted without remark. The Court was cleared for deliberation, and after mature consideration find the accused as follows.
>
> Of the specification: Guilty
>
> Of the Charge: Guilty
>
> And the Court does therefore sentence him the said William W. Hawkins, a private of Co. D 15th Reg't Cav. Mo vol, to be imprisoned in the Penitentiary at such place as the Commanding General May direct for the period of two (2) years.

If this sentence had been carried out, Hawkins would have remained in prison until the spring of 1867 and probably would have missed his chance to get to Colorado and become the experienced mountain man Powell hired for his 1868 exploration of the Rockies, which led to Hawkins going on the river expedition the next year. But Brigadier General Sanborn, who had authority over the court, decided that the conviction was unjustified, writing, "The evidence in the case seems at least to raise a reasonable doubt as to whether the accused ever intended to convert the property taken to his own use. The finding and sentence is therefore disapproved. The accused will be released from arrest and returned to duty with his company."

Hawkins's next muster roll records him simply as "present." His muster rolls and discharge form in July make no further mention of his arrest, but it appears he was not paid any more after his arrest, which might have been a form of punishment. In his pension files there is a brief, disinterested mention of his arrest, but no mention of mutiny, and Hawkins was honorably discharged. Yet such an experience could indeed have prompted years of bad dreams about being pursued by a sheriff.

However, Hawkins did end his service in arrears. When the army discharged him on July 1, 1865, fulfilling his twenty-month contract, his discharge form lists him as, "Indebted to U.S. for 1 Waist Belt and Plate, 1 Gun Sling, 1 shoulder sling and Plate." Perhaps Hawkins had been merely sloppy and lost some of his gear, or perhaps, since the gear was gun-related, stealing was his way of getting a bit of revenge for an arrest, jailing, and trial he considered unjust and humiliating.

There is nothing in Hawkins's military record that defines him as "a fugitive from justice" or "wanted by the law in Missouri." It's unlikely Hawkins got into legal trouble in Missouri after leaving the service, for in a deposition in his brother's pension file William states that he left the state "right away after discharge."[12] According to William's own pension file, a month after leaving the army he was in Leavenworth, Kansas, and by May 1866 he was in Denver. He might have headed west driving a wagon, for almost the only description that Powell offered of Hawkins was, "Our cook has been an ox-driver, or 'bull-whacker,' on the plains, in one of those long trains now no longer seen."[13] In 1867 Hawkins was in Nevada and then Wyoming. We don't know what Hawkins was doing in either place, but these were gold rush years there, Wild West years, with lots of temptations and chaos, so it is always possible Hawkins got into some sort of trouble in the three years between leaving Missouri and meeting Powell.

Or perhaps when Hawkins met John Wesley Powell, a Union officer who was looking for men he could rely on in the way he had relied on his troops in the war, Hawkins did not want Powell to check into his military record and discover that he had been arrested for theft, jailed for mutiny, court-martialed, and had finally run off with a few army items. Powell would not be eager to take a mutineer on a difficult journey into a remote wilderness, where discipline might make the difference between life and death. Perhaps Hawkins offered the name "Rhodes" to hide his past from Powell.

Where did Hawkins get the name Rhodes? Darrah's William H. Rhodes was a cavalryman who fought in some of the same battles as Hawkins, so it is possible Hawkins knew him and borrowed his more honorable name. More likely, it came from a famous mountain man named Bill Rhodes who roamed the West for a quarter of a century and was in the Wyoming gold rush in 1867, as was Hawkins. Mountain man Rhodes was killed by Indians in 1868, so the name was available. Hawkins could have been trying to borrow some of the stature of the veteran mountain man. Or perhaps the name had some private meaning for Hawkins.

Ironically, Hawkins's secret past could have made an important contribution to the success of the Powell expedition. When the Howlands and Bill Dunn "mutinied" at Separation Rapid, Hawkins faced a choice. He had already tasted the shame of being branded as a mutineer. If Hawkins went with the Howlands and Dunn, he might permanently reinforce this negative identity.

Or he could prove his loyalty to his commanding officer, and show his bravery. Both Powell and Hawkins agree that when the crew was wrestling with its decision at Separation Rapid, Hawkins was the first (after Powell's brother Walter) to pledge to continue down the river. Hawkins could have been eager to prove he was no mutineer.

Hawkins got into another ordeal with the military when he applied for a military pension in 1890. Until that year, pensions were granted only for disabilities suffered in the line of duty, but in 1890 the president signed a new law granting pensions for any veteran too disabled to work, as long as they had served a sufficient time in the army and been honorably discharged. The law was highly controversial and one of the leading issues of the 1888 presidential election, for critics charged it was wide open to fraud. Indeed, William's pension application makes me wonder. Though he was applying under the new law, he claimed he had been disabled in the army in 1864, when his horse fell on him. Hawkins blamed this injury for a wide assortment of maladies: "heart and lung trouble, asthma, and affection of left side," including broken ribs, partial left-ear deafness, partial loss of left-eye vision, and an injured back and shoulder.[14] He was now so disabled that he could perform only half the labor of an able-bodied person, which for a farmer prevented him from making a living.

The U.S. Department of War (or War Department) was highly skeptical, because there was no mention of such an accident in Hawkins's record. Hawkins replied that he could not provide further evidence as he could not find any of the doctors who had treated him, and all his officers were deceased. It probably didn't help that Hawkins was a suspected mutineer who had disappeared with $1.61 of army property rather than filing for the kind of discharge that could have earned him a disability pension. Hawkins hired a Washington, DC, law firm to pursue his case and for years continued filing affidavits. Perhaps he realized that his fame as a Colorado River superman wasn't consistent with being disabled in 1864, for on one document he claimed that his "simptoms" didn't appear until 1870.[15] He eventually did get a pension of $30 per month.

NOTES

1. Darrah, *Powell of the Colorado*, 114.
2. Stegner, *Beyond the Hundredth Meridian*, 44.
3. Darrah, *Utah Historical Quarterly* 15 (1947): 106.
4. Lewis Keplinger, "The First Ascent of Long's Peak," *The Trail* (June 1919).
5. Ibid.
6. Darrah, *Utah Historical Quarterly* 15 (1947): 107.

7. Keplinger, "First Ascent."

8. Darrah, *Utah Historical Quarterly* 15 (1947): 105.

9. Darrah, *Powell of the Colorado*, 114.

10. In an article published in the *Boatman's Quarterly Review* I assumed that Hawkins had taken part in the battle, but this now appears to have been wrong. Don Lago, "Billy Hawkins: Abducted by Alias!," *Boatman's Quarterly Review,* 14, no. 3 (Fall 2001), 10–11.

11. All quotes from court-martial proceedings are from William W. Hawkins Court-Martial File, File 16W3/15/20/6/, Box 1058, National Archives, Washington, DC.

12. John Hawkins, Military Pension File, File #WL706-634, National Archives, Washington, DC.

13. Powell, *Exploration,* 147–48.

14. William Hawkins, Military Pension File, File #SC911-532, National Archives, Washington, DC.

15. Ibid.

·16·

The Promotion of Andy Hall

A CURIOUS THING HAPPENED to Andy Hall between 1947 and 1951, between the time historian William Culp Darrah introduced Hall to the public in the *Utah Historical Quarterly* and the time Darrah published his biography *Powell of the Colorado*: Andy Hall became a much wiser man. He went from being a hell-raising young "character" to being "a genius…with judgment far beyond his years."[1] Darrah needed to improve Andy Hall's image because Hall had suddenly become crucial to Darrah's desire to absolve Powell of blame for the Howlands and Dunn walking off the trip.

Darrah spent years searching for letters, journals, and other documents about the Powell expedition, but by the time he organized them into a special issue of the *Utah Historical Quarterly* in 1947 he had not found Andy Hall's family or any letters or documents from or about Hall. He had to settle for a brief introduction cobbled together out of comments from other crewmembers:

> In the Major's words, [Hall was] "The Character" of the party. Although but 18 years of age, he had already spent five years on the loose in the plains as a bullwhacker, mule driver, and Indian scout. He had engaged in numerous Indian skirmishes and had raised hell wherever he found it.… He seems to have had some knowledge of English literature. It was Andy who suggested the name "Lodore" after the poem by Robert Southey, and on several occasions Powell makes direct references to the young fellow's pertinent comments and objectives. The Major first met Andy, a skilled boatman, resting upon the oars of a home-made craft of nondescript design. He engaged the lad on the spot. On many occasions it was Andy's good humor that enlivened the monotonous and gradually vanishing fare until starvation faced the whole party.[2]

After his *Utah Historical Quarterly* article was published, Darrah was informed by Wallace Stegner, who was researching his own Powell biography, that the museum at Grand Canyon National Park had been given a copy of a letter Hall had written from the river. Through the park Darrah got in touch with the letter's donor, Mamie Hall Laughlin, Andy Hall's niece, and she put Darrah in touch with another niece, Martha Stetson, who possessed other letters, two of them about the expedition. Of these three letters, one was written from Green River, Wyoming, as the trip was ready to launch, another was sent from the Uinta Indian Agency along the way, and the last was written from Fort Mohave at the end of the trip. This last letter contained Andy Hall's very brief account of what had happened at Separation Rapid: he wrote that the Howlands and Dunn left because they were afraid to run it. When Darrah received Hall's letter he wrote to Martha Stetson that he was "more than pleased with the information they give" because he could now prove his case that the fault lay in the river and in the weakness of the three deserters, not in Powell, and certainly not in Powell ordering the men to leave, as some historians had suggested: "Any lingering mystery as to the true reason has been completely solved." Considering that Hall was offering only one sentence to stack up against the detailed testimony of Sumner and Hawkins, Darrah might be a bit over-eager in saying that the case was "completely solved."[3] Darrah had been conducting a lively correspondence with Dock Marston, who was fond of psychological theory and had proposed that the chair Powell rigged on his boat on his second expedition was a Freudian throne that proved Powell's megalomania, an idea that exasperated Darrah. Now Darrah wrote Dock Marston that the information in Hall's letters "adds incontestable proof that the Howlands and Dunn left voluntarily because they refused to go further."[4] Marston answered that, no, Hall's letters didn't settle it: "Why did the three decide to quit at Separation after all those miles above them?" At the bottom of Marston's letter Darrah noted, "Not answered. I'm through with his prejudice and blindness."[5] It was the end of their "friendship."

Hall's letter was now crucial to Darrah, but it also presented a problem. Hall's letters were riddled with errors of format, spelling, grammar, capitalization, and punctuation. Hall looked like some kind of dummy. In truth, he was no more illiterate than millions of American youths of the time. But now Hall's feeble letter was supposed to discredit Oramel Howland, who as a newspaper printer had a good command of the English language and who wrote eloquent letters from the river. Now Hall's letter was supposed to vanquish Jack Sumner, whose lack of education did not stop him from telling vivid stories. Hall's writings conveyed little authority. Even Darrah's statement that Hall "seems to have had some knowledge of English literature" now seemed questionable. And indeed, there is no source for Darrah's claim that it was Hall who took the name "Lodore" from an English poem; no one on the expedition ever said it was Hall. Darrah seems to have invented this, and now his discovery of Hall's letters was calling his bluff.

Darrah's solution was to doctor Hall's letters to a major degree. In the Separation Rapid letter, which had 397 words, Darrah made about a hundred improvements. Hall's "perlos vorg" became Darrah's "perilous voyage." Hall's "me and bill Rhoads" became Darrah's "Bill Rhoads and I." Hall's "the made of the canion" became Darrah's "*The Maid of the Canyon.*" Hall's "wrapped" or "rapped" became Darrah's "rapid." Hall's "the magor" became Darrah's "the Major." In the crucial sentence about Separation Rapid, Hall's, "They was a frade to run it so they left us in abad place," became Darrah's "They were afraid to run it so they left us in a bad place."

Darrah did not change the meaning of Hall's words, but Hall's letter now read very smoothly, as if it were written by a smart, authoritative, fully trustworthy man. Darrah also doctored the first letter, written from Green River. By some standards of scholarly editing, Darrah's changes might be acceptable, showing mercy and true meaning to readers with limited patience for playing decoding games. Yet scholarly rules also require editors to disclose they are intervening and not presenting the original text. This was not Darrah's course. And Darrah had a big dilemma. The second letter, sent from the Uinta Agency, was now on file at Grand Canyon National Park, where other scholars could see it and compare it with Darrah's version, if he made changes to it. Darrah decided to publish the second letter as it was, packed with errors. It was sandwiched between his two doctored, literate letters. The discrepancy between the styles of the three letters wasn't hard to notice. Darrah did leave a few errors in his two doctored letters, changing "grene river" only into "Grene river." In his introduction to the letters Darrah then committed a bold falsehood, saying, "The original letters pay little heed to spelling or paragraphing. Nevertheless, so far as possible, they are here reproduced faithfully. Their simplicity, affection, and impulsiveness would be destroyed by alteration."[6]

Darrah published these letters as an appendix to a 1949 special edition of the *Utah Historical Quarterly* devoted to documents from the second Powell expedition. He presented the Hall letters with, "Here then is the final link in the chain of proof that the separation of the Howland brothers and Dunn was simple desertion—they refused to go farther."[7] With his new information from the Hall family, Darrah was now able to correct Hall's age from eighteen to twenty-one and to fill in more details about his origins and wandering life on the plains.

Darrah went back to work on his Powell biography, and when he introduced Andy Hall in it he left him a hell-raiser but raised him quite a bit higher: "Too young to join the Union Army, Andy Hall left his home in Illinois to seek his fortune. For four years he roamed the plains, engaged in a dozen Indian skirmishes, and generally raised hell wherever he found it. He was in a sense a genius, full of fun, strong and daring. With judgment far beyond his years and with a humor that never failed him, Andy was the life of the party."[8]

Powell agreed that Hall was entertaining, but Darrah did not repeat the rest of what Powell said about Hall, which would not have enhanced Hall's credibility: "He can tell a good story, and is never encumbered by unnecessary scruples in giving his narratives those embellishments which help to make a story complete."[9] When Darrah came to the events at Separation Rapid, which he discussed not in the text but in a long footnote, he declared, "The simple fact is they were afraid to go farther and deserted."[10] He then quoted Andy Hall's Fort Mohave letter as proof.

Darrah did not publish a letter Hall wrote to his family from Ehrenberg, Arizona, six months after the end of the expedition, in which he mentioned his motivations for going on it and his feelings about the results. In making his comments on Indians, Hall could have been thinking of the fate of the Howlands and Dunn:

> Ehrenburg, arizona ter
> March 6, 1870
> Dear sis
> it is a long time sins I have herd frome home on acount of drifting about so much frome one place to another I have ben in seven or eight diferent teritorys and part of california i amnow on the collorado river that runs betweene irasona and california whare I think I will stop this sommer this is the hotest place i ever was in snow is never knowne here I dont like this warme climate in the foul I will either come home or go to colorado and start a rencio [ranch?] my last years work has beene all throne away exploring this river i started with the intention of finding some god farming land and failed to find any there is some good land nere prescot and vegtebels and grane is very hy but the indians will not let the country git setled a man can not go out to the plow withought his gun and pistole with him and carful as they

The only known image of Andy Hall. Photo courtesy of
Huntington Library.

are theyre is always some one geting killed the country is so rough
around there that the soldiers can't follow them I have no more newes
at present if you get this leter write soon give my love to all yours truly
from your wild nefue A Hall[11]

Did Hall really go through the canyons of the Colorado River searching
for good farmland? It was, of course, the Great Unknown, but Hall could have
found plenty of good farmland back on the prairie he had left. It's more likely
he was motivated by the same taste for adventure that had led to his years of
wandering the West. Hall could have intended his words about farmland to reassure his family back in Illinois, where a respectable life consisted of farming;
his family had opposed his heading west. Hall began many of his letters home
by reassuring his family that he was still alive.

Who was Andy Hall and how did he come to be on the Powell expedition?

The first public record of Andy Hall, located by British historian Christopher Penn, is in the 1851 British census, which shows Mary Hall and her three children, Helen (whom the family often called Ellen), William, and Andrew. Andrew was born in Scotland in 1848, but his father soon died. Mary's brother, Henry Scott, had immigrated to America and taken part in the 1849 California gold rush but had decided there was better pay dirt in the farmlands of Illinois. Henry was still a bachelor and invited Mary to join him and become his housekeeper. She immigrated to America in 1854, taking six weeks to sail across the Atlantic, and settled in a neighborhood full of transplanted Scots in the town of Toulon, Illinois, in Stark County, only thirty miles from the town of Hennepin where John Wesley Powell would soon be teaching school. Andrew grew up hearing Uncle Henry's tales of the West and its amazing landscapes and adventures; this could have planted the seeds of wanderlust and adventure in the young boy. His niece Mamie Hall Laughlin told historian Darrah, "My father often told us children of Andy's love of adventure and of his fearless disposition."[12] Among his schoolmates Andy soon got a reputation as a daredevil. "One day," explained Laughlin, "a revolver he was holding was discharged accidentally and his hand was injured. Just as soon as the wound was attended to he was ready to get hold of the gun again."[13]

Curiously, the 1860 U.S. census seems to show Andrew Hall living in two places: in Toulon with his mother and in the town of Wethersfield in next-door Henry County with Peter and Helen Inglis, both born in Scotland. Inglis was a farmer with three kids too young to help with the labor of running a farm, so perhaps Mary Hall rented out Andy as a farmhand, which also left one less mouth for her to feed.

Farm work probably did not satisfy Andy's appetite for adventure. When the Civil War broke out, Andy's older brother William enlisted, "but Andy was refused," as niece Martha Stetson told Dock Marston, "as being too young which made him rather indignant, so to off set his disappointment and in spite of his family's objections he joined a wagon train that was headed west. He was only 16 at the time, but had already acquired the nick name of 'Dare Devil Dick.'"[14]

Andy wandered from place to place and from job to job—trapping, hunting, bullwhacking, sheep herding, apprenticing with a Denver gunsmith, tending a store, and getting into fights with Indians, whom Hall commented would love to scalp his fourteen-inch-long hair. In October 1868 he wrote his mother that he was at Green River, Wyoming, hauling wood for the railroad.[15]

In January 1869 he wrote his brother William that he was "in Denver waiting for a job."[16] This job must not have come through or lasted, for a few months later he was back in Green River, where Powell spotted him and signed him up.

Powell must have been impressed that Hall had already explored at least a bit of the Green River, at least by land. In one of his years in the Rockies, Hall had made winter camp at Brown's Hole, a valley along the Green River and a longtime favorite camp for mountain men. Hall wrote two letters from Brown's Hole, one to his brother and the other to his mother, though unfortunately neither letter has a date so we don't know which winter it was. To his brother he wrote,

> I am now in winter quarters in the lovliest place in the rocy mountains it is what is called browns holes on greenriver Utah ter write close to the unty valley whare the unty Indians ar camped we have vennasn in abundance all the time I am getting fat for once in my life. I waied to day 150 lbs the heaviest I ever waied in my life.
>
> O sweet is the vaill whare this river jently glides through the mountains so easy and free but sweeter by farr to my childhoodse joyes days is old spoon river to me.[17]

Four months after his 1870 letter to home, Andy Hall was still in Ehrenberg, where the 1870 U.S. census listed him as being twenty years old and born in Scotland. In a letter to his mother he reported that he was not doing well financially.[18] From an 1897 letter written by William H. Hardy we know that at some point Andy Hall came to him and got a job driving his stage from Hardyville to Prescott. By 1872 Hall had moved to Prescott and was running the Grey Eagle Stables, owned by Captain W. J. Ross, who had fought Indians under General Crook. A letter to his brother makes clear that Hall was still caught up in Wild West dreams of wealth, this time a rumor of diamonds, and he said he would not come home to Illinois till he had made enough money to live on for the rest of his days—he never did go home. He assured his brother that while he was no longer the quiet boy they had known, he did not drink or gamble. By 1875 Hall was back to driving, judging from a brief mention in the (Prescott) *Arizona Weekly Miner* on January 8, 1875: "Andrew Hall, driver of the Mohave county mail wagon, informs us that the Moss mill…is being hauled to the Sandy." In the winter of 1875–76 he was a special constable in Tucson. In the spring of 1876 Hall moved to Florence, Arizona, where the 1880 census lists him as married to a thirty-two-year-old lady named Francisca, who was born in Sonoma, Mexico. They had a son, Amota, age thirteen, and a daughter, Amilia, age four, both of whose parents are listed as being from Sonoma, so it seems Francisca had a previous husband. When Francisca died twenty years later, an article in the Florence *Arizona Blade,* on August 10, 1900, gave what little we know about her life: "Mrs. Francisca Santacruz, died Thursday, of dropsy. She was about fifty years of age and leaves a large family of children all of whom, except one, are married. She was the widow of Andy Hall, the Wells Fargo messenger, who was killed by the stage robbers, Hawley and Grimes, near Pioneer, fifteen years ago. She had one son by Hall, named Andy, who now resides in Florence. She was a good woman, and was highly esteemed by her people."

Powell historians were unaware that Andy Hall had a wife or son; this was pointed out to me by British researcher Christopher Penn. Penn also notes that the many newspaper articles about Andy Hall's death in 1882 never mentioned him having a wife or son, so he wonders if their arrangement was informal or if they had parted ways by that time. The further life of Andy Hall's son is unknown.

At some point, Hall began working for Wells Fargo as a messenger and guard in their freight route between Casa Grande and Globe. On the evening of March 18, 1879, Hall ate in a Chinese restaurant on the main street of Globe, walked out the back door, and was confronted by an angry dog. Hall tried to kick the dog away, but it continued lunging and snapping at him, so Hall pulled out his pistol and shot the dog. The dog belonged to the restaurant owner, Fan Gee, who came out and found his dog dead and saw Hall heading away. Fan Gee went inside and got his pistol and went searching for Hall. He found Hall in Klein's Store and angrily berated him for killing his dog, then lifted his gun toward Hall, whereupon Hall yelled, "Don't you do it." Hall shot him, killing him. Hall walked down the street and went into Kerr's saloon, whose owner was a deputy sheriff, told him what had just happened, and surrendered his gun. The next day Hall came before the local justice of the peace, and when onlookers testified that Hall had acted in self-defense, he was released. But the county attorney and district judge decided that the justice of the peace had not handled the matter properly, since there was no attorney and no witnesses for the victim. Hall was arrested but let out on bail, and on April 27 he came before a grand jury and was indicted for murder. He was let out on bail again. Hall's case remained in limbo, not going to trial, possibly because the creation of a new county was reshuffling the legal jurisdiction of the case. Hall still had not been tried when, on August 20, 1882, he was guarding a Wells Fargo pack train with a $5,000 gold shipment, which was attacked by robbers. He could have allowed them to get away, but he pursued them. If this was his taste for adventure at work again, it finally betrayed him. Hall was shot eight times, and killed. He was thirty-four. When his funeral procession wound its way through Globe, the man ringing the church bell was one of the three men who had committed the robbery and murder. They would soon be captured, and two would be lynched.

Hall has proven elusive even in death. According to more than one source, including the records of the Wells Fargo Company, which paid $109.50 for his funeral, Hall was buried in the Globe cemetery. Several people and I have searched the cemetery for his gravestone and have not found it. The most extensive search was done by river guide Art Christiansen, who not only searched the cemetery thoroughly three times, but also looked through all the cemetery records from 1882 and later and found no mention of Hall. There should have been a gravestone: a few weeks after the funeral the local newspaper reported that deputy U.S. Marshall Gabriel, a friend of Andy Hall who had taken charge of the murder investigation, had pledged to donate his share of the reward to buying Hall a gravestone and a fence around his grave. But the cemetery does hold many old graves without markers, and many with wooden and stone markers so eroded they no longer hold any names. One Grand Canyon hiker, to remain nameless, might have committed the most honorable of violations of the law against removing anything from a national park when he climbed both Hawkins Butte and Hall Butte and took rocks from them to place on the graves of William Hawkins and Andy Hall. The Hall stone is still waiting for its proper resting place.

NOTES

1. "Character" in Darrah, *Utah Historical Quarterly* 15 (1947): 107; "a genius" in Darrah, *Powell of the Colorado*, 258.

2. Darrah, *Utah Historical Quarterly* 15 (1947): 107.

3. Darrah to Martha Stetson, December 23, 1948, Darrah Collection.

4. Darrah to Otis "Dock" Marston, June 17, 1949, Darrah Collection.

5. Marston to Darrah, July 7, 1949, Darrah Collection.

6. Darrah, *Utah Historical Quarterly* 16–17 (1948–49): 506.

7. Ibid.

8. Darrah, *Powell of the Colorado*, 115.

9. Powell, *Exploration*, 123.

10. Darrah, *Powell of the Colorado*, 141 (fn).

11. Andy Hall to his sister Ellen, March 6, 1870, Darrah Collection.

12. Mamie Hall Laughlin to Darrah, Nov. 18, 1948, Darrah Collection.

13. Laughlin to Darrah, Nov. 26, 1948, Darrah Collection.

14. Stetson to Marston, Nov. 14, 1960. Andy Hall File, Marston Collection, Huntington Library, San Marino, CA (hereafter Marston Collection).

15. Andrew Hall to Mary Hall, Oct. 24, 1868, Andy Hall File, Marston Collection.

16. Andy Hall to William Hall, Jan. 30, 1869, Andy Hall File, Marston Collection.

17. Andy Hall to William Hall, n.d., Andy Hall File, Marston Collection. Spoon River is the pastoral river that ran close to Hall's Illinois childhood home, and that later became famous in Edgar Lee Masters's *Spoon River Anthology*.

18. Andy Hall to William Hall, Jan. 30, 1869, Andy Hall File, Marston Collection.

•17•

The Westering Star of Jack Sumner

JOHN COLTON "JACK" SUMNER was born under a wandering star. The Sumner family story is a quintessential story of the American frontier, and of a young America full of endless horizons, possibilities, and confidence. It is a story of people moving on in search of adventure and opportunity, a story of family bonds that repeatedly stretched to keep up with the American Dream.

It seems symbolic of the mobility of Americans on the mid-nineteenth-century frontier that even governors moved onward. Robert Lucas, the grandfather of Jack Sumner, had been governor of Ohio in the early 1830s; in 1838 he moved to Iowa and became Iowa's first territorial governor. It was probably to follow Lucas that the Sumner family moved to Iowa a few years after him. With his first wife Lucas had one daughter, Minerva. After his wife's death, Lucas married a woman named Friendly Sumner. Friendly's youngest brother was named Horatio Nelson Sumner, and Minerva married him. Thus Horatio Sumner was both the brother-in-law and the son-in-law of Governor Lucas. In moving to Iowa, Horatio was following his sister and Minerva was following her father. They settled in the town of West Liberty, which was only fifteen miles from the state capital of Iowa City, where the Lucas family home, Plum Grove, is preserved today as an Iowa State Historic Site.

Horatio and Minerva's departure from Ohio was probably encouraged by Horatio's financial troubles. Financial recklessness became a continuing theme of Sumner family history; decades later Jack Sumner would commit similar recklessness and thus precipitate a family crisis. So it is worth taking a look at the first evidence of this syndrome, a letter that Minerva wrote to her father on November 6, 1833. Horatio and Minerva were living just south of Columbus, Ohio, where Lucas was governor. Horatio seems to have signed a promissory note he was unable to pay off. Minerva wrote to her father, pleading for help:

My Dear Father,

I will write you a few lines to inform you of our unexpected trouble.
Mr. Knight was hear yesterday demanding his money witch was do in
October he says it is impossible for him to wate but a few days and if
we cannot make the money he will sell the Note, to a man who will collect it we have nothing to make the money with but our young calves
and thay will not sell for half the value of them Horatio has asked me
to ask you for money he says you will not lend it to him but I don't
think my father will see me deprived of the few comforts I now have
while his wife and children are enjoying all the comforts they can wish
O my Dear father if you will lend Horatio two hundred dollars you will
confer an everlasting favour on your unworthy daughter…pleas pray
for your affectionate child

    Pleas write amediately

                            Minerva E. B. Sumner[1]

However this turned out, Horatio didn't learn much from a bad experience. On leaving Ohio, Horatio and Minerva moved to Indiana, where Horatio
had a nephew named Edward C. Sumner, who had moved to northwestern Indiana and become a ranching and real estate baron, sometimes using dishonest
tactics, such as moving his cattle back and forth across the Indiana–Illinois
border to evade the tax appraisers in both states. Horatio could have gone to
work for Edward, or at least followed his example, for he bought too much land
he could not pay off. The national financial panic of 1837, which depressed real
estate prices and left many investors stranded, didn't help. A series of documents from Tippecanoe County, Indiana, where Horatio moved in early 1838,
shows Horatio failing to pay off a note worth $120 and being arrested. Two
years later, with his wife pregnant with Jack, Horatio was again hauled to jail
for debts, for a month. These troubles probably encouraged the Sumners to
soon move on to Iowa.

Into this turmoil Jack Sumner was born on May 16, 1840. There has been
some confusion about Jack's birthplace, and he contributed to it by listing
Tippecanoe County in his Civil War enlistment form. Powell historians have
listed his birthplace as Newton, Indiana, based on Sumner family sources,
but there has never been any Newton in Tippecanoe County. Lucas family researchers have found that Jack was actually born in Newtown, Indiana, which
was in Fountain County. Edward Sumner owned extensive lands in Fountain
County, so perhaps Minerva took refuge there when Horatio was hauled to jail.

It's interesting that Minerva's future son-in-law, William Byers, had an uncle near Newtown. Byers's diary for 1850 mentions his visit to this uncle.

Yet one Sumner family source says that the Sumner family didn't meet the Byers family until both families were in Iowa. Chauncey Thomas, who would marry Jack Sumner's youngest sister Flora and whose father worked with William Byers at his Denver newspaper, said that shortly after Horatio Sumner settled in West Liberty in 1841, a covered wagon pulled up at his gate. The driver asked about the roads ahead and about land to settle, and Horatio told him there were no good roads ahead and no bridges and he might as well settle on the good land right next door to Horatio. And he did. The newcomer, Mr. Byers, had a ten-year-old son named William, and Horatio had a seven-year-old daughter named Elizabeth, and thirteen years later they married. Thus Jack Sumner grew up next door to William Byers, and it was Byers who would now pull the Sumner family farther west.

Byers became a surveyor and worked his way to Oregon and California. After his marriage he settled in Omaha, helped lay out its streets, and became a leading citizen, serving in the first Nebraska state legislature. One day a drunken brawl broke out in the street outside his surveying office and Byers went out to stop it, and got a shotgun blast in the shoulder. Since surveyors had to haul heavy equipment on their shoulders, Byers's career was ruined. Yet fate soon intervened: a man who owed Byers several hundred dollars was going broke trying to run a nearby town newspaper, and he gave Byers his printing press as payment for his debt. Byers was now a newspaperman.

Byers was hearing the call of the Colorado gold rush, so he decided to become a Colorado newspaperman. He bought some wagons and horses, one of which he named "Jack" in honor of Jack Sumner. It would take two wagons to haul his printing press, weighing 3,200 pounds. Jack Sumner's brothers Ed and Robert would drive the teams to Colorado. On February 27, 1859, Robert wrote a long letter to Jack, who was back with his parents on the farm in Iowa. Robert reported, "We have got nearly all fixed ready for the trip, will probably start next week." Robert expressed doubt that Byers could succeed with the newspaper: "He will wish he had of had nothing to do with it. My opinion is it will not pay, it will be a fizzle."[2] Yet Byers arrived at the right time and picked the right place, Denver, to succeed, and his business gave him free time to indulge his own prospecting fever.

Robert was more optimistic about the prospects of those selling supplies to the prospectors: "John tell Dad now is the time to lay the foundation for a nice little fortune. He can do it by buying a lot of young cattle. The thing is working precisely as it did in 1849 when the California gold fever broke out. It is the case here when a man comes in, wants to buy an ox team, he will give most any price. They don't stand on trifles. You farmers had better stay at home and raise a good crop, all probability is that you will find some gold in Iowa."[3] This and later comments suggest that Jack Sumner was feeling left out of a great adventure; even his younger brother Charlie had gone with Ed and Robert to Omaha, although Charlie would stay there for school. Two weeks earlier Charlie had written home about their arrival in Omaha, and how the view from the Missouri River bluff was "the finest view that we ever saw before in our lives."[4]

Soon Charlie wrote, "The boys have just started for the mines. This is an eventful day. This Tuesday the 8th of March has separated us all from each other, perhaps forever."[5] In that letter he went on ruminating on the possibility that the family would never be together again. A week later he wrote, "After supper I will write to the brats, John included. I am not a brat anymore, I am a student. All I want of you John is simply this: Write to me often, yes often."[6] Another week later he reported that he had heard from "the boys" and berated Jack for not writing him more often.[7] On April 26 Charlie addressed Jack's wanderlust: "You stay where you are. I would not go on the boat this summer. John wait until we all come home and then if you must go, then you can be spared a little better. It would leave the old folks in a bad situation. No don't go!!"[8] It's not clear what boat Jack was yearning for, but the Sumner farm was only twenty miles from the Mississippi River, and this was the heyday of the steamboat. Two weeks later Charlie expressed his homesickness: "Golly sometimes I can see John and Will up in the woods by the little prairie or Cedarville Crossing, Will with a squirrel on his back trudging along behind John."[9]

Elizabeth Byers and her two young children remained in Omaha while her husband and her Sumner brothers immigrated to Colorado; when they gave her the go-ahead she, too, crossed the plains, with only a few companions, and showed pioneer fortitude in encountering Indians and fording the quicksand of the Platte River. Growing up with Jack and four other brothers, Elizabeth had become as tough as they were, including being good with a gun. Yet when she got to Denver, where she estimated she was only the eighth white woman there, she looked at the village of crude cabins and decided it was her mission to civilize Colorado. She organized Colorado's first charity and helped build its first Methodist church.

Early in 1861 William Byers wrote an enthusiastic letter to Charlie Sumner in Omaha urging him to come to Denver, promising him a job: "[I] can give you a good one, in the office, on a farm, or in the mines."[10] Charlie went home to Iowa to visit his parents and siblings, and then headed for Colorado. Upon arriving in Denver, Charlie wrote back glowing accounts of the beauty of the Rockies, the progress of the city, the booming mines, and the success of the Byers newspaper. Charlie went to work for Byers, carrying newspapers to the mountain towns for $30 a week. This must have finally proven too much for Jack, for now he, too, headed west. He arranged to meet up with his brother Ed, who was working as a clerk for Byers, for a trapping expedition. On June 9 Minerva used the back of a recent letter from Charlie to write to Ed and Jack, a letter full of motherly concern for a son who was now facing the wilderness. After much religious sentiment and moral instruction, she advised, referring to the outbreak of the Civil War, "Don't go among the Indians, they won't suffer you to trap on their land. They are all anxious to join the fight and devide the United States with the whites.... Be careful. A wrong step is fatel. God bless you and keep you."[11] Jack had written her on April 28, but the letter, which does not survive, took over a month to reach Iowa, and Minerva complained about the slowness of the mail and expressed anxiety to hear from Jack and Ed. Minerva soon received a letter from Charlie, and he, too, was anxious about his brothers: "Where is John and why don't he and Ed write?"[12]

We never do learn exactly where Jack was on his first Western adventure. The next time we can place him is from his Union army enlistment form, signed in Iowa more than a year later. But this mere glimpse of Jack Sumner in the West makes an important correction to an unfortunate habit of some Powell historians. Under the impression that Sumner didn't go West until 1866, some historians have ridiculed Sumner for putting on the airs of a veteran mountain man to Powell a year later. Yet back in 1861, at the age of twenty-one, Jack Sumner was already living a mountain man's life, dealing with trapping and Indians.

It's possible that while Jack Sumner was out West he found his way to Denver in the wake of a family tragedy. After only a month of hauling newspapers into the mountains, Charlie was stricken with mountain fever. A doctor gave him a prescription for quinine, but by mistake Charlie bought a bottle of morphine, and became violently sick and died.

Returning to Iowa, Jack Sumner enlisted in the 32nd Iowa Volunteer Infantry in August 1862, four months after the Battle of Shiloh (where Powell lost his arm) had given the nation more grim proof that the war was going to be both long and bloody. The 32nd was sent down the Mississippi River and several of its companies were stationed at Cape Girardeau, Missouri, where a year previously Powell had supervised the construction of its earthen fortifications. (One of them, Fort D, is still there today; a local tourist brochure promotes it as "Fort John Wesley Powell.") But Jack Sumner's Company E was sent farther downriver to New Madrid, Missouri, where perhaps a few old-timers remembered the massive earthquake, half a century earlier, that had sent the Mississippi River flowing backward. The 32nd Iowa was there to prevent the Confederates from flowing upstream. Then Sumner was sent to Columbus, Kentucky, another Mississippi River town, for six months. In January 1864, the 32nd Iowa boarded a steamboat and headed down the river to Vicksburg, where Sumner saw more earthworks whose construction had been supervised by John Wesley Powell.

In early 1864 Jack Sumner was part of the Union army's Red River Campaign to take Louisiana from Confederate control. On April 9, near the town of Pleasant Hill, a smaller Confederate force launched a determined attack against the Union line, and broke it. The 32nd Iowa, in the center of the line, was entirely cut off. Taking fire from every direction, they suffered heavy casualties—210 men, half of their total, and one fifth the Union's 994 casualties in that battle. But by holding their ground the 32nd helped prevent a rout. An artillery shell exploded near Jack Sumner and broke both his legs and dislocated both hips, and a shell fragment struck him in the head. As the 32nd made its escape, just barely in time, they had to leave their wounded on the field, many to die, but someone must have helped Jack get away. Because the Confederates withdrew, the battle was counted as a Union victory, but the Union forces, too, ended up retreating, to the dismay of its soldiers, and the Red River Campaign was considered a failure.

Two decades later Jack Sumner reported that this head wound still caused him severe headaches. Civil War pension records are often a game of cat and mouse, with the veteran making claims and the officials doubting them; that would happen to Sumner, but there's no doubt Sumner was badly off at the end of the war, judging from a December 1865 letter Ed Sumner wrote to his sister Elizabeth back in Iowa: "You tell me that Jack is getting better—am glad to hear of that—I feared he would never get well again."[13] Two years later, on November 12, 1867, the *Rocky Mountain News* printed some news items from Hot Sulphur Springs, the outpost owned by William Byers and operated by Jack Sumner, and the article described Sumner: "An ex-soldier, he seeks here to recuperate a constitution badly shattered in the swamps and trenches of the far south." Yet this came right after the same article described Sumner as a hunter and trapper, which would require considerable fitness and energy. It appears that Sumner, like Powell, was one of the many veterans who refused to allow injuries and pain to stop them.

William and Elizabeth Byers went back to Iowa at the end of 1865, and
Elizabeth and her children stayed until spring. Then she took charge of getting
Jack out to Colorado. It is a likely sign of Jack's continuing precarious health
that Elizabeth purchased an ambulance and team of horses to carry him across
Iowa to Omaha. Elizabeth drew on Byers's old connections with the Union
Pacific Railroad, based in Omaha, and arranged for a special train to carry just
their family out to Fort Kearney, the end of the line at that moment. At Fort
Kearney they joined a wagon train heavy with supplies bound for Montana,
and after a hundred miles they broke off and headed for Denver on their own.
There were plenty of Indian troubles on the plains that spring, and Elizabeth
was quite aware of the risk they were taking, but this was her seventh trek
across the plains and she had the confidence of a tough pioneer woman.[14] Years
later she recalled her trek west with Jack:

> My horses were high spirited and rebelled at being kept back by this
> freight train, so my brother would find out where we were expected to
> camp in the evening, then we would go ahead and stop at the camping
> place and have a restful time before the train came. I have so often
> thought since what a daring thing we did.... I have no doubt but what
> our little party would have been watched many times by roving bands
> of Indians. We left the wagon train at North Platte coming from there
> all alone, camping one night near a station with our horses tethered
> not far from the tent, and a tremendous thunder storm came up, with
> the most vivid lightning I ever saw. In the midst of the storm I heard
> an unusual noise. It seemed to me like a snort from one of the horses. I
> reached over and touched my brother who sprang awake in an instant.
> We sat up watching and just then there was a most terrific flash of
> lightning that enabled us to see two men creeping on their hands and
> knees towards our horses. My heart stood still, for I realized in an
> instant what our plight would have been had we been left there with-
> out our team. A few shots from John's revolver sent them flying. We
> tied the horses close to the tent and tried to get a little sleep.[15]

When John Wesley Powell met Jack Sumner a year later, he was meeting
a man who embodied the toughness and experience of an entire family of important Colorado pioneers.

Yet embodying a family's qualities can bring trouble, too. In a Greek tragedy,
a character flaw combined with the wrong circumstances will lead inevitably
to disaster. Sometime shortly before 1880, Jack Sumner signed a note worth

John C. "Jack" Sumner. Photo courtesy of Ray Sumner.

a considerable amount of money. Later Jack would claim that an old trapper friend of his had forged his name to this note, but the court issued its judgment against Sumner. The holder of the note, a man named Martin, came to William Byers and demanded to know Sumner's whereabouts, but it seems that Byers didn't tell him.[16]

Years later, in 1886, Minerva Sumner died in Denver, where she had lived after following her children to that city; since her children had invested for her in the booming Denver real estate market, Minerva, who had once been disgraced by real estate debt, ended up leaving $26,000 in real estate to her children. Byers became executor of Minerva's estate, and wrote to Jack Sumner in Grand Junction saying that he needed Jack's signature on the estate documents; his siblings were quite eager to sell their lots in a peaking real estate market. Jack wrote back and asked if his Martin debt meant that Martin could lay claim to the estate, and Byers answered that while he wouldn't voluntarily tell Martin anything or give him any money, Martin could probably get a court order and force the issue. Byers told Jack to get an attorney and to sign his share of the estate over to his wife. Jack's wife then signed her share over to their children, who were minors, and since minors could not legally own real estate, the whole estate was frozen in legal limbo for a decade until Jack's children came of age.[17]

Jack's siblings were not pleased. Byers fired off a series of angry letters to Jack's attorney: "You have got this matter into a fine muddle by your blundering. I cannot undertake to untangle your work."[18] To Jack, Byers wrote, "He does not seem to know how to help you out. He has gotten you into a nice scrape and now appears to be a way beyond his depth and can't swim." Byers urged Jack to fire his attorney: "Don't delay. It is harvest time here now on real estate."[19] In the midst of this, Jack Sumner disappeared for two months, perhaps on another of his prospecting trips. When Jack reappeared, Byers wrote to him furiously: "Please do not leave home again until you have fixed that trust deed matter. I cannot do a thing until that is adjusted. Have applications for lots almost every day but cannot make deeds until you fix that up."[20] Byers tried to maneuver to sell some land, but now Jack's attorney threatened to sue Byers to stop him. A full year had passed since Minerva's death and now everyone in the family was exasperated with Jack, the baby who had been born under a shady real estate star. Finally, Byers threatened to sue Jack to force the court to annul the Catch-22. It is here that Byers's letter ledger book ends, and there's no further ledger book, so we don't know how this saga turned out. But it must have left some bad feelings, for Jack would not return to Denver and visit his siblings for another fifteen years.

The Sumners recognized that they were somehow doomed to follow a difficult star. Decades later, in 1931, nearly a full century after Minerva wrote to Governor Lucas pleading for money, a son of Jack Sumner, Ed, wrote to a son of William Byers, Frank, to plead for money. Ed Sumner was deeply in debt and about to lose his home, which was the only thing he could leave to his children. In the middle of detailing his failed mining and other ventures and his debts and his desire to get a little money together to get into the chicken business, Ed paused and reflected on Sumner destiny: "But it seems strange that the Sumner blood in you must have let loose in some other way, than it has with the rest of us. Father was not contented: for just what reason I do not know. Only he wanted a plenty of this worlds good, but would not stop long enough for it to catch up with him, therefore was always on the go."[21]

NOTES

1. Robert Lucas Papers, State Historical Society of Iowa, Des Moines.

2. Robert Sumner to Jack Sumner, February 27, 1859, Byers Collection. Published with permission.

3. Ibid.

4. Charlie Sumner to Jack Sumner, Feb. 13, 1859, Byers Collection.

5. Charlie Sumner to Minerva Sumner, March 8, 1859, Byers Collection.

6. Charlie Sumner to Minerva Sumner, March 15, 1859, Byers Collection.

7. Charlie Sumner to Minerva Sumner, March 23, 1859, Byers Collection.

8. Charlie Sumner to Jack Sumner, April 26, 1859, Byers Collection.

9. Charlie Sumner to Jack Sumner, May 8, 1859, Byers Collection.

10. William Byers to Charlie Sumner, March 14, 1861, Byers Collection.

11. Minerva Sumner to Ed and Jack Sumner, June 9, 1861, Byers Collection.

12. Charlie Sumner to Elizabeth Byers, May 29, 1861, Byers Collection.

13. Ed Sumner to Elizabeth Byers, Dec. 19, 1865, Byers Collection.

14. Byers Collection.

15. Elizabeth M. Byers, "The Experiences of One Pioneer Woman by Mrs. William N. Byers," William N. Byers and Family Papers, WH55, FF43 (c. 1900–20), Western History Collection, Denver Public Library, CO.

16. Byers Collection.

17. Ibid.

18. William Byers to W. J. Miller, April 8, 1887, Byers Collection.

19. William Byers to Jack Sumner, April 8, 1887, Byers Collection.

20. William Byers to Jack Sumner, March 30, 1887, Byers Collection.

21. Ed Sumner to Frank Byers, June 8, 1931, Byers Collection.

·18·

Why Jack Sumner Stayed

WHEN ORAMEL HOWLAND, Seneca Howland, and Bill Dunn walked off the Powell expedition and disappeared without a trace, they never had a chance to explain their reasons for leaving, and historians have filled the void with surmises and hot debates. Yet historians have given little consideration to why the other crewmembers did not leave. This question is especially interesting in the case of Jack Sumner, who clearly resented Powell's personality and leadership, and who had stronger personal ties with Dunn and the Howlands than did the other crewmembers. Sumner had tramped the Rockies for years and faced enough dangers that a trek across the Arizona Strip and into southern Utah should not have scared him.

Sumner did vacillate. When the Howlands and Dunn announced their plans to leave, Sumner "did what I could to knock such notions out of their heads, but as I was not sure of my own side of the argument, I fear I did not make the case very strong, certainly not strong enough to dissuade them from their plans."[1]

Powell, too, admitted that he considered quitting the river. All the men were exhausted, hungry, and ragged; after thinking they were nearly at the end of the trip, the canyon threw a shockingly difficult rapid at them, left them wondering what else lay ahead, and left them badly demoralized. They had to choose between a visible danger on the river or the unknown dangers of trekking fifty or more miles across the desert.

Only a sentence after admitting his vacillation, Sumner said he became determined to continue down the river: "I talked with Major Powell quietly on the subject. He seemed dazed by the proposition confronting us. I then declared that I was going on by the river route, and explained my plans to him how to surmount the difficulty, plans which were carried out next morning."[2] This statement was rather typical of Sumner's tendency to claim all the credit and portray Powell as a weakling. Sumner's claims were annoying to Powell-admiring historians, prompting them to try to discredit Sumner, and Sumner made it easier for them by claiming too much.

At Separation Rapid, Jack Sumner might indeed have decided they could deal with the rapid, but it's likely something else was running through his mind that night as they debated what to do. Jack Sumner knew that southern Utah was a dangerous place for anyone with the name of Sumner.

In 1869 "Sumner" was one of the most despised names in America. It was despised by three groups that otherwise had little in common: Southerners, Mormons, and Navajos. All three groups might be encountered on the trek Jack Sumner would need to make to southern Utah. Sumner also probably assumed that the Mormons still held a grudge against his grandfather, Robert Lucas, who as governor of Ohio in the 1830s had helped destroy the Mormon's attempt to build their own theocratic homeland in Ohio, one of three failures that eventually sent them to Utah to get far away from men like Robert Lucas.

Hatred for the name "Sumner" inspired the most notorious event ever to take place on the floor of the U.S. Senate. On May 22, 1856, two days after he gave a combative antislavery speech, Senator Charles Sumner of Massachusetts was sitting at his desk on the nearly empty Senate floor when he was attacked by Representative Preston Brooks of South Carolina, wielding a walking cane with a heavy gold knob. Brooks continued striking Sumner until he was bloody and unconscious, and stopped only when his cane broke. Other senators who tried to help Sumner were held at bay by another South Carolina representative wielding a pistol.

Brooks became a hero in the South, which loudly declared that Sumner, one of the leading abolitionist firebrands, deserved what he got. Northerners were shocked by the ferocity of Southern feelings; they finally realized that slavery would never yield to moral persuasion, but only to blood. The Sumner beating polarized the nation and energized it toward war. Sumner, who remained disabled for months, became a Northern martyr. After the war, he helped lead the Radical Republicans in punishing the South and upholding the rights of freed slaves, which for Southerners was an added humiliation atop their military defeat and economic ruin, giving them continuing new reasons to hate Charles Sumner.

The Southern dislike for the name of Sumner was reinforced when General Edwin V. Sumner, a distant cousin of Charles, led Union troops in some of the major battles of the Civil War, including Antietam and Fredericksburg. Edwin Sumner, born in Boston in 1797, was a passionate Unionist; in 1856 he took command of Fort Leavenworth in Kansas and defended antislavery Kansans against proslavery raiders from Missouri. (The next year, a new Kansas county was named Sumner County for Charles Sumner.) In the Civil War, Edwin was the oldest field general on either side and commanded the largest corps in the Army of the Potomac, with 18,000 veteran troops. Sumner had already been in the army for nearly three decades when he led troops in the Mexican–American War (1846–48). Yet his longevity meant that he had learned military tactics in another era, and he was poorly equipped to go up against Stonewall Jackson and Robert E. Lee at Antietam; Civil War historians have graded Sumner harshly for many mistakes that cost his side 2,200 casualties and threw chaos into the Union battle plan.

Jack Sumner was related to Charles and Edwin Sumner—not closely, but through the sprawling Sumner family tree that began in 1636 when William Sumner arrived in the Massachusetts Bay Colony, then settled in Dorchester. Jack Sumner's line branched off early from the branch that produced Charles and Edwin Sumner: Jack descended from William's son William, and Charles and Edwin came from William's son Deacon. Jack was seven generations down the line from William Sumner. Like many of the leading New England families, the Sumners turned their early arrival into many successes; in 1782 Governor John Hancock appointed Increase Sumner to the Massachusetts Supreme Court, where the next year he helped rule that the state constitution had indeed outlawed slavery. In 1797 Increase Sumner was elected the fifth governor of Massachusetts.

Why would Charles and Edwin Sumner have any relevance to Jack Sumner brooding at Separation Rapid? Because the Mormon settlements in southern Utah, where he would end up, were heavily populated with Southerners. Most Mormons came from Northern states or from Europe, but when Mormon leader Brigham Young, who wanted the Mormons to be self-sufficient in everything, decided that the Mormons should set up cotton farms and factories in the cotton-favorable climate of southern Utah, he gathered the only Mormons who knew anything about cotton—the Southerners. Their loyalties are still evident today in places like Dixie National Forest, in southern Utah.

Yet is it plausible that Jack Sumner would have thought of this? Wasn't the distribution of Southerners in Utah just an obscure demographic detail that Sumner could not possibly have known? This might have been true, except for one thing: Southern Utah had become nationally infamous in 1857 for the Mountain Meadows Massacre, and the man whom both Mormon authorities and Americans blamed for the massacre was named Lee. John D. Lee came from the same Virginia clan of Lees that had produced Robert E. Lee, which was why John D. Lee made the perfect scapegoat. In the 1860s Yankees would believe anything about the name "Lee." Lees were fiendishly clever, bold, scheming, traitorous, and bloodthirsty. Mountain Meadows was just another Lee blood picnic on the way to Antietam. The national publicity given to the massacre and to John D. Lee had informed the nation that there were not only Southerners in southern Utah, but treacherous Southerners. In 1869 John D. Lee was still hiding out somewhere in southern Utah. Jack Sumner undoubtedly knew that when a Sumner foolishly went up against a Lee at Antietam in 1862, it had been a disaster. Was another man named Sumner now going to walk defenseless into the realm of another Lee?

Mormons had a second reason for disliking Edwin Sumner.

The Mormons had migrated to Utah in 1847 to create their own Zion, far away from religious persecution and unfriendly governments. Over the next decade Americans watched with growing exasperation as the Mormons proliferated and prospered and openly defied American laws and authority, especially with regard to polygamy. In 1857 President Buchanan decided it was time to force the Mormons to submit. In May of that year Edwin Sumner marched out of Fort Leavenworth with a large force, with orders to secretly approach Utah, launch a surprise attack, capture the Mormon leaders, and execute them. At least this is what Brigham Young believed, obsessively.

In reality, Sumner was marching against the Cheyenne on the plains. The real Utah expedition would leave Fort Leavenworth two months behind him, and would not march into Salt Lake City until June 1858. But the army was somewhat secretive about Sumner's mission, and Young became convinced that Sumner's rumored Cheyenne mission was merely a ruse to cover his approach to Utah. In response, Young organized a Mormon cavalry unit to patrol the plains as far east as Fort Laramie, four hundred miles from Salt Lake City, ostensibly to assist Mormon emigrants on their way west, but actually to locate, reconnoiter, and harass the approaching enemy. Young began mobilizing Utah for war. Utah anxiously awaited Edwin Sumner's arrival, and rumors about him became wilder and spread to other states.

In late August 1857, California newspapers ran the headline, "IMPORTANT NEWS FROM SALT LAKE. BRIGHAM YOUNG ARRESTED FOR TREASON. YOUNG CARRIED OFF A PRISONER BY COL. SUMNER TO WASHINGTON." The story went on to say that the leader of a wagon train recently arrived from Utah "reports that Col. Sumner with 86 dragoons, of Company G., U.S. Army, arrived in that city on June 25th, at 7 P.M., and took

Brigham Young prisoner, on a charge of treason and other crimes, and started with him for Washington city, within two hours after his arrival, meeting with no opposition on the part of the Mormons."[3] Such erroneous articles prompted George Q. Cannon, editor of the San Francisco Mormon newspaper *Western Standard,* to write Young a mocking letter:

> It is astonishing how easily they are sold on every thing pertaining to us, as a people; they greedily swallow the most absurd lies, and prefer them, all the time, to plain straight-forward, reasonable truth. The latest lie in circulation here, is one concerning your arrest, on a charge of treason, by Col. Sumner.... This happened on the 25th of June, and as you did not seem to be aware of it on the 4th of July, the date of your letter, I send you the news.[4]

Cannon seemed especially annoyed by the suggestion that Mormons would surrender without a fight. Such rumors only made Young more nervous.

One of Young's war preparations was to send George A. Smith, the church apostle who for a decade had been in charge of southern Utah, to warn the settlers there of Colonel Sumner's imminent arrival. As recorded by local militia member James H. Martineau, Smith warned,

> They intend to hang about 300 of the most obnoxious Mormons; Brigham to be hung any how—no trial necessary for him or the principle leaders.... They expect that one half the women will leave their husbands and cut their throats, and that one half of the men will join them.... The United States are sending out 2,500 infantry, besides Col. Sumner's dragoons, which are to rendezvous in G.S.L. City this winter, and 1000 teamsters, the worst description of men, picked up on the frontiers, which are more to be dreaded than the soldiers. They are making great calculations for "Booty and Beauty."...If the troops come among us, and we have to flee into the mountains, we will haunt them as long as they live.[5]

According to historian William P. MacKinnon, who compiled a five-hundred-page documentary history of the Utah War, "in isolated southern Utah—alerted by George A. Smith's preaching and his explicit references to Sumner—concern about a possible descent from the east by the Cheyenne Expedition seemed strongest. As a result, during the period 3-11 September 1857 Lt. James H. Martineau again took to the field with three comrades to scout through the high peaks and alpine plateaus above the Sevier River Valley."[6]

Martineau had "heard the cavalry under Col. Sumner would enter the country that way."[7] His patrol was one of at least three sent out to watch for Sumner, under orders from Mormon general Daniel Wells to southern Utah's colonel William Dame.

On September 11, at Mountain Meadows, on the Old Spanish Trail, the route by which Edwin Sumner was expected to appear and attack southern Utah, the hysteria that George A. Smith helped whip up found an outlet, against a pioneer wagon train. A dozen years later, in 1869, the fearful, angry energy that Edwin Sumner had helped set loose in southern Utah was still there, partly in hiding but still ready to strike at a man named Sumner.

In a way, Brigham Young was right about Edwin Sumner: when Sumner was near Fort Laramie he received orders to leave much of his force at that fort, to be incorporated into the Utah expedition that was coming along behind him. Sumner himself didn't get to Utah, but he soon became commander of the Department of the West, headquartered in St. Louis, and the Utah campaign was under his jurisdiction.

Jack Sumner also had a loaded political legacy from the family tree of his mother, Minerva Lucas Sumner.

The Lucas family, with deep Quaker roots in England, arrived in the colonies in 1679. A Robert Lucas joined William Penn in founding a colony for Quakers; Pennsylvania had democratic values, including respect for Indians, far ahead of the rest of the other colonies.[8] The leadership of the abolitionist movement included many Quakers, including the Howland family of New Bedford, Massachusetts. It was a coincidence that three of Powell's crewmembers had famous abolitionist names, but it did fit in with Powell's own convictions.

Perhaps Jack Sumner got his westering spirit from his Lucas ancestors. When Pennsylvania became too crowded, Edward Lucas (Jack's great-great-grandfather) lit out for the Western mountains, which for him were near the junction of the Shenandoah and Potomac Rivers in today's West Virginia. In 1787 the seven-year-old Robert Lucas probably watched his uncle Joseph Barnes guide up the Potomac River the primitive steamboat Barnes had built, two decades before Robert Fulton got credit for inventing the steamboat.

When the American Revolution arrived, William Lucas (Jack Sumner's great-grandfather) disregarded the Quaker disapproval of war and joined Washington's army. The Lucas family had also lapsed from Quaker principles by becoming slave owners. But this troubled the conscience of William Lucas, who in 1800 moved to Ohio, taking many of his slaves with him, and giving them their freedom. As the country became more polarized over slavery in the

mid-1800s, Robert Lucas (Jack's grandfather), who had served as the Democratic governor of both Ohio (1832-36) and Iowa (1838-41), could no longer tolerate the Democrats' defense of slavery, and he quit the party to join the Whigs
in 1852. As governor of Iowa, Lucas had championed Iowa in a boundary dispute
with Missouri involving 2,600 square miles, which became a more energetic,
national controversy because Missouri was a slave state and Iowa a free state.

After serving as Iowa's governor, Lucas returned to Ohio to sell his lands,
and he was drafted to run for Congress in the 8th congressional district, whose
residents included nine-year-old John Wesley Powell; the Powells lived about
twenty-five miles from Lucas's town of Piketon. We don't know if Powell's
father voted for Jack Sumner's grandfather, but Lucas lost and returned to Iowa.
The Powells had come to Ohio on the Ohio Canal, which ran between Lake
Erie and the Ohio River; the state senator who had chaired the canal committee and shepherded the canal bill was Robert Lucas. The course of John Wesley
Powell's westward migration had been guided by Jack Sumner's grandfather.

Robert Lucas's terms as governor of Ohio coincided with the attempt of the
Mormons to build their own realm in Ohio. Mormon prophet Joseph Smith
arrived there in 1831, and Robert Lucas became governor in 1832. It was in
Kirtland, Ohio, that Joseph Smith received many of his theological revelations
and wrote many key Mormon texts, both religious and civil. In Kirtland the
Mormons built their first temple, determined church hierarchy and practices,
developed their cooperative economic system, developed a theocratic style of
government, initiated polygamy, and began aggressively harassing opponents.

As the Mormon presence and power grew, so did resistance from local
and state newspapers, preachers, and politicians. Local businessmen refused
to hire Mormons or sell them goods. Mormons had to guard their temple,
homes, and stores against mob attack and arson. A mob tarred and feathered
Joseph Smith, who afterward had to be accompanied by a bodyguard. Smith
raised animosity by organizing a militia, performing marriages without legal
authority, and starting a bank without a legal charter. The Mormons took over
some local political offices, tried to relocate the county seat, and demanded
that a hostile justice of the peace leave office and leave town—an act of intimi-
dation that would soon lead to the birth of the Danites, a secret society willing
to murder political opponents.

The Kirtland colony ended disastrously, mainly because of the collapse of
its church-run bank. Joseph Smith blamed this collapse on religious persecution by Ohio's political leaders, which included Robert Lucas. As with Brigham
Young's conviction that Edwin Sumner was out to get him, Joseph Smith's

conviction that Robert Lucas was out to get him was largely imaginary—but politically convenient.

In the 1830s America was undergoing a frenzy of growth and financial speculation, and Joseph Smith got caught up in the bubble, his bank engaging in many reckless practices, even as he promised his followers that the bank was divinely inspired and guaranteed. In the national financial panic of 1837 the bubble burst, and the Kirtland bank failed along with numerous others. Many Mormons felt deceived and betrayed, believing that Joseph Smith had swindled them, and turned against him bitterly, creating the worst crisis yet for him and the church. Smith claimed that the bank had failed because the state of Ohio, out of religious bigotry, had refused to grant it a state charter that would have allowed it to operate with greater freedom, efficiency, and public trust: "Because we were 'Mormons,' the legislature raised some frivolous excuses on which they refused to grant us those banking privileges they so freely granted to others."[9]

It was true that, once started, the bank faced considerable opposition because of its church affiliation. Newspapers campaigned against the bank and many non-Mormons refused to patronize it, and even tried to ruin it. The Mormons feared physical violence against the bank. Wilford Woodruff wrote in his diary that they were "threatened by a mob from Panesville to visit us that night & Demolish our Bank & take our property. The wrath of our enemies appears to be kindled against us."[10] A guard was organized to defend the bank, and they debated whether to use clubs or guns, to merely break legs or to aim for the heart. One of these guards was nineteen-year-old George A. Smith, who spent the entire winter watching the roads for an approaching mob, and who two decades later would be traveling southern Utah to spread the alarm about the approach of Edwin Sumner's mob.

But it was not true that the bank charter was refused out of religious bigotry.

In these years America was grappling with the dilemma of how to combine its democratic ideals with a capitalist economy that was booming and generating concentrations of wealth and power, especially in its banks. Andrew Jackson had been elected president in 1828 on a promise to control the runaway financial system. Four years later Robert Lucas got elected governor as an anti-bank Jacksonian, and in 1834 Ohioans elected a state legislature that was even more Jacksonian, full of working-class reformers hostile to banks. Between 1830 and 1834 the number of chartered banks in Ohio had risen from eleven to thirty-one, but now the Jacksonian legislators called a halt. In 1835 they rejected all new requests for bank charters, and in 1836 they approved only one of seventeen requests. Joseph Smith founded his bank in late 1836. He asked the state legislature for a charter, and was rejected. He applied again in 1837 and was rejected again. This certainly hurt Joseph Smith's bank, but he was not singled out by Robert Lucas and the Jacksonians.

There is only skimpy evidence for how Robert Lucas regarded the Mormons, but it suggests he had no animosity toward them. Joseph Smith had announced his support for President Jackson and his policies, including his antibank policies, and the Kirtland Mormons published a pro-Jacksonian newspaper. Lucas should have regarded the Mormons as a friendly voting bloc. In 1839 when Joseph Smith was in a Missouri jail, Mormon leader Sidney Rigdon traveled to Iowa confident of enlisting Governor Lucas's support for Smith and of getting a letter of introduction to President Van Buren. Lucas declined to write anything complimentary about Smith as a person, but he did write that during his time in Ohio he had regarded the Mormons as "an industrious, inoffensive people." Ignoring the fact that Smith had been hauled into court for illegal banking practices under Ohio law and fined $1,000, Lucas added that he didn't recall that the Mormons had been charged with breaking any laws. According to a church-published history book from 1976, *The Story of the Latter-day Saints,* when the Mormons had fled Missouri in 1839 and were searching for a new home, Governor Lucas was ready to welcome them to Iowa.[11] Iowa historians mention a letter or letters Governor Lucas wrote to the Mormons, praising the Mormons' good character and promising them a welcome and fair treatment in Iowa, though Iowa historian Leland Sage notes that these supposed letters "have never been found by researchers."[12] The Mormons did buy thousands of Iowa acres that they might have turned into their new homeland, but they chose to settle just across the Mississippi River in Illinois, where they built the town of Nauvoo.

Yet Lucas made a good scapegoat. Most Mormon-written history books have followed Joseph Smith's cue and blamed the Kirtland bank collapse and resulting chaos on religious persecution by Ohio politicians. In 1869 there were plenty of Utah Mormons, such as George A. Smith, who had bitter personal memories of Kirtland. It would not have been prudent for Jack Sumner to walk into a Mormon town and introduce himself as the grandson of Robert Lucas.

Jack Sumner did exhibit a dislike and distrust of Mormons, which his family seems to have shared years before. Back in 1861 his brother Charles was migrating from Omaha to join the Sumner family in Colorado when he received news of the first shots of the Civil War. He wrote to his parents and

Jack in Iowa: "Heard the news of the fighting at Ft. Sumpter, made me feel bad.... let things come on as they may, I am prepared to die anywhere I don't care much where but should prefer to die fighting for my country against the accursed Mormons."[13]

Jack Sumner thought the Mormons capable of murdering Powell crew-members. Years later Sumner recalled the conversation of the remaining crewmen after the Howlands and Dunn left: "They all seemed to think the red bellies would surely get them. But I could not believe that the reds would get them, as I had trained Dunn for two years in how to avoid a surprise, and I did not think the red devils would make open attack on three armed men. But I did have some misgiving that they would not escape the double-dyed white devils that infested that part of the country. Grapevine reports convinced me later that that was their fate."[14]

Sumner didn't explain these "grapevine reports." On several more occasions he expressed his opinion that the Mormons were the culprits. In 1906 Sumner wrote to Lewis Keplinger, who had roamed the Rockies with Powell and Sumner in 1868, and listed the fate of the Powell crewmembers: "the two howlands and Dunn were killed. Powell says by Indians and I Say Killed by the Mormons, Part of the Same old 'Mountain Meadows massacre gang.'"[15]

We can't tell how much of Sumner's distrust of Mormons came from his family history, or from his personal experiences, or from later grapevine reports. But it is notable that Sumner feared the Mormons more than he feared Native Americans. In 1869 a man named Sumner had good reasons to fear Native Americans.

General Edwin Sumner spent most of his forty-four-year military career as an Indian fighter. When he started his career in 1819 the American frontier lay in Illinois, and he saw it shift westward to California; all along the way Native Americans resisted and had to be subdued, sometimes slaughtered, sometimes relocated. Edwin Sumner's humanitarian principles did not apply to Indians. Sumner fought in the Black Hawk War of 1832; the next year, when the U.S. Army created a cavalry to fight Indians across the Great Plains, Sumner became one of the first cavalry commanders. In 1838 he began training cavalry troops at Carlisle Barracks in Pennsylvania. He took part in campaigns that relocated the Winnebago from Wisconsin to Iowa and rounded up Sioux and forced them to Fort Snelling. Sumner helped to establish more Western forts than almost any other commander.

In 1851 Sumner was appointed the military commander of the newly established New Mexico Territory, and his first task was to subdue the Navajos.

He organized an expedition of four companies of cavalry, three of infantry, and one of artillery, and marched into Navajo country, shooting Navajo warriors on sight. When Sumner reached Canyon de Chelly he burned all the crops, engaging in scorched-earth tactics that Kit Carson would apply more thoroughly a decade later. Sumner believed that territorial governor James Calhoun was naïve in trying to placate the Navajos with gifts or treaties, and that they would yield only to "a rod of iron over their heads." Indians had to be forced to give up their traditional ways and become "good Americans": "I am convinced that the only way to subdue Indians effectively and permanently, is to improve their condition, and the best way to do this is to establish posts in the heart of their country, where we can bring them about us, and instruct them in agriculture and other useful arts." It was this philosophy that inspired Major Carleton and Kit Carson to round up the Navajos and force them on the Long Walk to captivity at Fort Sumner. After the captivity went disastrously wrong, the Navajos were released in June 1868, and they went away hating the name "Sumner." Edwin Sumner didn't establish Fort Sumner: it was simply named in his honor, but the Navajos didn't make a distinction. Edwin Sumner did establish Fort Defiance to intimidate and dominate the Navajos. "If this post," he wrote to his superior officer, "does not put a stop to Navajo depredations, nothing will do it but their entire extermination."[16]

When Kit Carson marched on the Navajos from the east, they fled west and took refuge in the most remote areas they could find, especially at Navajo Mountain and the South Rim of the Grand Canyon. Halfway between those locations was a Colorado River crossing, the future Lees Ferry, and the Navajos did indeed cross and flee onto the Arizona Strip, where they engaged in conflicts with Mormon settlers through the 1860s. Jack Sumner could not have known where he might or might not encounter Navajos on a trek across the Arizona Strip to Utah, but he surely knew that a Sumner falling into Navajo hands would be given no mercy.

In the end, we don't know for sure what was going through Jack Sumner's mind at Separation Rapid; this chapter remains an exercise in speculation. Perhaps the power of the rapid versus the great unknown of a desert trek was enough information on which to make a decision. And we should grant that Jack Sumner had an adventuresome spirit, which would lead him and Andy Hall to continue the river voyage all the way to the ocean. Yet it's likely that some Sumner family history at least rippled through Jack Sumner's imagination, and in the end he choose the route that had no Sumner connection.

NOTES

1. Quoted in Stanton, *Controversies,* 203.

2. Ibid.

3. This story was originally published in the San Francisco *Daily Evening Bulletin* on August 22, 1857, and was repeated by other newspapers.

4. George Q. Cannon to Brigham Young, August 31, 1857, LDS Church History Library, Salt Lake City.

5. Martineau Record, Transcript, William R. Palmer Collection, Sherratt Library, Southern Utah University, Cedar City, UT, 21–25.

6. William P. MacKinnon, *At Sword's Point, Part 1: A Documentary History of the Utah War to 1858* (Norman: University of Oklahoma Press, 2008), 251.

7. James H. Martineau, "My Life," Diary of James Henry Martineau, Huntington Library, San Marino, CA.

8. According to one modern genealogical source, the Lucas and Penn families intermarried, although this was not mentioned in the main biography of Robert Lucas by Robert Parish.

9. Quoted in Joseph Smith Jr., *History of the Church of Jesus Christ of Latter-day Saints,* ed. Brigham H. Roberts (Salt Lake City: Deseret Book, 1930), vol. 2: 468.

10. Scott G. Kenney, ed., *Wilford Woodruff's Journal, 1833–1898* (Midvale, UT: Signature Books, 1983), Vol. 1: 123.

11. James B. Allen and Glen M Leonard, *The Story of the Latter-day Saints* (Salt Lake City: Deseret Book, 1976).

12. Leland Sage, *A History of Iowa* (Ames: Iowa State University Press, 1974), 73.

13. Charles Sumner to the Sumner family, April 14, 1861, Byers Collection.

14. Quoted in Stanton, *Controversies,* 205–6.

15. Letter from Jack Sumner to Lewis Keplinger, Sept. 14, 1906, Lewis Keplinger Collection, Kansas State Historical Society.

16. Quoted in F. Stanley, *E. V. Sumner* (Borger, TX: Jim Hess Printers, 1969), 148, 155, 144.

·19·

The Madness of Jack Sumner

O N MAY 24, 1902, exactly thirty-three years after the day John Wesley Powell and Jack Sumner launched their expedition into the great unknown, the *Rocky Mountain News* carried a bulletin:

> CAPTAIN JACK SUMNER VICTIM
> OF MYSTERIOUS STABBING IN UTAH
>
> Special to The News.
> GRAND JUNCTION, Colo., May 23—
> Captain Jack Sumner, who left this city on Tuesday for Utah, was found about noon Wednesday near the town of Green River in an unconscious condition. He was brought to this city last night and taken to St. Mary's hospital. Dr. Hanson was called and found that Mr. Sumner was in a serious condition from a wound in the groin. He has since been in a half dazed condition and from what he says at times he must have been drugged and then stabbed. Word from the hospital this evening is that the captain is resting easy and that if no complications set in he will recover.

An accompanying article recalled Sumner's life, including the Powell expedition:

> POOR OLD JACK
>
> The success of the trip was largely due to Jack Sumner's resourceful nerve and daring and utter indifference to all danger.... What motive anyone could have had for stabbing him, except for purposes of robbery, his friends in this city are at a loss to understand. While as brave as a lion, he was as tender-hearted as a child, and has frequently given his last dollar and divided his last supply of provisions with persons in distress. While he has possessed a rugged constitution, he has seen

much exposure and endured many hardships, and is now 64 years of age, all of which will render his recovery slow, if not doubtful.

But there was more to this story, and it offers a deep look into Jack Sumner's psyche. A third of a century after Sumner had set off on the bold hopeful adventure of his youth, an ailing and defeated Sumner set off for the Green River again. Upon seeing the Green River, he needed little imagination to see the ghosts of himself and Powell going down it. Yet while Powell's river had carried Powell to great fame and power and security, Sumner's river had led to decades of obscurity, broken dreams, frustration, and poverty. Perhaps Sumner had heard that during the past January Powell had suffered a stroke, which in September would end Powell's life. This third-of-a-century anniversary offered Sumner a powerful focus for assessing his own life and passing judgment on its value. All we know for sure is that Jack Sumner, standing there quite alone, took out his knife, lowered his pants, and castrated himself.

He did an effective job of it too, judging from the notes Dr. K. Hanson made on his medical examination of Sumner four years later, on July 4, 1906: "Both testicles have been removed by himself. Operation was very successful. Done at a time of supposed temporary insanity." Given the severity of such a wound, and given Sumner's apparent isolation, we have to wonder if this was actually a suicide attempt. Dr. Hanson might have been thinking so when he said the insanity was "supposed." In an examination two years earlier, Dr. Hanson said simply, "He did this while in state of despondency." At the end of his 1906 examination of Sumner, Dr. Hanson added, "Amendment: Senile debility: He is stooped and slow of motion. His mind is clouded, and he sits in deep study or rather with a blank expression for quite a while at times. His speech is broken and slow. He appears very old for a man of his age."[1]

Jack Sumner had good reason to be despondent about his life. Years of trouble had left him with little to show for it. At the end of the Powell expedition, Sumner went through ten months of trouble just to get back to Denver. William Byers had already sent Powell a scolding letter for leaving Sumner so far from home without any money, and when Sumner finally got back, Byers published, in the *Rocky Mountain News* on August 9, 1870, a tribute to him and a denunciation of Powell:

> The expedition was a success, thanks to the dauntless man who *led* it, as much as to him who has clothed a portion of its history in the elegant diction of the lecture room. Last evening he returned and was

welcomed as one who had escaped the jaws of death and who, after dangers untold, hardships unrecounted, and perils unnumbered, was once more among those who could call him friend and brother. We give him a warm and generous welcome; we congratulate him that he is once more home; and finally we promise our readers at no distant day a new unwritten chapter in the history of the Powell expedition which may demonstrate that truth may really be stranger than fiction.

Some Powell historians, eager to defend Powell against Sumner's complaints against him, have held that it was only late in life that Sumner became embittered against Powell. But here in the summer of 1870 the Sumner grievance is already filed, and not by Sumner but by a man who had been one of Powell's most important backers. Sumner was only one of many who made a consistent complaint that Powell had insufficient loyalty to historical facts or to those who served him.

Byers never did publish his promised truth about the Powell expedition. He was an astute promoter of Colorado who had cultivated friendships with major shapers of Western expansion and he must have recognized that Powell was emerging as a major shaper. For Sumner, the fact that even his own brother-in-law was reluctant to challenge Powell's self-aggrandizing legend must have made it seem futile to hope for validation for his own leadership role. For the next thirty years, Sumner carried this frustration.

When Powell died four months after Sumner's self-mutilation and the *Denver Post* published an obituary honoring Powell, Sumner's resentment welled up and, from his camp in the Henry Mountains in Utah, he wrote the newspaper a long letter complaining about their "many errors," and about other published accounts of the expedition that were "all more or less misleading," and he offered his own account. On November 2, 1902, the *Denver Post* published his complaint: "Personally I care not but seems to me that thirty three years is a long time to wait for some recognition of the services of the men. Fremont give credit to all of his men. Powell give credit to none."[2] Sumner wasn't content to merely stake credit for his river skills but claimed that the whole idea of a geological expedition down the Colorado River originated with him.

Sumner's life after the expedition piled on many more frustrations, many opportunities for him to measure himself against the Colorado River hero he had been. Through years of trapping and prospecting he seldom did better than survive, yet he remained loyal to the American frontier myth with its promise of not just wealth but also of heroism, loyal even after Americans had relegated the frontiersman to the nostalgia shows of Buffalo Bill and begun to worship inventors, Wall Street financiers, and industrialists.

An April 18, 1901, article in the Denver *Republican* perfectly captured Sumner's status as a relic of a vanished era. The article shows some fondness for Sumner, but also ridicule:

J.C. SUMNER HATES TRAINS AND HOUSES AND IS WORRIED BY CHANGES IN DENVER

"If I can find my way out of these box canyons I'll look up some of my relatives. I've been camping since 1847 and I haven't been in Denver since the Tabor Opera House was built [1879, in Leadville], and I ain't much used to these skyscrapers. Where is 'F' Street?"

It was J.C. Sumner who wanted to know. He had just come out of the Equitable building when he made the inquiry. "Jack," as he is known, has prospected all over the west, but has an aversion for railroads and towns, and prefers a camp in a snow storm in a muddy arroyo to a parlor suite in the finest hotel.

Any building higher than a Mexican dobe house reminds him of the treacherous box canons that are the terror of the old prospector. It is sometimes necessary to spend days in getting out after entering a box canon.

"A train's bad enough, but these elevators make a fellow think he's drowning and falling over a cliff at the same time.... I wouldn't get into that cage again if I had to walk to the top of Pike's Peak.

"But what did they change the names of the streets for? I want to go to 'F' near Holliday street. Shoe me where 'F' is and I can find Holliday—maybe.

"Or, say if you will just take me to W. N. Byers, or W. F. Robinson, or W. R. Thomas, I'd be all right, for they married relatives of mine, and I guess maybe they know the town by this time."

Mr. Sumner is on his way to examine a district in New Mexico, where rumor has it that rich ore exists in abundance.

"You bet I will go both ways on a burro—it will only take about four weeks longer than to go by train, and I never ride in the cars unless I have a broken leg....

"I've been camping most of my life and houses are no use except to look at."

The images of canyons and falling over cliffs and drowning are notable when applied to a man who had mastered the greatest of canyons and rivers.

Wallace Stegner spent years exploring the theme of what happens to a man who persists in trying to live by the American frontier myth long after that myth has ceased to function. Stegner knew this story too well, for it was the story of his own father and childhood. In his most ambitious novel, *The Big Rock Candy Mountain,* Stegner portrayed his father as futilely pursuing the frontier myth at great cost to himself and his family, until he despairs and commits suicide. In Jack Sumner, Stegner had an identical character and storyline and fate, yet ironically when Stegner turned to writing Powell history, he, too, was eager to dismiss Sumner.

Sumner's life was also hard on his family. In 1884 Sumner's wife Alcinda filed for divorce, after eleven years of marriage, charging that Sumner "has become an habitual drunkard," and had abandoned her and their children for a whole year to go prospecting when he could be supporting her through "ordinary industry."[3] Yet eighteen months later they got remarried. They might have worked out an arrangement that offered more stability, for now they would settle in a house in Grand Junction, Colorado, and remain there for more than twenty years; they took advantage of Grand Junction's growth by buying property and building cottages. Yet Jack could not get over his Wild West fever and continued prospecting and mining, playing big roles in several big projects (such as three years at a mining operation on the Dolores River), but his gains often turned back into losses. Then came the fiasco of Jack's inheritance from his mother, embittering his siblings against him, probably contributing to Jack not returning to Denver until the befuddled 1901 visit that made the newspaper. Perhaps Sumner's foggy state of mind contributed to his falling twenty-four feet off a scaffold at the Grand Junction smelter in August 1903, breaking five ribs and dislocating his hip.

Jack Sumner was a lost man in the modern world of technological and legal complexities. It must have been galling that after remaining true to the frontier myth, Sumner was forgotten, while John Wesley Powell, who had long since become a Washington bureaucrat, remained a mythic hero. Sumner felt that a promise to him had been broken, and if he didn't have the sophistication of a Wallace Stegner to understand how such things could happen, he attached that sense of betrayal wholly to Powell. Comparing himself to the Powell legend, Sumner felt, shall we say, emasculated. We are venturing into Freudian territory here, and perhaps this chapter is speculative enough without wading into the quicksand of psychological theory. But even if you have no use for Freudian symbolism, consider the value of literary symbolism. Wallace Stegner could not have invented a more potent symbolism for the end of the American frontier than a man who traveled a hundred miles in one day—Sumner must have taken the train!—to try to end his life beside the river in whose reflection he was still a hero.

NOTES

1. Quoted in Jack Sumner army pension file, National Archives, Washington, DC, WC-644-311: "Both testicles," July 4, 1906; "He did this," Nov. 2, 1904; "Amendment," July 4, 1906.

2. Jack Sumner army pension file, Oct. 22, 1884, decree of Wyoming court granting divorce to Alcinda Sumner, National Archives, Washington, DC.

3. Jack Sumner army pension file, Oct. 22, 1884.

·20·

Jack Sumner Looks Back

LESS THAN A YEAR before he died, Jack Sumner received a letter that prompted him to reflect on his life, especially on the Powell expedition. The letter was from Lewis Keplinger, whom Sumner had met in 1868 when Keplinger came west with John Wesley Powell on Powell's second summer exploring the Rocky Mountains.[1] Sumner and Keplinger had helped Powell make the first ascent of Longs Peak, and Sumner was probably impressed by Keplinger's abilities, since it was Keplinger who found the tricky route to the top.

Born in Illinois in 1841, Keplinger joined the Union army at the start of the Civil War, marched with General Sherman across the South, and rose to the rank of second lieutenant. Yet Keplinger was essentially a bookish person and after the war he attended Illinois Wesleyan University, where Powell was teaching. Like Powell, Keplinger had a keen interest in science, and in his later years he would write poems, essays, and books pondering the meanings of geology and Darwin. His 1868 experiences in the Rockies left a deep impression on him: forty years later he returned to climb Longs Peak again, and his poems contained many images of mountains and rivers. After 1868 Keplinger studied law; he settled in Kansas City, Kansas, and became highly respected as a lawyer, judge, state legislator, and community leader. Jack Sumner lived a very different life, remaining a hardscrabble frontiersman, searching for bonanzas he never found.

In 1906, from across this divide of years and fates, Sumner wrote back to Keplinger.[2] Sumner's letter is the first document to surface in decades in which a participant discusses the Powell expedition.

Sumner's letter is largely consistent with the accounts he gave to Robert Stanton in this same time period, but this consistency is news in itself. Sumner knew that Stanton was writing a book, and Sumner wanted to influence history's verdict on Powell and on Sumner himself. Sumner's private letter to

Keplinger had no such motive, and thus offers a sincerity check on his controversial anti-Powell statements. If anything, Sumner is even more blunt with
Keplinger, declaring that he overthrew Powell's abusive leadership and assumed total command of the expedition.

What did Keplinger make of Sumner's complaints about Powell? Years
later, in 1919, Keplinger wrote to Stanton: "I know that Jack Sumner felt un-
kindly to Major Powell. I knew both and some allowances may be made for
any derogatory statements Jack may have made."[3] In 1912, apparently unaware
that Sumner was long dead, Keplinger wrote to Enos Mills, the man behind the
creation of Rocky Mountain National Park: "He is a very forceful character....
The success of that expedition was largely due to Mr. Sumner. Major Powell
himself has told me since that but for Sumner he never would have got through
the cañon alive."[4]

What's new in the 1906 letter is Sumner's account of his post-Powell adventures.

A few notes: A. C. Lanken was the mountain man who helped guide Powell's 1868 group. When Sumner says that Walter Powell is in "the bug house," he
means a mental institution, and when he speculates that Walter Powell suffered
from "peticoat dementia," he presumably means syphilis, perhaps a Powell
family secret. Sumner was not correct that William Hawkins, now a Mormon,
had at least two wives; Hawkins did outlive two wives and get married three
times, but it was one wife at a time.

> Paradox, Colorado
> Sept 14, 1906
> Mr. L. W. Keplinger
> Kansas City, Kansas
> Dear Old Friend,
> It seems that after 38 years you Remember your old Friend "Jack."
> Well I am greatly Pleased to get a letter from you and will try to answer
> it. things have not went as well with me as they have with you. I will try
> to give you an Idea of the ups and downs since you Parted with us on
> oak Creek. I Remember the Long's Peak Episode very well. But I think
> it was August 4th 1868 that we reached the top. It is of no consequence
> now. After you left us we proceeded on to White River where we Built
> cabins and Spent the winter Hunting and Exploring the Country. in
> March we left that camp and proceeded to old Fort Bridger where we
> sold our stock and came Back to Green River Wyoming where we took
> Boats for the great unknown and we had a Hell of a time of it getting

through. After you left I had to take charge of the Sextant so it kept me Pretty Busy for 20 hours out of the 24. Must catch a Star as you can for about 800 miles. lost a boat and lots of Supplies in Green River. at the Mouth of uinta river Powell neglected to get Supplies and we were nearly Starved in consequence. we were 111 days from Green River Wyoming to the Mouth of the Virgin River where the Powells left us and went to Salt Lake and I have seen neither of them Since. I took the two Boats left and with Bradley, Hawkins and Hall proceeded on down the Colorado River. Bradley and Hawkins Stopped at EhrenBurg Arizona. Hall and I went on to the head of the Gulf of California then came back up the River about Old Fort Yuma and Being Level Broke we commenced Killing a few Deer to Sell to the Mexicans and what few whites were there. one day while hunting the Apaches Jumped me and I had to kill two of them. as they appeared to be Government pets I had to walk from the Colorado River to owen's valley—500 miles—California. as you probably know I am a little too Hot-headed to Submit to an arrest under such trivial pretexts. When I struck Owens valley I found a job and went to work cutting cord wood for a Mining Company. After working two months I wanted my money so I could Start back to the Rocky mts. the Boss Refused to give me my money or a horse he owned. Which of course caused a row. there was nothing left for me to do but adopt drastic measures. So I took Horse saddle and Bridle away from him and his Pet henchman who happen to be the Sheriff at the time. I Rode the Horse alone across that Sink of Hell, Death Valley; across Nevada Desert; Utah and Back to Green River Wyoming. lived on my Gun the entire distance. after that went onto the plains and Hunted Buffalo, Wolves, and occasionally a Damed Sioux to vary the monotony of my life. for the last 25 years I have lived west of the range Engaged most of my time in Mining with various ups and downs. Mostly downs. I have a wife and three grown Sons all Doing for themselves two of them Publishing Newspapers and one a farmer. I am the same old wanderer that I always was and will Probably wind up under a cedar tree fit Subject for Wolf Bait. this is a great Copper Country and I have some pretty fair Prospects and if I have good luck with them I may be able to make you a visit a K. C. when we can smoke a pipe and perhaps Boost a bottle. you ask about the Colorado River party. here is the list as far as I know and Believe Correct. ten started from Green River. J. W. Powell. Walter Powell. O. G. Howland. Seneca Howland. George Bradley. Frank Goodman. and Jack Sumner. Andrew Hall. Bill Dunn. Goodman quit us at uinta river. the two howlands and Dunn were killed. Powell states by Indians & I Say Killed by the Mormons, Part of the Same old "Mountain Meadows" massacre gang.

Of course you know J. W. Powell is Dead. Walter Powell is in the Bug House. Bradley Killed accidently at San Diego California. Hall Killed by Road agents in Arizona. all that are left are Wm R Hawkins and myself. Hawkins Joined the Mormons and has two or more women and had when I saw down on the Gila River three years ago a good sized Kindergarten of his own which he has doubtless increased since.

I Presume you remember A. C. Lankin [Lanken], the fellow that stole the mule and grub on your first trip to Bear River. Well he Scrimped and Saved until he had accumulated $30,000 then went into his room in Rawlins Wyoming, whrote on a card "life is not worth living" and Sent a Bullet through his head.

So J. W. Powell Says I Saved his Bacon a time or two did he? Well from Reading his Report one would think there was no one in the Party but Capt Powell and himself. he Evidently didn't tell you of the row in Cataract Canon when I got so damed mad at his abuse of howland and Dunn that I had to "Speak out in meeting", which culminated in my taking full command of the Expedition and Keep it to the end. Poor Walter was crazy when he was in the Park and got worse. Peticoat Dementia or a plain case of rats in the Garret I don't Know which.

Well I Guess I have written enough to tire you, so I will close. hoping to hear from you again soon. If you know of any one wanting Copper prospects tell them to drop me a line. If you want some Specimens of the copper will send them.

Yours most truly Jack Sumner

Paradox Montrose Co. Colorado[5]

NOTES

1. Keplinger to Jack Sumner; no date, and no known surviving copy.

2. Jack Sumner to Keplinger, Sept. 14, 1906, Keplinger Papers, Kansas State Historical Society, Topeka (hereafter Keplinger Papers).

3 Keplinger to Stanton, Nov. 1, 1919, Stanton Papers, New York Public Library, New York.

4. Keplinger to Enos Mills, March 1, 1912, Keplinger Papers.

5. Sumner to Keplinger, Sept. 14, 1906.

PART III

John Wesley Powell

·21·

Horse Feathers

SOLDIERS AND RIVER RUNNERS do love to tell stories. Sometimes, their stories get a bit exaggerated.

John Wesley Powell loved to tell a story about the Battle of Shiloh. Powell had plenty of genuine Shiloh heroism to talk about proudly. Shiloh is often called the Gettysburg of the West, a massive battle where the course of the war could have swung decisively either way. General Grant was leading the Union army's first deep intrusion into the South when he was surprise-attacked by the Confederate army, thrown into chaos, thrown back, and nearly broken. Powell was an artillery commander at Shiloh's most pivotal, most famous event—the Hornet's Nest—where a few thousand Union solders stopped a much larger Confederate force, giving General Grant crucial hours in which to turn the battle around. Losing an arm at Shiloh brought Powell respect for the rest of his life.

Yet this wasn't quite good enough. Powell's longtime assistant, Marcus Baker, related this story the year after Powell's death:

> He told me how, at the time of the battle of Shiloh, where he lost his right forearm, his superior officer, General W. H. L. Wallace, a tall and handsome soldier, mounted on a fine large chestnut thorough-bred, seeing him wounded and the enemy closing in, said: "Here, Lieutenant, we're going to be captured in a few minutes; get onto my horse and go back to the landing at once." So saying, General Wallace dismounted, and, strong-armed as he was, picked up this mere boy-lieutenant who might have weighed 125 lbs., set him in the saddle and sent him away. It was only a few minutes later that this noble officer received his death-wound. Midst the hissing and singing of bullets and screeching of shells Powell galloped back to the landing, about half a mile distant, the red blood spurting from his wounded arm, and soon arrived white and faint.[1]

In footnoting part of this quote, Powell's biographer William Culp Darrah commented, "Powell described this incident to many persons."[2]

As General Wallace foresaw, the Hornet's Nest was soon surrounded. Some Union troops, including Powell's artillery unit, escaped just in time, while others, realizing they were trapped, tried to run the gauntlet of Confederate fire and break out, with little success. About 2,200 Union soldiers, including General Benjamin Prentiss, surrendered.

Yet there was a big flaw in Powell's story. When General W. H. L. Wallace was shot (closer to an hour than "a few minutes" after helping Powell), Wallace was still riding his horse, Prince. Shiloh historian Timothy B. Smith described the scene: "Wallace led the way, continually turning and directing his troops.... Rising in his stirrups to get a better view, he was hit in the head and tumbled from his horse.... Staff officers repositioning the division's artillery near the landing knew something was amiss when they saw Wallace's riderless horse: 'I saw poor Prince, the General's horse, coming on a lope without a rider,' staff officer I. P. Rumsey wrote. He added that it 'was the saddest moment of my life.'"[3]

There was no need for Wallace to give Powell a horse, for Powell already had his own horse. Shiloh National Military Park historian Stacy D. Allen told me, "As an organizational commander of a field artillery battery, Captain Powell was authorized and required to have a personal mount, and based on his own account, he rode into battle in command of his battery."[4]

General Wallace would not have given away his horse on the grounds that he expected to be captured; according to Smith, Wallace never had any such plan or expectation:

> Prentiss's claims to the contrary, he and Wallace apparently did not make any decision to specifically sacrifice themselves. Prentiss later wrote an extremely self-centered report in which he argued that he and Wallace "consulted and agreed to hold our positions at all hazards, believing that we could thus save the army from destruction." He added that they had been told the other divisions had fallen back to the river, making the case that they purposefully held when everyone else had retreated and did so knowing they would be sacrificed. Such is post-battle fabrication; no other evidence is needed than the fact that both Prentiss and Wallace were either mortally wounded or captured in the act of falling back.... Grant did not need Wallace and Prentiss to hold on and sacrifice themselves; he had a third major line already formed to save the day.[5]

Smith is making a revisionist case in suggesting that the Hornet's Nest was not as crucial as Shiloh histories usually say, but he makes a valid point that General Prentiss, in writing his battle history, had a motive for turning his surrender into a heroic, Alamo-like sacrifice. In the immediate aftermath of the battle, when the only thing people heard about Prentiss was that he had surrendered with 2,200 troops, he was angrily denounced by newspapers, politicians, and military leaders, some calling for him to be court-martialed and shot. When Prentiss was released from Confederate captivity after six months he began giving speeches defending his role, and over time he exaggerated that role. Prentiss was fortunate that, years later, the most important historian of the battle was a soldier who had fought in the Hornet's Nest and was eager to portray it not as incompetent leadership or ignominious surrender, but as a heroic stand that saved the day. General Wallace was dead so never had a chance to explain his own actions or intentions, but historians have tended to accept Prentiss's claim that Wallace was a fellow "Davy Crockett," bravely sacrificing himself and being shot off his horse, Prince.

It was Prentiss's version of events that Powell was hearing and reading—and embellishing further: Prentiss and Wallace were going to stand until the end, so obviously Wallace did not need his horse. Indeed, Wallace would probably prefer that his horse not be captured, so Powell was doing Wallace a favor by saving his horse. Powell might be severely wounded and bleeding, he might have only one arm to grip the reins, but he was still tough enough to do one more heroic deed. Wallace recognized that Powell was a man strong enough and trustworthy enough to save his beloved Prince.

Then, in 1896, Powell received a letter that must have given him pause.[6] It was from Colonel Cadle, chairman of the Shiloh National Military Park Battlefield Commission, which was gathering testimonials that would become part of the official history of the battle. Powell might get away with telling an exaggerated story to his friends, but the public record was a different matter, especially for someone who had served in high government positions and been the focus of great controversy. General Wallace might not be around to contradict Powell's story about Prince, but others who had been there, perhaps beginning with Colonel Cadle, would recognize it was nonsense. Powell probably would not have approved of Marcus Baker publishing his tale about Wallace's horse, but Baker published it a year after Powell died and Baker wouldn't have known he was contradicting Powell's official testimony. In his reply to Cadle, Powell retreated from any claim about Wallace's horse and admitted that he was riding his own horse and that Wallace helped him onto his own horse:

About four o'clock, as I have always remembered the time, Gen. Wallace asked me if I could not plant a section to his left…. Soon I discovered that there was a line of men concealing themselves in the fence and I dismounted and pointed one of the pieces along the fence loaded with solid shell. As I raised my hand for a signal to the gunners to stand clear of the recoil a musket ball struck my arm above the wrist which I scarcely noticed until I attempted to mount my horse…. At about this juncture a medical officer rode up to me and commenced to cut my sleeve for the purpose of examining the wound; but immediately Gen. Wallace himself rode up and dismounting picked me up, for he was a tall athletic man, and put me on my horse and directed the sergeant to take me back to the landing.[7]

In the 1940s William Culp Darrah was researching his Powell biography and contacted Shiloh National Military Park; in his book's acknowledgments Darrah thanks two historians at that park. It is highly likely that the Shiloh historians sent Darrah Powell's 1896 testimony about having his own horse and riding it away from the battle. Yet Darrah chose to ignore this, made no reference to it, and instead included Baker's more heroic version. Other historians have copied Darrah.

Perhaps we should forgive Powell for his horse story, for he was only one of millions of Civil War veterans who enjoyed dwelling on their youthful heroic deeds and who stretched the facts. On the other hand, Powell was probably the only soldier who concocted a story about a general giving him his own magnificent horse. General Wallace was giving Powell not just a horse but also a blessing, protection against any image of Powell ignominiously fleeing a great battle. For Powell, W. H. L. Wallace held special authority: as a lawyer and U.S. state attorney, Wallace was one of the leading citizens of LaSalle County, Illinois, which was five miles from the town of Hennepin where Powell taught school for three years before the war. Illinois political leaders were talking of sending Wallace to the U.S. Congress when the war was over.

Prince the horse, too, became an honored citizen in Wallace's hometown, Ottawa, Illinois. Led by Wallace's personal servant, Prince marched in Wallace's funeral procession. Years later Prince was buried next to Wallace and his wife. The Ottawa Episcopal Church holds a memorial stained-glass window, made in 1872 by artisans Mrs. Wallace sought out in Dresden, Germany, depicting Wallace's life, including a scene of Prince running—without a rider—from the battlefield to the boat landing. Downtown Ottawa holds a mural showing Wallace astride Prince, with soldiers reaching out to pet Prince.

In his letter to Colonel Cadle, Powell could have come clean about Wallace's horse, but he made two other claims that a later park historian declared to be bogus. Powell wrote, "On the 5th, the day before the commencement of the battle, I rode with General Grant and his staff over much of the site of the subsequent battle."[8] Yet according to park ranger Charles M. Spearman, "Powell's ride across the battlefield with Grant and his staff on April 5th is doubtful since Grant was severely injured in a fall from his horse on the evening of April 4th and there is no record of him visiting the battlefield area on the 5th." Spearman also questioned Powell's claims about his cannons: "Powell also states that the battery consisted of 4 twelve-pounder Napoleons and 2 twelve-pounder howitzers which is in contradiction with the Illinois Adjutant-General's Report which records that Battery F. 2nd Illinois Light Artillery was armed with six 6-pounder guns. The Adjutant-General's Report is considered the more accurate report for this period. Later the battery was re-armed with other types of ordnance and Powell may be remembering later guns used by the battery when he returned to the unit."[9]

Powell's claims about Wallace's horse, his ride with Grant, and the larger cannons showed a grandiosity that fit in with the complaints that some of Powell's Colorado River boatmen would make against him. Indeed, perhaps such grandiosity was necessary for a man to have the self-confidence it took to be the first to take boats into the "Great Unknown."

NOTES

1. Marcus Baker, "Major J. W. Powell: Personal Reminiscences of One of His Staff," *Open Court* 17 (1903): 348.

2. Darrah, *Powell of the Colorado,* 57.

3. Timothy B. Smith, *Shiloh: Conquer or Perish* (Lawrence: University Press of Kansas, 2014), 213.

4. Stacy D. Allen, personal communication, May 15, 2001.

5. Smith, *Shiloh,* 219.

6. Cadle to Powell, 1896; no known surviving copy.

7. Powell to Cadle, May 15, 1896, Ser. 1, Box 14, Folder 169, Shiloh National Military Park, Shiloh, TN.

8. Ibid.

9. Charles M. Spearman, personal communication, Jan. 13, 2009.

·22·

Major Powell, I Presume

J OHN WESLEY POWELL has been an inspiration to generations of river runners, yet historians might have overlooked his most important act of inspiration.

On one of my visits to Shiloh National Military Park in Tennessee I found the park historian, who gave me an hour-by-hour account of Powell's fateful day in the battle. The historian corrected several mistakes in the usual accounts: The park's own battlefield marker showing the location of Powell's artillery battery was in the wrong spot. The books about Powell said he was wounded by a bullet, when it was actually cannonball shrapnel. One otherwise authoritative book on the battle said Powell's unit was Missouri artillery, when it was Illinois.

The biggest error about Powell and Shiloh might be an error of omission. In the park's Visitor Center I read a display about people who fought at Shiloh and went on to great things. There were two U.S. presidents—Ulysses S. Grant and James A. Garfield. There was Ambrose Bierce, who wrote noir stories about the war. And there was a famous river runner—but it was not John Wesley Powell. Actually, the display didn't mention that this individual had been a river runner. Today the only thing most people remember about this person is that long ago, somewhere in Africa, he uttered four words, "Dr. Livingstone, I presume?" That person, in fact, was Henry M. Stanley, who not only found Livingstone but also became the first person to descend the Congo River, in an ordeal that made Powell's river expedition seem mellow in comparison.

It wasn't just in the Visitor Center that Shiloh lore has featured Stanley and ignored Powell. In 2012 Winston Groom, best known for his novel *Forrest Gump* but also a Civil War historian, published a book about Shiloh that includes a photo of Stanley in his African explorer's garb and mentions him on seventeen pages, including a dozen quotes, but makes no mention of Powell.[1]

Perhaps this was partly because Groom had two ancestors who fought for the Confederacy at Shiloh, alongside Stanley, and because Stanley used his journalist's skills to write a dramatic account of the battle. Yet Groom was also following a tradition among Shiloh historians, whose books usually mention Stanley but not Powell. This isn't because Stanley played a larger role in the battle than did Powell—on the contrary. Nor does it reflect the importance of their future achievements, at least in American history: Powell's "finding" the Grand Canyon counted for more than Stanley's finding Livingstone, who never regarded himself as lost. This discrepancy might be another case of historians following one another's tracks.

As a river explorer Stanley might have outdone Powell, and indeed this could have been Stanley's ambition. The Congo is about twice as long as the Green-Colorado and has a much larger volume and more-difficult rapids. Powell rode the railroad to his launching spot, but Stanley struggled through the jungle for two years just to reach his put-in. Stanley spent twice as long on the river as did Powell.

Stanley began his Congo expedition in 1874, two years after Powell's second Colorado River expedition. Stanley started with more than two hundred native helpers, of which half died along the way—some from disease, some from attacks by native warriors. Stanley retaliated by looting and burning villages. When dozens of his helpers deserted, Stanley had them recaptured and locked in slave chains. Stanley's men lugged a forty-foot boat, cut into sections, across a thousand miles of jungles and deserts. When Stanley finally started his nearly two-thousand-mile descent of the Congo he had only a hundred men left, most of them using canoes stolen from natives. For the next thousand miles Stanley fought off ambushes and fleets of huge war canoes. The rapids, too, were deadly. Stanley soon came to a series of cataracts and rapids stretching for fifty miles, today called Stanley Falls. At each cataract and impassible rapid Stanley's men had to drag their heavy, fifty-foot-long canoes out of the water and cut a portage trail through the jungle slopes, even over a 1,500-foot mountain. Like Powell, Stanley started out knowing little about river running and learned as he went, but his learning was paid for with many deaths. At another gorge of cataracts 150 miles long, Stanley took thirty-seven days to progress thirty-four miles, with the loss of three canoes. Even while stealing food from the natives, Stanley's men were near starvation. When they got within fifty miles of their goal, they abandoned the river and walked out of the jungle, more than two and a half years after starting. Stanley soon learned that his fiancée in America had married someone else eighteen months before.

As I compared the lives of John Wesley Powell and Henry M. Stanley, I found that they were closely linked, both during the Battle of Shiloh and during their lives as explorers.

Powell and Stanley came to Shiloh from sharply different directions, and not just geographically. Powell's father was an abolitionist involved with the Underground Railroad, and Powell inherited those values, which propelled him to join the Union army and at one point led him to train black troops. And unlike the large portion of his contemporaries who regarded Native Americans as subhuman, perhaps deserving genocide, Powell respected Native Americans and founded the U.S. Bureau of Ethnology to study their cultures. Stanley, as you might have guessed from his brutal treatment of Africans during his expedition, was comfortably racist. Born illegitimate in Wales, he immigrated to New Orleans at age sixteen and was aided by a wealthy cotton merchant named Henry Stanley, whose name he adopted. Young Stanley also adopted the values of Southern society: its feudalistic hierarchy, code of honor, obsession with military valor, and contempt for non-whites. When the Civil War broke out, Stanley regarded abolitionists as robbers who were trying to deprive Southerners of their legitimate property: "Why a sooty-faced nigger from a distant land should be an element of disturbance between white brothers was a puzzle to me.... As I had seen him in the South, he was a half-savage, who had been exported by his own countrymen, and sold in the open market, agreeable to time-honored custom."[2] In his career in Africa Stanley helped to establish Belgian rule over the Congo, which became one of the most brutal in the history of European colonization. Of Native Americans, Stanley held that whites "had as much right to the plains as the Indians, and it would not be a difficult task to prove that they had a better right.... Savage and implacable humanity of the Indian type need expect no other fate than extinction."[3]

Powell enlisted in the army with far more determination than Stanley, who at first thought that as a foreigner he was not expected to fight; when an anonymous detractor sent him a petticoat in the mail he was shamed into enlisting. He joined the 6th Arkansas Infantry, which called itself the Dixie Greys, under the command of Colonel Robert Shaver. Shaver's troops had an especially intense experience at Shiloh, repeatedly being in the thickest fighting. In two of those encounters Henry M. Stanley could have been facing John Wesley Powell.[4]

General Grant, following the Tennessee River southward, unloaded his troops at Pittsburg Landing in southern Tennessee, near a rustic little church called Shiloh, and organized them to invade Mississippi. Grant was overconfident about his safety and neglected precautions, such as digging in. Confederate general Albert Sidney Johnston outnumbered Grant and knew he had to act boldly before Grant's gradually arriving forces were fully assembled and outnumbered Johnston's forces; Johnston marched on Grant and took him largely by surprise at dawn on April 6, 1862. Many Union troops were still in their tents or making breakfast.

Shaver's troops were among the first Confederates to meet significant resistance, but they soon drove this line of Yankees away and occupied their camp; Henry Stanley imagined the battle was already won. Shaver's troops soon encountered stronger resistance from Union colonel Everett Peabody, but again the Union troops were too disorganized to hold out for long. The Confederates continued advancing through the morning. Stanley was awed by the furor of the guns and the gore of dead and dying men. At one point a bullet struck him and knocked him down, though he discovered that the bullet had hit his belt buckle, denting it, and saving his life.

At Duncan Field, one of many clearings amid a landscape full of thick woods and ravines, Powell and Shaver had the same experience of advancing too far, being dangerously exposed to enemy fire, and retreating. "Shaver's right," in the words of historian Timothy B. Smith, "stumbled into W. H. L. Wallace's forming division in Duncan Field. Shaver found out quickly that more Federals were on this line than expected, but it only took him a moment to reform his startled units behind the brow of a hill."[5] At about 11:30 AM the Confederates, including Shaver's troops, attempted a charge into Duncan Field but quickly retreated into the woods.

Shaver's troops were waiting when John Wesley Powell raced up the road toward Duncan Field and saw Union troops there. An officer ordered Powell to join the Union line on the edge of the field; Powell replied that he was supposed to report to General McClernand and raced right through the line and into the middle of the field. Powell had been waiting among reserve units at Pittsburg Landing, where the previous day Grant's efforts to reorganize his forces had reassigned Powell's battery to three different divisions, one after the other, only for him to end up back in the unassigned category at day's end. According to Larry J. Daniel (one of the few Shiloh historians to mention Powell), "Receiving no orders, and fearing that he had been forgotten in the reorganizational shuffling, Powell struck out with his battery to the front. Arriving near the Duncan cabins, his men strayed into a volley from Shaver's brigade in the Review Field sector. Two gunners and several horses fell wounded. The captain had his two Napoleon guns wheel about and unlimber, but the fire was so intense that several of his men panicked. Powell managed to get five of his cannon out, but left a Napoleon gun and battery wagon by the roadside."[6] As Powell recalled thirty years later, "I was in a position where I was not only surprised but fully at the mercy of the enemy."[7]

Powell had rushed straight into a noose that continued tightening around several thousand Union troops, leading to such an intensity of combat that the Confederates called it the Hornet's Nest (see chapter 21). Both Powell and Shaver were soon repositioned to the southern end of the battle. Around 3 PM Shaver's men launched one of the main assaults on the Union line, only to be driven back by cannon fire, mainly from Emil Munch's 1st Minnesota Artillery but also likely from Powell's 2nd Illinois Artillery, which was posted farther back and was firing over the heads of Powell's own troops.

Of course, we can't know for sure which way Powell's cannons were pointing, so we can't say for sure that Powell was shooting right at Stanley. We also can't be sure that Stanley was shooting at Powell at Duncan Field: Stanley recalled that after he was hit in the belt buckle he took a long time to find his unit again, so he probably missed his chance to shoot at Powell.

Powell was soon wounded and escaped the Hornet's Nest just before it was surrounded. The next morning Stanley, shamed by an officer's comment that he was moving too slowly, charged ahead so energetically that he outran his own men and ended up alone and surrounded by Union troops.

Stanley was captured and shipped to a prisoner-of-war camp near Chicago, Camp Douglas; in his first week there he witnessed the deaths of 220 prisoners from dysentery and typhoid. There was an easy way to escape the camp: renounce the Confederacy and join the Union army. Stanley did so and, just like John Wesley Powell, he was enlisted in a battery of the Illinois Light Artillery. Stanley's battery was sent to Harper's Ferry, West Virginia, but he soon came down with dysentery and was sent to a hospital. Stanley was under orders to report to his unit when he recovered, but instead he deserted the Union cause.

I found it an unlikely coincidence that two men who explored two of the world's most difficult whitewater rivers within a few years of one another had been so closely interlinked at a famous battle. But perhaps it was not a coincidence. Perhaps Powell helped to inspire Stanley.

For the first month of the Powell expedition the newspaper coverage of it was limited mainly to papers to which crewmembers sent a few letters from the river—newspapers in Denver, Chicago, and Bloomington, Illinois. Additionally, when Powell stopped at the Uinta Agency at the end of June he dispatched to the St. Louis *Missouri Democrat* the first month of Jack Sumner's river journal, which was published at the end of August. It has never been clear why Powell chose the *Democrat,* but the *Democrat* did have a good reputation for covering Western news, partly due to its star reporter, Henry M. Stanley.

The *Democrat* first employed Stanley in 1865 as a freelance reporter. He wanted to explore the West and talked the *Democrat* into letting him send them stories. He got as far as California but spent the most time in the mining towns of the Colorado Rockies. He found that freelance reporting would not pay his way, so he took occasional jobs. In Central City he apprenticed as a printer at the town newspaper, the same office where Oramel Howland worked as a printer. We don't know exactly when Howland worked there: we can only locate him in Central City in the spring of 1864. Stanley's timeline, too, is vague, but he would have been there in later 1865 or early 1866. It's possible Howland and Stanley worked there at the same time and knew one another, and even possible that it was Howland who was teaching Stanley to be a printer. Stanley got a good feel for Central City society, and wrote about it.

In May 1866 Stanley and a friend built a flat-bottomed boat and attempted to row six hundred miles down the Platte River from Denver to Omaha. This was the same journey attempted five years previously by some members of the party of men from Bloomington who had spent that summer exploring the mountains, led by Linus Graves, a distant cousin of Oramel Howland. The Bloomington men didn't get far on the ungenerous Platte River, and indeed Stanley says he was told in Denver that others had tried it but all had failed. Stanley, too, had a hard time, capsizing twice, losing his guns and supplies, and finally walking the last stretch to Omaha.

Stanley's taste for adventure then took him across the Atlantic and to Turkey, but at the start of 1867 he was back in St. Louis working as a staff reporter for the *Missouri Democrat,* which soon sent him west to cover the Indian uprisings on the plains. He also visited Colorado, including Central City. In the spring of 1867 Powell was paying keen attention to news of the Indian uprisings since he and his party of Illinois men were heading into those plains, and in fact the news prompted him to cancel his plans to go to the Dakota Badlands. Powell was in Colorado at the same time as Stanley, but Stanley would not have read about Powell in the Colorado newspapers, which covered Powell's arrival and departure but said nothing about him while Stanley was there in late August and early September. However, it is possible Stanley heard about Powell, because Stanley paid visits to newspaper editors, which he wrote about, saying the *Rocky Mountain News* was "characterized by boldness of speech and extreme partisanship," and the Central City *Register* was "full of queer mountainisms."[8]

Stanley's connection with the *Missouri Democrat,* which would publish Jack Sumner's river journal, made it more likely that he would notice news of Powell's 1869 river expedition. Stanley also published a few articles in the *Chicago Tribune,* to which Powell sent six letters from his expedition, and in the *Missouri Republican;* the *Republican* was reprinting Powell's letters to the *Chicago Tribune* and also printed a letter Powell sent to a St. Louis–area friend, Henry Wing.[9]

In early July 1869 newspapers all over the country ran stories about the Powell expedition, inspired by hoaxer John Risdon, who claimed to have been a crewmember, and who claimed the expedition had ended in tragedy and death. This was the first time most people had heard about the expedition. Powell's wife declared that Risdon's reports didn't make sense, and that she had a letter from her husband dated after his supposed death. Soon letters with even later dates, which Powell had sent from the Uinta Agency, arrived in the Midwest, and there was a new round of publicity, with more denunciations of Risdon.

Powell was not the only missing river explorer who was making the newspapers that summer. On September 7, 1869, only days after Powell emerged from the Grand Canyon, the San Francisco *Daily Examiner* ran this item: "The discussion of the probable fate of Dr. Livingstone has been renewed in England. Capt. Burton, the African traveler, believes that the Doctor is a prisoner in the town of Lusccula, the capital of the kingdom of Cossebee, and an expedition in search of him is talked of." David Livingstone had set out in March 1866 to find the source of the Nile and had not been heard from since.

That same day, Salt Lake City's *Deseret Evening News* became the first newspaper to announce that John Wesley Powell had survived the Grand Canyon, and soon newspapers across the country, their audiences stimulated by the Risdon hoax, began repeating the news.

A few weeks later, Stanley, who was now working for the New York *Herald,* met with his editor, James Bennett, and discussed the other river explorer who had been given up for dead, Dr. Livingstone. They came up with a plan for Stanley to go find Livingstone.

In the books he wrote about his adventures, Stanley never mentions that Powell might have been an inspiration for his search for Livingstone. He gives all the credit to Bennett.[10] Yet Stanley's biographers have found it quite unlikely that the idea originated with Bennett, who showed little urgency about pursuing the search. Biographer John Bierman points out many discrepancies in Stanley's account:

Clearly, then, Stanley's account of his meeting with Bennett was in large part fictional. Even the date he ascribed to it was a lie…. As if to conceal that mendacity, the pages for October 17 and the next eight days were at some point torn out of his journal.

But if Bennett was as lukewarm as he seems to have been about the Livingstone assignment, why did Stanley choose to twist the truth and give his boss a large share of the credit?

When he wrote his bestselling *How I Found Livingstone* and dedicated it to Bennett, Stanley was still in the *Herald's* employ and hoping that the paper would finance his second expedition to Africa. He was no doubt also aware how resentful Bennett was that he should be basking in world celebrity while Bennett's own role was overlooked.[11]

Bierman and other biographers suggest that it was Stanley's idea.

Yet there is one good objection to the idea that Powell might have inspired Stanley. During the spring and summer of 1869, while Powell was on the river, Stanley was working as a journalist roaming Spain to cover its civil war. When he met with Bennett, it was in Paris. Would Stanley have seen American newspapers in Spain or Paris? Few people would, but of course Stanley was a newspaperman with a professional need to stay in touch with the news from back home. He was probably especially interested in the paper that launched his career, the *Missouri Democrat*.

Stanley could have been inspired by Powell merely from the newspaper stories about Powell's expedition, but if Stanley figured out how their days at Shiloh were so intertwined, he would have taken Powell even more personally. Stanley remembered how frightened he had been by the Yankee cannonballs screaming overhead, cannonballs that turned out to have been fired by Powell. Powell had come out of Shiloh a hero, Stanley a fool and a prisoner. And now, even with only one arm, Powell had become an even bigger hero who had accomplished something bigger than anything the proud and ambitious Stanley had even fanaticized about. Stanley clearly already had a hunger for adventure and fame, but Powell's story might have increased it. However, the problem with this theory is that the newspaper coverage of Powell seldom mentioned anything about his Civil War record; Jack Sumner's journal in the *Missouri Democrat* mentioned that Powell had only one arm, but didn't explain why.[12] Stanley would have needed to pick up this story from the veteran's grapevine. As Stanley compared his actions at Shiloh with Powell's, he might have figured out that he and Powell had faced one another twice.

There could have been one further, haunting echo of Shiloh's guns in Powell's story. The commander of Confederate forces at Shiloh was General Albert Sidney Johnston. Johnston's death early on the first afternoon of the battle threw confusion into the Confederate attack and tilted it toward defeat. Five years previously, Johnston had led the federal expedition against the Mormons, which caused the Mormons great alarm, triggered the Mountain Meadows Massacre, and left them deeply wary of federal power. With the beginning of the Civil War, the Mormons were left alone for years. In isolated southern Utah, the first federal soldiers the Mormons had seen in a decade could have been three men wandering through the desert, offering the dubious story that they had just boated through the Grand Canyon. If it is true that the Mormons killed Powell's three men, then it was a strange twist of fate through which General Johnston and Henry M. Stanley enacted their revenge against John Wesley Powell.

NOTES

1. Winston Groom, *Shiloh 1862* (Washington, DC: National Geographic, 2012).

2. Henry M. Stanley, *The Autobiography of H. M. Stanley*, ed. Dorothy Stanley (New York: Houghton Mifflin, 1937), 213.

3. Henry M. Stanley, *My Early Travels and Adventures in America* (Lincoln: University of Nebraska Press, 1982), xvi–xvii.

4. My matchup of the actions of John Wesley Powell and Henry Stanley in the Battle of Shiloh combines many sources, including correspondence with historians, two visits to the battlefield, and several books, including Smith, *Shiloh*; Wiley Sword, *Shiloh: Bloody April* (Dayton, OH: Morningside Bookshop, 1988); James Lee McDonough, *Shiloh: In Hell before Night* (Knoxville: University of Tennessee Press, 1977); and Larry J. Daniel, *Shiloh: The Battle That Changed the Civil War* (New York: Simon & Schuster, 1977). Henry Stanley's actions are alwo detailed in his *The Autobiography of Henry M. Stanley* (Boston: Houghton Mifflin, 1937).

5. Smith, *Shiloh*, 158.

6. Larry J. Daniel, *Shiloh: The Battle That Changed the Civil War* (New York: Simon and Schuster, 1997), 180.

7. John Wesley Powell to Cornelius Cadle, May 15, 1896, Ser. 1, Box 14, Folder 169, Shiloh National Military Park, Shiloh, TN.

8. Stanley, *My Early Travels*, 176.

9. All letters published in Darrah, *Utah Historical Quarterly* 15 (1947).

10. Henry M. Stanley, *How I Found Livingstone* (London: Sampson Low, 1872).

11. John Bierman, *Dark Safari: The Life Behind the Legend of Henry Morton Stanley* (New York: Alfred Knopf, 1990), 76–78.

12. Jack Sumner journals, *Missouri Democrat*, August 24 and 25, 1889.

·23·

The Impeachment of John Wesley Powell

I N THE SPRING OF 1868 John Wesley Powell was preparing for his second summer of exploring the natural history of the Rocky Mountains, and he was looking beyond that to leading an expedition down the Colorado River. For his first summer in the Rockies, Powell had obtained support from several sources, including General Ulysses S. Grant. Grant issued an order allowing Powell to purchase supplies from military posts at a low price, and assigned a military escort for Powell in the Dakota Territory, which was troubled with Indian unrest. Powell changed his mind about going through the Dakota Territory and so never needed this military escort, but Grant's approval of it was a badge of legitimacy for Powell. Powell also obtained scientific instruments from the Smithsonian Institution.

With the success of Powell's 1867 expedition, his legitimacy as an expedition leader seemed proven, and he had every right to expect further support from Washington, DC.

But a great deal had changed in Washington since 1867. The nation was now gripped by one of the worst political crises in its history. The angry divisions that had led to the Civil War had been stirred anew by the policies of President Andrew Johnson. Most Northerners felt that Johnson had betrayed the cause and the blood and the victory of Union armies, and was allowing Southerners to reassert their power, including brutal power over the freed slaves. On February 24, 1868, the U.S. House of Representatives voted to impeach Johnson. On March 30 the Senate began the impeachment trial. Both sides in the trial declared that the fate of American democracy was at stake.

According to the *Bloomington Pantagraph* on March 24, 1868, one week before the impeachment trial began, Powell left Bloomington on August 23 for Washington, DC, to enlist government support for his plans. Powell's hopes depended on getting help from two men: General Grant and Illinois senator

Lyman Trumbull. But both Grant and Trumbull had become lightning rods for the anger swirling around Andrew Johnson. Many senators would soon be furious at Lyman Trumbull, blaming him for the failure of the impeachment, which was finally abandoned on May 26.

The day before that, on May 25, Lyman Trumbull stood up in the U.S. Senate to advocate a trivial measure, which normally should have drawn little notice among numerous other, larger requests for government aid. But four pro-impeachment senators rose to challenge Trumbull and to criticize his petitioner, and the ensuing debate consumed probably about two hours of valuable Senate time. Trumbull's petitioner was John Wesley Powell. The fate of the Powell expedition down the Colorado River would be decided by the furious waves and eddies of powerful historical forces.

In 1867 Powell had won federal support easily. He had traveled to Washington and consulted with General Grant, whom he had first met in 1861 at Cape Girardeau, Missouri, where Powell was an artillery captain. In 1867 Grant was general of the U.S. Army and an iconic hero with tremendous influence. Powell submitted an official letter to Grant on April 29, 1867, asking "that the officers of the Commissary Department, on the route traveled by the party, may be instructed to sell supplies to it at government rates."[1] On that same date General Grant, or at least his staff officer George K. Leet, endorsed Powell's request, and Leet sent an endorsement to General Winfield S. Hancock, the army commander on Powell's route.

Nearly a year later, on April 2, 1868, Powell submitted a similar letter to General Grant. There was one difference. This time Powell wasn't asking for low-cost provisions, but free provisions: "I most respectfully request that the proper Officers be instructed to issue rations to this party while thus engaged, the party to consist of not more than twenty-five persons."[2]

The rest of Powell's letter shows he was an astute politician. He tried to give his expedition high official status, identifying himself as the secretary of the Illinois Natural History Society, and stating that the expedition was "under the auspices of the State Normal University of Illinois," where Powell was on the faculty. In truth, both organizations were only ten years old and quite small and humble; Powell had been dismayed to find that the natural history collection shared by these two institutions was an amateurish mess. Powell's Western expeditions were energized mainly by Powell's personal enthusiasm. Powell proposed to survey the Colorado River "from its source to the point where the survey made by Lieutenant Ives was stopped." Powell justified this survey as crucial science: "The grand cañon of the Colorado will give the best geological section on the continent." Yet like NASA advocates a century later, Powell had no shame about justifying exploration in the name of national defense: "Nor is it necessary to plead the value to the War Department of a topographical survey of that wonderful region, inhabited as it is by powerful tribes of Indians that will doubtless become hostile as the prospector and the pioneer encroach upon their hunting grounds." Powell insisted that his financial request was trivial compared with the costs of other Western surveys.[3]

The next day, General Grant endorsed Powell's request, noting, "The work is one of national interest."[4]

Three days later the War Department rejected Grant's request. Commissary General of Subsistence A. E. Eaton declared "that 'rations' cannot be 'issued' to the party as requested without the sanction of law, as its members are not the employees of or in the service of the United States." Eaton was willing for Powell to purchase supplies from army posts, "at the total cost to the United States," but only if local commanders decided they could spare such supplies. "If this is not deemed satisfactory to the principle of the party it is respectfully suggested that he should obtain the enactment of a law according him such other aid as he may seek."[5]

Commissary General Eaton's job did include guarding the military purse, but it was extraordinary for a War Department bureaucrat to overrule General Grant, especially for an expenditure that was indeed trivial. At least, this overruling would have been extraordinary only a year before—but then General Grant became embroiled in the impeachment of Andrew Johnson.

Andrew Johnson faced the difficult task of succeeding Abraham Lincoln, who was rapidly being elevated to sainthood. Many Americans resented Johnson's mere presence in the White House, and Johnson gave them lots more to resent. In contrast with Lincoln's generous spirit, Johnson was a crude, pugnacious, and vindictive man. Johnson was drunk at his vice presidential inauguration, made a shambles of his inaugural speech, and appalled everyone. Lincoln had chosen Johnson to be vice president in his second term because Lincoln wanted to reassure the South that they would be welcomed back into the Union. Johnson, a Tennessee senator, was the only Southern senator who had remained loyal to the Union. But Johnson had retained many Southern habits, including crude racism: he believed that blacks belonged to an inferior race who didn't deserve equality with whites. Johnson was also a Democrat in a government dominated by the Republican Party, founded to combat slavery.

With the end of the Civil War many Northern congressmen were determined to reconstruct Southern society, break up its feudalistic social order, redistribute its plantation lands, and ensure equality—or at least safety—for the freed slaves. White Southerners began resisting, passing laws to restrict rights for blacks, and launching organized violence against them. President Johnson refused to use federal authority to protect blacks, and in fact tried to sabotage Reconstruction efforts.

The tensions between President Johnson and Congress mounted steadily, and they rose seriously when Johnson vetoed two major pieces of Reconstruction legislation: the Freedmen's Bureau bill and the Civil Rights Act. The Freedmen's Bureau was an agency to protect and aid freed slaves, and the Civil Rights Act declared that blacks were American citizens, with legal rights. Both pieces of legislation were authored by Senator Lyman Trumbull of Illinois, the chairman of the Senate Judiciary Committee. Trumbull had also authored the Thirteenth Amendment to the U.S. Constitution, which outlawed slavery. Congress failed to muster the two thirds vote needed to override Johnson's veto of the Freedmen's Bureau bill, but by one vote it did override Johnson on the Civil Rights Act. Trumbull would help see that the core of the Civil Rights Act was soon cemented into the U.S. Constitution as the Fourteenth Amendment, which would be the foundation for much of the civil rights progress of the twentieth century. Lyman Trumbull was ahead of his times—the Civil Rights Act even declared that Native Americans and Chinese Americans were American citizens—but his regard for equality was tempered by his regard for the U.S. Constitution. Radical Republicans were often annoyed at Trumbull for hedging on civil rights for the sake of constitutionality. But this meant that when Trumbull authored civil rights legislation, his bills were legally unquestionable.

President Johnson further heightened tensions by ousting some of Lincoln's cabinet choices and replacing them with his own supporters, and by firing military commanders who were enforcing Reconstruction measures in the South. Congress tried to restrict Johnson's power with two major laws. One law required that any presidential orders to the military had to go through the general of the U.S. Army, Ulysses S. Grant, who was now a determined opponent of Andrew Johnson. The other law, the Tenure of Office Act, required Johnson to get approval from Congress before he removed any cabinet member or other federal executive whose appointment had required congressional approval to begin with. The Tenure of Office Act contained a trap, for it defined a violation of it as a high misdemeanor, which would fit the Constitution's requirements for a presidential impeachment, requirements defined as "Treason, Bribery, and other high Crimes and Misdemeanors."

Trapped between Congress and President Johnson was General Grant. At first Grant tried to be neutral, but he became more and more disgusted with

Johnson and his policies and began resisting Johnson's efforts—first passively, then actively, even countermanding Johnson's orders. Johnson called Grant a traitor, but knew he couldn't fire a national hero.

Radical Republicans made several efforts to organize the impeachment of President Johnson, but their efforts floundered because their charges against Johnson were too nakedly political, and too weak legally.

In late February 1868 President Johnson walked right into the trap in the Tenure of Office Act. He fired Secretary of War Edwin Stanton, who had been resisting Johnson's policies. But Stanton refused to go, and barricaded himself in his office, where he would remain for three months, cooking meals in his office fireplace. Nearly three years of frustration and furor over Andrew Johnson now centered on the question of who controlled the War Department.

The firing of Stanton threw the nation into an uproar. There was rage in newspapers, pulpits, and taverns. There was talk of a new civil war, of armies marching from the South to support Johnson, or armies marching from the North to overthrow Johnson. Radical Republicans drew up articles of impeachment, almost all dealing with Johnson's attempted, illegal seizure of the War Department.

It was only a few weeks later that a War Department bureaucrat snubbed General Grant, refusing to honor his trivial request for "Somebody" Powell. Was this just another shot in the furious battle over who controlled the War Department?

Commissary General A. B. Eaton has left little trace in the historical record, so it's hard to gauge his motives in overruling Grant's request for Powell. Eaton was a West Pointer and career soldier who had spent a dozen years in the Commissary Department before becoming commissary general in 1864. Grant's papers mention only a few, routine interactions with Eaton before 1868; in the only interaction of significance, Eaton's 1865 complaint about excessive requisitions for Fort Leavenworth, Grant agreed, writing to General William T. Sherman, who was in charge of Western operations: "Look into them and stop all unnecessary expenditures and reduce all necessary ones to actual requirements."[6] President Johnson had promoted Eaton to brevet major general in 1865, so was Eaton beholden to Johnson and scoring a point against Grant by turning down Grant's request for Powell? Then again, Grant retained Eaton in office through most of Grant's presidency.

After Eaton's insistence that it would take a law for Powell to obtain his requested aid, Powell had no choice but to go to Congress. Powell went to his U.S. representative, Shelby Cullom, and to Senator Lyman Trumbull, who would become his advocate on the Senate floor. Why did Powell turn to Trumbull and not the other senator from Illinois, Richard Yates? Because Yates was newly elected and held little influence, whereas Trumbull had been in the Senate for a dozen years and, as the chairman of the Senate Judiciary Committee, was a respected and powerful senator. Congressman Cullom was the protégé of Senator Trumbull, and they often worked together. Trumbull was one of two Senate regents of the Smithsonian Institution; he cared about science and exploration. One year after Powell ran the Colorado River, Senator Trumbull's twenty-four-year-old son Walter would be part of the first major party of Americans to explore Yellowstone. Powell had a ready link to Trumbull through Jesse Fell, a leading citizen of Bloomington, and one of the founders of the Illinois State Normal University, Powell's college. Fell was a high-powered political operative who was Lincoln's floor manager at the 1860 Republican convention and who helped manage Trumbull's tough 1866 reelection campaign and pay off Trumbull's campaign debts. And given Powell's abolitionist sentiments, Powell must have admired Trumbull for his civil rights initiatives.

At the time that Powell went to Senator Trumbull, Trumbull's intentions concerning the impeachment vote were still unknown. Most people assumed that Trumbull was a safe vote for impeachment, since Trumbull had authored many of the Reconstruction measures Johnson had sabotaged. On the campaign trail in 1866 Trumbull had called for Johnson's impeachment. Shelby Cullom was confident Trumbull would vote for impeachment.

On April 16, 1868, Congressman Cullom introduced joint resolution HR 251 that would authorize the War Department to provide Powell with army supplies. Without any discussion, the bill was sent to the House Committee on Military Affairs, chaired by Ohio congressman James Garfield. Garfield would become an important Powell ally for years to come; it was Garfield who would persuade Powell to write a popular book about his expedition. It was Garfield who on May 11 submitted HR 251 to the House of Representatives. Garfield presented the letter Powell had written to Grant, and Grant's endorsement, and Eaton's refusal. Garfield added an April 21 letter from Joseph Henry, the director of the Smithsonian Institution.

Henry said that Powell's expedition had "the entire approval of the Smithsonian Institution," which would supply it with scientific instruments. Henry emphasized that Powell was not pursuing any monetary or personal interest but rather serving natural history. But Henry had plenty of experience at selling science to money-minded congressmen, so he promised some Teflon-and-Tang spinoffs in a letter to Garfield: "Though the object of the exploration is the advance of science, its results will be of much practical value. The professor intends to give special attention to the hydrology of the mountain system in relation to agriculture."[7] Agriculture at the bottom of the Grand Canyon?

There was no debate over Powell's request, and no one called for a recording of the yeas and nays. The resolution was passed by voice vote. If anyone voted against Powell, there is no record of it. The next day, May 12, the House of Representatives sent Powell's resolution to the Senate. The Senate referred the Powell resolution to the Senate Committee on Military Affairs.

The Senate had scheduled its first vote on impeachment for May 16. There were eleven articles of impeachment, and the Senate would vote first on the eleventh article, since that was judged the most general and the one most likely to pass. Impeachment required the votes of two thirds of the Senate, and the vote was expected to be very close.

Lyman Trumbull loathed Andrew Johnson and his policies, but as the impeachment process went on, Trumbull had more and more misgivings about it. Trumbull had served as a justice on the Illinois Supreme Court, and now he was chairman of the Senate Judiciary Committee, and his judicial mind honored the importance of law and the Constitution. The Constitution said that impeachment might be justified by "Treason, Bribery, and other high Crimes and Misdemeanors," which was rather vague, but clearly implied criminal actions, not political actions. And, clearly, Johnson was being impeached for political actions. The Tenure of Office Act might be law, but it was a dubious law. If Johnson could be removed for his policies, it would be like a coup d'état, permanently weakening the presidency and American democracy.

In a closed Senate session on May 11, the same day the House of Representatives was voting on the Powell resolution, Lyman Trumbull announced that, reluctantly, he had to vote against impeachment. His fellow senators gasped.

The next night, thousands of people gathered in the streets of Chicago to denounce Lyman Trumbull. Anti-Trumbull meetings were held all over Illinois. The Illinois Republican congressional delegation prepared a letter demanding that Trumbull resign from office. Thousands of angry letters poured in, accusing Trumbull of being a traitor, a Benedict Arnold, a madman. Some people threatened physical harm: if Trumbull showed up on the streets of Chicago, he'd be lynched from the nearest lamppost. Newspapers around the country denounced Trumbull. When the *Chicago Tribune,* a longtime Trumbull supporter, said that Trumbull's vote might be regrettable but remained honorable, subscribers and advertisers bombarded the newspaper with outrage.

But in contrast with a few of the other Republican senators who would vote against impeachment, Trumbull was not accused of taking bribes for his vote. Trumbull was too respected for that, which is why his decision against impeachment was so threatening to the pro-impeachment side. Trumbull created safe cover for other Republican senators to oppose impeachment.

The first vote on impeachment was taken on May 16, and it came up one vote short. Thirty-five senators voted for impeachment and nineteen against, including seven Republicans.

Congress adjourned for a week so that members could attend the Republican National Convention, which would nominate Ulysses S. Grant for president. The convention also offered a good chance to pressure the defecting Republican senators. The next vote on further articles of impeachment was scheduled for May 26. The prosecutors were still hoping to find one vote to shift, but it looked bleak.

On May 25 Senator Henry Wilson of Massachusetts rose to introduce HR 251, authorizing the War Department to grant supplies to John Wesley Powell. Like James Garfield in the house, Wilson was the chairman of the Senate Committee on Military Affairs. It might have been protocol for the chairman of the Committee on Military Affairs to introduce a bill his committee had approved, but it was also smart politics. Henry Wilson was a highly respected senator, whom Ulysses S. Grant would choose to be his vice president in his second term. Wilson had become respected for his role as a watchdog over military spending during the war; no one could accuse Wilson of encouraging wasteful raids on military supplies. Wilson was also pro-impeachment. Wilson made a brief introduction of the Powell resolution, but when it was challenged by other senators, Wilson turned over its defense to Lyman Trumbull.

There could have been another reason why it was Wilson and not Trumbull who introduced the Powell resolution: Senator Ben Wade, the president pro tem of the Senate, who controlled access to the Senate floor and thus the ability to introduce legislation, was furious at Lyman Trumbull. Wade was a firebrand abolitionist and a leader of the impeachment movement. At that time, the office of Senate president pro tem was next in line after the vice president to succeed to the presidency. Because there was no vice president under Andrew Johnson, a Johnson impeachment would have made Ben Wade president. "Benjamin F. Wade never forgave Trumbull," wrote Trumbull biographer Ralph J. Roske. "He took a revenge against Trumbull that was stained with smallness. As Senate presiding officer, during the remainder of the session, he never saw Trumbull when the Illinoisan asked for recognition."[8] If Wade's ostracism of Trumbull had already begun, someone else needed to introduce the Powell resolution.

Four senators rose to criticize the Powell resolution, all of them pro-impeachment: George Edmunds of Vermont, John Sherman of Ohio, Timothy Howe of Wisconsin, and Lot Morrill of Maine. Lyman Trumbull offered most of the defense, but then he was joined by John Conness of California, who was pro-impeachment but also pro-Western exploration. Conness would play a large role in preserving Yosemite, where a mountain is named for him. "I know it is difficult," declared Conness, "for gentlemen who live in the East to understand or sufficiently estimate the extent of that West belonging to their own country which is not yet understood. It is only twenty-five years since… Frémont was authorized to explore what is at this day as well understood as the city of Washington, but was then unknown to this country. Now portions of it may be said to be teeming with population, industry, and civilization, but it is the result in part of the exploration that he made."[9]

The debate over Powell totaled about nine thousand words, which probably took about two hours.

The attacking senators seemed embarrassed by the time and energy they were devoting to Professor Powell; they knew they were engaging in overkill. The leading attacker, George Edmunds, repeatedly belittled his own objections: "Here is a private party, for some purpose, undoubtedly a good one—I have nothing to say about that, for I do not know anything about it," "To be sure it is a small matter," "To be sure it is a picayune matter," "Of course, as everyone says, this is a very small matter," "Of course, I sympathize with the object of the expedition," "Professor Powell, with that accuracy and modesty which almost always characterize learned men and true men, merely applies to the War Department for rations for twenty-five men, which is a trifling thing.… General Grant thinks that is a trifling matter," "I do not know but that the Senate has cost the United States more in talking about this bill than it would to have given the rations." Senator Howe called it, "This little resolution, no bigger than a grain of mustard."[10]

But the attacking senators refused to stop attacking.

They attacked the necessity of Powell's explorations. Senator Sherman, who had heard from General William Palmer about his encounter with James White, declared that the whole of the Colorado River had already been explored by White, and that the river's lower region was then being surveyed by General Palmer. Trumbull was befuddled by this declaration, having heard nothing about White, and he replied that Senator Sherman's own brother, General William T. Sherman, had in 1867 endorsed Powell's efforts. Senator Conness explained that General Palmer had merely surveyed a line that crossed the

Colorado River, and that "he was not in this region at all. But it is very essential to their further operations that they ascertain as much as they can of this region." Senator Edmonds twice suggested that the Colorado River was of value only if it was navigable, and Lieutenant Ives "had gone as far up the Colorado as it seemed to be useful to the interests of man or of government that anybody could go." Senator Conness conceded that the Colorado was unnavigable but that "it is nevertheless important to ascertain and determine the course of the river, and not only that but to determine the country adjacent to it." Senator Howe seemed to be admitting that Powell's plans had practical value when he said, "But this river, I understand, runs through a territory supposed to be rich in mines and not very much explored," but then Howe said that "enterprising mining companies should take it into their heads that this was a good opportunity to employ Professor Powell to make surveys in their interest."[11] Thus, Powell didn't need government help.

The attacking senators repeatedly questioned Powell's credentials and character. Senator Edmunds demanded to know if Powell was a trained geologist and a salaried professor, and if he had any government authority. Senator Wilson replied, "I do not personally know him: but I understand that he is a gentleman of capacity and character, a learned man."Senator Conness called Powell "one of the best men in the nation." Senator Edmunds played along with this, saying, "I admire and respect [Powell] as much as my friend from Illinois does—that is not what I am combating by any means." But when the pro-Powell senators made it clear that Powell's was a private party without government authority, the other senators took this as further reason to oppose him. Powell had no right to government aid. The pro-Powell senators insisted that Powell's private status made his expedition a bargain. Senator Conness: "If the Government should organize an expedition to make the exploration in which Professor Powell is engaged it would probably cost $100,000 before it were done, while in all human probability the expenditures to be made under this resolution, if it shall pass, will not reach more than a few thousand dollars." But Senator Howe answered that since the government had no control over Powell, he could use his explorations of a region "rich in mines" for personal gain, and the government shouldn't help him do so: "That it would be so used of course I cannot know. That it would not be so used nobody can know who does not know thoroughly the character of Professor Powell." Senator Morrill complained that not only would the government have no control over Powell's explorations or results, but it couldn't even limit the amount of supplies Powell took. This would be, said Morrill, up to "the judgment of Professor Powell, over which the government has not the slightest control.... How much that may be nobody here sees and nobody can know, of course. How well defined the expedition is I do not know, and I have not heard it stated. Any one can see that if the expedition is to expand to the extent of exploring the entire river on a grand scale...that your quartermaster's stores and commissary stores will be called on to a very great amount." Senator Edmunds emphasized that everyone in Washington and the country was calling out for better economy in government spending, but "it is always some other bill, some abstraction that may come up hereafter that we are to be economical about."[12] Edmunds insisted that this economy might as well begin with Powell's request.

The curious thing about Senators Edmunds and Howe is that after all the fuss they made about Powell's request, they didn't even bother to vote on it. But Powell's four critics were quite successful at bedeviling Lyman Trumbull, which might have been their primary impulse.

Powell's critics were also probably motivated by an impulse and a target larger than Trumbull. The impeachment had been triggered by the intense fight over who controlled the War Department: Congress or President Johnson. Now, with the failure of the first vote on impeachment, it was pretty clear that Johnson had won. The day after the Senate debated the Powell resolution, the Senate voted on another article of impeachment, and it, too, failed, by the same vote totals. Impeachment supporters gave up, and that afternoon Edwin Stanton abandoned his office at the War Department and let President Johnson take it over. The Powell resolution, too, was all about the authority of the War Department. The anti-Powell senators were bothered that the War Department was being given the authority to essentially give away the store, and they were trying to impose congressional control over the War Department—President Johnson's War Department. Controlling Powell's supplies might be a trivial victory indeed compared with controlling Reconstruction policy, but it might offer some symbolic satisfaction. Repeatedly in the debate, the anti-Powell senators claimed that they didn't oppose Professor Powell or the idea of exploration or the "trifling" sums involved, but they did oppose giving the War Department a free hand. Senator Edmunds: "Then, what kind of bill do we get here? We get a bill which says that the War Department is authorized and directed to furnish to the expedition, without limit as to the number of men, all the quartermaster's stores and commissary stores, which includes a great deal more than the rations, that may be necessary for the expedition to prosecute its work." Senator Morrill: "It [his objections] is in regard to the unlimited character of this resolution. The Secretary of War is authorized and empowered to issue indefinitely commissary stores for this expedition.... There is not the slightest limitation; all the resources of the Government put at the command of this expedition."[13] By opposing Powell, pro-impeachment senators could take a jab at both Trumbull and the War Department.

In the end, Powell's supporters agreed to amend the resolution to limit it to supplies for twenty-five men, which is all that Powell had requested and that Grant had endorsed to begin with.

The yeas and nays were called. Twenty-five senators voted in favor of Powell and seven voted against. Twenty-two senators did not vote. Five of the seven votes against Powell were pro-impeachment senators.

The vote tally offers some statistical support, but only mild support, for the theory that votes against Powell were motivated by pro-impeachment sentiments. Among senators voting against impeachment, only 10.5 percent voted against Powell. Among senators voting for impeachment, 14.2 percent voted against Powell. If Edmunds and Howe had bothered to vote, this would have been 20 percent. Perhaps their absence proves they never really cared much about Powell's request.

A stronger factor than impeachment sentiments was regional loyalties. All senators from west of the Mississippi River, if they voted at all, voted in favor of Powell. Four of the seven votes against Powell were from New England. Five New England senators voted for Powell, meaning that New England was 45 percent against Powell. The other three anti-Powell votes were from New York, Ohio, and Kentucky.

In the end, the scenario presented here is a plausible theory, but a few steps short of proven. It's not as if Commissary General Eaton admitted that he was refusing Powell because he was trying to snub Grant. It's not as if any senators announced they were voting against Powell because they were trying to snub Trumbull or President Johnson's War Department. The statistics on the vote lend support to this scenario, but only modest support. Clearly, regional differences played a larger role. However, it does stand out that after the House of Representatives passed Powell's request without any comment, the Senate spewed a lot of heat over it, all brought by pro-impeachment senators, who readily admitted how overdone their complaints were.

Yet among the senators who voted against Powell, we can find other, reasonable motives.

Ohio senator John Sherman can be forgiven for imagining that the entire West had been explored already. For twenty years John Sherman had been receiving letters from his brother (and future general) William T. Sherman, who was traveling widely in the West and reporting that California and Colorado were swarming with prospectors and the Great Plains with settlers, and, during the impeachment trial, that New Mexico was worthless land. Additionally, John Sherman's skepticism about Powell was fueled by his skepticism about previous railroad-initiated surveys that cost millions of dollars. "All these surveys," said Sherman in the Senate debate, "are got up either for the purpose of furnishing jobs or for scientific display, and their reports are generally of very little practical value. I shall not vote for any bill of this kind."[14] John Sherman's distrust of railroads led him to write the Sherman Anti-Trust Act of 1890, a landmark law that limited the power of railroads and other monopolies.

The biggest exception to this scenario is that of Ohio's other senator, Ben Wade, who would have become president if Johnson were impeached. Yet Wade voted for Powell.

Wade's life story offers good reasons why Powell's plans would have appealed to him. Wade grew up on the frontier and adopted the identity and manners of a frontiersman. In the Senate, Wade became chairman of the Committee on Territories, overseeing much of the exploration and settlement of the West. Wade also saw the West as votes, pro-Northern votes. The admission of Nevada as a state in 1864 had added three electoral votes to Lincoln's reelection margin. Wade saw Colorado and Nebraska as potential counterweights to Andrew Johnson's power. Wade waited until late one night when the Senate chamber was empty of opponents to bring Colorado statehood to a vote. But President Johnson vetoed Colorado statehood, and Wade couldn't rally the two-thirds vote needed to override Johnson's veto. If this Powell guy wanted to go explore Colorado, his findings might encourage settlement and statehood. Wade soon got a confirmation that he had made the right vote on Powell. That summer his niece, Nellie Wade, went to Colorado in a group headed by Schulyer Colfax, the speaker of the U.S. House of Representatives and then Grant's vice presidential running mate. In the mountains, the Colfax group ran into John Wesley Powell, and Colfax and Nellie Wade were very impressed by him.

Another exception to this scenario was Senator William Pitt Fessenden of Maine. Fessenden voted against impeachment, and also against Powell. Along with Trumbull, Fessenden was the other of two Senate regents of the Smithsonian Institution, so he should have been friendly to science and exploration. But Fessenden was also a staunch guardian of the federal budget, first as chairman of the Senate Finance Committee, then as Lincoln's secretary of the Treasury. More significantly, Fessenden had become famous as a New England chauvinist who snubbed the West. "Most western Republican senators," wrote Fessenden biographer Robert J. Cook, "regarded him not only as an inveterate promoter of New England interests but also as an opponent of their own rapidly developing section…. Personally, he had no great love for a region he had not visited since [1837] and which, in a sarcastic aside on the hyperbolic rhetoric of western politicians, he once referred to as 'the great West, the almighty West, the all-pervading West, the without-which-nothing-else-lives-in-the-world…West.'"[15]

If Powell ever imagined that having Jack Sumner on his crew would score a few political points with his distant relative Senator Charles Sumner, he was disappointed: Charles Sumner didn't bother to vote.

It was Powell's political astuteness that led him, in 1870, to give the name "Mount Trumbull" to a prominent mountain near the Grand Canyon. Powell knew how to thank his patrons. Powell also named a nearby mountain Mount Logan, after Illinois congressman John Logan. Powell was playing both sides—Trumbull and Logan were bitter political rivals. In 1866 Logan had run against Trumbull when Trumbull was seeking reelection. In 1868 Logan was one of the congressmen-lawyers who prosecuted the Johnson impeachment case in the Senate. Powell couldn't afford to annoy Logan. But he made sure that Trumbull's mountain was higher than Logan's mountain, by 163 feet.

Powell was politically astute enough that he should have known that there was another risk in giving the name of Trumbull to a mountain on the Arizona Strip, which the Mormons regarded as part of their homeland. The Mormons hated Lyman Trumbull. Trumbull was one of the leading congressional advocates of using federal power to suppress the Mormons. In mid-July 1869, as the Powell expedition was on the river in Utah, Senator Trumbull arrived in Salt Lake City and had an angry confrontation with Mormon leader Brigham Young, which was covered in newspapers around the country.

After his 1869 Colorado River expedition, Powell planned to further explore the region, especially southern Utah. To accomplish this, Powell would be heavily dependent on the cooperation of the Mormons, including Brigham Young. Was Powell ignorant of Mormon feelings against Lyman Trumbull? It seems more likely that his debt to Trumbull and his needs for future federal funding were so great that Powell was willing to risk annoying the Mormons.

NOTES

1. *Papers of Ulysses S. Grant*, Vol. 17, Jan. 1–Sept. 30 1867, ed. John Y. Simon (Carbondale: Southern Illinois University Press, 1967), 406.

2. Ibid., 407. Powell's 1868 letter and Grant's reply are included in the 1867 volume of Grant's papers, but not in the 1868 volume.

3. Powell letter to General Grant, April 2, 1868, in *Congressional Globe,* May 25, 1868, 2564.

4. General Grant order of April 3, 1868, in *Congressional Globe,* May 25, 1868.

5. Letter from Commissary General of Subsistence A. B. Eaton to Grant, April 6, 1868, in *Congressional Globe,* May 25, 1868.

6. Letter from Grant to Sherman, July 28, 1865, in *Papers of Ulysses S. Grant,* Vol. 15, 287.

7. Joseph Henry to Congressman James Garfield, April 21, 1868, in *Congressional Globe,* May 11, 1868, 3407–8.

8. Ralph J. Roske, *His Own Counsel: The Life and Times of Lyman Trumbull* (Reno: University of Nevada Press, 1979), 152.

9. *Congressional Globe,* May 25, 1868, 2564.

10. Ibid., 2563–66.

11. Ibid., 2564, 2565, 2564.

12. Ibid., 2563, 2564, 2564, 2564, 2566, 2565.

13. Ibid., 2565, 2566.

14. Ibid., 2563.

15. Robert J. Cook, *Civil War Senator: William Pitt Fessenden and the Fight to Save the American Republic* (Baton Rouge: Louisiana State University Press, 2011), 148–49.

PART IV

Naming Names

·24·

The *Maid of the Cañon*

ONE OF THE DETAILS of the 1869 Powell expedition that has received little attention from historians is the origin of the name of one of Powell's boats, the *Maid of the Cañon*. This inattention to the *Maid* began with John Wesley Powell himself, who in his 1875 book assigned it to the wrong crew. Powell said it was manned by William Hawkins and Andy Hall, and almost every author since has repeated this error. Eventually historian Marty Anderson pointed out that according to the journals and letters of the crewmembers, Hawkins and Hall rowed *Kitty Clyde's Sister* and it was really Walter Powell and George Bradley who crewed the *Maid of the Cañon*.[1] It is at least symbolic of Powell's neglect of his crewmembers that after spending three months with them on the river he could not even place his own brother in the correct boat.

Historians have supposed that the name *Maid of the Cañon* reflected the long maritime tradition of naming ships for females, which would be even more natural for a boat rowed by two young men. Yet a more elaborate explanation for this name is not hard to find.

In the late 1980s I attended the world premiere of an IMAX movie at the Science Museum of Minnesota in Saint Paul. This movie had been produced by the same creative team that had produced the *Grand Canyon* IMAX movie two or three years before. The new movie was about Niagara, and, like the Grand Canyon movie, it was created to be the sole movie in its own theater for tourists.[2]

For its Grand Canyon film the filmmakers had gone to considerable effort to make accurate replicas of Powell's boats and to take them down the river, which was the movie's central story and dramatic highlight. We see the *Maid of the Cañon* (although none of the boats have names painted on them) plunging through Lava Falls and other rapids, rowed by veteran dory guides in period costumes. Yet with other story elements the filmmakers were less devoted to

Powell's boats in Grand Canyon, second expedition. Photo courtesy of Grand Canyon National Park Museum Collection.

reality, freely inventing scenes for the sake of drama. A decade later the same writer-director would make a film about Zion for a theater just outside Zion National Park, and, as with his Grand Canyon and Niagara films he was lazy with the facts, especially with his romanticized scenes and stories about Native Americans.[3]

The Niagara film begins with a long sequence showing the Native American story of the "Maid of the Mist." Never mind that the Iroquois and other area tribes had been complaining for years that they'd never had any legend of a Maid of the Mist, that the whole stupid thing had been fabricated by whites, that it was insulting to Native Americans.

There are numerous versions of the Maid of the Mist story, and the most common is that a chief chose his daughter as a human sacrifice to a great god who resided in Niagara Falls, placed her in a canoe, and sent her over the falls to her death. In the artwork and postcards depicting the Maid, she is usually naked. Other versions say that her father felt guilty and joined her in going over the falls, or that her lover rescued her and that they still live behind the waterfall, behind its mist. In some versions, the sacrifice of a maiden is an annual event, performed at the first full moon of the spring.

Yet in the entire ethnological record, starting with meticulous Jesuit missionaries in the 1500s, there had never been any mention of such a legend or human sacrifice ritual. The story might have derived from a real event in the 1750s, when an Iroquois man was paddling his canoe across the river above the falls and got caught in the powerful currents and swept to his death. There could have been a legitimate Native American legend of a girl who attempted suicide by going over the falls but was rescued by the gods and taught how to appreciate life. As American and Canadian settlers retold and embellished this legend in the early 1800s it was subjected to their contradictory attitudes toward Indians—romanticizing and demonizing them—and the protagonist became a beautiful, innocent nature nymph who was cruelly destroyed by pagan barbarism, the same barbarism that justified taking away Indian lands for a Christian civilization. In 1996, after Native Americans had complained for decades, the company that runs the *Maid of the Mist* sightseeing boats finally agreed to cease telling the maid story.

The Maid of the Mist legend had become so well established by the mid-1800s that when in 1846 a seventy-two-foot steamer began crossing beneath Niagara Falls it was christened the *Maid of the Mist*. This boat was not intended as a sightseeing craft but as a ferry service to link New York City and Toronto. Two years later a new suspension bridge took away most of the ferry's business, so the owners, who had already noticed that many passengers came just to enjoy the falls, turned their ferry into a sightseeing boat, with a route that approached the Falls. The tour's popularity soon motivated the introduction of a more luxurious and powerful boat (though still a mere hundred horsepower) that toured eight times a day. Niagara Falls was fast becoming a major tourist attraction; in 1860 it attracted the Prince of Wales (the future King Edward VII), who rode on the *Maid*. He came partly because of the enormous publicity generated by Niagara's tightrope walkers. Yet by 1861, with the outbreak of the Civil War, the *Maid of the Mist* had gone bankrupt. Its owners sold it at auction, to be turned into a ferry on the St. Lawrence River. But there was a big problem. The only way to deliver the *Maid* to its new owners was to run the most monstrous whitewater in America.

Three miles below Niagara Falls, in a deep gorge, is a set of rapids called Whirlpool Rapids, with a drop of fifty feet; three miles below that is Lower Rapids, with a drop of nearly fifty feet. The largest drop in the Grand Canyon is "only" thirty feet. Through the Niagara Gorge flows the volume and power of the Great Lakes, which hold one-fifth of all the fresh water on Earth.

On June 6, 1861, the *Maid* ran it at 250,000 cubic feet per second, a level seen on the Colorado River only during extreme spring floods. In the century and a half since the *Maid*'s run, only a few people have attempted it, and fewer have survived. In 1883 Captain Matthew Webb, who had successfully swum the English Channel, tried to swim Niagara Gorge with thousands of people watching from above—four days later his body was found seven miles down-river. Undeterred, James Scott, a fisherman who had grown up on the banks of the Niagara and imagined he was its master, tried to swim the Gorge, and he, too, drowned. In 1887 a man made it through in a barrel, and a few other craft have made it through, including a motorboat. In 1982 a team of kayakers made a first descent at 120,000 cubic feet per second, and it was filmed for the TV series *American Sportsman*. In 1976 there was a brief attempt at commercial rafting, which ended on its twelfth run when four people drowned.

Back in 1861 the *Maid*'s owners gave its three-man crew a $500 incentive to risk their lives. Captain Joel Robinson was up to the challenge and steered the *Maid* through with only modest damage, including a toppled smokestack. After repairs, the *Maid* served the Isle of Orleans on the St. Lawrence River for several years, went on to other jobs, and was retired by 1902. A new *Maid of the Mist* began its career in 1885, the first of several. Since no boat could make it upriver through Niagara Gorge, all the *Maids* were built along shore near the falls or built on the rim above and lowered down the cliffs by cranes and cables.

For many viewers, including me, the highlight of the Niagara IMAX movie was the *Maid of the Mist* running the Niagara Gorge. As with the Powell boats, the filmmakers went to considerable expense and trouble to make a replica of the 1861 *Maid* and to run it down the Niagara River, a scene that allowed no retakes. We see the *Maid of the Mist* rocking through the waves, twenty-foot-tall waves crashing over its upper deck and inundating its main deck. We see the smokestack breaking off, on cue, although the IMAX boat was diesel-powered and the smokestack and paddlewheel casing were for show. The scene reminded me of watching the *Maid of the Cañon* rocking its way through Lava Falls in the *Grand Canyon* movie. And it seemed to me that the narrated voice of Captain Robinson was done by the same guy who had done the voice of Major Powell in the other movie.

The 1861 run was terrifying for its crew, as the boat rocked and trembled and groaned so violently that they feared it would capsize or be torn apart. Robinson and mechanic James McIntyre gripped the wheel as hard as they could, hoping to steer down the inside curve of the rapids, but the current shot them into the most violent wave train. At one point McIntyre was knocked down and might have been swept overboard except for Robinson's boot holding him down.

Niagara historian Pierre Berton summarized it: "Robinson never really recovered his sangfroid. His wife declared that he 'was twenty years older when he came home that day than when he went out.' He sank wearily into his chair, determined to abandon the river forever. In his neighbor's words, 'his manner and appearance were changed…. He had been borne, as it were, in the arms of a power so mighty that its impress was stamped on his features and on his mind. Through a slightly opened door he had seen a vision which awed and subdued him.'"[4]

The *Maid*'s 1861 run got considerable publicity. On June 22, 1861, the national magazine *Harper's Weekly,* amid all its urgent Civil War news, ran an illustration of the *Maid of the Mist* shooting the rapids. On June 9 the *New York Times* gushed about the attempt:

> The idea that anything made of wood could outlive a voyage down those terrible rapids, was regarded absurd. The prospect of its being tried, however, drew at least three or four hundred people to the banks of the river…. Readers know how Niagara looks just under, and just below the bridge. The giant offspring of four lakes writhes like a chained monster…ominous, voracious, deadly…. The water tortured into foam dashes down the stair-case of rocks…. As she passed under the bridge, the crowd rushed to the other side and trembled for the safety of the daring crew…. Again and again she shot overhead in foam, and again and again, as she all but disappeared, it was thought that the river had claimed its own. But the Maid was native to the cataract and bore a charmed life.

The *Maid*'s triumph even got mentioned in the July 1861 edition of *Illinois Teacher,* the professional journal of school teachers in Illinois, which included John Wesley Powell and Walter Powell. Amid news items that were otherwise entirely about education matters, the editor noted that the *Maid* had "gone safely over the fearful Rapids and the dreaded Whirlpool…. No craft of any sort has ever before ventured on this perilous route. The bold navigator was Mr. Robinson, previously famous for daring feats on the river." Three pages later an article about the annual meeting of the Illinois Natural History Society noted that Dr. George Vasey—for whom Powell later named a Grand Canyon spring "Vasey's Paradise"—had donated 1,800 Illinois botanical specimens to their museum, and that the society had been required to elect a new trustee "in place of J. W. Powell, of Wheaton, who has gone to the war."[5]

Even before the tightrope walkers, Niagara Falls had defined itself as a place of sensational stunts. It began grotesquely in 1827 when local hotel owners took an old schooner, placed bears and bison and other wildlife on it, and sent it down the river and over the falls, with an estimated 10,000 people watching. Tightrope walking and going over the falls in a barrel might require skill and nerve but they also fit right in with the mummies and murder-and-vice wax museums that soon defined Niagara as a tacky carnival. Newspaper editors of 1861 greeted the *Maid*'s feat as another sensation.

It's highly likely, then, that John Wesley Powell and his men had heard of the *Maid of the Mist* and its triumph in the rapids. Powell was born only sixty-five miles from Niagara Falls, in Mount Morris, New York, in 1834, only seven years after the zoo schooner stunt, which was the sort of story that would fascinate a young boy. The Powell family left New York when John was four, and we don't know that he ever saw Niagara Falls. In 1858 he began three years of teaching public school in the Illinois town of Hennepin, named for French explorer Louis Hennepin, whose 1683 book had made Niagara Falls famous. Yet John's brother Walter and George Bradley, who would row the *Maid,* had no geographical connection with Niagara Falls: Walter was born in Ohio and Bradley on the Massachusetts coast. Historians have assumed that the boats were named by the men who rowed them, though we don't know this for sure about the *Maid.* Bradley is believed to have spent some time at sea (though we know no details), where he could have picked up some appreciation for ships and sailing skills. Yet for anyone planning a journey down a dangerous whitewater river, the triumph of the *Maid of the Mist* would have made it a good omen. In the deep insecurity of life at sea, sailors have always craved good omens and mascots. In seeking information about the unknown Colorado River and its canyons, Powell was being warned they might hold Niagara-scale waterfalls or monster whirlpools that would kill him. Powell knew of very few precedents for running whitewater rivers; what he did know was mostly from a few mountain men in canoes, who sometimes didn't know what they were getting into. The crew of the *Maid of the Mist* had accomplished the greatest feat of river running in human history, as far as anyone could recall. For Powell and his men, invoking the *Maid of the Mist* was invoking river running courage, skill, and triumph.

The legend of Niagara's Indian maid was only one of numerous American tales involving Indian maids, if perhaps the most dramatic one. It is often hard to trace the origins of these tales. Some could have derived from genuine Native American stories, based either on real events or on the natives' own legends. But many tales clearly originated from the American imagination latching onto Native Americans as raw material, in the same way it might use George

Washington or old European tales to spin new American stories. Of course, for Americans, Native Americans were not safely remote Hans Christian Andersen fantasy figures but a troubling reality, both appealing and frightening, and American tales about Indians were often loaded with national psychology and agendas.

The most common Indian maid story was the lover's leap story, of which there were many variations. An Indian maid refuses a forced marriage to someone she disdains, perhaps because she loves someone else, and leaps to her death. Sometimes she falsely believes her lover is dead and can't bear to live without him. Sometimes she is spurned for another woman. Sometimes two lovers come from enemy families or tribes, and they leap together. Star-crossed lovers are a universally appealing theme, from *Romeo and Juliet* to Goethe's *Werther* to *West Side Story* to *Titanic*. Some versions of the Niagara story are lover's leap stories. Mark Twain said in *Life on the Mississippi* that there were fifty named lover's leaps along the Mississippi River, whose upper half holds a lot of limestone cliffs. He had grown up below one of the most famous lover's leaps, a cliff that towers over Hannibal, Missouri. Efforts to trace the origins of the Hannibal Lover's Leap lead to confusion, but one finger points at Twain's own brother Orion Clemens, who edited the town newspaper and published a local lover's leap story in 1840.

Another famous lover's leap is at one of Illinois's most popular tourist attractions, Starved Rock State Park. This is only thirty-four miles upstream from Hennepin, where John Wesley Powell taught school. In the summer of 1858 Powell launched a skiff on the Illinois River at the town of Ottawa, a few miles upstream from Starved Rock, and rowed right under Lover's Leap and 273 miles to the river's junction with the Mississippi. His trip should have stoked his imagination about river explorers, for he was following the 1680 journey down the Illinois of Louis Hennepin, and the 1673 journey of Jacques Marquette and Louis Jolliet up the Illinois. When the French began exploring midwestern rivers they were hoping that the Mississippi would turn out to be the route to the Orient, the river that emptied into the Gulf of California, the Colorado River.

Starved Rock is one of the few places in the Midwest where you can readily imagine yourself to be in old Glen Canyon or some other Utah sandstone canyon. For several miles along the Illinois River a sandstone layer, 425 million years old, outcrops and forms cliffs. Creeks dropping steeply from the plateau above have carved out eighteen side canyons—not quite slot canyons but still narrow and sinuous, full of waterfalls, waterslides, pools, streams, overhangs, ledges, moss, wildflowers, and eerie green light filtered through the trees. A botanist, like George Vasey, would not mistake it for Utah, but for Chicagoans these grottoes seem like an enchanted world. Starved Rock became so popular with tourists that in 1891 an entrepreneur built a three-story hotel there and in the 1930s the Civilian Conservation Corps built a grand lodge worthy of the great Western national parks; by the year 2000 Starved Rock was receiving 2 million visitors annually, nearly half the number who annually visit Grand Canyon National Park.

Powell became fascinated by the geology of the area. His secretary, M. D. Lincoln, recalled, "The town of Hennepin standing on a bluff of the Illinois River, was of itself a study. The underlying country for miles around was a deep accumulation of drift-like material.... During the winter Powell became greatly interested in this body of drift material and the peculiar characteristics of the country, and early in the spring he commenced a more thorough examination of it and the adjacent county of La Salle [home of Starved Rock]. He devoted several weeks to this work, up and down the valley of the Illinois."[6] Powell's fascination with the grottoes of Starved Rock could have fueled his fascination with the southwestern canyons he was hearing about.

The name "Starved Rock" derives from the 1760s, when area Native American tribes were warring with one another; one group took refuge atop a 125-foot-tall butte beside the river, where their enemies surrounded them and starved them to death. At least, that's the legend, another Native American legend that has gotten bungled by whites. Right next to the Starved Rock butte is Lover's Leap, from which a heartbroken Indian maid threw herself. Once again, there's more than one version, and their origins are hard to trace.

Did the legend of the Starved Rock Indian maid reinforce the imagery and the appeal of "the maid of the canyon"? Starved Rock historian Mark Walczynski cautions us that Powell might not have known this story. In researching the two books he wrote about the park, Walczynski didn't find this story mentioned in documents until the late 1890s. The name "Lover's Leap" arose at about this time, as tourism promoters were changing old pioneer names to more picturesque names such as Eagle Cliff. Then again, Lover's Leap was originally Maiden Rock, which suggests it already bore its Indian maid legend, if only in oral tradition. I found it surprising that someone might be inventing a new lover's leap legend as late as 1900: Most Indian lover's leaps seem to have arisen in pioneer days, when Indians were more of a living presence, and by 1900 this fashion seems to have passed. The best evidence for this is the Grand Canyon, the best landscape in America for lovers to leap in, but there is no lover's leap there. The Santa Fe Railway was skilled at exploiting Indian lore to charm tourists, but even they did not affix a lover's leap to the canyon rim. Yet Walczynski says that a late invention of the legend would be consistent with the other Indian romanticizing that was going on at Starved Rock at that time.[7]

Considering the tangled and vague origins of so many Indian legends, it seems appropriate that we might never know for sure the origins of the name *Maid of the Cañon.*

When I asked Walczynski why Powell started his river trip at Ottawa and not his own Hennepin, which was on the Illinois River, he offered an important new insight into Powell. We've never known where Powell got his desire to run a major whitewater river like the Colorado. Powell's 1850s rowing trips on the Mississippi and Ohio Rivers suggested he was fascinated by river adventure, but a Mississippi River swarming with steamboats was a different world from the world of the Colorado. Walczynski says that by starting at Ottawa, Powell was seeking out whitewater:

> The Illinois River is really two rivers; a new river that is only about 14,000 years old, and an old river, one that is approximately 2 million years old…. The river flows nearly due west, and then makes a 90 degree turn toward the south, just above Hennepin…. Unlike the lethargic and slow moving Illinois River below the big bend, the upper Illinois River is a swifter flowing stream, shallow, rocky, and with several sets of rapids especially in the Starved Rock area. The most challenging part of the river is…about three miles below Starved Rock…. In fact the reason why the town of Hennepin was located where it was, is because it was below the rapids of the upper Illinois…. In 1858, and because of the rapids, only small boats, canoes, and the like could navigate the Illinois River between Starved Rock and Ottawa. Only during times of high water could a large boat travel as far upstream as Ottawa. Hennepin for a decade or two was the primary port on the Illinois River above Peoria.[8]

There could have been practical reasons why Powell chose Ottawa as a put-in. He needed to buy a boat, and Ottawa, as the largest nearby city, located on the canal system that bypassed the river rapids, probably had plenty of boats. But surely Hennepin, too, had boats. It appears that ten years before he headed west, Powell was already seeking out whitewater, and for the sheer adventure of it.

NOTES

1. Marty Anderson, Marty Anderson Collection, Special Collections, Cline Library, Northern Arizona University, Flagstaff.

2. Kieth Merrill [producer and director], *Grand Canyon: The Hidden Secrets* (Destination Cinema, United States, 1984); Kieth Merrill [director] and Nicholas J. Gray and Richard W. James [producers], *Niagara: Miracles, Myths and Magic* (Destination Cinema, United States, 1986).

3. Kieth Merrill [director], *Zion Canyon: Treasure of the Gods* (World Cinemax Productions, United States, 1996).

4. Pierre Berton, *Niagara: A History of the Falls* (Albany, NY: SUNY Press, 1992), 160.

5. *Illinois Teacher* 7, no. 7 (July 1861): 259, 262. The statement that Powell was "of Wheaton" meant that it was his family home.

6. M. D. Lincoln, "John Wesley Powell," *Open Court* 16 (December 1902): 715.

7. Mark Walczynski, personal communication, e-mails, 2015.

8. Ibid.

· 25 ·

Lodore

The Cataract strong
Then plunges along,
Striking and raging,
As if a war waging.

—Robert Southey, "The Cataract of Lodore."[1]

WHEN JOHN WESLEY POWELL descended the Green River in 1869, he named one Utah canyon the Canyon of Lodore. Today, historians attribute this name to a famous poem, "The Cataract of Lodore," written in 1820 by English poet Robert Southey. Yet neither Powell nor his crewmembers ever mentioned Southey or his poem. This identification did not arise until four decades later, in Frederick Dellenbaugh's 1908 account of the second Powell expedition, *A Canyon Voyage.*[2] Dellenbaugh did have some credibility: he had journeyed through the Canyon of Lodore with Powell and could have heard the story from him. On the other hand, a few years before publication of *A Canyon Voyage,* Dellenbaugh had published another river history book, *The Romance of the Colorado River,* and he'd made no mention of Southey. None of the diaries or letters of the second expedition's crew, who approached and ran Lodore with considerable worry and comment, made any mention of Southey.[3]

There is another possibility: in 1835 Mary Shelley, the author of *Frankenstein,* published a novel titled *Lodore,* which became very popular in America.

As for who affixed the name "Lodore," Dellenbaugh said only that it came "at the suggestion of one of the men."[4] In this he was following Powell, who, in both the letter he wrote on June 18, 1869, to the *Chicago Tribune* and in his book years later, said only that it was one of the men. Nor did any of the other crewmembers, in their diaries and letters, name anyone as the source. It was only in 1947 that the name of Andy Hall became attached to this story.

William Culp Darrah was researching his Powell biography, *Powell of the Colorado,* and presented many of the trip diaries and letters in a special volume of the *Utah Historical Quarterly.* In his brief biographical sketch of Hall, Darrah wrote, "He seems to have had some knowledge of English literature. It was Andy who suggested the name 'Lodore' after the poem by Robert Southey."[5] Four years later in his Powell biography Darrah wrote, "Andy surprised the Major with a display of learning by suggesting that the canyon be named Lodore after the waterfall...in Southey's poem."[6] Darrah offered no source for this claim, and today no one knows any source for it. Two years later Wallace Stegner, in his Powell biography, adopted Darrah's claim and, with a bit of his novelist's flair, made it more specific: "[The] rapids [were] so furious that Andy Hall, remembering some schoolboy lesson, was led to exclaim, 'Oh, how the waters come down at Lodore!' They named it the canyon of Lodore."[7] Subsequent historians have repeated Darrah's claim as a fact.

Perhaps Darrah, not satisfied with "one of the men," selected Hall at random. Or perhaps he selected Hall because Southey's poem was popular with kids and Hall was the youngest crewmember. Another possible fit is that the poem was from Great Britain and Hall was born in Scotland—but it does not appear that Darrah was aware of Hall's birthplace at the time he wrote his 1947 biographical profile.

Historian Dock Marston seemed hesitant about Darrah's claim that Hall was the source of the name "Lodore." Marston had seen Andy Hall's original letters, loaded with misspellings and awkwardness that suggested Hall was barely literate, and Marston might have wondered if Hall would be familiar with a long-dead English poet. Also, Marston recognized that Darrah had been dishonest in claiming he had published Hall's letters accurately. In 1960, corresponding with Andy Hall's niece, Martha Stetson (who was then still living in the longtime Hall hometown of Kewanee, Illinois), Marston asked her, "Do you have any idea where Andy got his knowledge of English poetry? He is credited with being the source of the name CANYON OF LODORE on the Green River which is named for the poem by Southey."[8] Stetson replied that the source might have been her mother (Hall's sister): "I wouldn't know where my uncle gained his knowledge of English poetry unless from my mother as she was an avid reader and told of reading aloud to the family in the evenings. She would often recite poetry to us."[9]

Southey's poem was popular with children because of its Dr. Seuss–like rhythm and wordplay. Indeed, the poem is still alive: in 1991 an American publisher brought it out as a picture book for kids.

And shocking and rocking…
And hitting and splitting…
And rattling and battling,
And shaking and quaking,
And pouring and roaring,
And waving and raving,
And tossing and crossing,
And flowing and going,
And running and stunning.[10]

Like Andy Hall and most of Powell's crew, Jack Sumner had never been to college, but he clearly recognized that the name "Lodore" came from an old and foreign literary source, and in his journal on June 20, 1869, he disapproved: "It has been named Ladore Canyon by the Professor, but the idea of diving into musty trash to find names for new discoveries on a new continent is un-American, to say the least."[11] At least Sumner's comment eliminates him as the source for the name. But his "musty trash" comment could apply to either Southey's poem or Shelley's novel.

Robert Southey was one of the most famous poets of his time. Along with William Wordsworth and Samuel Taylor Coleridge, Southey was a Lake District poet who thrived at the peak of Romanticism and its celebration of nature. For the Romantics, the highest goal was "the sublime," landscapes where nature showed its greatest powers and hushed humans into awe. Cataracts and waterfalls were among the foremost abodes of the sublime; in early nineteenth-century America, before Americans had discovered their Western wonders, their ultimate locale for the sublime was Niagara Falls. Not far from Southey's home at Keswick was a waterfall named Lodore. Wordsworth visited Lodore in his poem "An Evening Walk": "And listens to the roar/ that stuns the tremulous cliffs of high Lodore."[12] Coleridge spoke of the falls as "The Precipitation of the fallen angels from Heaven, Flight and Confusion and Distraction but all harmonized into one majestic Thing."[13] It's likely Powell was aware of Southey for another reason: Southey had written a major biography of John Wesley, the religious leader for whom Powell was named, a book controversial among Methodists, especially Methodist preachers like Powell's father.

It's also likely that Powell was aware of Mary Shelley's novel *Lodore,* part of which was set in Illinois, Powell's home state. It was Andy Hall's home state too.

Mary Shelley was born into the center of the intellectual world of the Enlightenment and Romanticism. Her mother was Mary Wollstonecraft, whose

Powell boat (second expedition) in Canyon of Lodore. Photo courtesy of Grand Canyon National Park Museum Collection.

1792 book *A Vindication of the Rights of Women* was a pioneering feminist manifesto, adding women's rights to the intense discussions of human rights going on in the wake of the American and French revolutions. Mary's father was William Godwin, whose 1793 book *An Inquiry Concerning Political Justice,* advocating a rational, democratic, and egalitarian society, made him a leading social reformer. Mary's husband was Percy Bysshe Shelley, one of the demigods of Romanticism. This intense milieu made it possible for the nineteen-year-old Mary to create an enduring modern myth, *Frankenstein,* that dealt with the dreams and nightmares of a rational age.

Lodore, too, deals with the dreams, contradictions, and disappointments of the Enlightenment and Romanticism, especially the Rousseauian ideal of the natural person. Rousseau held that everything that was wrong with humans was a result of the corrupting influences of human civilization, and that humans who were immersed in nature would be naturally good and happy. Rousseau inspired both loyalty and loathing, and not just among intellectuals. When George Howland Sr. of New Bedford had acquired a used whaling ship named *Rousseau* in 1834, the year before Mary Shelley published *Lodore,* he immediately had its masthead referencing the "French infidel" ripped off and thrown in the mud, and he would have effaced its name if he were not under the mistaken impression that he could not legally change a ship's name. So he settled for mispronouncing the name as "Russ-O" for the rest of his life, and he hated to acknowledge it was one of his most profitable ships. You could say that Oramel and Seneca Howland were conducting their own experiment on the sublimity of nature, and cataracts in particular, which turned out badly when they wrecked their *No Name* in the Canyon of Lodore.

Mary Shelley sets up her literary Rousseauian experiment by having Lord Lodore, unhappy in his marriage, exile himself from England to the American wilderness, where he raises his little girl Ethel immersed in nature. As a young woman Ethel returns to Europe, and as a natural woman she confronts the dysfunctions of civilization. Yet when Shelley wrote *Lodore* in the early 1830s it was clear that the Rousseauian ideal had some serious flaws, and Shelley also explores its shortcomings. This wasn't just an abstract story, for in her personal life she had lived out the shortcomings of Romanticism's ideals; she and Percy had lived in poverty and fled from creditors, just as Ethel and her husband do in *Lodore.*

Mary Shelley has Lord Lodore go to Illinois in 1818; this choice reflects the lively discussion in England that year when English writer Morris Birkbeck published two books, *Letters from Illinois* and *Notes on a Journey to America,* describing his idyllic life in a cabin in the woods, plucking delicious wild grapes and enjoying the freedom and equality of a republic. In 1816 Birkbeck helped establish a utopian settlement in southern Illinois, including the town of Albion, which drew hundreds of English settlers. Birkbeck's books drew a strong rebuttal from William Corbett in *A Year's Residence in the United States of America,* published in 1819, which accused Birkbeck of being a wealthy intellectual lazily living in a cabin lined with books and fancy ideas, while the average American pioneer faced struggle and poverty. In 1821 Francis Wright weighed in on Illinois with *Views of Society and Manners in America,* defending the Rousseauian virtues of Birkbeck's colony. Wright went on to found a utopian community, Nashoba, in Tennessee in 1826. The previous year Englishman Robert Owen founded the utopian community of New Harmony in Indiana, only twenty miles from Albion. Years before, Southey and Coleridge had discussed founding a utopian town, based on the ideals of Mary Shelley's father William Godwin, in Pennsylvania. To the European Romantic imagination, America was the proving ground for the Rousseauian ideal. Birkbeck did play an important role in Illinois history, for in 1824 Illinois voted on whether to continue being a slavery-free state, and Birkbeck, under the pen name Jonathan Freeman, campaigned energetically against slavery. John Wesley Powell, as an Illinois abolitionist, probably knew this history.

In selecting the name "Lodore" for her novel and lead characters, Mary Shelley was invoking Romanticism's fascination with waterfalls and mountain heights as the epitome of the sublime. Shelley has Lord Lodore visit Niagara Falls: "He stood watching that vast and celebrated cataract, whose everlasting and impetuous flow mirrored the dauntless but rash energy of his own soul." Shelley would have been familiar with the Lodore waterfall, and not just from literary sources. In 1805 Coleridge had written to Shelley's father about the beauty of the falls, and in 1811 Percy Bysshe Shelley made a pilgrimage to visit Southey and saw the falls. Before he left England, Lord Lodore sought out the sublime: "He was charmed with the scenery and solitude.... Amidst romantic mountains, and in immediate vicinity to a cataract of the Wye...he passed his day, loitering beside waterfalls, clambering the steep mountains, or making longer excursions on horseback, always directing his course away from high roads or towns."[14] The foolishness and dangers of towns and human society are ultimately proven when Lodore leaves his Illinois idyll and has his English aristocratic code of honor reawakened when he gets into a duel and is killed.

When Ethel gets back to England she is dazed by the smoke, noise, and traffic of London, and even more by the pretensions, scheming, and unkindness

of aristocratic society. She repeatedly longs for the "wilds of Illinois—the sim-
plest abode, food, and attire, were all I knew of human refinements, and I was
satisfied."[15]

While her aunt worries about so improper an enjoyment, Ethel the natural
woman goes boating on a river:

> Boating was a pleasure that she enjoyed almost more than any other.…
> The river sped swiftly on, calm and free. There is always life in a
> stream, of which a lake is frequently deprived, when sleeping beneath
> a windless sky. A river pursues for ever its course, accomplishing the
> task its Creator has imposed, and its waters are forever changing while
> they seem the same. It was a balmy summer evening; the air seemed to
> brood over the earth, warming and nourishing it.… The equal splash
> of the oar, or its dripping when suspended, the clear reflection of tree
> and lawn in the river, the very color of the stream, stolen as it was
> from heaven itself.… Every sound and every appearance was beauti-
> ful, harmonious, and soothing. Ethel's soul was at peace; grateful to
> Heaven, and satisfied with everything around her.[16]

Yet as the financial troubles of Ethel's new husband worsen, Ethel's innocence isn't quite so charming. Of her Rousseauian expectations about human
kindness, her husband upbraids her: "My little wild American, this is a philosophy for the back-woods only."[17] Even as Shelley observes the flaws of society,
she leaves the Rousseauian ideal looking painfully naïve. In the real Illinois
story, Morris Birkbeck drowned crossing the Fox River while returning from a
visit with Robert Owen in New Harmony in 1825.

Ethel was John Wesley Powell's kind of heroine, and he himself could have
been nicknamed Lodore for containing the soul of cataracts. Yet is it likely that
Powell was familiar with Shelley's *Lodore*?

We get some good glimpses of Powell's reading habits in the diaries of his
crewmembers. Powell himself mentioned "an illustrated copy of Shakespeare
which tumbles around the camp" on the first expedition.[18] His second expedition crew was much better educated than the first and included some teachers;
Powell brought along a good selection of novels and poetry and often read
them aloud over the campfire. Sir Walter Scott provided three books, including
the knightly romance *Marmion,* which Powell shared aloud while in Lodore
Canyon. He also brought Longfellow's *Hiawatha,* Whittier's poetry, and Emer-
son's essays. He even read on the river, as reported by John F. Steward: "The
day being fine, the boats were lashed together, and the Major, in the middle

one, read his favorite selections from Scott."[19] Powell's cousin Walter Clement Powell reported, "The Maj. read Whittier till 9 o'clock, then we all turned in."[20]

Powell's college education came at a time when the study of literature often consisted of little outside the Greek and Latin classics. "Modern" novelists like Mary Shelley were unlikely to show up on a college curriculum. But Powell had an intense curiosity, which is what drove him down the Colorado River; in natural history he was largely self-educated, and it's likely that he also educated himself in the literature of the day. Powell did attend two colleges in Illinois in the 1850s and then started teaching at Illinois Wesleyan University in the 1860s. Powell's mentors and colleagues included people of wide interests and learning. In literature there were hardly any novels that featured Illinois, so a novel set in Illinois and written by a world-famous author would have been a source of great curiosity, if not pride. For Powell, who was intensely interested in the unfolding world of science, Mary Shelley could have held special interest, for her *Frankenstein* was already considered an important statement on the culture of science. Powell's political sympathies would have made him aware of, and perhaps sympathetic with, the names of Godwin and Wollstonecraft. Powell's interest in nature would have made him aware of the poetry of Percy Bysshe Shelley. All of this makes it quite likely that Powell was familiar with Mary Shelley's *Lodore*.

Powell's own writings, which can be quite poetic, make it clear that he was absorbing the literary culture of his time, including Romanticism's style and view of nature. Much of his rhetoric is classic Romanticism. His most famous lines about starting down "the Great Unknown" ring with an invocation of the sublime, of humans being tiny, threatened, and awed amid nature's grandeur: "We are three quarters of a mile in the depths of the earth, and the great river shrinks into insignificance as it dashes its angry waves against the walls and cliffs that rise to the world above; the waves are but puny ripples, and we but pigmies, running up and down the sands or lost among the boulders." In the Grand Canyon Powell had found literary raw materials that vastly outdid the Lodore waterfall and the other English landscapes used by Southey and his colleagues. Powell seems to imitate the Romantic's strategy of finding correspondences between the Earthly realm and more spiritual realities: "The clouds are children of the heavens, and when they play among the rocks they lift them to the region above." No Romantic landscape would be complete without ruins, and fortunately Powell has Ancestral Puebloan ruins, however humble beside English castles, to add to his images. The only major ingredient missing from Powell's writing is an invocation of fairyland, the Romantic's habit of filling nature with enchantment stories, with giants' castles and fairies' gardens. As a geologist and as a river runner struggling for survival, Powell was content to see real rocks and dangerous waves. Yet Powell does close his book with some grand Romantic flourishes, comparing the Grand Canyon with a symphony, and concluding that in the canyon "a concept of sublimity can be obtained never again to be equaled on the hither side of Paradise."[21]

If one of Powell's men suggested the name "Lodore," it is much more likely he was thinking of the Southey poem, known even to children, than the Shelley novel. Powell's first crew were smart men, but smart more with regard to mountains than to philosophical novels. Then again, Andy Hall was from Illinois and his sister loved to read aloud to the family, so a novel set in Illinois might have stirred her interest. Whatever the origin, Powell likely recognized that the name "Lodore" had a double association with nature's grandeur, and this doubly encouraged him to adopt the name. Since Powell adopted the name before Disaster Falls, perhaps Shelley's *Lodore* invoked Ethel's blissful harmony with nature's beauty, but after Disaster Falls it might have seemed more evocative of Lord Lodore's foolish pride and death and Ethel's loss of Rousseauian innocence. After Oramel and Seneca Howland wrecked their boat, George Howland Sr., who had wrecked numerous whaling ships or had them disappear without a trace, might have said, "I could have warned you about those foolish Rousseau ideas." John Wesley Powell was in the grip of a life-and-death confrontation between the dreams of humans and the realities of nature, and he left imprinted on remote canyon walls the efforts of European intellectuals to decide if nature was the mirror of heaven or a Frankenstein monster.

NOTES

1. Robert Southey, *Poems of Robert Southey* (London: Oxford University Press, 1909), 348.
2. Frederick Dellenbaugh, *A Canyon Voyage: The Narrative of the Second Powell Expedition* (1908; repr. Tucson: University of Arizona Press, 1988), 32. Page references to 1988 ed.
3. Frederick Dellenbaugh, *The Romance of the Colorado River* (New York: G. P. Putnam's Sons, 1902).
4. Ibid., 196.
5. Darrah, *Utah Historical Quarterly* 15 (1947): 107.
6. Darrah, *Powell of the Colorado*, 124.
7. Stegner, *Beyond the Hundredth Meridian*, 62.
8. Marston to Stetson, Nov. 23, 1960, Andy Hall file, Marston Collection.
9. Stetson to Marston, Dec. 11, 1960, Andy Hall file, Marston Collection.
10. Southey, *Poems of Robert Southey*.
11. Quoted in Ghiglieri, *First Through the Grand Canyon*, 135.

12. William Wordsworth, "An Evening Walk," *The Poems,* Vol. 1 (1793; repr. London: Penguin Books, 1977), 77. Page references to 1977 ed.

13. Quoted in Penelope Hughes-Hallett, *The Wordsworths and the Lakes: Home at Grasmere* (London: Collins and Brown, 1993), 38.

14. Mary Shelley, *Lodore* (1835; repr. Peterborough, Ont.: Broadview Literary Texts, 1997), 147, 92. Page references to 1997 ed.

15. Ibid., 282.

16. Ibid., 236.

17. Ibid., 337.

18. Powell, *Exploration,* 123.

19. John F. Steward, "Journal of John F. Steward," *Utah Historical Quarterly* 16–17 (1948–49): 189.

20. Walter Clement Powell, "Journal of Walter Clement Powell," *Utah Historical Quarterly* 16–17 (1948–49): 313.

21. Powell, *Exploration,* 247, 256, 397.

PART V

The End of the Adventure

·26·

Hats Off to Bishop Leithead

M OST OF OUR UNDERSTANDING of the Powell expedition comes from the diaries and letters written by the participants. Yet there was one firsthand account that was written by someone not on the expedition, someone who encountered it at its end, an account long unnoticed by historians.

Shortly after Powell passed the Grand Wash Cliffs, which marked the end of the Grand Canyon, he came to the mouth of the Virgin River and found three men and a boy fishing with nets. One of these men was Joseph Asay, who with his wife and three sons had built a cabin near the Colorado River to supply fish to the Mormon colony centered in the town of St. Thomas about twenty miles up the Virgin River, where the Virgin was joined by the Muddy River. St. Thomas was founded in 1865 as part of Brigham Young's effort to set up a cotton-growing colony; in the 1930s, with the completion of Hoover Dam, St. Thomas was swallowed by the spreading waters of Lake Mead, only to reemerge around 2000, a ghost town of foundations. For the Asay family the fishing that day had proved to be excellent, and they took Powell and his men up to their cabin and cooked them a feast of fish, which the long-hungry men greatly appreciated.

Powell had recognized that St. Thomas would be the first town he would encounter after the Grand Canyon, so he arranged to have his mail sent there. The last chance Powell had had, more than two months previously, to receive or send mail was at the Uinta Indian Agency, so he had relied on the Utah superintendent of Indian Affairs, Colonel Frederick H. Head, to send his mail to St. Thomas. Given the tensions between Mormons and outsiders, Powell might have trusted his mail to a Wisconsin lawyer like Head more than to local authorities, but the Mormons strongly distrusted Head; a few years previously, during Utah's Black Hawk War, a Mormon militia had threatened to kill Head for siding with the Indians over the white settlers.

The fishermen arranged to send an Indian to town, and George Bradley wrote a letter to take along: "I wrote a line and sent it to Lucy to assure Mother I was all-right, but I was so intoxicated with joy at getting through so soon and so well that I don't know what I wrote to her."[1]

The St. Thomas postmaster was James Leithead, who was also the LDS bishop in charge of the colony and the owner of a flour mill and cotton gin. Leithead got Andrew S. Gibbons and headed down to the river to meet Powell. Gibbons was the right person to take along, for he had more experience with the Colorado River than almost any other Mormon. In 1863 Gibbons had accompanied Jacob Hamblin on an exploratory expedition that located a crossing of the Colorado River just below the Grand Canyon. Gibbons helped find the best location for a road and helped build a raft to cross the river and go downstream a bit. Seven years after Powell, the Mormons set up a ferry at this site, operated by Harrison Pearce. Ten months before Powell came along, Leithead and Gibbons built a fourteen-foot boat, and Gibbons, along with Octavius Gass, one of the leaders of nearby Callville (where James White came ashore), took it hundreds of miles down the Colorado River to Yuma, from which they went overland to Tucson to represent the Mormons in the Arizona state legislature. Gibbons and Gass had an alarming time getting through the rapids of Black Canyon, with Gass clinging to the railing of the boat and yelling at Gibbons to keep it straight. It didn't help that, from a fear of Indian attack, they tried to keep their boat in the middle of the river.

Later in life Leithead wrote a brief memoir.[2] He must have been impressed by his meeting with John Wesley Powell, for Leithead devoted about 10 percent of his memoir to the final night of the Powell expedition.

Leithead's account closed with a complaint that sounds rather familiar. Though Leithead had known Powell for only a day, he lodged the same complaint that many of Powell's boatmen would make: that Powell had taken their loyal services and given no gratitude in return. Or worse, that he had taken the truth and replaced it with a self-aggrandizing legend, in this case the story that Mormon leader Brigham Young was so worried about Powell that he put his outposts on alert for him. Powell's defenders have dismissed such complaints as the petty jealousy of grumpy old boatmen, but when it comes from a Mormon bishop, perhaps it has a higher authority.

When Major Powell made his first trip down the Colorado River he landed at the mouth of the Rio Virgin twenty five miles from St. Thomas. He sent an Indian with a note directed to the postmaster, stating that he had landed and would stay a few days before proceeding farther and to send any letters or papers for him or his men. He also intimated that they were short of everything at that time.

I was postmaster at St. Thomas. The Indian arrived in the night. I wrote a note stating that I would be down the next morning and would bring his mail with me. In the morning I got Brother Gibbons to go with me, taking one hundred pounds of flour, some tea, coffee, sugar, tobacco, and about twenty five very nice melons. It was after night before reaching his camp, but he was expecting us and met us a short distance from camp bare headed, having lost his hat during the perilous trip down the river. They had a blazing fire burning when we drove up and when we tumbled out the melons they went into them with a will after being for months running the fearful rapids of the river wet day after day, it was a treat unlooked for. After talking until after midnight we made our bed to take some rest. In a short time the Major came and asked us if we were asleep. When we told him no, he said you may as well get up. I want to talk and want to hear the news. We got up and after satisfying him he gave us some account of his trip down the river. He had one of his boats smashed all to pieces and its occupants thrown into the raging rapids, but escaped with their lives. Another boat they left at the head of the last rapids; two of his men refused to run the rapids and he left the boat with the hope that after seeing him thru safe would follow in the boat. He also left them a part of the bedding, food, guns, and ammunition and they attempted to cross the country to St. George or some of the settlements in southern Utah, were killed by the Indians. When I afterwards learned of their fate I wrote Major Powell and acquainted him of the fact. He was very much concerned about them, feared they would perish and so they did in that way.

In the morning before Brother Gibbons and I were ready to start, the Major had concluded to go with us to St. Thomas, him and his brother and let his other men have the boats and everything else left from the ravages of the river and pursue their way to Ft. Mohave. He gave them an order on the commandment [commandant?] there for sixty days rations. And we returned to St. Thomas, arriving there before night, we learned that Brother Henry Nebeker had started that morning with a four horse and wagon for Payson. I furnished the Major a hat his brother a pair of shoes and some other articles which

I do not remember now. We prepared food to last them to St. George, got some young men to overtake Nebeker during the night and he would give them passage to Payson. All of this I furnished myself as well as what I took to the river; and in the Major's book he gave all credit to Brigham Young, so I have been told. He did not even send me a copy of his book.[3]

Powell did not even spell Leithead's name correctly in the book.

NOTES

1. Quoted in Ghiglieri, *First Through Grand Canyon,* 230.

2. Leithead, *Diary of James Leithead,* L. Tom Perry Special Collections, Harold B. Lee Library, Brigham Young University, Provo, UT, unpublished. Published here with permission.

3. Ibid.

·27·

A Hardy Welcome

WHEN THE POWELL expedition emerged from the Grand Canyon they encountered two prominent individuals who wrote accounts of meeting them: first Bishop James Leithead of St. Thomas, and then William H. Hardy, the founder of Hardyville.

Hardyville was an important early ferry crossing and steamboat port on the Colorado River, located on the present site of Bullhead City. William H. Hardy lived out a classic story of the Wild West, chasing adventure and finding abundant opportunity. He was drawn West by the 1849 California gold rush but soon realized there was less profit in mining than in owning a store selling supplies to miners. When mining started booming in Arizona, Hardy headed there, scoped out the geography, and found a location that was both a likely crossing on the Colorado River between Arizona and California and one of the northernmost ports for steamboats (though the Mormons soon built their own port, Callville, farther upstream). There Hardy built a store, hotel, saloon, and ferry, and from there he built a road, stage line, and freight line to Prescott, where he also opened a store. Hardy knew that a railroad would soon be built across Arizona and he was hoping it would cross the river at Hardyville. This put Hardy in touch with General William J. Palmer, who was surveying the Southwest for the Kansas Pacific Railway. Palmer needed the knowledge and logistical support of local leaders like Hardy. They began corresponding.

In 1869 many still hoped that the Colorado River would have great potential for commerce, that it might be—or could be engineered to be—navigable far beyond Hardyville, perhaps through the Grand Canyon, even all the way to Colorado. This would benefit a southwestern railroad, and thus William Palmer took a keen interest in the arrival of James White at Callville in 1867 and proclaimed that White had indeed run the Grand Canyon. Now Palmer was eager to see how Powell's expedition came out and what it had to report. In the summer of 1869 Palmer wrote to Hardy asking about Powell, and on August 5 Hardy replied: "Neither of the two parties that have undertaken the exploration of the Colorado River have made their appearance at this place yet and as the river is low I hardly believe that one soul of either party will come out safe but I believe that all have perished. Both Adams and Powell are crazy and know not what they were doing."[1] William Hardy does not sound like a believer in the navigability of the Colorado River.

A few weeks later the remainder of Powell's party arrived at Hardyville. Now there were only four men; the Howlands and Bill Dunn had left at Separation Rapid, and Powell and his brother Walter had left at the Virgin River. On September 4 Hardy wrote a note to the Prescott *Weekly Arizona Miner,* which they published on October 2, 1869:

> The "Powell Expedition" is heard from at last. Four men with two of the boats—*Kitty Clyde's Sister* and *Maid of the Canyon*—belong to the outfit arrived here at noon today. They report one hundred and ten days from Green River City, and thirty-five days from the junction of the Grand with the Green River. They say they encountered numerous rapids and precipitous falls over which they dared not risk the boats, but were compelled to make frequent portages, laborious and danger-ous in the extreme. Maj. Powell left the expedition at the mouth of the Rio Virgin and proceeded to Salt Lake City, taking with him the notes of the trip together with the geological and other "ological" specimens gathered along the route.

Two weeks later, on September 20, 1869, Hardy wrote to General Palmer and reported that he had talked with one of Powell's men, though it's not clear which of the men. It couldn't have been George Bradley, for Bradley was in the boat that the speaker describes lowering over Lava Cliff Rapid. This leaves Andy Hall, Jack Sumner, and William Hawkins. The speaker describes himself as a former bull wrangler, which suggests Andy Hall, the only crewmember known to have driven bulls, but then the speaker says that three others on the crew had once driven bulls. According to an 1897 letter that Hardy wrote to Professor George Davidson, Hardy later hired Andy Hall to drive his stage between Hardyville and Prescott.[2] Perhaps this connection was made in the meeting Hardy described in his 1869 letters. In any case, Hardy's two letters to Palmer that are here reproduced make it clear that Hardy was not too im-pressed by the Powell expedition.[3]

Hardyville
September 20th 1869
Gen Wm J. Palmer
Dear sir,
Since I last wrote I have had an opportunity to converse with one of
the men that came through the great canyon with Maj Powell.

To numerous questions that I asked he said:

There was but one of our party that had any experience with a
boat. He was not an expert. As to me I used to drive bulls as did three
others of our party. We soon learned to roe but we were afraid of the
water, would get frightened in passing over the rapids.

The journey was a lonesome monotinous and hard one and money
would not hire me to try the trip over again. We found sand bars on
one side or the other of the river nearly all the way. The walls of the
canyon was not perpendicular as had been described but benched off
or flared out at the top and generally was two or three miles across at
the top of the mountain. We found different kinds of rock. One place
the bank was marble, again volcanic lava, finally all kinds of rock was
passed in making the ascent but little timber was noticed except on
the high mountains near the San Juan and Grand rivers.

One time I undertook to lower one of our party over the worst
rapid and the rope slipped and down he went sideways all right and
we took the chances and followed. Here our boats took in some water
but not bad.

(Note:) From this man's description I would think that a man
used to running the rivers of Maine or Wisconsin would make sport
of the worst falls encountered by this party. First their boats were not
properly constructed but were the common square end short skiffs.
Should have been of the bateau pattern and thirty feet long.

Mr. Powell took the barrings of the canyons and can make a perfect chart of the whole river. We see more indications of mineral along
the banks, no valuable agricultural land in sight.

It would cost more to make this river navigable than it would to
build a Pacific railroad across the continent. The fourgoing is all that I
could learn of this man that seamed to be important.

Maj Powell sent a copy of his report to have it signed by the commander of the post but I did not learn of this untile it had been sent
away or I would have got a copy of it—however it will be published
soon and then we can learn all about it....

The Colorado River is very lowe and will probably be lower in
December than it has been in years....

Yours truly, Wm H Hardy

Hardyville

Sept. 28, 1869

Gen Wm Palmer

Dear General,

Your letter of the 16th of Aug came to hand per last mail. I have written all the facts connected with the Powell expedition that I could gather. The fact of Powell's leaving the party at Callville and three others leaving the expedition at a point about one hundred miles above Callville left none of the party to pass this place that were reliable or acquainted with exploring to give an intelligent report. I learned however that it was the intention of Prof Powell to at once publish his report. I am satisfied that the lay of the country will not suit you or help your enterprise....

Wm H Hardy

NOTES

1. All letters from Hardy to Palmer are from William Palmer Papers, Colorado Historical Society, Box 5, Folder 368. Published with permission.

2. Hardy to George Davidson, 1897; no further details available.

3. Hardy wrote in run-on sentences (which the Prescott newspaper probably cleaned up for publication) so I have supplied some punctuation and capitals to make reading easier.

·28·

The Afterlife of a Boat

A T THE SMITHSONIAN INSTITUTION in Washington, DC, some of the largest crowds gather around the iconic craft of American exploration: the Wright brothers' airplane *Flyer,* Charles Lindbergh's *Spirit of St. Louis,* and the Apollo 11 command module *Columbia.* Crowds would also be admiring the boats used in the Lewis and Clark expedition and the Powell expedition, but those boats aren't there; they quietly disappeared after the expeditions. Only a few historians have ever wondered publicly where they went.

Long after Powell's crewmembers were scattered far from the Colorado River, one of Powell's boats seems to have lived a long and productive life on it.

It wasn't the *No Name,* which was smashed in the Canyon of Lodore early in the trip. Some of its nails are probably still lying at the bottom of the river, long covered by mud, rusting away.

It wasn't the *Emma Dean,* which was left tied to shore above Separation Rapid in case the Howland brothers and Bill Dunn changed their minds about hiking out of the canyon. The *Emma Dean* might have remained there for months and finally been torn loose by a spring flood, swept into the rapid and then downstream, and smashed apart on boulders or against cliffs, becoming mere driftwood.

We can't be sure which of the two remaining boats it was. When Powell and his brother Walter left the trip at the Virgin River, the four remaining men continued downriver in the two boats that had survived the voyage. George Bradley and William Hawkins stopped at Ehrenberg, Arizona, a ferry crossing and port town recently developed by brothers Michael and Joseph Goldwater, who were importing goods from California and New Mexico to supply the miners and military outposts in western Arizona. Bradley and Hawkins headed off to new lives, Bradley as a ranch or orchard owner in Southern California, Hawkins as a farmer and Mormon in Utah and later Arizona. The men had received little financial payout from Powell and were threadbare. They faced uncertain journeys, and their boat was almost the only asset they had, so they would not have simply abandoned it but tried to sell it. Good boats were hard to come by on the lower Colorado River, which was rapidly being settled and developing into a shipping corridor. Local trees made lousy, brittle lumber. Powell's boats had been built by a master shipbuilder in Chicago; even after all the battering they had taken on the river they were probably better than the boats made locally. Perhaps the men sold their boat to the main merchants in town, the Goldwaters, who could have added it to their ferry service. Then again, if the Goldwaters had owned a historic boat they might have left a memory of it with their grandson Barry, who in 1940 became one of the first hundred people to ride a boat through the Grand Canyon and who was quite interested in the subject. Perhaps the boat ended up in the hands of a fisherman whose entire ambition was to row from one quiet eddy to another.

Jack Sumner and Andy Hall couldn't seem to get the river out of their veins, for they continued their journey to the Gulf of California. In their brief mentions of this journey, neither man mentioned which boat they used, the *Maid of the Cañon* or *Kitty Clyde's Sister*. Sumner had gone through the canyon with Powell in the *Emma Dean*, Hall in *Kitty Clyde's Sister*, but with the abandonment of two boats the crews had rearranged themselves. Considering the bonds that sailors make with their boats, it's likely Hall would have preferred completing the voyage in the boat in which he'd begun it, but Hall was the youngest crewmember and Jack Sumner the guide of the expedition, and he could have had some reason for favoring the *Maid of the Cañon*. Whichever boat it was, Sumner and Hall took it to the delta and the sea, and with the help of a tarp as a sail, the upstream tides, and some hard rowing, they returned upstream to Fort Yuma. There they left the river, and their boat. It's likely this was the boat that ended up in the hands of one of the most legendary steamboat captains of the Colorado River, Jack Mellon.

Mellon is legendary not just in the sense of being a famous steamboat captain, but also in the sense of being mysterious. Carol Brooks, curator of the Arizona Historical Society in Yuma, pursued Mellon's biographical trail for a decade and came up with only scraps about him. This could be because Mellon ran away from home at age nine and was not eager to recall his own story. In newspaper articles over the years Mellon said he was born in both Nova Scotia and Massachusetts, and in the U.S. census he listed himself as born in Ireland in 1842. One of the few personal accounts of him comes from Godfrey Sykes, who explored the Colorado River delta and wrote a book about it. Sykes wrote that Mellon was

One of the best known, and perhaps the most skillful, of the Colorado steamboat captains and pilots…. "Captain Jack," as he was generally called, was one of the leading citizens of Yuma—the home port of the flotilla of river steamers and barges—and a most remarkable man. We became close friends in his later years and I learned much about his earlier experiences. He was of British-Irish stock, had been at sea ever since he was about ten years old and had reached the mouth of the Colorado River in the early sixties as an ordinary seaman on a small coasting brig. He could neither read nor write, at that time, his sole accomplishment, apart from his seamanship, being more than average ability as a rough and tumble fighter…. He had started his river experiences as a deck-hand but quickly developed a river sense and ability to read the channel which put him into the pilot-house…. The other captains and pilots got into the habit of trusting his memory implicitly and it seldom led them astray. His knowledge of the river and estuary was intimate and accurate, and not only covered existing conditions but former alignments and trends towards future changes…. Perhaps his best known feat, which remained as a tradition amongst other steamboat men on the river for many years, was his piloting and steering the steamer *Cocopah* downstream from Fort Mojave to Yuma between dawn and dusk of a single day upon the crest of a great flood. The distance was approximately three-hundred river-miles and he held the wheel for the whole wild trip without slowing down or hesitating for a moment in situations where quick decisions were necessary.[1]

Mellon said he once took a 178-foot steamboat up the Colorado to the mouth of the Virgin River, twenty-five miles above Callville, which had been considered the end of navigability.

In 1917, seven years before his death, Mellon received a letter from Colorado historian Thomas F. Dawson, who was sending Mellon a copy of his book making the case that James White had preceded Powell down the Colorado River.[2] Dawson should have contacted Mellon sooner, for Mellon replied that while he had not met White he was well acquainted with two of the men who had talked with White at Callville, and Mellon considered them "reliable," which helped convince Mellon that White had done it. Then Mellon declared that White's raft was a more plausible craft than Powell's boats. And Mellon should know: he had owned one of Powell's boats.

White's chances for coming down on the raft were better than Powell's with the class of boats he used. They were keel boats, and would strike on a hundred rocks in the rapids that the raft would pass over. I owned one of the boats and used her in tide water at the mouth of the Colorado. They were well built, but entirely unsuited for swift water navigation.

A friend of mine, Clark Flevell, some time about '95, went to Green River crossing, and there built a boat suited to the river. He and another man made the trip from Green River crossing to Yuma in six weeks. Clark never got out of his boat in any of the rapids—he ran every one of them. He told me he could easily make the trip starting in May, from Green River Crossing to Yuma, which is 410 miles below Callville, in thirteen days. White coming through was no miracle, but Powell's was on account of the model of boats he used, and the same can be said of Stanton.[3]

Mellon doesn't tell us how he came to own the boat—whether he bought it directly from Jack Sumner and Andy Hall, or secondhand. And since Mellon traveled well up the Colorado, it's possible he bought the other Powell boat, which Hawkins and Bradley had left in Ehrenburg.

When Mellon says he was using the boat "in tide water at the mouth of the Colorado," he was probably using it as a scout boat to find the best route through sandbars. The Colorado's enormous load of sediment and its spring floods meant that it was often shifting its sandbars and channels, and this was further exaggerated by the powerful tidal bores in its delta. Steamboat pilots and captains had to carefully watch for changes, and constantly relearn the river. In low-water months the channel could become dangerously shallow. While the Colorado River didn't have as many driftwood snags as the Mississippi River, snags notorious for ripping the bottoms off steamboats, it, too, could be tough on hulls. Even experienced captains like Mellon sometimes ran aground on sandbars. Extracting a heavy steamboat from a sandbar could be a miserable experience, and some boats ended up being abandoned, a costly loss for a shipping company and a devastating blow to a captain's career. A steamboat carried rowboats the crew could launch to take soundings and get a closer look. Rowboats also ferried men and supplies and messages to and from shore or other boats, and served as lifeboats in case boilers exploded and steamboats went down.

When Lieutenant George Wheeler surveyed the Colorado River from Fort Mohave upriver to the mouth of Diamond Creek in 1871, torturing his men and his boats for more than a month, he might have heard that Captain Mellon had acquired one of Powell's boats. At the end of his trip Wheeler left his battered boats at Fort Mohave, and a few months later he wrote to the camp commander, Captain R. H. Pond, directing him to give his boats to Mellon. Pond replied that the boats were in such terrible condition that Mellon would not want them. But he did give Mellon the best boat.[4]

I have examined photographs of rowboats carried on steamboats or riding in the Colorado River near Yuma, but have not seen any obvious Powell boat. Unfortunately, Yuma had no newspaper in 1869, and today it offers very few documents about activities in Yuma then, so there is no mention of Powell's men or boats being there. I made inquiries, but no one in town knew anything.

What would have happened to Powell's boats? After all their bravery in the canyons, they could have hit an ignominious rock and sunk, and rotted in the river. They could have gotten buried in a sandbar after being abandoned along shore or swept away in a flood. If it was the right sandbar, such as one now outside the river, a boat might still be there, preserved by Yuma's dryness, like an Egyptian mummy waiting to be unearthed. Or a boat could have been swept out to sea. Or it could have worn out, ended up in a backyard or junkyard, and been torn up for firewood. It could have ended up in the hands of someone with no knowledge of its past, no respect for its achievements. But would Captain Mellon, with his appreciation for boats, have causally discarded such a historically important boat? Carol Brooks, the Yuma historian, is afraid he would have. The people of Yuma were no different from Americans all over the frontier: They were in love with the future, not the past. If something was old, it needed to be discarded to make way for the new.

Whatever the fates of the boats, at least fate seems to have been on their side in the rapids and canyons.

NOTES

1. Godfrey Sykes, *A Westerly Trend* (Tucson: Arizona Pioneers Historical Society, 1944), 212–13.

2. Dawson to Mellon, 1917 Thomas Dawson Papers, Colorado Historical Society, Denver.

3. J. A. Mellon to Thomas F. Dawson, December 31, 1917, Thomas F. Dawson Collection, Colorado Historical Society.

4. Letter from R. H. Pond to George Wheeler, June 18, 1872. No further details available.

PART VI

The Fate of the Howland Brothers and William Dunn

·29·

Introduction

ALMOST FROM THE MOMENT that Oramel Howland, Seneca Howland, and William Dunn left the Powell expedition at Separation Rapid and headed for the Mormon towns of southern Utah, people began wondering about their fate. Their fellow crewmembers began wondering about their fate even before they had met any fate. Their fate was to disappear without a trace.

Jack Sumner, in the account he provided to Robert Stanton in 1907, recalled the crew's conversation soon after they had successfully run Separation Rapid: "While we repaired the boats the boys discussed the conduct and the fate of the three men left above. They all seemed to think the red bellies would get them. But I could not believe that the reds would get them, as I had trained Dunn for two years in how to avoid a surprise, and I did not think the red devils would make open attack on three armed men. But I did have some misgiving that they would not escape the double-dyed white devils that infested that part of the country."[1] Sumner was referring to the Mormons, almost the only white inhabitants of the Arizona Strip and southern Utah.

The crew's discussion contained some intriguing sociology, for in 1869 Americans hated both Indians and Mormons. Sumner wasn't wondering whether the men would get killed, only who would do it, whether "red devils" or "white devils." The American public, too, wasn't always sure which devil was worse, and was ready to believe accounts of any depravity or treachery ascribed to either. Americans had a 250-year tradition of regarding Indians as enemies of Americans, but the Mormon sect had sprung up recently, and Americans were still baffled and infuriated by Mormon claims that they were the only genuine Christians. The 1857 Mountain Meadows Massacre, in which the Mormons slaughtered a wagon train of some 120 people migrating through the state, contributed to American demonization of Mormons, though the Mormons tried to hide behind American demonization of Indians.

Separation Rapid. Photo courtesy of Grand Canyon National Park Museum Collection.

In some respects, discussions of what happened to the Howlands and Dunn have not advanced very far beyond the crew's original discussion. We are still debating whether the Indians or the Mormons represented a greater danger to those three men. Perhaps this discussion can best be summarized by a plaque that river runners placed on the cliff at Separation Canyon in the 1930s, partly in answer to the absence of the names "Howland" and "Dunn" from the Powell Memorial on the rim at Grand Canyon National Park. The plaque reads, "Here on August 28, 1869, Seneca Howland, O. G. Howland, and William H. Dunn separated from the original Powell party, climbed to the North Rim and were killed by the Indians." Every so often, river runners place duct tape over the word *Indians* and write *Mormons* on it. The duct tape remains up for a while, and other river trips come along and view it as amusing mischief or as good scholarship, until eventually another river runner, not necessarily a Mormon, comes along and rips the tape off, and once again the Indians get the blame.

Even today this discussion has sociological undercurrents, with prejudices that steer it, but over the last century these currents have shifted substantially. It is no longer acceptable to demonize Native Americans for defending their lives, land, families, and ancient way of life from invaders. Yet even many

liberal academics who teach tolerance for everyone have made an exemption
for the Mormons, whom they often regard with scorn. Anti-Mormon prejudice
has made it downright chic to blame the Mormons for the killing of Powell's
men, and it fueled the widespread, uncritical, and often enthusiastic accep-
tance of a blatant hoax that claimed to offer evidence against the Mormons, a
claim I will scrutinize in chapter 31.

In the history books, as on the plaque at Separation Canyon, the guilt of
Native Americans has remained much better embedded. And the Indians did

Plaque at Separation Rapid. Photo Courtesy of Grand Canyon National Park Museum
Collection.

have plausible motives for killing Powell's men. By 1869 the Southern Paiutes of the region had been under serious pressure for more than a decade. Mormon settlers had arrived in large, well-organized numbers and evicted the Paiutes from the springs and other water sources crucial for survival in an arid environment. The Mormons had taken over old Paiute farming areas and were expanding cattle and sheep grazing onto the grasslands that were essential for Paiute hunting. The Mormons were cutting down pinyon pine trees to use as firewood and for miles of fence posts, depriving the Paiutes of pine nuts, a crucial source of nutrition. The Paiutes had always lived in a marginal environment, and now they had been pushed into a life-and-death crisis. By some estimates, including the estimate of John Wesley Powell in 1874, the population of the Kaibab Paiutes, one of the Paiute bands on the Arizona Strip, dropped by about 80 percent in the decade after the Mormons arrived, not from disease as was often the case elsewhere, but from resource loss—from starvation. Death came faster when whites simply massacred the Paiutes. In the face of such pressures, some members of the Shivwits Paiute band, which lived west of the Kaibab Paiutes, removed themselves across the Colorado River and lived with the Hualapai, whom they helped to resist the U.S. Army.

Then one day, in an area where whites almost never traveled, the Shivwits Paiutes might have heard some distant gunfire. Whites were trespassing on their land, poaching the wildlife they needed for survival. The Howlands and Dunn had no choice but to hunt, for the Powell expedition had been almost entirely out of food, and Powell could give his departing men only rifles and ammunition for hunting. Their gunfire would have been heard from miles away and drawn attention that would not be welcoming.

Another possibility is that the Howlands and Dunn ran into a Navajo raiding party that had crossed the Colorado River at (the future) Lees Ferry to steal horses from the Mormons, something that had been occurring for years and that occurred at least twice in 1869, prompting the Mormon militia to pursue and attack the Navajos.

Yet in the history books the Paiutes got the blame for killing the Howlands and Dunn, because of a series of reports that emerged soon after they disappeared. At first these reports came entirely from Mormon sources, but a year later they seemed confirmed when John Wesley Powell met with some of the Shivwits Paiutes and they confessed they had killed his men in revenge for a crime that had been falsely attributed to the men. Yet this confession contradicted several accounts the Mormons had given about Paiute actions, and it came at the end of a series of accounts that had undergone several substantial

Powell with Southern Paiute, Chief Chuarumpeak, 1873. Photo courtesy of Grand Canyon National Park Museum Collection.

changes. This book will further complicate previous accounts, adding several new documents, including letters written and received by Nathan Howland, the brother of Oramel and Seneca Howland, who conducted his own investigation into his brothers' disappearance. When their circumstances are examined carefully, these changing Mormon accounts invite questions about motives.

There were two other odd things about the theory that Paiutes killed the Howlands and Dunn. In all of Utah for all of 1869, Powell's men were the only whites killed by Indians. The Indian rebellion of a few years before, the Black Hawk War, had been thoroughly smothered. In a New Year's editorial on January 5, 1870, Salt Lake City's *Deseret News* summarized: "So far as Utah is concerned the year 1869 has been one of peace and prosperity.... The Indians have driven off stock from some places in the South, yet there has been no war upon the settlers; and, with the exception of the three men belonging to Major Powell's party who left him on the Colorado River, no lives have been taken by them." (In the 1860s Mormon mind, the Arizona Strip was part of Utah.) Amid the deep conflict and bitterness between Mormons and Indians, it was only three strangers who had barely set foot in the state who were killed. Another odd thing was that the Mormons never sought to punish the killers of Powell's men, a leniency that was far from normal on the American frontier. Nor did the Mormons ever make any effort to bury the bodies.

The Shivwits confession never persuaded Jack Sumner, who made several claims blaming the Mormons. Sumner cited grapevine reports as his source, and indeed since Sumner spent several years prospecting and working in Utah he was in the right place to hear such reports. Yet when Sumner got specific, his claims became highly dubious. He pointed an accusing finger at Andy Gibbons, one of the Mormons who met the Powell expedition at the mouth of the Virgin River. Sumner told Robert Stanton, "When Major Powell made the foolish break of telling them the amount of valuables the boys had, I noticed a complete change in the actions of a certain one of the men present. From one with a listless demeanor he instantly changed to a wide-awake, intensely interested listener, and his eyes snapped and burned like a rattlesnake's, particularly when Major Powell told him of an especially valuable chronometer for which he had paid six hundred and fifty dollars."[2]

Yet this conversation was taking place two days and, by the crew's own count, at least seventy miles downriver from where the Howlands and Dunn had headed overland. Andy Gibbons was separated from them by vast and very difficult terrain, and he couldn't guess their route, so for Gibbons to try to find them was geographically absurd. Sumner also told Stanton,

> I am positive I saw some years afterwards the silver watch that I had given Howland. I was with some men in a carousal. One of them had a watch and boasted how he came by it. I tried to get hold of it so as to identify it by a certain screw that I had made and put in myself, but it was spirited away, and I was never afterwards able to get sight of it. Such evidence is not conclusive, but all of it was enough to convince me that the Indians were not at the head of the murder, if they had anything to do with it.[3]

When Sumner says "carousal" with an "a," he means not a merry-go-round but a drunken spree, and this alone diminishes the reliability of his observations. Even if Sumner was correct that this was the watch he entrusted to Oramel Howland to give to Sumner's family in case he didn't make it, this does not prove that a Mormon snatched it from Oramel's dead body. If Indians took the watch, they would have had no use for it and would have traded it to the Mormons for something they could use. Jack Sumner seems excessively ready to blame the Mormons.

Yet there are more solid grounds for wondering if the Mormons were responsible for the deaths of the Howlands and Dunn. Previous inquiries into this possibility have paid very little attention to the historical and political context of the Powell expedition. It wasn't just the Paiutes who believed that their way of life was under siege in 1869. The Mormons, too, after more than two decades of feeling they were safely far away from their persecutors, felt they were being invaded in 1869, an invasion spearheaded by the newly completed transcontinental railroad and articulated by Washington politicians newly determined to crush Mormon independence. Two of the most prominent anti-Mormon politicians, widely hated in Utah, had strong ties with John Wesley Powell. By carefully examining the intense political dramas that were occurring even as Powell was on the river in Utah, and by presenting a series of documents, facts, and circumstances that have not been considered before, we arrive at some scenarios in which it becomes plausible for the Mormons to have killed Powell's men: not because of any misunderstanding, as has sometimes been assumed, but precisely because they were associated with Powell. This will become an elaborate story, with many layers and branches. Some of it will rest on solid ground, and some will be an exercise in speculation, and I will try to mark the boundaries between the two. But a large part of this investigation will consist of mapping out circumstances and circumstantial evidence; as we pile up layer upon layer of circumstances and scenarios, they will definitely outpace the proof for them, by quite a distance. It is entirely possible I will end up building a house of cards. But there are some possibilities that need to be taken seriously and mapped out carefully, even if at the end they remain mere possibilities, some more plausible than others.

As soon as I mention looking into Mormon history in a way that might find something amiss, some readers undoubtedly will begin wondering if I have any sort of personal agenda. And they have a right to wonder. Almost all of Mormon history has been written by authors with agendas. The writing of Mormon history has been more polarized between positive and negative than writing about almost any other topic in American history, perhaps even more than the Civil War. Most Mormon history has been written either by church historians or church members who were determined to make the church look good, no matter what, or by lapsed members or critical outsiders who were determined to dig up dirt, even to make up dirt, to make the church look bad. There have been few entirely neutral historians. The normal protocols of historians do not require them to discuss their possible biases, and indeed doing so might be regarded as bad form. But in this case, it's only fair.

I do not come from an LDS family, but my family has long been curious about Mormon history. Back in the 1930s, at the University of Oklahoma, my uncle Nils wrote his master's thesis in history on the federal expedition to Utah in 1857, which helped trigger the Mountain Meadows Massacre. Half a century later his study was still being cited by Mormon historians, for instance by Leonard J. Arrington in his 1985 biography of Brigham Young. In the 1950s and 1960s my uncle's brother-in-law and sister-in-law, Max and Marjorie, lived in "the Hamblin House" in Kanab, Utah, built by the family of Jacob Hamblin, the Mormons' most famous explorer. You might say that living in the Hamblin House made them thoroughly insiders in southern Utah history, but in fact they always remained outsiders, for they were almost the only non-Mormons in town at that time; Max worked for the Bureau of Land Management (BLM) and was in charge of managing BLM resources across a wide area, enforcing policies that were often strongly resented by local residents. This gave Max and Marjorie a long and very close-up view of the century-old tension between the Mormons and federal authority.

The conflict between the Mormons and federal authority is at the heart of my exploration of the fate of the Howlands and Dunn. I believe I have been motivated by simple curiosity, and have gone where the evidence has led, forming scenarios along the way and discarding them when they did not seem to fit the facts. I have been well aware of the longstanding temptations and failures of people writing Mormon history, and have done my best to avoid them. My uncle's master's thesis still resides in the grand, Ivy League–style reading room at the library at the University of Oklahoma, and the next time I visit there, I don't want to feel I might be an embarrassment to him.

NOTES

1. Quoted in Stanton, *Controversies*, 205–6.
2. Quoted in ibid., 208–9.
3. Quoted in ibid., 209.

·30·

Toab

FOR THREE DECADES the story remained pretty much where Powell had left it: the Shivwits killed his men in retaliation for a crime against them. (I'll further explore this claim in chapter 33.) The account was rather vague, with no location or names and or many details. In 1902 Frederick S. Dellenbaugh, in his *The Romance of the Colorado River,* added a location, which he learned through Jacob Hamblin: "Northward they went," wrote Dellenbaugh, "to a large water-pocket, a favourite camping ground for the Shewits, a basin in the rocky channel of an intermittent stream, discharging into the Colorado.... The trail to the water leads down under a basaltic cliff perhaps thirty or forty feet high, as I remember the spot, which I visited about six years later. As the unfortunate men turned to come up from filling their canteens, they were shot down from ambush. In consequence I have called this the Ambush Water-pocket."[1] Area residents had called it Penns Pockets.

If the Howlands and Dunn were killed at Ambush Water-pocket, then it renders a verdict on another of the mysteries surrounding their route and their deaths. North of there, farther away from the canyon, is Mount Dellenbaugh, which Powell named in 1872 for Frederick Dellenbaugh, a distant relative of his brother-in-law Almon Thompson; Dellenbaugh was Powell's artist and assistant topographer on his second river expedition. At the top of Mount Dellenbaugh, carved into the black volcanic rock, is a vague inscription: "Dunn, 1869, Water" with an arrow pointing to the north. It is plausible that the Howlands and Dunn might have been motivated to climb Mount Dellenbaugh, which was about a twenty-mile walk from where they would have exited Separation Canyon; as the tallest peak for many miles around it offered their best chance of getting a view of the landscape to the north, perhaps including trails. It is also plausible that Bill Dunn might have felt triumphant about having completed the Colorado River journey and might have wanted to leave his mark atop a mountain. Yet here the plausibility ends. If the three men were killed at Ambush Water-pocket to the south, they never would have made it this far north. And since the men would still have been heading north at Mount Dellenbaugh, how could they have known about a water source they had not yet reached? Since this was the rainy season, there should have been plentiful rock pockets holding water and little reason to point out one distant water source. It would also be questionable for three men who had been starving and eager to get to the Mormon towns to have taken the time and effort to carve an inscription on a rock, especially in a remote area where there were almost no other whites to find it. The biggest problem is that Almon Thompson later visited Mount Dellenbaugh, and Frederick Dellenbaugh himself visited it twice, and Dellenbaugh even mentioned what he found: "On the summit is a circular ruin about twenty feet in diameter with walls remaining two feet high."[2] Neither man saw a Dunn inscription. A century would pass before a report of it showed up in print. More-recent examiners have expressed doubts about its authenticity. On the whole, the inscription seems likely to be a prank, perhaps done long ago by a local cowboy.

It was another twenty years after Dellenbaugh's book that something new was added to the story, a different location and the name of the perpetrator. The source had high credibility within the Mormon world. In 1861 Anthony W. Ivins, then age nine, was one of the original settlers of St. George, and he later served as constable, city counselor, county assessor, county prosecuting attorney, Indian agent, and president of the St. George church stake, and in the overall church became an apostle and first counselor to the church president. Ivins also owned a ranch far out on the Arizona Strip, on the Shivwits Plateau, a few miles north of Mount Dellenbaugh. Ivins was the first white person to build a house on the Shivwits Plateau. He knew the Shivwits Indians better than almost anyone, both as their neighbor and as their Indian agent. Local Mormon histories say the Shivwits liked and trusted Ivins, but this seems a typical Manifest Destiny version of events. In truth, Ivins and other settlers wanted the Indians' springs and land for their own cattle and sheep businesses, and Ivins took the lead in removing the Indians from the Arizona Strip and relocating them to a small reservation near St. George. The Shivwits resented and resisted being forced off their longtime homelands.

In September 1924 Ivins published an article about the fate of Powell's men in an LDS Church magazine called *Improvement Era,* which didn't get much attention in Grand Canyon history circles. Ivins did not repeat the initial 1869 Mormon stories in which the Howlands and Dunn were killed in retaliation for misdeeds done to the Indians. Ivins decided that Powell's men had been

killed near his own homestead, at a spring called Log Spring. But his reasons
for believing this were hardly compelling:

> More than twenty years after the Howlands and Dunn were killed,
> the writer was one day riding alone on the range, a short distance
> east, and a little north of the Parashont Ranch House. A heavy growth
> of cedars covered the mesa, it was an ideal place for an ambuscade.
> Passing through a dense growth of cedars the horse emerged into a
> small clearing, and stopped. It was evident that someone had long
> before camped on the spot, dead cedars had been pulled down, a tem-
> porary shelter improvised, and a fire built. Like a bolt from the blue
> the thought came—This is the spot where Powell's men were killed.[3]

Ivins told a more dramatic version of this story to Jimmy Guererro, a cowboy who went to work on the Arizona Strip in 1902. As a high church official
writing in a church magazine, Ivins might not have felt comfortable revealing
what he took to be his horse's nearly supernatural reaction to a place of horrible
death. Guererro told an interviewer, "Right across the knoll from Parashaunt
House there is a knoll over there running down to a point. On this knoll there
is where 'Tone' Ivins figured they burned those people, the three fellows." The
interviewer was Wallace Mathis, also a longtime rancher on the Arizona Strip.
Mathis had never heard this part of the story, and he queried, "Burned them?"

> GUERERRO: Burned them.
> INTERVIEWER: Did they just shoot them?
> GUERERRO: No, they burned them.
> INTERVIEWER: They burned them?
> GUERERRO: "Tone" told me the reason [he] figured out on the knoll
> [was] where they burned those people. He said "I used to try to ride
> my horse up over that knoll. I couldn't get my horse more than halfway
> up over it. They wanted to go back down."[4]

As a constable and prosecuting attorney, Ivins knew that a horse's refusal
to climb a ridge wasn't evidence that would go far in a courtroom, and he refrained from telling anyone else his belief that Powell's men had been burned.

Ivins also identified the killer, a Shivwits named Toab, and here Ivins was
backed up by far more than "a bolt from the blue." Residents of the Arizona
Strip and St. George knew Toab as a mean and violent man who had killed
at least two Indians. Starting in the 1960s, St. George historians obtained
many oral histories from Arizona Strip old-timers, and when the subject of

Indian relations came up, many volunteered stories about Toab. At some point, Toab got mixed into the Howland/Dunn story, perhaps following the lead of Anthony Ivins. Ivins's version of events: "It appears that when they first met the Shevwit Indians the white men were received with protestations of friendship. After they had passed, a council was held to determine whether they should be permitted to proceed in peace, or should be attacked and killed. The majority of the Indians were in favor of treating the strangers as friends. But To-ab insisted that they be dealt with as enemies. Persuading two young Indians to go with him, he followed the men...[and] attacked them from ambush, and killed them."[5]

In 1997 longtime Arizona Strip rancher Spencer Esplin seemed to sum up the current standing of the story:

> I've heard several stories and have tried to follow it.... They come up out of the river there and they...ran into these Indians. There [are] different stories. Supposedly an old fellow, Toab, was at that time one of the renegade Indians in the country, and he was the one they suspected of killing them, or being kind of the man who was in charge of doing it with the Indians. But this fellow claimed that Toab told him that they'd come up and they fed them and they started out and he says "They begged for their lives but we killed them anyway." But nobody really knows exactly where they were killed. A friend of mine and I went out and put up a little sign out there and it kind of gives the history.... Nobody knows exactly where they were killed or what happened to them, or what happened to their bodies.[6]

Wallace Mathis, the rancher who interviewed Jimmy Guererro, had his own memories of Toab, which he shared when he was interviewed in 1975: "He was known as an Indian that hated the white man. He used to walk up and down the middle of the road, as I remember, with a long knife on his side, and everybody respected him. When he'd come to get something at the door, the housewives would give it to him readily because they were afraid of him. In fact, he was reported to have killed several white men."[7]

One time when Mathis was about twelve years old he and another boy were left alone at the ranch when their fathers went off on a trip:

> The first afternoon after they left, here comes ol' Toab, leading his old rawboned horse up the canyon right to our place. We were almost petrified because we'd heard so much. Now it is a fact that he was

mean. Ben Sorenson woke up one night and old Toab was right over him. He'd had some kind of fight with him that day…. He woke up and Toab was right over him with a knife. He woke up just in time to save himself. Anyway, we didn't [know what] to do with Toab…. We stayed there till about dark and found out that he wasn't going to leave, and if he'd gone, we wouldn't have dared to go to sleep anyhow…. We watched for our chance and grabbed him and got a rope and tied his hands behind him and tied him to a tree…. When our dads came home they said that was the thing to do, not to take a chance, leaving him loose.[8]

Another close call with Toab was reported by two ore freighters, Harvey Frehner and Martie Bunker, on a remote road. Frehner noticed that Bunker was no longer following close behind him and stopped his wagon and went back around a bend. He found that Bunker had had some sort of mechanical problem and was lying under his wagon working on it, and right above him stood Toab holding a big rock, ready to hit him with it. Frehner called out a warning, Bunker got away, and Toab fled.[9]

Oliver Stratton recalled a Toab murder:

Toab…came and told John [Pymm] he wanted a horse. So Johnny let him have one of the horses to save any trouble…. Then he said, "You want to see something, Pymm?"…[They] went up around a ways where some rocks that came together this way, and there was a squaw lying in there dead. He said, "I killed my squaw last night. I get heap jealous and I cut her throat like a sheep."…The squaw was just stuck in between the rocks, lying there…. I guess people don't really know how many people old Toab and his scouts killed. The Arizona Strip was their territory, and he was a renegade. If anyone went out there alone, they were taking a chance…. He would be out in the hills, and he was clever. He'd catch someone out there and they'd just disappear it seemed like, to never be heard again.[10]

Loren Miles recalled how as a boy he ran into Toab in a narrow passage and fled: "I could hear Toab cussing but I was afraid to look back. I was too scared. Had I known at the time (what I later learned) that he had killed three men from Powell's Colorado River party some time before, I think I would have been unable to think or move out of my tracks. Toab spent the last few years of his life in the Utah State Prison for the above-mentioned crime."[11]

Actually, Toab was sent to prison for killing another Indian by hitting him in the head with a hoe, a fact reported by historian Juanita Brooks, whose father-in-law, George Brooks, was the county sheriff who escorted Toab to prison. Tales like that of Loren Miles warn us that stories about Toab and Powell's men have gotten seriously garbled.[12] Another Arizona Strip resident suggested that Toab had killed Glen and Bessie Hyde, a newlywed couple who attempted to boat the Grand Canyon and who disappeared, though Toab died years before their 1928 trip. Among the many legends that got connected with Toab was that he was openly carrying a watch he had taken from Powell's men, or that he wore pasted on his forehead, as a trophy, a dollar bill he had taken from them. Loren Miles's report does raise the question of why Toab would be punished for killing an Indian but not for killing Powell's men. Anthony Ivins explained: "From the time this Indian, To-ab, came to the reservation I had suspected he was connected with, if not entirely responsible for, the murder of the Howland Brothers and Dunn, but neither by persuasion, nor offer of reward or threats, could the Indians be induced to give a word that would incriminate him."[13]

Ivins did claim that years later he found one Indian, Old Simon, who said that it happened exactly as Ivins said, with Toab as the killer and Log Spring as the location. And if Jimmy Guererro is to be believed, Toab did confess the crime to him:

I was talking to old Toab.... We all fed the old buggar. We fed him good.... He was sitting there one day and he started telling me about it. I just can't stand to have people tell me about torching things, especially people. He began to tell me. He said, "I was a little bit of a boy when that happened. They just cried and begged and cried and begged," and laughing all the time. Finally I said "God damn you, Toab, you were anything but a boy then. I was a little boy. You were a big boy. You were the first one that struck the match." [Toab answered:] "No, no, no."[14]

As for Toab's age, a Shivwits census in 1898 counted Toab as sixty-five years old, which would have made him thirty-six in 1869.

The southern Utah and Arizona Strip pioneers were tough people who had endured many difficulties, but clearly they were so intimidated by Toab that they would swallow their pride and give away their hard-earned food to avoid provoking him. The Mormons did have an informal policy of tolerating Indian begging as a way of pacifying them, but Toab seems to have gotten special indulgence due to his violent temper. Toab does seem to have been capable of murdering Powell's men, perhaps to steal their possessions, perhaps out of sheer meanness. Yet he and the other Shivwits had another possible motive.

When Powell's men wandered onto the Shivwits Plateau, it had been less than eight years since 250 Mormon families arrived at the future site of St. George in a church-organized colonization effort. For the Southern Paiutes, who lived in small groups scattered across a land with limited springs and food resources, this Mormon wagon train was probably the largest mass of humanity they had ever seen, and perhaps the first white people many had seen. At first it was probably not obvious that the Mormons were going to extinguish the Paiutes' way of life. The Mormons got off to a poor start, failing to grow enough crops to sustain themselves, and in 1864-65 a severe drought forced them to survive by hunting rabbits, squirrels, gophers, and snakes, just like the Paiutes. But soon the Mormons were greatly expanding their farmlands and livestock herds, which required that they take over the springs and lands on which the Shivwits had always depended. More settlers arrived, and new towns were founded and grew.

The pressure of Mormon expansion led to the Black Hawk War, named for a Ute chief, which involved much of Utah. Starting in 1865, Utes, Paiutes, and Navajos engaged in cattle raids, killings, and skirmishes against the Mormons, and the Mormons organized militias and struck back, sometimes with little regard for whether they were retaliating against the right Indians. The Indians preferred to ambush a handful of isolated Mormons and get away before any militia could respond. Two such attacks, by Navajos, occurred on the Arizona Strip near the Utah border in 1866. St. George was spared any direct attacks, but residents were nervous and alert. The Shivwits were less involved in the war than other Southern Paiute bands, but they were aware of the conflict going on around them. The Howlands and Dunn could have been killed in the same sort of ambush that had been going on elsewhere.

In the same article in which he theorized about the killing of Powell's men, Anthony Ivins explained the context:

> It at once became evident that ranching could not be successfully carried on, while the Shevwitts remained on the land.... They became insolent, frequently killed cattle for food, and when remonstrated with replied that the country was theirs, and that the white man, with his flocks and herds, should move away, and leave them in peaceful possession. Representation was made to the Indian Department, at

Washington, and the suggestion offered that the Shivwits be removed to a reservation on the Santa Clara River, where they would be among civilized people, and subject to proper Government supervision. The suggestion was approved, funds were appropriated for the purchase and improvement of land, and the writer was appointed to establish an agency, and place the Shevwits upon it. The Indians were reluctant to leave their old home, and a few, in the beginning, refused to come in.... There was one man who was a constant source of trouble. He was obstinate, uncontrollable, a constant mischief maker. He pretended to be possessed of supernatural power, was a medicine man, and pretended to see, in dreams and visions, the past, present, and future. His Indian name was To-ab.[15]

The Shivwits took Toab more seriously as a medicine man and warrior. Toab was the son-in-law of Quetuse, the longtime chief of the Parashant-area Indians, who was said to be so strong he could easily swim across the Colorado River—though the Shivwits, when wanting to visit tribes on the opposite side of the canyon, made boats out of driftwood tied together with yucca fibers. LaVan Martineau, a white orphan raised by a Southern Paiute family, recorded some of their lore about Toab: "Toab had the power to heal and would heal people.... Toab was also bulletproof and one time while he was healing someone he allowed himself to be shot in the chest with a muzzle loader to show his power. He just spit the bullet out."[16] Martineau's mother-in-law was Toab's granddaughter, and she maintained that the Shivwits held a council to decide what to do about Powell's men, and the younger braves decided to kill them.

The Shivwits resistance and relocation went on through the 1870s and 1880s, with their reservation being established in 1891. In the meantime, the Mormons did their best to convert and "civilize" the Shivwits, with mixed results. As elsewhere in Utah, the Paiutes became an important source of menial labor for the Mormons, picking their crops and hauling their wood, usually for modest payments of food. Yet this meant the Paiutes were increasingly hanging out near Mormon villages, resulting in conflicts, dependency, resentments, and cultural misunderstandings. One year the St. George Mormons were gratified at how many Shivwits showed up to be baptized as Christians, yet when the same people showed up again the next year and the Mormons explained that they only needed to be baptized once, the Shivwits answered that they had gotten baptized only to claim the free clothing being offered as a reward.

By 1869 the Shivwits had probably figured out where the trend of Mormon expansion was going. They had also figured out that it would be suicidal to attack a well-armed town like St. George, but it might be safe to attack three threadbare men far from the towns. When Frederick Dellenbaugh ventured onto the Shivwits Plateau in the mid-1870s he recognized the Shivwits' hostility: "I have always had a lurking suspicion that the Shewits were glad of an excuse (if they had one at the time) for killing the men. When I was there they were in an ugly mood."[17] Mormon pioneers often defined Toab as a *renegade*, not a normal term for a mere psychopath but more a way of describing someone resisting their agenda. Even in Ivins's own telling, Toab comes across not just as a psychopath but also as a leader stirring up resistance. George Seegmiller told a story in which Toab was ready to die to resist white encroachment. Some white miners forced Toab to take them to a rumored copper deposit: "I remember this old Wren Bryson he took him and he shook him. He said, 'You tell us where that mine is or I'll kill you right here.' Old Toab says, 'Maybe so, Mormon steal'm.' He wouldn't tell them anything. 'Maybe so, Mormon steal'm. I can't find it.'"[18]

A scenario in which the Howlands and Dunn were killed as part of a larger conflict over land dispossession also gives the Mormons a motive for demonizing the Shivwits, for portraying them not as innocent victims of Mormon expansion but as barbaric killers who needed to be brought under control. No one had a stronger psychological temptation than Anthony Ivins, who had pushed the Shivwits off their land and then, as their Indian agent, had to face the consequences of his actions: their poverty, social breakdown, despair, begging, alcoholism, violence, and resentment and harassment of whites. It was convenient if his main political opponent was also a vicious killer of white men and if the killing took place on his own land, which justified his taking that land away from the Indians and turning it to civilized purposes.

At some point Toab headed across the Nevada border and lived with two Indian friends near the town of St. Thomas, friends whom the local whites considered to be chronic troublemakers. After the Mormons abandoned St. Thomas in 1871 it became an enclave for outlaws seeking a place far from the authorities. After the regional Indian agent moved from St. Thomas to the county seat of Pioche about a hundred miles away, the Paiutes, too, found less restraint from authority. According to regional historian Arabell Lee Hafner, "Toab, another Indian, went around with them for a long time. It was believed he was once an Indian chief from one of the other tribes, but had done something wrong and had to leave."[19] Hafner attaches no date to this report, but her book includes a photograph of Toab, apparently older, sitting with his two friends, which suggests he fled to St. Thomas long after 1869.

Toab did seem to have the personality of a killer, and he had a plausible mo-tive. But the case against him becomes seriously problematic when it depends on Anthony Ivins's "bolt from the blue" in which a horse who is unenthusiastic about climbing a hill leads to a revelation about a crime location and burned bodies. Ivins's eagerness to blame Toab also unavoidably reminds us of the Mountain Meadows Massacre, where Mormon attackers dressed up as Indians and painted their faces with war paint, then spent decades publicly placing the blame on the Indians. On the other hand, distrust of Mormons could become so prevalent that they would get blamed when they probably didn't deserve it, as with the Gunnison Massacre of 1853.

Along with Anthony Ivins's version, other Arizona Strip families have their own versions of where and how the Howlands and Dunn were killed. But the credibility of Arizona Strip folklore drops considerably when people believe that Toab went to prison for killing Powell's men, or that he killed Glen and Bessie Hyde. The Shivwits, too, have their folklore: in one version, the Howlands and Dunn left the river trip to look for gold, and were living in a cave somewhere on the Shivwits Plateau and panning for gold—geologically unlikely—which prompted the Shivwits to kill them for trespassing. In the end, Toab's role, if any, remains blurred thanks to the workings of folklore and the temptations of Mormon political agendas.

NOTES

1. Dellenbaugh, *Romance*, 228–30.

2. Ibid., 310.

3. Anthony W. Ivins, "Traveling Over Forgotten Trails: A Mystery of the Grand Canyon Solved," *Improvement Era* 27, no. 11 (Sept. 1924): 1023.

4. James "Jimmy" Guererro, undated interview, Grand Canyon-Parashant National Monument Oral History Collection, Special Collections, Dixie State University, St. George, UT, 13-008AB, 11.

5. Ivins, "Forgotten Trails," 1025.

6. Spencer "Spence" Esplin, interview, "Ranching on the Arizona Strip," January 22, 1997, Dixie Pioneers and Story Tellers Oral History Collection, Special Collections, Dixie State University, St. George, UT, 97-006A.

7. Gordon Wallace Mathis, interview, May 1, 1975, Delmar D. Gott Oral History Collec-tion, Special Collections, Dixie State University, St. George, UT (hereafter Gott Collection), 75-007, 10.

8. Ibid., 10–11.

9. Rex Jensen, "Grand Gulch Trail Was Stuff of Legend," *Las Vegas Review–Journal Nevadan*, Oct. 25, 1981.

10. Oliver L. "Ivy" and Jennie Higgins Stratton, interview, January 14, 1975, Gott Collec-tion, 75-001.

11. Loren Miles's journal, quoted in public talk by his daughter Marilyn Fotheringham, January 21, 1998, at the Institute of Continued Learning at Dixie College, St. George, Washington County, Utah. Found in Dixie Pioneers and Story Tellers Oral History Collection, Special Collections, Dixie State University, St. George, UT, 98-003.

12. Juanita Brooks, "Old Toab," *Utah Magazine* (April 1946): 20–47.

13. Ivins, "Forgotten Trails," 1023.

14. Guererro, undated interview, 11.

15. Ivins, "Forgotten Trails," 1021–22.

16. LaVan Martineau, *Southern Paiutes: Legends, Lore, Language, and Lineage* (Las Vegas, NV: KC Publications, 1992), 66.

17. Dellenbaugh, *Romance,* 230.

18. George and Maudie Miles Seegmiller, interview, May 6, 1975, Gott Collection, 75-008.

19. Arabell Lee Hafner, *100 Years on the Muddy* (Springdale, UT: Art City, 1967), 113.

·31·

The Toquerville Hoax

IT WOULD BE ANOTHER seventy years after Anthony Ivins's article before another major twist was added to the story. In 1993 historian Wesley P. Larsen published an article in the regional history journal *Canyon Legacy* asserting that Powell's men had been killed by Mormons in the town of Toquerville.[1] As a Mormon and as the former dean of the college of sciences at Southern Utah University, Larsen had good credentials. His story got media exposure and was spread through the river-running community and told around campfires in the Grand Canyon. In 2003 Larsen's story gained a national audience when it was included by Jon Krakauer in his bestseller *Under the Banner of Heaven,* which examined 1984 murders committed by polygamist fanatics. Krakauer argued that these murders were the outcome of nearly two centuries of Mormon fanaticism, which also led to the Mountain Meadows Massacre and the murder of Powell's men.[2]

Yet when Larsen's claims are examined with a light more penetrating than a campfire, they quickly melt away.

Larsen's thesis is based on an 1883 letter found in a long-neglected trunk by the great-grandson of southern Utah pioneer John Steele. The letter was written to Steele by fellow Mormon pioneer William Leany, and it mentioned a triple killing that had occurred "in our ward," including the words "the murderer killed to stop the shedding of more blood."[3] One of Larsen's central claims is that the only time Leany and Steele lived in the same ward was at the time of the Powell expedition. But this was not true. According to public LDS biographical sources, there were four periods when Leany and Steele lived in the same place at the same time: first in Nauvoo, Illinois; then in Salt Lake City; then for years in Parowan, Utah, where Leany served in the militia for a year under the command of John Steele; and finally in the St. George–area settlements, where Leany lived in Harrisburg and Steele lived in Toquerville.

Furthermore, at the time of the Powell expedition, Leany and Steele were not in the same ward. According to the official LDS record, *Annals of the Southern Utah Mission,* compiled by James G. Bleak, it was only in November 1869, two months after Powell's men disappeared, that the semiannual conference of the LDS Southern Mission combined Harrisburg and Toquerville into the same ward, where they would remain until they were split up again in March 1874.[4]

If you allow that Leany was writing his letter years later and might have been using a blurred definition of when they shared "our ward," then you open the door to an event, a triple murder, that was also a bit outside the exact timeline but that fits the Toquerville letter perfectly. According to the *Annals of the Southern Utah Mission,* "At Toquerville a terrible calamity occurred on this date [March 1875]. Richard Fryer who for some time had, at intervals been subject to attacks of insanity, this date shot his wife and babe, and also Thomas Batty, who had been trying to subdue the frenzied man. Fryer was killed by the Sheriff's posse, who were attempting to capture him. Mrs. Fryer died soon after being shot. Thomas Batty, died on the 17th, and the babe on the 18th."[5]

In his discussion of the Leany letter, Larsen insisted on referring to the "three men" mentioned in it, but in fact the original letter never said anything about "three men," only "the three" and "those three." A wife and baby fit the description. The posse killing Fryer fits the Leany letter's contention that "the murderer killed to stop the shedding of more blood."

The Toquerville murders received major publicity in Utah newspapers. The *Deseret Evening News,* which as the voice of the LDS Church could be hesitant about publishing negative news that might get national attention and make the Mormons look bad, could not resist the tabloid horror of this story. After a series of bulletins starting on March 16, 1875, it carried a long report from a witness, William W. Hammond, on March 23:

> Richard Fryer has been at times, for a year or two, laboring under fits of temporary insanity, but of late has acted in so rational a manner as not to be considered dangerous, and but yesterday did a faithful day's work at plastering. He some time ago ordered his wife, Teresa Fryer, to leave his house and take her infant son, which she did, and has since lived most of the time with Thomas Batty and family, whose residence is but a short distance from her former home.
>
> Fryer went this morning, about 7 o'clock, and knocked at the door of Thomas Batty's house, and upon being asked, went in, and asked if his wife was there. Being answered in the affirmative, he asked her

if she had not brought disgrace and shame enough upon him? Fryer then drew a loaded revolver and fired a shot at Thomas Batty, the ball entering below the left eye and coming out at the back of the head. Batty then fell into the arms and upon the shoulder of Henry Willis, who was present when Fryer fired a second shot, the ball entering the back part of the head and coming out through the right eye. Fryer then turned and fired at his wife, who was yet in bed, the ball entering below the left ear and lodging in the head, near the right eye, which shot produced instant death. Fryer then shot his infant son, who was in bed with his deceased mother, the ball entering the child's forehead and coming out the back of the head.

After completing the tragedy, Fryer went to his house.... The sheriff of Kane County, as soon as he was notified of the facts, went as near the house of Fryer as was deemed safe and called from the bystanders a posse, instructing them to arm themselves, which they did. The sheriff and posse then approached the house as near as was wisdom, when the sheriff called and asked Fryer if he would surrender. The first time he answered, "I will not, if you want me, come and take me." The second time his answer was, "I will not; I have had enough of you and Bishop Bringhurst."

The position occupied by Fryer precluded the possibility of taking him without a further sacrifice of life. After viewing the position and believing that unless immediate action was taken more innocent blood should be shed, the sheriff ordered his posse to open fire, which they did, killing Fryer instantly.

The phrase in Leany's letter, "the murderer killed to stop the shedding of more blood," is close to a quotation of the newspaper's "unless immediate action was taken more innocent blood would be shed."

The newspaper followed this account with the coroner's report on the bodies of Richard and Teresa Fryer and, two days later, the baby Fryer and Thomas Batty.

The other Salt Lake City newspaper, the *Tribune*, was founded by non-Mormons and missed few chances to make the church look bad. It introduced a further element into the Toquerville story, blaming Fryer's actions on Mormon fanaticism. It concluded its March 17 article with, "Fryer has been subject for some time to fits of insanity.... He had since driven his wife from home. When the Sheriff went to take him he told him to keep away, as he was the Lord." And the *Tribune* concluded a March 26 article with the following:

INSANITY PRODUCED BY RELIGIOUS EXCITEMENT
This man Fryer, was sometime ago a steady, industrious man, and a
very zealous Mormon. He had, no doubt, built his faith and hopes on
Brigham, the false Prophet, and when he learned that Brig. had been
sent to prison, and that he had denied polygamy, and all his teachings
were false, it affected his mind to that extent that he became insane,
and caused him to commit this terrible deed.

The element of religious fanaticism in Fryer's actions fits well with the
strong tone of religious apocalypse in Leany's letter.

The Toquerville murders were not forgotten by history. In the 1980s a
Toquerville historian published two books on Toquerville history, and he included the Fryer/Batty murders in both of his books. The historian's name was
Wesley Larsen. A decade before the Toquerville letter was discovered, Larsen
had already published the perfect explanation for almost every detail of it. He
had even offered a bit of sympathy for Fryer: "There were people in the community who thought that Fryer considered himself better than the rest of the
town and resented it. Fryer was assaulted and mistreated. For example, a few
young men caught him, tied his feet to a single tree that was fastened to a har-
nessed work horse, and raced through the streets of Toquerville dragging him
behind them. These cruel incidents might have injured him and caused a mental breakdown.... Richard began to have temporary spells of insanity and had
them for a year or two before an undreamed of tragedy took place."[6] Yet when
Larsen presented the Toquerville letter to the public, he omitted mentioning
that he possessed an alternative and thorough explanation for it. If Larsen had
related the Fryer/Batty story, his Powell theory would have been ignored. Lars-
en's books were readily available in the public libraries of the region, but no one
bothered to check them.

Larsen made several other claims for the Toquerville letter that don't
stand up.

The Toquerville letter speaks of "the killing of the three in one room of our
ward." A ward is an ecclesiastical district, in the same sense as a political ward.
Larsen tried to conjure the mere word *ward* into a *ward house,* and suggested
that because only Toquerville had a ward house with more than one room, the
killing must have occurred in the Toquerville ward house. This was a leap of
illogic. (Regarding "in one room," the Toquerville letter could diverge from the
Deseret News, which initially reported the murders took place in two rooms,

but then Hammond's eyewitness report said that after killing Batty, "Fryer then turned and fired at his wife," which makes no mention of a second room.)

Larsen suggested that Powell's men, intercepted by Mormons, were taken to Toquerville because it was the county seat. At that time Toquerville was indeed the seat of Kane County, but the much larger St. George was the seat of Washington County as well as the government and church capital of the Southern Mission. It's unlikely Powell's men would have reached Toquerville on their own, because they would have had to pass St. George or the trails leading to it. When you are coming north from the Arizona Strip, old St. George is highly visible on its heights, and the only way to (just barely) miss spotting it is to follow the base of the Hurricane Cliffs. But then Powell's men would have seen Fort Pearce and the major trail coming down the Hurricane Cliffs and heading for St. George, which soon become known as the Honeymoon Trail.

Larsen emphasized that the murder of Powell's men became a secret carefully guarded by the LDS Church, but if it was, William Leany would have been the very last person to be told about it. In September 1869 Leany was on trial by LDS authorities for being a heretical troublemaker.

In trying to explain the phrase "the murderer killed to stop the shedding of more blood," Larsen suggested a high-level LDS conspiracy to silence the killer of Powell's men and thus save the church from serious retaliation. Larsen pointed the finger at Eli Pace, the son-in-law of John D. Lee, who was shot in late January 1870 under strange circumstances. Larsen suggested there was a cover-up surrounding Pace's death; on this point Larsen might be quite correct, but at the time it seems to have been an open secret as to why Pace was killed and why the real reason was covered up. Lee's daughter Nancy had already been abandoned by her first husband, and now Eli, her second husband, was planning to leave her, too. According to a letter from John D. Lee's former neighbor, who signs himself "Bosco," published in the *Salt Lake Daily Tribune* on January 1, 1875, soon after Lee's arrest for the Mountain Meadows Massacre,

> Her [Nancy's] next husband was a young Mormon boy by the name of Eli Pace; it is believed by many that he got tired of her and was going to leave her. ONE NIGHT HE WAS KILLED, when no one but his wife was present. He was shot through the heart, not with a shot-gun but with a Colt's revolver. His wife got a light, and then gave the alarm, stating that Eli had shot himself. A post mortem examination was held, but no evidence was brought to prove that Lee's daughter killed him. Lee is a great visionist; he was not long in settling the matter, for the spirit

of Eli Pace came back and told Lee that he had killed himself. He, the spirit, was happy in Heaven, and wanted his father to take care of his loving wife Nancy. Of course, no one believed in Lee's vision, as he never fails to try his visions or dreams when occasion requires.

Historians, too, have been known to see ghosts. I won't speculate on Larsen's motives, but clearly he had his own agenda. He not only withheld the Fryer/Batty explanation, but he also was ready to warp the facts to make them fit. For example, "The murdered men must have been highly important if the killer was executed. As in the case of the Mountain Meadows Massacre, the people involved may have made a 'covenant of silence.'"[7]

Larsen's story in 1993 was quickly circulated by the media and by word of mouth, and it won a special welcome among people inclined against the Mormons. The *Salt Lake Tribune* had totally forgotten its tabloid-style coverage of the Fryer/Batty murders 118 years earlier but it had not forgotten its skeptical stance toward the church, and now it published Larsen's theory and implied that the Mormon murder of Powell's men proved the villainy of Mormons. Michael Quinn, a Brigham Young University historian who was excommunicated by the church in 1993 for treading on forbidden ground, mentioned Larsen's theory in a 1997 book and signed onto the idea that the killer "was killed to avoid retribution on the LDS community."[8] Sandra Tanner, publisher of LDS-skeptical books, published the Larsen story on her website.[9] The Larsen story found its warmest reception in the river-runner community. There were ironies here. In the nineteenth century, anti-Mormon feelings arose from Christians who were outraged by Mormon theology, immorality (polygamy), socialist economics, and interference with America's Manifest Destiny. Yet by the latter decades of the twentieth century Mormons were perceived as conservatives, ultra-patriotic, the epitome of family values, perhaps more religious and moralistic than Baptists who, after all, still indulged in drinking and smoking. In the lingo of the cultural divide that opened up in the 1960s, Mormons were thoroughly "square." Meanwhile, the river-runner culture that evolved from the 1960s onward had a distinct countercultural accent, freewheeling in lifestyle, language, dress, drinking, sex, drugs, rock and roll, environmental radicalism, and religion—if it had any religion at all. The 1960s had also spawned a culture of historical revisionism in which it was no longer correct to portray Native Americans as demons when they were simply trying to defend themselves from American imperialism. The idea that three scruffy river runners had been murdered by the ultimate squares had a resonance that set river guides smiling mischievously and righteously as they relayed the story. Jon Krakauer published his book soon after the September 11, 2001, terrorist attacks, when Americans had started a debate about the dangers of religious fanaticism, and he pointed out that the Mountain Meadows Massacre had occurred on another September 11th and originated from a homegrown religion. In only ten years, Larsen's tampering with a few details of small-town 1860s Utah history had become part of a global debate about the survival of human civilization.

The hazards of indulging in anti-Mormon prejudice is something I will try to keep in mind while developing the remainder of this inquiry.

NOTES

1. Wesley P. Larsen, "The Letter, or Were the Powell Men Really Killed by Indians?," *Canyon Legacy* (Spring 1993).

2. Jon Krakauer, *Under the Banner of Heaven* (New York: Random House, 2003).

3. Larsen, "The Letter."

4. James G. Bleak, *Annals of the Southern Utah Mission,* Special Collections, Dixie State University Library, St. George, UT, Book B. 1874 entry is p. 220; 1869 entry is p. 17.

5. Ibid., Book B, 399.

6. Wesley P. Larsen and Lois Meyers, *Tales from Toquerville and Other Southern Utah Towns* (self-published, 1986).

7. Larsen, "The Letter."

8. Michael Quinn, *The Mormon Hierarchy: Extensions of Power* (Salt Lake City: Signature Books, 1997), 534.

9. Utah Lighthouse Ministry, http://www.utlm.org.

·32·

Three Men Sentenced to Be Shot

I N THE SUMMER OF 1869 the people of Utah felt themselves to be under siege. After being persecuted and driven from place to place in the Midwest, and after mobs had killed their prophet Joseph Smith and many other Mormons, they had gone to a great deal of trouble to find a place where they would be safe. They had abandoned homes, farms, and many of their possessions and trekked more than a thousand miles, over mountains and deserts, to a land outside the boundaries of the United States. They were hoping to create their own domain. For more than two decades they had labored and sacrificed to build dozens of towns. They were prospering, their population was growing, and they felt they were preparing a place for God on Earth.

Yet from the start the world had begun closing in on them again. The year after they arrived in Utah, the United States acquired Utah from Mexico and made it a territory, ending Mormon hopes of independence, and placing them under unfriendly authorities. The Mormons couldn't even hope for statehood and the self-government it would have brought, as long as they practiced polygamy. Two years after the Mormons arrived in Utah the California gold rush created a much larger flow of Americans to the West and across their lands. In 1857 President Buchanan sent an army to Utah to subdue the Mormons, who were too independent, especially in their open practice of polygamy. The army action didn't go well, and triggered the Mountain Meadows Massacre. Because of the Civil War, Americans had withdrawn their attention from the Mormons for a decade, but now they were ready to act, and in 1869 federal authorities were finally pursuing the massacre perpetrators. The completion of the transcontinental railroad, right through Utah, made it much easier for outsiders to reach Utah, including federal officials and troops, and including non-Mormons who might compete against Mormons for land and business and political power. The discovery of several rich mining areas in Utah in the 1860s drew in thousands of rough miners and led to the building of towns full of vice. Washington politicians had already carved several large slices off the Utah Territory and added them to other states or territories, and new plans might cut up Utah even more drastically, depriving the Mormons of a political power base. Ulysses S. Grant took office in March 1869, determined to assert federal authority over Utah. On July 15, 1869, as John Wesley Powell was progressing down Utah canyons, another threat stepped off the new railroad into Utah: Alexander and David Smith, the sons of Mormon prophet Joseph Smith and now missionaries for the rival Reorganized Church started by Joseph Smith's widow Emma, came to preach that Brigham Young was an imposter who had gotten their religion badly wrong.

In 1856 the Republican Party platform included a determination to pro- hibit "those twin relics of barbarism–polygamy and slavery." Opposing slavery occupied them for the next decade, but by 1869 the Republicans were ready to turn their attention to the Mormons, who like Southerners were defying not just the federal government but also their definition of Christian morality. Anti-Mormon sentiments were especially strong in Illinois, where in the 1840s the Mormons had built the city of Nauvoo as their capital. At its peak in 1844 Nauvoo held around 10,000 people, perhaps more than Chicago. Non- Mormon area residents strongly resented and feared the Mormons for their theology, polygamy, theocratic government, cooperative economics, and po- litical influence in western Illinois. After a mob killed Mormon prophet Joseph Smith in 1844, the Mormons decided to leave Illinois, a bitter decision after all the hope, effort, and money they had put into building Nauvoo. Even after migrating more than a thousand miles, the Mormons hadn't left behind their bitterness toward Illinois and its governor Thomas Ford, whom they blamed for Smith's murder. Illinois, in its turn, retained a strong dislike for the Mor- mons. Thus it was not surprising that when the U.S. Congress moved to clamp down on the Mormons, the effort was led by two Illinoisans, Senator Lyman Trumbull and Representative Shelby Cullom. Both men chaired committees that gave them special power. Trumbull was the chairman of the Senate Judi- ciary Committee, and he would seek to use the court system in Utah to break Mormon power. Cullom was chairman of the House Committee on Territories, which gave him jurisdiction over the governing of Utah, and he would seek to outlaw polygamy and to greatly curtail the rights and power of the Mormons, even if this required marching the U.S. Army into Utah. If you asked Mormons in 1869 which American politicians they despised most, Lyman Trumbull and Shelby Cullom would be at the top of the list.

Trumbull and Cullom were also John Wesley Powell's senator and congressman. When Powell tried to get federal support for his planned river expedition, he turned to Trumbull and Cullom, and they introduced bills in the Senate and the House of Representatives to grant supplies to Powell. The official sponsors of the Powell expedition were the two politicians who posed the greatest threat to the survival of Mormon Utah.

Shelby Cullom was elected to the U.S. House in 1864 from a district that had been gerrymandered to include the now reliably Republican McLean County, the home of Bloomington and Illinois Wesleyan University, where Powell came to live and teach in 1865. Like Powell, Cullom came from a devout Methodist background, but Cullom didn't escape from his mother's intensely puritanical outlook; he applied it to the political world, seeing issues like slavery and polygamy as choices between God and the devil. The Lincoln–Douglas debates converted Cullom into an abolitionist Republican, and he was so impressed by Lincoln that he grew a beard to match Lincoln's. After the Civil War, Cullom ardently supported Radical Republican efforts to reform Southern society and to impeach President Johnson. In 1869 he prepared a bill, HR 1089, that would impose a different sort of reconstruction in Utah. Introducing his bill in the U.S. House, he declared,

> Are we to have any legislation that will effectively crush out this bold and defiant iniquity, or are we to go on as we have been for over thirty years, allowing the practice of bigamy and polygamy to flourish in violation of human and divine laws, cloaked by the title of "Latter-day Saints" and a pretended system of religion?…The great mass of the Mormons are either actively or passively in hostility to the Government of the United States. A great majority of them are of foreign birth, brought from their homes by persons assuming the garb of bishops or apostles of the church, and have never known, and never would know under the present system, anything of the institutions of this country. The power of these priests and presidents and apostles and bishops over them must be destroyed, so that the light of Christianity and civilization may reach their benighted understandings…. Polygamy has gone hand in hand with murder, idolatry, and every secret abomination. Misery, wretchedness, and woe have always marked its path. Instead of being a holy principle, receiving the sanction of Heaven, it is an institution founded in the lustful and unbridled passions of men, devised by Satan himself to destroy purity and authorize whoredom.[1]

Cullom's zealotry did not abate with the years. In 1884 he got elected to the U.S. Senate and within a month he took the Senate floor to denounce the Mormons:

> There is scarcely a page of their history that is not marred by a recital of some foul deed. The whole history of the Mormon Church abounds in illustrations of the selfishness, deceit, and lawlessness of its leaders and members. Founded in fraud, built up by the most audacious deception, this organization has been so notoriously corrupt and immoral in its practices, teachings, and tendencies as to justify the Government in assuming absolute control of the Territory and in giving the Church or its followers no voice in the administration of public affairs. The progress of Mormonism to its present strength and power has been attended by a continual series of murders, robberies, and outrages of every description; but there is one dark spot in its disgraceful record that can never be effaced, one crime so heinous that the blood of the betrayed victims still calls out for vengeance.[2]

He was referring to the Mountain Meadows Massacre in early September 1857.

In this 1884 speech Cullom was trying again to pass a law like the one he had introduced fourteen years before, which had passed in the House of Representatives but failed in the Senate because even legislators who sympathized with his opinions on polygamy were disturbed by the bill's severe curtailment of citizen rights. That first bill had been drafted, early in 1869, by Robert N. Baskin, an Ohio-born, Harvard-educated lawyer based in Salt Lake City. Ferociously anti-Mormon, Baskin spent decades leading efforts to curtail Mormon power; he served as the prosecutor of John D. Lee in his 1875 trial for the Mountain Meadows Massacre.

The bill that Baskin presented to Cullom in 1869 would turn polygamy into a crime punishable by a $1,000 fine and five years in prison, and it would bar polygamists from voting, holding public office, serving on some juries, benefiting from the Homestead Act and other federal generosities, and gaining U.S. citizenship if they were emigrants. It would prescribe a loyalty oath similar to that taken by ex-Confederates. It would remove marriages in Utah from the authority of the LDS Church and make them civil procedures. To break the power of the Mormon authorities, it would remove their power to appoint judges and sheriffs and give this power to the territorial governor, who as a Washington appointee would be reliably independent and probably anti-Mormon. It would give federal marshals the power to enforce these measures, and would authorize the president to send the army to Utah to subdue the Mormons.

The military consequences of Cullom's bill were disturbing to many Northerners, who were exhausted by years of war. The *New York World,* for instance, declared "*This bill means war,*" that the Mormons would certainly resist, and that the U.S. Army would need two or three years and half a billion dollars to win such a war.

The Mormons were indeed indignant. Since Cullom had portrayed polygamy as a crime against women, whom Mormon men turned into slaves and prostitutes, the Mormons organized a series of "indignation rallies" around the state in which women attacked Cullom's bill as outrageously misguided and heartless. Women testified about how their ancestors had fought in the American Revolution to secure the constitutional rights that Cullom was now trying to destroy. The largest rally gathered some five thousand women in the Tabernacle in Salt Lake City on January 14, 1870; they launched some very personal attacks against Cullom. Mrs. H. Y. King declared,

> Who is the man who framed this incomparable document? What ideas he must have of women! In what academy was he tutored, or to what school does he belong, that he should so coolly and systematically *command* the *women* of this people to turn traitors to their husbands, their brothers, and their sons?…Let *us* the women of this people, the sisterhood of Utah, rise *en masse* and tell this man to defer "the bill," until he has studied the character of *woman* such as God intended she should be, *then* he will discover that *devotion, veneration*, and faithfulness are her peculiar attributes.[3]

Mrs. Miner declared, "While the hearts of many of my sisters are burning with indignation at the author of this last-named bill, I own that mine is filled with pity; for, after having carefully read it, I have come to the candid conclusion that he never knew the happiness of domestic life." Mrs. Wilmarth East seemed to be summoning Patrick Henry: "What is life to me if I see the galling yoke of oppression placed upon the necks of my husband, sons, and brothers, as Mr. Cullom would have it?"[4]

However, we do need to be cautious about trying to connect the rage against Shelby Cullom with the fate of the Howlands and Bill Dunn, for the timeline could be slightly off. Though the Cullom bill was progressing behind the political scenes throughout 1869, and while Mormon leaders were likely aware of it, the bill had not broken into the newspapers or generated public outrage by September 1869. Remember, the Salt Lake City women's rally was not until January 1870, four months after the Howlands and Dunn disappeared. It is not clear that the average person in southern Utah would have had much reaction to the name "Cullom" in the fall of 1869.

But this cannot be said about the other sponsor of the Powell expedition, Senator Lyman Trumbull. Brigham Young himself was in a rage against Trumbull during the summer of 1869, a rage echoed across Utah.

At the end of June 1869, the Mormons solemnly observed the twenty-fifth anniversary of the death of Joseph Smith. Thousands gathered in the Tabernacle to hear John Taylor, who had been riddled with bullets and left for dead by the same Illinois mob that had murdered Smith. From pulpits and newspapers all over the state there were plenty of reminders of the villainy of Illinoisans, and perhaps reminders of the vow made in Nauvoo to seek blood vengeance for the death of their prophet. Only two weeks later, with incredibly poor timing, a train came through Utah and off stepped Illinois senator Lyman Trumbull and many other prominent Illinoisans, including an ex-governor, the editor of the *Chicago Tribune,* the president of the Chicago Board of Trade, and many other business leaders. Two months after the completion of the transcontinental railroad, they were heading to San Francisco and making many stops along the way to encourage Westerners to do business with Chicago and Illinois. Yet, for the Mormons, Trumbull's arrival was also an ominous reminder that after more than two decades of isolation, Utah was now easily within reach of its worst enemies.

A dozen years previously, Senator Trumbull had given a speech on the "twin relics of barbarism," denouncing the Mormons for polygamy, and denouncing congressional Democrats, who were in charge of administering the territories, for giving the Mormons too much free rein. Trumbull was an early advocate of women's rights, including equal pay for equal work, and for him polygamy was not just degrading but also a form of slavery. Trumbull had a long history of advocating human rights causes, including in his private law practice both before and after his Senate career. In 1845 he had argued a case before the Illinois Supreme Court that resulted in Illinois outlawing slavery. Half a century later he and Clarence Darrow went before the U.S. Supreme Court to defend Eugene Debs in the Pullman strike. Trumbull's protégés included William Jennings Bryan and Shelby Cullom—Cullom's views on the Mormons echoed Trumbull's views. Another Trumbull protégé was his Chicago law partner Cyrus M. Hawley, whom President Grant appointed, at Trumbull's urging, as one of three district judges in Utah only a few weeks before Trumbull arrived there in 1869. Grant was removing Mormon-friendly or even Mormon-neutral judges and replacing them with adversaries like Hawley. Trumbull had always believed in using the power of the federal government to attack undemocratic practices, and thus, as another anti-Mormon tactic, he had introduced a bill to amputate northern Utah and attach it to Idaho. Cyrus Hawley's mission in Utah was to break the power of the Mormon court system and to impose federal authority on Utah.

From early in the history of the LDS Church, Joseph Smith had encouraged Mormons to settle their disputes outside the civil court system, partly because he wanted them to behave like brethren and not litigants, and partly because he knew the civil courts would be prejudiced against Mormons. Under the church's auspices the Mormons tried to resolve their own problems, including serious crimes like murder. In Utah, which as a territory lacked the autonomy of a state and was subject to considerable federal influence over its territorial government and courts, the Mormons sought to evade federal control by turning the probate court system into their alternative court system. Most of the probate judges were church elders. Probate judges presided over both civil and criminal cases, even murder trials. One of Judge Hawley's assignments was to impeach the probate court system and to drag the legal affairs of Utah back under the authority of civil courts. The failure of the Utah justice system was most obvious to a national audience in the lack of justice for the perpetrators of the Mountain Meadows Massacre, and Hawley was determined to finally catch and punish them. Within weeks of his arrival, Cyrus Hawley would be one of the most hated men in Utah.

The meeting of Senator Trumbull and Brigham Young turned into a confrontation that got into newspapers across the country. On July 12, 1869, the Chicago *Evening Journal* published the following report:

> The interview was at first entirely friendly. No one introduced the subject of polygamy, but treated the Mormon President with all due respect. As the party was retiring, Brigham remarked to Senator Trumbull that on returning to Congress he might hear of some persons being put out of the Territory.... "If such federal officials are sent here as sometimes have come, they will be guilty, and in an orderly way put out of Utah for good cause." To this uncalled for and atrocious manifesto the Senator very judiciously replied, "Before you take any step of that kind, allow me to request that you make known your grievances to President Grant. He is a just man, intending to do justice to all; but he will not permit a violation of law to go unpunished. It will not be safe to molest public officers in the discharge of their duties."

The Chicago *Evening Journal* reporter followed up:

Touching the Trumbull interview, Brigham tells me that he did get a little excited by what he deemed impertinent advice on the part of his visitors, and that, under the influence of this feeling, he told the wise men of the East, in effect, to mind their affairs and he would mind his.... From the declaration of Young and his foremost men...I cannot doubt that the monarch of Utah contemplates forcible resistance in certain emergencies, or more probably a show of force wherein to overawe the timid party or the nation at large. Brigham has an organized militia of 15,000. This force has existed for some time, but there seems to be an unusual activity pervading it at present. Regiments are being mustered and drilled.... What show this body of militant fanatics might make in a case of actual collision can only be surmised.

Such reports touched off discussions in many newspapers in many states; one such is this editorial, headlined "The Mormon Problem," in the Quincy, Illinois, *Weekly Whig* on July 29:

The conversation between Senator Trumbull and Brigham Young... illustrates in a striking degree the spirit of Mormonism. For nearly a quarter of a century past, there has existed far away in the heart of the continent, surrounded by almost insurmountable barriers of mountain and desert, a people defiant of the restraints of law...[with] a spirit of murderous intolerance toward the weak, and of fawning sycophancy and cajolery toward those in power....

But the completion of the Pacific Railroad...promised to change all this and inaugurate a new era. It seemed to the Mormon Prophet all the more important, therefore, that he should make a firm stand.... He seems to have begun upon Senator Trumbull with the same impudent bravado, imperiousness and flattery which he had already employed so successfully upon others. But never did he try his arts upon a more unpromising subject; and his discomfiture must have given him new assurance that the days of Mormon domination in Utah, even, are numbered. Senator Trumbull is entitled to the thanks of the moral and law-abiding citizens of the whole country.

When Brigham Young was threatening to throw troublesome federal officials out of Utah, he was likely thinking of Senator Trumbull's friend Cyrus Hawley. Young had good reason to be nervous: two years later, Hawley and his allies would have Young arrested and put on trial for "lewd and lascivious cohabitation."[5] Hawley would take many other aggressive actions to disrupt Mormon society. He went all the way to the U.S. Supreme Court to crush the authority of the Utah probate courts. He outlawed the activities of Mormon militias. When Utah elected George Q. Cannon as its territorial delegate to the U.S. Congress, Hawley went to Washington and lobbied to prevent Cannon from being seated, on the grounds he was too loyal to his church.

It's likely that while Senator Trumbull was in Salt Lake City, he met with Hawley and encouraged him to resist Brigham Young's threats, to stand up to him.

Soon after Hawley had arrived in Salt Lake City in June 1869, he was attending a reception when Young approached him and aggressively demanded to know whether he was planning to persecute his people. Hawley tried to stay calm and replied that no, he was not going to persecute the Mormons, but was only going to administer the law as he found it.

The Mormon newspaper, the *Deseret News,* offered Hawley a more satirical welcome on June 16, 1869:

> Mr. Hawley is the law partner of Senator Trumbull and has had a very extensive practice for the last twenty-two years in Chicago. His health being somewhat impaired by excessive labor he has found it necessary to change his occupation for awhile in order to obtain rest, and relaxation from the cases and anxieties of business.
>
> We think the Judge is extremely fortunate in being appointed to his present position, for if there is a place in the world where a judge has little to do in it, Utah certainly is that place. We trust that his intercourse with the citizens of Utah may be very pleasant and that his health may soon be fully reestablished.

Hawley had not come to Utah for his health. He had long been politically engaged, once running for Congress. Being forty-five years old at the outbreak of the Civil War, too old to fight, he had made his contribution by writing a series of widely read articles that discredited, on legal and constitutional terms, the South's arguments that it had a right to be left alone to practice its own system and morality. Mormon arguments about being left alone reminded Hawley of Confederate arguments.

On July 20, 1869, the day that Senator Trumbull left Salt Lake City, Judge Hawley began the first of many court cases that would leave Utahans enraged at him. Utah had three district courts, and also a Supreme Court, which consisted of the three district judges convening together. Hawley and another district court judge, O. F. Strickland, who was appointed at the same time and for the same purpose as Hawley, met as the Supreme Court and overturned a verdict that had been delivered a few weeks previously by the third district judge, C. C. Wilson, in his own district court. Wilson, who was also the chief justice of the Utah Supreme Court, was considered pro-Mormon and would be sacked a year later by President Grant, who in an angry confrontation denounced Wilson to his face. During that year, Hawley and Wilson would engage in a bitter feud, with Hawley continually trying to undermine Wilson's authority. But Hawley began this process with a singularly terrible choice. He latched onto a murder trial over which Wilson had presided. Three non-Mormons had murdered a Utah man, even while—as a witness testified—he pleaded for mercy for the sake of his wife and children. Wilson found them guilty and sentenced them to be shot on July 26. With a few days to spare, on the premise that the trial proceedings had been improper, Judge Hawley brought their case up for appeal. The attorney who defended the three men was Robert Baskin, the author of the Cullom bill. If Cyrus Hawley had tried to invent a case that would most inflame Mormon passions, he could not have done any better than this, joining forces with Robert Baskin to defend three non-Mormons who had committed a brutal murder.

The murder took place in the railroad camp of Wasatch (also spelled Wahsatch) near the Wyoming border, which had sprung up in 1868 for the workers digging the 772-foot-long Echo Tunnel for the transcontinental railroad. As railroad construction had moved west, the railroad continued moving its camps, mostly tents, and moving its workers, who needed to be mobile and thus were mostly single young men. A camp of hundreds of rootless young men brought the troubles common in Wild West boom towns: drinking, gambling, theft, prostitution, gangs, and fighting, including many fatal shootings. Wasatch had little law enforcement, so the workers engaged in vigilante justice, including lynching. Wasatch, like several mining towns in Utah, was very offensive to the Mormons, partly because it was drawing outsiders and their vices into the Mormons' realm. When the transcontinental railroad was completed in May 1869, Wasatch was transitioning into a real town, with real wooden buildings, to serve as a base for the railroad, and it was attracting some local Mormons looking for jobs.

The murder first hit the *Deseret News* on May 12. Thomas Brannigan, "John Lowell" (the correct name was Jack Lavelle), and Charles Howard were in the Salt Lake City jail for murdering Calvin Russell in Wasatch around May 6:

RUFFIANS TAKEN CARE OF

The particulars of the murder of Russell, as far as we have been able to learn, are as follows: Brannigan assumed the title and authority of a policeman at Wasatch, and he, in connection with some others, passed a law that all parties found out after 9 o'clock at night should be arrested. Subsequently to the passing of this bogus law Russell entered a saloon in which were Brannigan and some of his gang, one evening after the prescribed hour, and was informed by them that he must consider himself arrested. They consented, finally, to let him go on the payment of a dollar. He paid the dollar but gave them to understand that they could not "blackmail" him again. An altercation ensued between him and Brannigan in which Russell struck the latter on the head with a bottle and then made his exit. On the night following Brannigan, Lowell, and Howard lay in ambush for Russell at a place where the latter kept his horse, and shot him, causing his death.

Neither this article nor the subsequent court documents mention if Russell, the victim, is a Mormon. His behavior suggests, at least, that he was not a very good Mormon, but the fact that he was married and had children sets him far apart from the typical resident of a railroad camp. The sympathy Russell received from the newspaper and the jury suggests he was a Mormon, but even if he was not, the Mormons could not allow three non-Mormons to get away with murder.

Within three weeks the three men had been tried and pronounced guilty. Judge Wilson hadn't found enough people to compose a proper grand jury, which was supposed to have twenty-four members, so he had drafted several bystanders, and even then he had only seventeen jurors. The accused were charged with second-degree murder, but the jury found them guilty of first-degree murder. In announcing the verdict, the *Deseret News* expressed pleasure that the court had acted so swiftly and decisively. The defense attorney filed an appeal, but Judge Wilson completed the appeal within one week. On June 9 his decision was published in full, more than two thousand words, in the *Deseret News*. At the end, Judge Wilson addressed the guilty, urging them to prepare to meet God:

There you will meet your murdered victim sent into the presence of his Maker by your hands without one moment's warning or preparation, and to whom you refused mercy, although with his dying breath he appealed to you in behalf of his wife and children, hoping thereby to awake if possible one spark of humanity in your souls. You heeded not his dying voice, but by one more fatal shot ushered his unprepared soul into eternity. But, not withstanding you hearkened not to the cries for pity uttered by your poor bleeding victim, still you may yet hope that the Great Ruler of the Universe will have mercy on your dying souls.

This sermon proved too much for one of the convicted, Jack Lavelle, who wrote a letter that the *Deseret News* published on June 23:

Salt Lake City Prison
June 11th, 1869
Mr. Editor:
Sir, thinking, that you perhaps, would insert this brief statement in your valuable paper, I have presumed to offer it to the public, not in justification of myself, but simply to state the truth in regard to a statement made on oath by one of the witnesses in the late murder case.... The statement is this, that Russel, while lying on the ground, called to us, the defendants, to spare him, in the name of his wife and children. Now, sir, my days in this world are numbered, and God knows I would not willingly go before his last Great Court with another sin added on my soul, but sir, I pronounce this statement false, as the man who uttered it.... The only reason I have for correcting this statement is because his Honor Judge Wilson cited it in his remarks, while passing our sentence and, those same remarks having been published in your paper I deem it a duty to correct this statement; and moreover, as it was read by a great many of the citizens of Utah, by whom, as bad as I am, I would not have it thought that I am devoid of all human feelings, and sir, in conclusion may God forgive the man who swore to this statement as I hope even in this late hour to be forgiven.

Yours very respectfully &c,
Jack Lavelle

Even as this letter was published, Judge Hawley was reviewing the case, and on July 27 he announced that he was annulling Judge Wilson's ruling and sending the men back to jail to await a new trial. The newspaper reported that attorney Robert Baskin wanted the three to be set free.

Being new in Utah, Cyrus Hawley was probably shocked by the hostility his action unleashed. Feeling lonely and vulnerable, he quickly wrote to Senator Trumbull to seek support:

Salt Lake City
July 29th 1869
Dear Senator,
On the meeting of our Supreme Court on Monday, the day you left us, Judge Hoge retired under protest and left the bench to me but said as he left that he should commence proceedings to regain his seat. Thereupon the appeal of the <u>three</u> men tried and sentenced to be shot by Judge Wilson in the District Court was argued for four days…. The record was found very defective & the rulings of the Court so erroneous as against the prisoners, that Judge Strickland and myself could do no less than set the Judgment aside and order a new trial. Judge Wilson, on learning this, became exceedingly angry, & construed the actions of the Supreme Court into a <u>personal affair</u> as <u>against himself</u>. I wrote most of the opinion & took especial care not to say anything that he could justly claim as personal. But he seemed to think that his rulings in the lower Court on the trial & on the motion for a new trial must be sustained right or wrong. The bar universally said that we could do no less than we did, and even went so far as to say that it was the most important & the ablest opinion that had been given in the Supreme Court, & requested that the opinion be published. Some of the bar called upon the publishers of the paper here and made arrangements for its publication. The Clerk of the Supreme Court furnished a copy to the publisher for publication. Judge Wilson on hearing of this issued his order under the seal of his District Court to the publisher forbidding its publication. Of course this is an unprecedented proceeding. The bar is greatly incensed by reason of it & so is Judge Strickland. To avoid any complications, I took my wife & went to the <u>Camp</u> to make a visit to Gen. Gibbons. The <u>only</u> occasion Judge Wilson has for his unwarrantable proceeding is the fact that the Supreme Court granted a new trial to the <u>three men</u> whom he had sentenced to be shot on the 26th inst. The beginning of his course had its origin in the removal of Judge Hoge. My appointment to his place—Judge Hoge was led by him & acquiesced in all his opinions, & by his support he controlled all the decisions of the Supreme Court. Judge Strickland & myself, being the majority of the Court, will order the opinion printed according to the request of the bar. When published I will send you a copy that you may know what a little matter has offended Judge Wilson. The bar…are getting very sick of Wilson & have threatened to ask for his removal. I…intend to keep clear of all such movements. Whatever Judge Wilson may do, and however foolish he may act, I intend to maintain my equilibrium & do what is right regardless of him.

I have always treated him well, both in private and upon the bench, while his conduct has been quite the reverse & so marked that even spectators noticed him and spoke of his ungentlemanly conduct. You will pardon me for the liberty I have taken in stating the above facts. I do not desire to trouble you, but it is natural for me to let my friend know all my troubles & difficulties.

In great haste,
Cordially your friend,
CM Hawley[6]

This is where matters still stood a month later. Three men who were supposed to have been shot, three men whom Judge Wilson had consigned to God, had been yanked by evil hands back to Utah and were still unpunished and unrepentant. This is where matters stood when three men left the Colorado River and headed for the Mormon towns of southern Utah. They had been sent by the same senator who had sent Cyrus Hawley to bring down the Mormons' world. Now Mormons had a chance to obtain justice and to strike a blow against Senator Trumbull's invasion of Utah, and a chance to obtain blood atonement for the death of Joseph Smith at the hands of an Illinois mob.

But would the Mormons have made any connection between three scruffy, wandering strangers and Senator Trumbull? Actually, this connection could have come up quickly and naturally. When the Howlands and Dunn explained that they had come from the Powell expedition, the Mormons, given the political realities of the moment, would have wanted to know if this was a federal expedition. Not exactly, the Howlands and Dunn would have answered, but it did receive some federal support through Senator Trumbull and Representative Cullom of Illinois.

Even apart from the Trumbull-Cullom connection, in 1869 federal surveys were not welcome in Utah. Geological surveys of the American West were usually intended to locate mineral wealth, which would only bring more outsiders and trouble pouring into Utah. Government surveyors had made it possible for Washington politicians to carve away large portions of the original Utah Territory and award them to other states. Government surveyors had inserted the worrisome transcontinental railroad into Utah. The Mormons had considered southern Utah their most inaccessible and safe frontier, but now this Powell guy was coming through, making it known, opening up unpredictable troubles.

The settlers of southern Utah were paying extra attention to Judge Hawley's activities. Hawley's judicial district consisted of southern Utah, including

Mountain Meadows and all the towns from which the massacre perpetrators had come and where they were still hiding, perhaps hiding in plain sight, but certainly trying to hide their participation. The towns of southern Utah had been more religiously fanatical than most of Utah, a big factor in their justifying killing 120 people in the name of God. Though a dozen years had passed since the massacre, the perpetrators knew that the American people—and perhaps more importantly, Brigham Young—were still irate about it and that if federal authorities ever came searching for them, they could not expect much sympathy or protection. After years of neglect, Judge Hawley set the investigation and pursuit rolling again in 1869.

In history books about the Mountain Meadows Massacre, and about this whole period in Utah history, Hawley's name is often peripheral, secondary to the role of Judge James McKean and Robert Baskin, or not mentioned at all. This is partly because by the time John D. Lee was arrested and brought to trial, Hawley had retired and gone home. But McKean would not arrive in Utah until the summer of 1870, when President Grant removed Judge Wilson and replaced him with McKean, and in 1869 Robert Baskin was still a private attorney, not yet the U.S. attorney who prosecuted Lee. In the fall of 1869 it was up to Cyrus Hawley to pursue the perpetrators. Hawley understood the animosity he was stirring up in Utah, so in 1872 he persuaded President Grant to build a U.S. Army fort in Beaver, the seat of his district court, and man it with 250 soldiers, to protect him as he investigated the massacre.

There was one prominent southern Utah family that must have felt especially uncomfortable about Judge Hawley's pursuit of the massacre participants. The brothers John Hawley, George Hawley, and William Hawley had—by some accounts—participated in the massacre. As their friends and neighbors began seeing the name Hawley being vilified in the newspapers, they likely asked John, George, and William if they were related to Judge Hawley. And they were: they were distant cousins. As the other massacre participants realized that the Hawley brothers, who had long disliked Brigham Young, were relatives of the judge who was seeking testimony against them, they likely looked askance at the Hawley brothers.

The family connection lay far in the past. In 1632 Joseph Hawley emigrated from England to the Connecticut Colony, where he founded one of those great New England families that spread far and achieved much. (Joseph Hawley settled a few miles from the town of Trumbull, named for another great Connecticut family, which would produce Lyman Trumbull.) Connecticut would have a Governor Hawley and a Senator Hawley, and Cyrus Hawley's great-grandfather was an officer in the American Revolution. But by then, the branch that would produce the Mormon Hawleys had already branched off. It's likely that the Mormon Hawleys and Cyrus Hawley had never heard of one another until 1869.

Pierce Hawley was working as a Methodist missionary to the Indians in Illinois when, in 1833, he converted to the LDS faith. He moved his family to join the Mormon gathering in Missouri. A mob nearly killed him and held knives to the throats of his sons John and George. When the Mormons were driven out of Missouri, the Hawleys moved to Nauvoo, Illinois. To cut lumber for the Nauvoo temple and other buildings, Pierce Hawley and his sons headed to Wisconsin—the beginning of a long family association with the lumber business. The church had promised that in exchange for the logs the Hawleys would float down the Mississippi River to Nauvoo, they would be given a small steamboat. But while they were in Wisconsin, Joseph Smith was murdered and succeeded by Brigham Young, and Young refused to honor the promise about the steamboat. The Hawleys believed Young had robbed them. They went back to Wisconsin and nearly starved that winter. When Young led the Mormons to Utah, the Hawleys rejected him and headed to Texas on a mission previously assigned by Joseph Smith and led by Lyman Wight, whom Young regarded as a renegade. The Hawleys remained in Texas for nearly a decade, running a sawmill. But the Hawleys gradually became dissatisfied with Wight's leadership. When a missionary from Utah came along and told them how the Mormons there were thriving, four Hawley sons decided to move to Utah, against the wishes of their father Pierce, who still detested Brigham Young. Pierce soon joined the Reorganized Church led by Joseph Smith's wife and sons and persuaded his two other sons to join, too, and to remain in the Midwest. The other four Hawley sons migrated to Utah in 1856; three of these were soon assigned to the cotton mission in southern Utah (the other son moved on to California). In April 1857 they settled in the town of Washington, where they built a molasses mill. They had many dealings with John D. Lee. Lee bought his Washington land from William Hawley, paying him $150 in cattle. In 1858 Lee bought the Hawleys' molasses mill, which proved very profitable, and the next year he paid John and George Hawley $82 to move it to his land and rebuild it. Late in 1859 the Hawleys went back into the lumber business, moving to Pine Valley to run a sawmill that fed lumber to the growing towns of southern Utah.

In September 1857 John Hawley was heading from Salt Lake City to the town of Washington, Utah, when for three days he fell in pace with a wagon train from Arkansas. The migrants told John of how Mormons along the way had harassed them. Hawley outpaced them and made it to Washington, where he found that John D. Lee and other local leaders were in a frenzy over this wagon train, or actually about the coming apocalypse between Mormons and their persecutors, whom this wagon train came to symbolize. From here, accounts vary greatly. John, George, and William Hawley were all sergeants in Company I of the Mormon militia of Washington, each in a different platoon. Company I was one of several militia units that marched from southern Utah towns to Mountain Meadows, where the Arkansas wagon train was now camped. The Washington men arrived on September 8, with the wagons already circled and under siege. John D. Lee claimed that all three Hawley brothers participated in the massacre on September 11. But Lee later made quite a few claims that did not show up in the testimony of other participants, claims presumably intended to deflect blame from himself and to widen the circle of guilt. No other massacre participant reported that George Hawley was ever there. But other participants did say that John and William were there and participated. Quite a few participants later claimed that when their leaders announced their plans for committing the massacre, including against women and children, they opposed it or refused to participate. William Hawley later claimed (though this story comes to us thirdhand) that he not only refused to participate, but also threatened to fight for the emigrants, whereupon his fellow militiamen chained him to a wagon wheel to subdue him. However, no other witness repeated William's wagon wheel story, which should have been a conspicuous event. In the memoir John Hawley wrote in 1885 he spoke somewhat peripherally about the massacre, as if he had not been there, insisting that he strongly opposed it and that afterward he condemned John D. Lee to his face in such strong terms that Lee held a secret council to decide if Hawley should be executed for disloyalty—a majority said no. But Lee planned to get his revenge from God, as Hawley wrote: "He said he had received more persecution from me about that mountain affair than all the rest and he wished me to understand he would look for a reward in heaven for my persecuting him. I told him if I had accused him wrongfully he might, but not without. Well the conversation ended with a mad spirit in him."[7] John Hawley was bothered that Lee had stated in print that he was a massacre participant; Hawley's friends continued asking him about this, and in a June 12, 1884, letter in the *Saints' Herald,* Hawley insisted that he was not there and that Lee must have gotten him confused with some other guy named John Hawley.

If the Hawley brothers did participate in the massacre, they might have believed, as others did, that they were justified by their religious faith and safe in their anonymity. But the Hawleys probably felt much less safe, much less lost in the militia crowd, when the person who showed up in 1869 to pursue the killers was named Hawley, probably proud of his distinguished family pedigree and unhappy at seeing it disgraced. Or if, as they claimed, the Hawleys were opposed to the massacre, they might have seemed the most sympathetic and likely people to defect and provide Judge Hawley with the testimony he needed to find and arrest the killers. Their guilty neighbors would now look at the Hawleys with distrust and hostility.

In any case, the year after Judge Hawley arrived in Utah, John and George Hawley fled Utah. They had been there fourteen years and built homes, businesses, and communities, but now they abandoned it all, renounced the LDS Church, denounced Brigham Young, and put a thousand miles between themselves and Utah. William Hawley remained in Utah for the rest of his life, but one source says he was rendered crazy by the Mountain Meadows Massacre and that he sometimes rose in church and denounced Brigham Young, though his brethren would tolerate this on the grounds that he had experienced something terrible.

In his 1885 memoir, John Hawley did not say that his leaving Utah had anything to do with evading the hunt for massacre perpetrators. But in 1869 he was under considerable pressure to prove more loyalty to the LDS Church. Erastus Snow, one of the twelve Mormon apostles and the leader of the LDS Southern Mission, told Hawley that to be fully holy he had to practice polygamy, but Hawley had always been happy with his one wife, and he refused. While he was in Salt Lake City, Hawley bought a new wagon from a non-church business, where it cost only $80 and not the $125 a church-affiliated business required, and he received a "solid reproof" from his brethren.[8] When a missionary for the Reorganized Church came through southern Utah, Hawley invited him to preach, bringing a rebuke from Erastus Snow. When Hawley publicly announced his judgment that Brigham Young had perverted the teachings of Joseph Smith, Snow came and berated him for three hours, not letting him reply, and cut him off from the LDS Church. In October 1870 John and George Hawley left for Iowa, where they joined their long-lost family and the Reorganized Church.

The Hawleys weren't the only people in southern Utah who were feeling under pressure in the summer of 1869. And it wasn't just the families connected with the Mountain Meadows Massacre who were worried. All Utah Mormons were feeling the world closing in on them. They were being invaded by enemies, by the members of the same Illinois mob who had killed Joseph Smith and who were now wearing judge's robes and defending thugs who would kill the fathers of innocent children. Yet just when people were feeling both outrage and powerlessness, along came a therapeutic opportunity, a chance for justice, a chance for blood atonement: three men showed up and no one would ever know if they disappeared, sent by the same senator and congressman who were trying to destroy the world.

Here's an example of the outraged righteousness that might have applied itself to the Howlands and Bill Dunn. When in 1871 the now-unified Utah judges had Brigham Young arrested for polygamy, it was on the same day as the great fire that destroyed Chicago, and many Mormons took this as God's punishment. From the diary of John Pulsipher:

> Bro. Brigham was arrested by an unjust court and ring of apostates and mobbers, headed by the notorious Judge McKean.
>
> That judge cares not for law or justice—but packs juries of sworn enemies, tries and condemns the innocent as he pleases....
>
> Here is an item of History worth remembering. The very day these arrests were made a terrible fire broke out in Chicago, and raged before a strong wind 'til it consumed 4 or 5 square miles of the business part of the city with all its vast buildings, stores, banking houses and factories! It was beyond the power of man to stop it....
>
> A terrible scourge on that Proud City.
>
> For be it remembered that in the city of Chicago was the political platform got up that declared slavery and Polygamy Twin Relics of Barbarism and must be put down what ever must be the consequences. So, we see, When they made the attack on polygamy, the Lord suffered that terrible calamity to come on them.[9]

Later on that same page Pulsipher noted news of the concurrent and massive Peshtigo fire in Wisconsin, and concluded, "The sayings of Prophets are being fulfilled."[10] If God was willing to destroy a great city to avenge a judicial action, he might not hesitate to throw in three more men.

As the Howlands and Dunn wandered toward St. George they could have run into the wrong people, perhaps out herding cattle or manning Fort Pearce, which protected St. George from Indian threats. In 1869 St. George and its neighboring towns held several people who had participated in the Mountain Meadows Massacre, people who might have had a volatile combination of righteousness, resentment of the persecution of Mormons, and fear of pursuit, which could have triggered a new act of violence.

This chapter has developed a scenario, a historical and political context that makes it psychologically plausible that the Mormons might have killed the Howlands and Dunn deliberately, yet this scenario is based entirely on circumstances. Circumstances are not evidence that this act actually happened. This chapter has offered nothing that could be called evidence or proof. Certainly, there is no letter from Judge Hawley to Senator Trumbull reporting that he has heard a rumor that the Mormons killed his protégé's men and that he is planning to investigate. Nor is there any other such letter or document.

Does this scenario now hit a dead end? Actually, it might still leave us with somewhere farther to go. By leaping forward to the aftermath of the killings of the Howlands and Dunn, by examining the response of the people of southern Utah, we might still be able to pick up the tracks of this scenario and follow it farther.

But first, I will briefly mention another event that might have gotten mixed up with the Howlands and Dunn. In the 1850s the Mormons set up a new colony on the Salmon River in today's Idaho, and they thought they were doing well and had pacified the area Indians. They were shocked when in 1858 the Indians attacked, forcing them to abandon their settlement. They placed all the blame on John W. Powell. No, not our John W. Powell—another John W. Powell, who came West as a government surveyor and remained as a mountaineer. To this day, Mormon-written history books blame the attack on the "evil-minded" Powell. (Powell testified to the War Department that the Indians attacked because the Mormons were taking their land and arming enemy tribes.) If the Howlands and Dunn ran into Mormons and explained they were from the expedition of John W. Powell, government surveyor of the West, the Mormons would not have believed there were two John W. Powells. They might have assumed that the evil-minded Powell was plotting more trouble.

NOTES

1. Shelby M. Cullom, "Enforcement of Laws in Utah," speech delivered in the US House of Representatives, February 17, 1870 (Washington, DC: F. & J. Rives & Geo A. Bailey, 1870), 14–15.

2. Shelby M. Cullom, *50 Years of Public Service* (Chicago: A.C. McClurg & Co., 1911), 222.

3. *Proceedings in Mass Meeting of the Ladies of Salt Lake City to Protest Against the Passage of Cullom's Bill, January 14, 1870*, 6, in Shelby M. Cullom Papers, Abraham Lincoln Presidential Library, Springfield, IL.

4. Ibid., 8, 3.

5. Legal charges against Young, mentioned in Robert N. Baskin, *Reminiscences of Early Utah* (1914; repr. Salt Lake City: Signature Books, 2006), 54. Page references to 2006 ed.

6. Cyrus Hawley to Senator Trumbull, July 29, 1869, Lyman Trumbull Papers, Abraham Lincoln Presidential Library, Springfield, IL.

7. John Pierce Hawley, *Autobiography of John Pierce Hawley,* Community of Christ Archives, 1885.

8. Ibid.

9. Diary of John Pulsipher, Special Collections, Harold B. Lee Library, Brigham Young University, Provo, UT (hereafter Pulsipher Diary), 1871.

10. Ibid.

·33·

The Aftermath

IN THE AFTERMATH of an event like the Howland–Dunn killings, which were done in a remote area by unknown assailants (who had good reasons to remain unknown), with no witnesses or reliable sources of information, it should not be surprising that there might be considerable uncertainty and confusion about it, or that accounts changed as the authorities tried to gather more information. This might be why the Mormons provided six varied explanations of what had happened. Some of these explanations were public, some private. Yet it also might be worth examining these accounts more closely, especially the circumstances in which they continued mutating, in case there was something more than mere confusion going on.

The first news of the fate of the Howlands and Dunn was a telegram received by President Erastus Snow, the leader of the southern Utah settlements, in St. George. This telegram was recorded by James G. Bleak, official and diligent chronicler, in his *Annals of the Southern Utah Mission*:

> On Sept 7th, at 5:15 p. pm. The following telegram was received at St. George: "Pres. Erastus Snow: Powell's three men killed by She-bits, five days ago, one Indian day's journey from Washington. Indians report that they were found in an exhausted state, fed by the She-bits and put on the trail leading to Washington; after which they saw a squaw gathering seeds and shot her. Whereupon the She-bits followed up and killed all three.
>
> Two of the She-bits who killed the men are in the Washington Indian camp with two of the guns. Indian George has gone to secure what papers and property there is left. Operater."[1]

This telegram has long puzzled historians. It included no explanation of where it came from, or who sent it. Since the telegram makes references to the town of Washington, just down the road from St. George, it seems to have originated there.

Yet another thing about this telegram was odd. When the sender sent it to Erastus Snow in St. George, Snow was not in St. George, and he would not be back for days, and the sender knew this, for everyone in Washington knew that Snow was leaving town for days. It's possible the sender watched Snow ride through Washington on the very morning that he sent the telegram in the other direction. It's possible that the sender waited until Snow was safely out of town. The sender not only sent the telegram to Snow, but he also sent a copy to the *Deseret News* in Salt Lake City, which published a near-verbatim account of it on September 8, turning it into the seemingly official account of what had happened, soon to be republished in newspapers around the country. But this version of events had not been authorized by Erastus Snow. It was released behind his back. He would soon disavow it.

Back on July 13 Erastus Snow had announced that the southern Utah militias would meet for a military drill starting on September 8, lasting three days for some, longer for others. They were to meet at Harmony, which is about thirty miles north of St. George as the raven flies, more by the wandering roads of the time. To get there in time Erastus Snow must have left St. George early on September 7, if not sooner. At Camp Harmony on September 8, roll call was taken at 9 AM and it was found that out of sixty-two members of the St. George Nauvoo Legion, only twenty-two were present—more than half of the members had asked to be excused from the drill for various reasons. The next morning, roll call counted twenty-seven men from St. George. Erastus Snow's presence was noted by John Pulsipher in his diary: "We met with the military men of this southern district—met at Harmony for 23 days drill. Brig. Gen. E. Snow commanding, a new drill is introduced into the legion—Upton's military tactics. We organized in the cavalry co. as we need to be mounted to do much more than our home guards."[2] The scale of the drill impressed militia member Orson Welcome Huntsman:

> This was the largest camp that I had seen for some time past. There was a string of wagons for over a mile long encamped side by side…. The bugle sounded and the whole army was called out on parade under the command of apostle Erastus Snow, brigadier general, and marched all day long on foot, the next day on horseback and the next day we charged the great train of wagons just as though they were the foe, and the next two or three days we fought one army against the

other. We went right into battle and fought like gallant soldiers, could hardly see the enemy for the dust and smoke, the firing of the rifles and the cannons and the great danger of being captured by the enemy, made great excitement for men and beast.[3]

Huntsman's regiment would not be dismissed until the 14th, but the St. George company was dismissed at sunrise on September 11. In the meantime, the emptiness of the town of Washington was noted in the diary of resident Charles Lowell Walker, who on September 11 wrote, "Very Warm. At work fixing up around home. The town is very quiet, the majority of the Men having gone to Harmony on a 3 days drill." Walker also noted that Snow was back in town by September 18.[4]

If Washington was "very quiet" when someone sent the telegram to St. George and Salt Lake City, who was there to send it? Even under normal circumstances, there were only a few people who had access to the telegraph in Washington. This telegraph was not, as in most Western towns and Western movies, a Western Union office on the main street where anyone could walk up, plunk down their coins, and send any kind of telegram to anyone. Like much else in Utah, Utah's telegraph system was set up and run by the LDS Church. It connected many towns so small and remote that a commercial telegraph company would not have bothered with them. In many years the Deseret Telegraph Company lost money. It was used, first of all, to conduct church and governmental business. In the 1860s it was used to alert towns about Indian movements during the Black Hawk War, and in the 1880s it was used to warn towns of the approach of federal agents on anti-polygamy raids. In most towns the telegraph was kept locked up inside a church building. In Washington, it was locked up inside a private home. Whoever sent that telegram, he was not just the "operator": he was also someone who had some authority. But we will return to this question later.

The telegram of September 7 soon put Erastus Snow in an uncomfortable position. Only two or three days before the telegram was sent, John Wesley Powell had come through St. George and met with Snow and asked him about his missing men. Snow later said that he expressed his concern to Powell and agreed to help him. But now Snow, who was supposed to be in charge of all things that came out of southern Utah, had effectively been put on record as saying that Powell's men were cold-blooded killers who had betrayed the Indians' kindness and murdered an innocent, helpless woman, thus bringing their deaths on themselves. Snow's situation then became worse because while he was still drilling, Powell was on his way to Salt Lake City, where he would give a well-attended public lecture about his journey, praised by the *Deseret News* on September 17, 1869, and win some friends and respect. As Powell continued back to the Midwest he responded strongly to the telegram report that his men had murdered anyone. On September 18 the *Cheyenne Leader* reported, "Concerning the death of three of his men, Major Powell informs us that these men left him a few days before the completion of his journey down the river, and struck across the country for the Mormon settlements. After his arrival in Salt Lake he received a dispatch from one of the Southern Mormon elders, stating that the dead bodies of three men had been discovered, but the Major does not deem it at all certain that they were his men, and utterly discredits the report that they killed a squaw, as he says they were honorable men and gentlemen." The "Southern Mormon" elder was most likely Erastus Snow, back home and trying to take charge of the situation. He had introduced a new element: the bodies had been found.

When Powell got back to Illinois he again denounced the telegram that called his men murderers. On September 28 the *Chicago Tribune* quoted Powell: "I have known O. G. Howland personally for many years and I have no hesitation in pronouncing this part of the story a libel. It was not in the man's faithful, genial nature to do such a thing."

Now the publishers of the *Deseret News* and the leaders of the LDS Church were seeing a newly important national figure denouncing, in national newspapers, the veracity of the Mormon newspaper. They did not need this sort of negative attention, and Erastus Snow did not need their blame.

The day after the *Chicago Tribune* story, on September 29, the *Deseret News* published a considerably different version of events:

> THE MURDERED MEN OF THE POWELL EXPEDITION.
> President Erastus Snow telegraphs from St. George, per Deseret Telegraph line, that after making a thorough investigation through reliable Indians, of the facts of the murder of the three men of the Powell expedition, he is satisfied they did not molest the squaw, as the first Indian reported, but that they were killed by an enraged Shebitt, some of whose friends had, a short time previously, been murdered by a party of miners on the other (east) side of the Colorado river.
>
> The Shebitts have since returned to their own country, but the Piedes [a Mormon term for Paiutes] of Southern Utah, say they (the Shebitts) burned the papers of the expedition the men had with them, after killing them. President Snow concludes his dispatch saying he will still continue the search.

The papers alluded to above are simply duplicates of those in the possession of Major Powell, which he gave to the men when they left the company, lest anything should happen to him and his party in the last kanyon, and the records of the expedition get lost; in which case these others would be preserved to tell the story of his voyage.

There are quite a few changes here. Powell's men are now totally innocent of having malicious personalities or committing any crime; they were merely victims of an Indian crime. Instead of a group of attackers, there was only one. The motive isn't entirely clear, whether the enraged Indian mistook Powell's men for the guilty party or simply took his revenge against a convenient target. There is no mention of the Indians feeding or directing Powell's men. Instead of the killers being camped in Washington with the murder weapons, the killer is long gone. The previous, badly erroneous report came from an unreliable Indian, but this one came from reliable Indians. And here Snow makes no mention of the bodies having been located.

These changes in the story are substantial enough that we have to ask what is going on. Was the first report simply the result of incompetence? Or did the sender of the September 7 telegram concoct a false story, which Snow then corrected? Or was the first story correct, and Snow concocted a false story to escape from Powell's condemnation in the national press? Or was the first story false and Snow now felt trapped by it, but was still trying to modify its details? Or was it some combination of these factors?

Snow did not make any offer to retrieve the bodies to send them to their families, but considering that this was summer in Arizona there was some biological logic to not doing so. Snow did not even make an offer to give the bodies a proper Christian burial. Nor did he pledge to track down the killer and punish him. In 1869 on the American frontier, with many Indian wars still being fought and with the Wounded Knee Massacre still two decades in the future, it was not at all normal to allow Indians to get away with murdering white people, even obscure whites, and especially not members of a nationally important expedition. Whites almost always retaliated, sometimes far out of proportion to the cause, sometimes indiscriminately, not caring if the Indians they were killing were the ones who had committed the killings.

The next shift in the story emerged in response to inquiries from Nathan Howland, the brother of Oramel and Seneca Howland, who began his own investigation into their disappearance. Nathan Howland's letters have remained in Howland family hands until now. Nathan Howland first contacted William

Byers, editor of the *Rocky Mountain News* and longtime employer of Oramel Howland, asking him for news about his brothers. Byers undoubtedly subscribed to the *Deseret News.* But Byers dismissed Mormon accounts:

Denver

Oct. 15, 1869

Mr. [N]. D. Howland

Dear Sir,

Your letter requesting information relative to the fate of your brothers is received. We are sorry to say that we cannot give you any definite news concerning them. All we know can be told in a few words. Major Powell says in a letter published in the "New York Tribune" that the Howlands and W. H. Dunn refused to go through the last canyon before reaching Callville as they did not consider it safe and that they said they would strike across the country to the settlements in Southern Utah distant some two or three hundred miles, and make their way to the Union Pacific Railroad and thence home (Denver). The slip enclosed being an extract from one of the Salt Lake papers throws no light on the matter. Another item appeared in the same paper a few days later stating that nothing further was known concerning them. While it is possible that they may have gone to prospecting for gold in the Mountains of Southern Utah, such a fact does not seem probable as they were without money, clothing or provisions and would have had to go to one of the settlements to procure supplies. Considerable interest was manifested in Utah as to their fate, and their arrival at a settlement would have been reported immediately to Salt Lake and we should have heard of it ere this. It seems to us that the only way to settle the matter definitely is for some one to go to Salt Lake and from there to the settlements in Southern Utah if necessary, which we think can be done quite easily. W. H. Dunn has no relatives that we know of. He was an old and experienced mountaineer and was highly esteemed by those acquainted with him. The Howland boys had hundreds of warm friends in this Territory. Should any of the other boys of the party who were left thousands of miles from home without any money ever get back we may know more of their reasons for leaving the expedition at the time they did, but until then we will have to take Major Powell's word for it.

We will gladly furnish you at any time all the information we have concerning them or their affairs.

We remain, very truly,

Byers and Daily[5]

It is not clear if the newspaper article Byers sent to Nathan Howland was one stating that the Howland brothers had been killed, which might not deserve to be dismissed as throwing "no light on the matter," but at least Byers was not endorsing this outcome and was holding out the hope they were still alive. Perhaps Byers was merely trying to be kind, or perhaps he was accustomed to thoroughly distrusting anything the Mormon newspaper said. Byers also seemed to distrust Powell's version of events.

Byers did not send out a search party, but this could have been because he had an easier option. Byers wrote a letter to Joseph E. Johnson, a longtime, trusted friend who lived in St. George. Byers and Johnson had known one another for fifteen years, beginning in Omaha, where both were business and civic leaders. After Byers left Omaha for Denver he tried to persuade Johnson to join him there, but Johnson felt called to Utah. Johnson grew up near Palmyra, New York, where Joseph Smith began preaching his new religion, and Johnson's siblings became some of Smith's first converts. Johnson, too, converted and settled near Nauvoo, and he accompanied Joseph Smith to the Carthage, Illinois, jail where Smith was killed. Driven from his home, Johnson moved to Kanesville, Iowa, the staging place for the Mormons' migration to Utah. Johnson became Kanesville postmaster, renamed the town "Council Bluffs," and started a newspaper and family, which led him to remain there when the Mormons left. Moving across the Missouri River, Johnson opened the first store in Omaha and got elected to the Nebraska state legislature, where Byers had served a short time before. Johnson moved to Utah in 1861 and to St. George in 1865, for its warmer climate. Johnson had long loved botany, and he patented some botanical cures, opened a St. George drugstore, and designed an elaborate garden and nursery, into which his next-door neighbor built a gate so he, too, could enjoy it—Johnson's neighbor was Brigham Young, who had built a winter home in St. George. From Nebraska, Johnson brought with him his printing press and started a St. George newspaper—which ceased publication in July 1869—and a botanical journal. It's plausible that one reason Oramel Howland left the river and set off for St. George was because he knew that William Byers had a trusted friend there.

Byers would have considered Johnson a well-informed source. When Powell came through St. George days after leaving the river, he sought out not only Erastus Snow but also Joseph Johnson to inquire about his missing men. Now Johnson wrote to Byers what he might have intended to be a private letter, but that Byers published on November 23:

THE POWELL EXPEDITION:

Fate of the Howlands and Dunn.

We are in receipt of the following letter from an old friend in southern Utah. It doubtless is conclusive as to the fate of the three missing men of the Powell party. We hope to learn more particulars before long:

St. George, Utah.

Nov. 11, '69

W. N. Byers:

Your letter received per last mail. In reply I will state that there were three men of the Colorado exploring expedition, under Major Powell, killed by Indians about thirty or forty miles from this place. Friendly Indians came in and stated that three white men were found in a perishing condition by the Kibatbels and were brought into their camp, fed, and recovered, and sent forward from this place on the regular trail; that on their way they came across a squaw gathering seeds, and that they debauched and shot her. This enraged the tribe and they were pursued, foully murdered and left for wolves to eat; not allowing whites even to go and bury them. It has been very well ascertained that the whole of this was a sheer fabrication, and that the Indians wantonly murdered the three for what they had.

I talked with Major Powell about these men but did not write down the names. They left the Major and party near the mouth of the Pah-sear, a creek emptying into the Colorado about 100 miles southeast of this. On account of the danger of passing down the rapids they chose the dangers of land travel. The Major gave them his firearms and ammunition. The party had little food, so they had to hunt for a living.

Maj. Powell arrived here in seven or eight days after the three left him, all safe, and was anxious about the others.

I will take all possible measures to obtain all the facts and particulars in the matter and write you. I don't think the bones have been buried. Some friendly Indians might be induced by good pay to go out and gather and bring in the bones, if desired.

Yours truly,

J. E. Johnson

Johnson has added a new element to the original telegram story: Powell's men had raped the Indian squaw. But then he repudiates this whole story, saying confidently that it was "a sheer fabrication." His new story is that the

Indians killed Powell's men in an act of robbery. He makes no mention of Snow's amended story about the miners. He makes no mention of Snow's promise, more than a month ago, to "continue the search."

When Johnson insists that the telegram story was "a sheer fabrication," he does not say whether it was fabricated by the Indians or by the Mormons. But an Indian robbery and killing of members of an important national expedition might have presented an image of chaos that the Mormons of southern Utah would find embarrassing; they might try to hide it by offering a story blaming the victims for their own murders. When this story brought a different form of embarrassment, with John Wesley Powell denying in the national press, perhaps Erastus Snow altered the story in a way that cleared from blame both Powell's men and the Mormons. But now Joseph Johnson, Brigham Young's next-door neighbor, has declared in a major newspaper that the story published by the Mormons was a "sheer fabrication," and he has repudiated Snow's version of this story.

Erastus Snow probably went and had a firm talk with Joseph Johnson, for Johnson soon wrote another letter to Byers, retracting his previous letter and adopting Snow's story. On December 20 Byers published the following:

> We are in receipt of the following additional information about the murder of the Powell party, written by Mr. J. E. Johnson, at St. George, Utah, December 6:
>
> "I have learned more in regard to the young men, your friends, that were murdered by the Indians, towards the Colorado. It was done by a band of Shebit Indians, who live across the Colorado, whose friend had been murdered evidently by some white men—miners. The Indians took them for miners, and killed them out of revenge. They had committed no crime against the Indians, but suffered for others' crimes. They were unburied."

Whether through Johnson's confusion or Snow's alteration, Johnson has introduced a different version of Snow's story. Now it was only one Indian who was murdered, and now it was more than one Indian who killed the Howlands and Dunn. It's still a bit vague, but now the killings look more like a case of mistaken identity.

There were indeed miners roaming around northern Arizona in the summer of 1869. William H. Hardy of Hardyville, who was in the business of selling supplies to miners, wrote to General William Palmer on August 16, 1869, "There are at present several hundred small prospecting parties traveling all through the southern part of Nevada and northern part of Arizona."[6]

Byers sent Johnson's new letter to Nathan Howland. Nathan Howland
had continued his efforts. He had contacted the editors of the *Deseret News,*
and they sent him issues "containing all the information we have concerning
them."[7] They advised Howland to contact Erastus Snow for further information. Howland wrote to Snow.

When Snow received Nathan Howland's letter, Snow could have recog-
nized a return address only two miles from the Vermont birthplace of Joseph
Smith. Snow would know this, for Snow, too, was born and raised in Vermont,
and he had converted to the LDS faith there. Snow came from a distinguished
Mayflower-era family, and thus of all the Mormon leaders Nathan Howland
could have contacted, Snow might have been the most likely to know, as the
Howland family had long known—from the family-tree obsession of most
Mayflower families—that Joseph Smith was descended from *Mayflower* pilgrim
John Howland. The murdered Oramel and Seneca Howland were indeed very
distant relatives of Joseph Smith. Perhaps Erastus Snow now realized that he
had left the bodies of two of Joseph Smith's relatives rotting in the desert, being
gnawed by coyotes. Snow answered:

> St. George
> December 9, 1869
> Mr. [N]. D. Howland
> South Royalton, Vt.
> Dear Sir,
> In answer to yours of the 19th ref: I communicate to you the following
> data in relation to the killing of your brothers by the Indians. Major
> Powell, who came through the city in the fore-part of September last
> stated to me that he had parted with three men of his expedition, men-
> tioning I think the names of your brothers as two of them, above the
> head of the Grand Falls of the Colorado, they preferring to take their
> chances over the desert to this place rather than run, as they thought,
> a greater risk in descending the falls. When Major Powell arrived
> here he had left those men 7 days previous and upon telling me the
> circumstances I felt concerned about their safety and immediately
> sent out some friendly Pah-Ute Indians to find them if possible and
> pilot them to this place.
>
> They returned unsuccessfully and reported that some Indians
> had told them that three white men had been killed about 100 miles
> S.E. from here by a band of Indians living near the Colorado.
>
> The country between the Colorado and this place is a barren
> desert without any running streams and only very few diminutive
> springs can be found. A white man hardly ever passes over it and

during the summer it is very unsafe for a stranger to the country to venture over that region on account of the scarcity of water.

From the best information I can obtain, I believe that the murdered men did not provoke the Indians by their own actions but were killed in revenge for others' faults. A short time previous to this affair some miners killed some Indians and ravished some squaws on the opposite side of the Colorado and some of the Indians belonging to the same tribe finding Major Powell's men, supposed them to be of the same class of men that had killed their friends and did not hesitate to take revenge.

I have not been able to get any particulars as to the remains of the men, the color of their hair, their clothing or papers. The Indians who reported to me did not see the bodies themselves and all they know is as they were told themselves.

I have offered rewards to the Indians for obtaining papers or other mementoes of the murdered men, should they ever come across any and I shall take pleasure in forwarding to you the same if any should reach me.

Sincerely sympathizing with yourself and other relatives of the deceased

I remain yours, very respectfully,

Erastus Snow

Snow has retained his basic story but made several major changes. Most significantly, he now says that upon meeting Powell he immediately sent out a search party to find the Howlands and guide them to St. George. He has not said this before—not to Powell, not to Johnson, not to the newspaper. He also says he offered rewards for bringing in the men's papers and other items, which is odd because Snow had previously reported that the Indians had burned those papers. Snow's offer of a reward to very poor Indians also makes it odd that the Indians never turned in anything else, not even a scrap of clothing. Snow is also reneging on his claim to Powell that the bodies had been located; now even his reliable Indians have only heard about them. Snow has also moved the bodies and the murders farther from St. George than anyone else has, "100 miles S.E. from here," which Snow must know is nonsense, for it would place the bodies on the other side of the Colorado River. It's also odd that Snow is offering rewards for "mementoes" of the men but saying nothing to Nathan Howland about finding and honorably burying his brothers. It's as if Snow does not want to find the bodies. Snow has even rebuked the Howland brothers for being dumb enough to try to cross the desert in summer, when

Snow knows it is actually monsoon season, with daily thunderstorms that leave plenty of puddles, at least. Snow then relates his story about the miners, but he adds the new element that the miners had raped several squaws. Snow now says definitely that the Indians did not mistake Powell's men for the guilty miners but only took them to be "of the same class," and thus a convenient target for revenge.

Since Snow is now talking directly with the brother of the deceased, it might be natural for him to want to make himself look better or to give the situation a bit more dignity, saying that the bodies were not found rather than admitting that the bodies had been left in the desert to be gnawed by coyotes. But we have no indication that Snow made any further efforts to locate or bury the bodies or to bring back "mementoes," which could have included important documents about the expedition, and not just duplicates of what Powell possessed. Nor did Snow ever try to bring any Indians to justice.

The next summer Powell returned to the Southwest to plan another river trip, and he made an effort to find out what had happened to his lost men. Powell and Mormon guide Jacob Hamblin and Howland cousin Walter Graves (the student from Bloomington, Illinois) traveled to the base of Mount Trumbull and met with the Shivwits. Mediated through Hamblin, who spoke the Shivwits language, a sixth version of events emerged, a new variation of Snow's story. Now there was no bunch of Indians killed, no squaws raped, no "same class" revenge. Now there was one squaw killed by miners in a drunken brawl, which the Shivwits learned about from one Indian who crossed the river. Upon seeing Powell's men, the Shivwits were sure these were the guilty men and took their revenge.

Was this, finally, the accurate story, and everything before it badly garbled? Yet on the American frontier it was quite unusual and dangerous for Indians to openly confess to killing whites, even by mistake. Even whites didn't get away with accidental murder. Or was this story yet another layer of story manipulation? Of course, suggesting such manipulation supposes that the Mormons were now manipulating the Indians into making a confession. The Mormons did hold considerable power over the Paiutes, but was it enough to coerce the Paiutes into making a self-endangering confession of murder?

Given the circumstances of the Howland–Dunn killings, there was plenty of room for honest confusion. Yet when we see how often and how dramatically the Mormons changed their stories, not only contradicting themselves but also offering outright nonsense, we have to wonder if something else was going on, if the Mormons did not want to produce the bodies and knew there were no Indians who deserved to be punished. We have to wonder if we are witnessing the ongoing invention of a story designed to hide something so serious that the Mormons would prefer being convicted of abandoning Joseph Smith's relatives to rot in the desert.

Now that we have raised a realistic possibility that the Mormons might have been engaging in a cover-up, it's time to return to the question of that first telegram. But once again we will be dealing with a possibility that is entirely circumstantial.

The telegraph system arrived in Washington and St. George in early 1867. In Washington the man in charge of the telegraph was Robert Covington, one of the original pioneers of the cotton mission and the bishop of Washington. Unlike in most towns, where the telegraph was kept in the church tithing office, in Washington the telegraph was placed in a private home, the home of Adolphus Whitehead, the manager of the cotton factory; the telegraph would help him keep cotton producers in touch with changing conditions. In Salt Lake City Whitehead had managed a woolen mill owned by Brigham Young, and Young had sent him to Washington to manage the factory there. But for church or state business, the most likely telegraph user was Robert Covington.

Only one month after the September 7 telegram was sent, Robert Covington, who had served as bishop for twelve years and deserved a lot of the credit for the success of the cotton mission, was removed as bishop and ordered to leave Utah. In reality, he was being sent on a mission to Mississippi, to last half a year. It was an assignment that most Mormons would find punishing, if not a form of punishment.

The Mormons had sent missionaries to the American South before the Civil War, with very little success. When Robert Covington arrived in Mississippi in November 1869 he had little church support in facing the grim realities of a collapsed society. Southerners saw Mormonism as a Northern religion and missionaries as more invaders trying to destroy their way of life. Southerners, with their code of chivalry toward women, were especially outraged by Mormon polygamy. They portrayed Mormon missionaries as lust-crazed barbarians who were trying to turn their daughters into prostitutes and lure them away to Utah. The same vigilante groups that were lynching former slaves also murdered Mormon missionaries and burned down churches. Historian Patrick Q. Mason, in his *The Mormon Menace: Violence and Anti-Mormonism in the Postbellum South*, found that the South was more militantly anti-Mormon than other regions: "Mormonism was unique in the way it inspired southerners to set aside general norms of civility and religious tolerance as they sought the eradication of the Mormon presence…. Southerners victimized Latter-day Saint missionaries and converts in well over three hundred documented cases of violence in the last quarter of the nineteenth century." One missionary, killed in 1879, was taken home to Salt Lake City and buried under a monument that read, "There is no law in Georgia for the Mormons."[8] Black churches fully enlisted in the anti-Mormon crusade. Reverend L. M. Hagood, a black Methodist, declared that Mormonism was "an institution more cruel than the Inquisition and more loathsome than the smallpox."[9] The leading black Methodist magazine called for the U.S. government to send an army of 150,000 to Utah to "wipe this blot off from our civilization."[10]

When Robert Covington returned to Utah, the *Deseret News* reported, on April 18, 1870, "The Bishop's account of matters in Mississippi is not very flattering. He says a general feeling of insecurity to life and property is very prevalent…. The Ku-Klux-Klan is very numerous and powerful and no man's life is considered safe whose course is offensive to them." It did make sense to send Covington to Mississippi, for like many in the cotton mission he had been born in the South (North Carolina), and he had once lived in Mississippi as a plantation overseer and slave owner, until converting to Mormonism in 1842 and moving to Nauvoo. Yet Mississippi was one of many Southern states that would later pass laws against practicing or even preaching polygamy—the sentence in Mississippi was ten years in prison. Mississippi was also one of the worst states for vigilante violence against Mormons.

Whatever the intentions behind sending Covington to Mississippi, he went through a punishing experience. When Covington returned to Washington, he was never reinstated as bishop. Were Brigham Young and Erastus Snow retaliating against Covington for sending a telegram, behind Snow's back, that caused embarrassment to the church? Were they punishing Covington for taking part in a cover-up?

On the other hand, it's possible the telegram originated not with anyone who lived in Washington, but with someone from elsewhere who went to Washington precisely because the telegraph there was not kept locked in a church office.

We could take a different approach by asking not who sent the telegram, but who received it. The editor of the *Deseret News,* who published the telegram, was George Q. Cannon; he was also the treasurer of the Deseret Telegraph Company. George's brother David H. Cannon lived in St. George and was one of the leaders of its church and its militia; at age twelve, David had served as the newspaper's first apprentice when it began publication. A third brother,

Angus, had been the first mayor of St. George and had now returned to Salt Lake City to serve as the newspaper's business manager. When Judge Cyrus Hawley went to Washington, DC, to try to stop Congress from seating George Q. Cannon as a congressman, he declared that Cannon was, according to Cannon's own diary, "one of the founders of a system of murder and an inaugurator of bloodshed."[11]

If the Mormons were engaging in a cover-up, there are three possibilities as to what they were trying to hide.

First, they could merely have been trying to hide their own inability to control the Indians in their backyard, which had now led to a tragedy and embarrassing national headlines.

Second, a few Mormons might have run into the Howlands and Dunn and killed them, then tried to blame the Indians, as they had done with the Mountain Meadows Massacre.

In their book *Massacre at Mountain Meadows,* LDS historians Ronald W. Walker, Richard E. Turley Jr., and Glen M. Leonard counted thirteen people from the town of Washington who had plausible involvement in the massacre. This number included some of the founders and civic leaders of the town and the cotton mission. (But this number did not include, it should be said, either Robert Covington or David H. Cannon.) Many of them were still living there or in the area in 1869. Many of them had large families in the area. Some of them held grazing rights south of St. George, in the areas where the Howlands and Dunn were most likely to appear (although grazing had been greatly curtailed during the Black Hawk War years). Some of them had helped build Fort Pearce south of St. George to help guard their towns against surprise attack, and in fact the fort was named for a family that had two members at the Mountain Meadows Massacre. Church tithing records, which record the labor Mormons donate to public works, show that quite a few area residents spent time doing construction projects at Fort Pearce in the summer and fall of 1869. Fort Pearce would have been the most likely place for the Howlands and Dunn to finally encounter someone. There were also massacre participants originally from other towns who might then have been in the St. George and Washington area. The next year, as Powell surveyed the region and prepared for his next river trip, he was assisted by some of the massacre's most notorious individuals, including John D. Lee, Isaac Haight, William Dame, and George Adair. Powell's men puzzled how men who could be quite "agreeable" in person could have done such a deed.

The Howlands and Dunn might also have run into a Mormon militia patrol on the Arizona Strip. According to the memoir of Edwin G. Woolley, there were two occasions in 1869, in February and November, when the Mormons sent militia patrols from St. George onto the Arizona Strip, both times in response to Navajo raids for horses. The November raid took place north of St. George, and as the Navajos fled toward the Colorado River the militia caught up with them and engaged in a rifle battle.

However, in the absence of any documents that point fingers at anyone in particular for the killing of Powell's men, it would be a mere guessing game to begin naming names.

There is a third possibility as to what the Mormons were trying to cover up. The Indians might have killed the Howlands and Dunn not for vengeance against them, but as an act of vengeance against the Mormons, who had committed a crime against the Indians three years before. This crime was still secret, and the Mormons could have feared that if outside authorities investigated the Howland–Dunn killings, it would lead to the disclosure of their crime. We will consider this possibility next.

NOTES

1. Bleak, *Annals,* Book B, 10. Telegraph received Sept. 7.

2. Pulsipher diary, Sept. 1869.

3. Orson Welcome Huntsman, *Diary of Orson Welcome Huntsman*, in *Collection of Mormon Diaries* [1935–38] (Washington, DC: Library of Congress), reel 4, item 5, vol. 1, 1–2.

4. *Diary of Charles Lowell Walker,* Vol. 1, ed. Karl Larson and Katherine Miles Larson (Logan: Utah State University Press, 1980), 298, Sept. 11, 1869.

5. Daily was Byers's publishing partner.

6. Hardy to Palmer, August 16, 1869, William Palmer Papers, Colorado Historical Society, Denver. Published by permission.

7. Nov. 9, 1869. Letters in hands of Howland family. Published by permission.

8. Patrick Q. Mason, *The Mormon Menace: Violence and Anti-Mormonism in the Postbellum South* (Oxford, UK: Oxford University Press, 2011), 13, 34.

9. Rev. H. L. Hagood, "Mormonism," *Southwestern Christian Advocate* (June 8, 1882).

10. "The Mormon Question," *Southwestern Christian Advocate* (Feb. 2, 1882).

11. George Q. Cannon journal, no date, quoted in Davis Bitton, *George Q. Cannon: A Biography* (Salt Lake City: Deseret Books, 1999), 186.

·34·

The Arizona Strip Massacre

OR A DECADE after the Mountain Meadows Massacre of 1857 the participants tried to cover up the nature of the massacre and their personal roles
in it. Yet as the truth about the massacre filtered out, it became a national scandal. For the LDS Church, it became the blackest mark in its history, and the
participants became a source of shame for the church. These men tried to re-
habilitate their reputations through loyal service and hard labor. But then, in
January 1866, the Mormons of southern Utah committed yet another massacre
against innocent people.

In 1864 the U.S. Army began rounding up Navajos and marching them to
captivity in New Mexico. Thousands of Navajos evaded capture and hid in the
more remote corners of Navajo lands, mainly in the areas closest to the Colorado River, where canyon mazes made them harder to find. The terrain also
made it harder for the Navajos to survive. For the Navajos living in the region
around what would become Lees Ferry, where crossing the Colorado River
wasn't so hard, one survival strategy was to raid the villages of southern Utah
for livestock. The Navajos saw it as a fair trade for everything that had been
stolen from them. The Mormons saw it as just another act of Indian treachery
and theft.

In January 1866 the Navajos struck at Pipe Spring, a ranch that had been
started by James Whitmore in 1863, far from the well-defended towns around
St. George. The Navajos stole a herd of sheep and some cattle and killed Whitmore and his son-in-law Robert McIntyre, who were a few miles from their
house. When Whitmore and McIntyre didn't return home, their family sent
for help, and Captain David H. Cannon rode out from St. George with his
cavalry. Cannon soon sent for reinforcements and got nearly fifty more men,
including his brother and militia officer Angus Cannon. After heavy snows
fell, they couldn't track Whitmore and McIntyre, the Indians, or the sheep,

but they did find the tracks of two Paiutes pursuing a cow and caught them in the act of butchering the cow. The Paiutes claimed that the Navajos had committed the raid and the murders, and that they were merely collecting the spoils. The Mormons didn't believe them and interrogated them, tortured them, and threatened to kill them. One Paiute declared he'd had a dream about how the Navajos did the killing and about the location of the bodies, which were indeed where he said. The Paiutes then led the militia to a nearby Paiute camp, where Paiutes possessed some of the clothing and personal items of the murdered men. Convinced of the guilt of the Paiutes, the Mormons fired a volley at them, hitting women, children, and elderly men, and killing several. They then brought five Paiute captives to where the bodies of Whitmore and McIntyre lay, turned them loose, and shot them down. The next day the militia came across an old Indian man hobbling along on his wounded leg from the camp shooting, and shot him in the head.

In their official reports, militia leaders stated that the Paiutes committed the murders and got their justified punishment; this version of events can still be found in some Mormon-written history books today. But at the time and in later documents, some of the militia objected to this version of events. The Paiutes weren't in possession of Whitmore's sheep, so obviously someone else stole them. The Paiutes insisted that the Navajos had done it, although in some versions Paiutes were forced to help or a few renegade Paiutes voluntarily helped. The Paiutes who possessed the clothing and items of the dead said they had simply scavenged it, or that the Navajos had given it to them. Some reports said that the Paiute prisoners were killed in a flare of anger when the Mormons saw the bodies of their dead friends, while others said there was a leadership council that deliberated on the fate of the prisoners and decided to execute them.

A memoir written by James Ott, who was the grandson of militia member Seth Johnson (apparently a relative of Joseph E. Johnson), recalled the incident:

> They reasoned that since Indians had done the work and these happened to be Indians they must be the guilty ones.… Grandfather's opinion was asked about it and his answer was: "They are no more guilty than I myself am." However, the verdict was that they must be shot.… They were shot down like dogs. Grandfather pleaded for their lives to such an extent that some of the members of the party said: "Treat him the same way—shoot him down."
>
> Several weeks after this occurrence, he happened to meet Jacob Hamblin, the great Indian friend, and told him of the affair as it had

happened. (Hamblin was very sick at the time of the expedition or he would have been there). After grandfather told him of the affair he stood in thought for a minute or two then said: "If I would have been there they would not have killed those Indians unless they did it over my dead body."[1]

Another participant, Edwin D. Woolley Jr., commented that seeing the pleasure some of his companions took in the killings made him more ashamed than he had ever been in his life. Even John D. Lee, to whom the Paiutes soon complained about the killings, recorded his regret about it. The Paiutes were angry about the killings and, according to Seth Johnson and also to militia officer John Steele, took their revenge for it by killing three random travelers—three Mormons, the brothers Joseph and Robert Berry and Robert's wife Isabella, two dozen miles from Pipe Spring in April 1866.

Did the Paiutes also take revenge against three other random travelers on the Arizona Strip three years later? Compared with the Navajos and some other tribes, the Paiutes were fewer in number, less organized, and less powerful, and they knew they didn't have the strength to attack a Mormon town. But three isolated travelers, like the Berrys or the Howlands and Dunn, dozens of miles from any town, were much more viable targets. On the other hand, both space and time might argue against the Howlands and Dunn being killed in retaliation for the Arizona Strip massacre. The Howlands and Dunn were some fifty miles west of Pipe Spring, and they were in the territory of a different band of Paiutes, the Shivwits, and not the Kaibab Paiutes who lived near Pipe Spring. The Shivwits might not take the massacre as personally, and more than three and a half years had then passed. The Berry killings had taken place during the Black Hawk War, when many tribes were rebelling against the Mormons, but by 1869 this rebellion had thoroughly died out.

Whether or not the Howlands and Dunn were killed in revenge for the Arizona Strip Massacre, the Mormons of the St. George area would have worried that this was the case. They would have worried that since Powell's men were part of a federal expedition, their disappearance might draw in federal investigators who might talk with the Shivwits or with Mormon dissenters like Jacob Hamblin or Seth Johnson and discover the massacre, and discover that the Mormons had covered it up, just as they had tried to cover up the Mountain Meadows Massacre. Investigators might discover that some of the militia members at the Mountain Meadows Massacre had also shown up at Pipe Spring. Still in trouble over the Mountain Meadows Massacre, the leaders of southern Utah did not need any more bad publicity. While it was true that Americans wouldn't care about massacred Indians in the way they cared about massacred American pioneers, the leaders of southern Utah did not want to get blamed for causing any further trouble for Brigham Young and the church, especially at a time when the federal authorities, like Judge Hawley, were looking for any ammunition they could get. Thus the Mormons might have tried to cover up the Howland-Dunn killings, even if they'd had nothing to do with it. They might have tried to come up with a story that would give the Shivwits another, relatively innocent motive for the killing, and they might have refrained from bringing in the Shivwits for trial and punishment out of fear that the Shivwits would cite the Pipe Spring events as their motive. They might have come up with a story that blamed the Howlands and Dunn for their own deaths, and when that didn't go over well, they might have concocted another story about how it was an act of retaliation against the wrong people. For more than three years the Mormons had been worrying about their own act of retaliation against the wrong people, and now this was the exact story they came up with to hide the guilt and motives of the Shivwits. The psychology at work here is intriguing: anxiety about retaliating against innocent people generates a story about retaliating against innocent people.

We now have a plausible cover-up and two plausible motives for a cover-up. Are there any leads that allow us to pursue this matter further?

NOTES

1. James A. Ott, "A Sketch of the Life of Seth Johnson," LDS Church History Library, Salt Lake City, c. 1922.

·35·

The Afterlife of William Hawkins

O NE OF THE MOST important statements about the fate of the Howland brothers and Bill Dunn has received the least scrutiny. It seems to have baffled everyone into silence. But perhaps it will lead our inquiry further.

In 1919 Grand Canyon pioneer William Wallace Bass contacted William Hawkins, who had settled in southern Arizona, and asked for his recollections of the Powell expedition. Toward the end of his recollections, Hawkins spoke of the departure at Separation Rapid: "This is the last time we ever saw Dunn and the two Howland brothers alive. Some years afterwards I, with a party of some others, buried their bones in the Shewits Mountains, below Kanab Wash."[1]

Hawkins offered no further explanation, and since he died a few months later, before Bass's booklet was published, no one had a chance to ask him for one. Bass himself might not have realized what a significant statement this was, being the first time someone had reported the fate of the bodies. Hawkins must have realized this was important, but he didn't explain where the bodies were, who this "party of some others" was, how they had found the bodies, what condition the bodies were in, what the bodies revealed about how they were killed, or whether there were any possessions nearby. This lack of explanation and context has prompted historians to treat Hawkins's statement as being just too weird to credit or pursue further. Additionally, Powell-admiring historians had already decided to ignore or discredit Hawkins, a Powell critic, as an unreliable if not dishonest source.

Yet when we learn about the life of William Hawkins after the Powell expedition, it becomes much more plausible that he might indeed have been in the right place with the right people to have come to bury the remains of his old friends.

We can locate William Hawkins in 1872 in the town of St. Thomas, the Mormon town from which Bishop Leithead had come to meet the Powell

William Hawkins at age 70, shortly before his death.
Photo courtesy of Hawkins family.

expedition when they first emerged from the Grand Canyon. Hawkins had not
seen St. Thomas then, for he had continued down the Colorado River, but if
he had he would have seen a pleasant, orderly, garden-filled town, intended
to be a Mormon home for the long term, unlike so many Wild West towns
that were temporary and shabby bases for skimming the resources off the land.
St. Thomas prospered and grew, but then a longstanding confusion about the
boundaries of Arizona, Nevada, and Utah was finally settled and St. Thomas became part of Nevada, which assessed far higher taxes than Utah and demanded
that St. Thomas residents pay back-taxes. The Mormons abandoned the town
and returned to Utah. St. Thomas was taken over by rougher characters, including numerous outlaws who decided that it was as far as they could get from the
law. The newspaper in Pioche, the county seat, suggested that the zone along
the Nevada/Utah border be called "Murderers' Paradise" since there was little
law, and when the law did show up, outlaws could easily hide in the wilderness

or slip across the Utah border. The newcomers turned Mormon stores and homes into saloons, gambling halls, and bordellos.

It was in St. Thomas on February 28, 1872, that William Hawkins became a killer and a fugitive from the law.

After parting from Powell, Hawkins and George Bradley continued downriver to Fort Mohave, near Hardyville. As both a river port and a river crossing on the trail to California, Hardyville offered jobs in transportation. At some point William Hardy hired Andy Hall to drive his stagecoach on the road between Hardyville and Prescott; it could also have been in Hardyville that Hawkins began a career as a freighter. The 1870 census located him in Prescott, working as a teamster. Two years later he was working for the Stansfield Company hauling freight. One day when they were stopped in St. Thomas, perhaps in one of its rowdy saloons, Hawkins got into a fight with a fellow teamster named either Reed or Reid, either George or James, and shot him dead. The Pioche newspaper carried an article about it, which was later mentioned by another newspaper, but unfortunately no issues of the Pioche newspaper from early 1872 have survived. We next pick up the story in the May 22 issue of the *Deseret News,* which, in a section of last-minute news from Beaver, where Judge Cyrus Hawley was holding court, paired the Hawkins story with its latest mocking of Judge Hawley. Hawkins probably felt the irony that the Bishop of St. Thomas had once greeted him as a hero and now Hawkins had fled St. Thomas as an outlaw. Perhaps it was nostalgia for the glory of the Powell expedition that led Hawkins to adopt the alias "Green River."

MURDERER CAUGHT—JUDGE HAWLEY'S COURT.

The following dispatch was received yesterday afternoon, as we were going to press:

Beaver, May 21.—

A murderer named W. W. Hawkins, *alias* "Green River," was arrested on Saturday by James Hunt, Sheriff of Beaver county. It appeared that Hawkins, and George Reid, the man he murdered, were teamsters in Stansfield's train, and on the 28th of February, while at St. Thomas, on the Muddy, Nevada, he shot the man without any provocation. There being no authorities at St. Thomas to take cognizance of the affray, the desperado managed to have the matter concealed, by threatening the other teamsters who were eye witnesses, if they let the truth be known; so the matter passed off as an accident until the arrival of J. D. Dunlap, deputy U. S. Marshal, from California, who was informed of the murder there and took the proper steps to bring the matter to light. The Sheriff of Lincoln County, Nev., will be here in a few days to take the prisoner to Pioche.

Judge Hawley's court has been in operation for the past week.... The people being generally busy, his majesty's court was poorly attended. His honor still weakly clings to his little naturalization catechism, and runs his court with a deputy U.S. Marshall, the decision of the [U.S.] Supreme Court notwithstanding. The Judge remarked the other day, in the presence of several gentlemen, that he would strictly adopt the rulings of the Supreme Court, but that the Supreme Court was entirely mistaken in its late decision on Utah affairs.

Hawley was refusing to abide by the U.S. Supreme Court's ruling a few weeks previously that Utah probate courts and territorial marshals did, after all, have authority over criminal cases in Utah, which meant that the Mormons and not federal judges like Hawley would continue to rule the judicial process.

The *Deseret News* continued the Hawkins story for the next two days, reporting on May 23 that the deputy sheriff had arrived to take charge of Hawkins, and on May 24 that Hawkins and "one of the teamsters in the above named train, a witness in the case, left here this morning for Pioche, by order of the sheriff of Pioche, to appear before the grand jury."

A few days later, on May 28, the Virginia City *Territorial Enterprise* reported on

the killing of James Reed by W. W. Hawkins, alias "Green River," on the Muddy River, on the 28th of February, the parties both being at the time employed as teamsters in Stansfield's wagon train, engaged at that time in freighting through the southern part of Nevada, Utah, and Arizona. Since the time the affair occurred, until Sunday last, no trace of Hawkins was found and the matter had quieted down somewhat. On Sunday last, however, Sheriff Kane received a telegraphic dispatch from Sheriff Hunt of Beaver county, Utah, informing him that he had arrested and was holding in custody W. W. Hawkins, on a charge of murder.

On June 5 the *Ely Record,* which was published in Pioche, reported that "Hawkins is now confined in the county jail awaiting his trial, and the witness is out on his own recognizance. It is hardly possible the case will be brought up for trial the present term of court, as the next Grand Jury will have to take the initiatory steps in the matter." To find out what had happened in the Hawkins trial I had to get the Lincoln County clerk to guide me into a cramped, musty, tomb-like vault full of files. The records showed that when the deputy got home on May 27, 1872, he filed an expense claim of $3.00 for arresting the prisoner, mileage expenses (150 miles) of $112.50, and road expenses of $100. Later I talked with a local historian, Bob Rowe, who said that these expenses were probably so high because stage companies refused to take prisoners, even in handcuffs, due to liability rules, so the sheriff probably had to rent the stage-coach. The Seventh District Court listed Hawkins as "M. W. Hawkins," assigned an attorney to him, and set no bond. The entire proceeding was summarized as only, "Defendant: Discharged, June 4, 1872." No further explanation. In both September and October the court announced its recent findings and ongoing cases, but there was no further mention of Hawkins.

The dismissal of Hawkins's case probably says more about violence and justice in Pioche in 1872 than it says about his case. Pioche was at the peak of its silver mining boom, and its population and violence had swollen much faster than its law enforcement. Pioche and its immediate area saw eleven homicides in 1872, and thirteen each in 1871 and 1873, two or three times as many murders as the worst years in the famously violent towns of Dodge City, Tombstone, and Deadwood. Only five of the thirty-seven killings in 1871-73 resulted in prison sentences, and the average sentence was about seven years. In many instances the sheriff or jury took no action, for killings were consid-ered justifiable or inconsequential. A Pioche prosecutor or judge or jury might be even less troubled by a crime that had happened in far-away St. Thomas. Hawkins might have received some extra sympathy because he was working as a freighter, a perilous job around Pioche, where freight wagons loaded with supplies and stagecoaches loaded with silver were frequently robbed, their drivers shot. The county jail in Pioche (whose dark, dungeon-like cells make it a tourist attraction today) was often full. Hawkins was going to have to be held until the next grand jury convened, adding more expenses atop the expenses of arresting and transporting him. The Pioche court was often clogged with mining disputes that involved powerful mining barons and millions of dollars, so perhaps the court did not want to be bothered with William Hawkins.

Another reason why so few killers were brought to justice in Pioche was that it was easy for them to make a getaway. The county was full of wilderness, but the quickest and safest escape was to cross the Utah border only twenty miles away, where Nevada sheriffs held no power. This part of Utah held ample forests and mountains in which to hide, and few towns. If outlaws ran low on funds or got lonely they often gravitated to the town of Pine Valley, which offered jobs in its sawmills. The former miners opened three bars in town and engaged in shady behavior. Yet the local Mormons tolerated them, partly because they were under pressure to produce a lot of lumber and were often short of labor. Besides, they sometimes succeeded in converting such needy outcasts into decent LDS Church members.

Pine Valley historian Mary Esther S. Putnam wrote, "Into Pine Valley during its boom period many notorious characters found their way—robbers and murderers fleeing from the law and looking for a place off the beaten highways where they could hole up until their crimes were forgotten. Saloons… helped keep them occupied. But they gave Pine Valley a bad name that most of the Mormon people there little deserved."[2]

When William Hawkins showed up in Pine Valley shortly after his release from jail, the locals took him to be just another criminal hiding from the law. This memory of Hawkins was still alive a century later when Bess Snow and Elizabeth S. Beckstrom wrote another town history: "Because of its secluded location, it became a retreat for men evading the law. If they heard that officers were anywhere in the vicinity, they could easily find refuge in the mountains. The following are some of the criminals: Jim Marshall, who had killed a man in Flagstaff, Arizona; Old Man Rapp, who had led a guerilla band during the Civil War; Perry Davis, who had killed a man while in a card game; Bill Hawkins, who had killed a man down on the Muddy. He had once lived with the Indians and fought the whites."[3]

This claim that Hawkins lived with Indians and even fought whites was taken from a Washington County history, *Under Dixie Sun,* compiled by the Daughters of Utah Pioneers in 1950.[4] Their source is unclear. The Hawkins family is not sure what to make of this claim. If he had lived with Indians when he was trapping in Colorado, Jack Sumner should have known about it, but he never mentioned it, and indeed Hawkins mentions getting into several fights with Indians. Perhaps he lived with Indians after the Powell expedition, when he was roaming Arizona.

In any case, in Pine Valley Hawkins went to work in one of its sawmills, and perhaps the Mormons went to work on him. He converted to the LDS faith and was baptized on May 11, 1873.[5] Perhaps he liked the idea of shedding his vagabond past and his outlaw identity and becoming a respectable member of a close-knit community.

If Hawkins had arrived in Pine Valley a bit earlier, he might have been baptized by Bishop John Hawley. Hawley was one of the pioneers of Pine Valley, and the town was still heavy with his imprint. This was the John Hawley who, by his own account, had resisted taking part in the Mountain Meadows Massacre, and who as of 1869 had to squirm as his distant relative Judge Cyrus Hawley very publicly pursued the massacre perpetrators and tried to suppress the Mormons.

The next time we can place Hawkins is at the end of that year, December 28, 1873, when he wrote a letter to John Wesley Powell. Hawkins addressed his letter from the Sevier River, where he reported that he was "at work fencing my place. i will have a fine place her next sumer." This must have been the ranch Hawkins was building at the north end of the Panguitch Valley, a few miles south of Circleville. Circleville's first settlers had abandoned it in 1866 due to the Black Hawk War, after they massacred Indian prisoners, but in 1873 whites were beginning to return to the area. (In 1879 the Parker family moved in, with a son named Robert Leroy Parker, who would become known as Butch Cassidy.) On November 11, 1875, an article in the Buffalo, Utah, *Daily Courier* would describe the reporter's journey down the Sevier Valley: "At the bend we emerge into the Panguitch division of the Sevier valley and soon pass Hawkins' ranch. Hawkins was one of the men who accompanied Major Powell on his famous first voyage down the Colorado canons." In his letter, Hawkins told Powell that "Joseph Kessler livs her with me. He lived on the Mudy at sent tomas in 69 when you come thrue.... I got a leter from pine Vally and the post master said they were a packedge for me. I suppose it is th picturs that you was going to send me. I will go out ther soon."[6] It's not clear when Hawkins moved permanently from Pine Valley to his ranch, but he was expecting to be there by the summer of 1874, and he was likely there when his first child was born in March 1875, though unfortunately the location of this birth was not recorded.

If Hawkins was still in Pine Valley in 1874 it is highly probable he received a summons to head not just for the Arizona Strip but also for the path that was likely followed by the Howland brothers and Bill Dunn. Yet even if Hawkins had already left Pine Valley, his experience working at the sawmills there would have made him likely to be summoned.

One of Joseph Smith's central revelations was that Christians had forgotten the proper design and purpose of temples, where the most important rites of faith needed to be performed. In the Midwest the Mormons had built or planned several temples, only to be forced to abandon them when they fled their persecutors. Brigham Young started building a great temple in Salt Lake City, but his health problems made him fear he would not live to see it completed, and he became determined to build another temple more quickly in St. George. This would strain the manpower and resources of the much smaller southern Utah population to the breaking point.

Some of the wood for the St. George temple came from the Pine Valley sawmills, but this was mostly the fine-grained wood used for fine-crafted interior features. The builders needed larger and sturdier logs for the temple's support and framework, and for this this they turned to the ponderosa pine forests around Mount Trumbull, from which they would take about a million board feet of lumber. The landscape in the eighty miles between Mount Trumbull and St. George was rough, and included the formidable Hurricane Cliffs and heavy winter snows around the mountain. The Mormons had to build a road to Mount Trumbull and a sawmill and a large boardinghouse there. They had to haul grain for their horses and oxen and food for themselves, and they had to haul the logs down the Hurricane Cliffs and to St. George. Robert Gardner, who had run the logging operations in Pine Valley, took charge of the Mount Trumbull operation and took with him all the experienced hands he had, though this was not enough and he had to enlist and train others, mostly volunteers. At the beginning of 1875 forty men were at work at Mount Trumbull, and more were working to haul the lumber. Unfortunately, there is no master list of these workers. James William Nixon, for whose father a spring near Mount Trumbull was named, mentioned in his autobiography a dozen men who worked there, including Ebenezer Bryce, who had left his name on Bryce Canyon, but Nixon makes no mention of Hawkins.[7]

Both Nixon and Robert Gardner mentioned that the first man in charge of hauling the lumber was Isaac C. Haight, one of the leaders of the Mountain Meadows Massacre. Nixon:

> At Trumbull during the running of the mill I remember certain characters who had connection with the Mountain Meadows Massacre had come to Trumbull for hiding while they were being searched for by the officers. Among them was a man named Hate (Horten), Stewart (alias Cameron), and another by the name of Higbee (Alias Juo Mount). I was impressed with the uneasiness of these men whenever strangers would drive up to the house. They would invariably run to hide. I remember one of them had a hut built out in the lava bed to which he would invariably flee if a stranger came in sight. These men had all taken part in the massacre, for which John D. Lee paid the supreme penalty of death.[8]

Isaac Haight, John Higbee, and William Stewart were nervous not just because they each had a $500 bounty on their heads and because federal authorities were searching for them, but also because John D. Lee, furious about being singled out to take the blame for the massacre, was trying to organize his friends to find and capture the three.

The three probably felt the bitter irony that they were hiding out at Mount Trumbull, which that idiot John Wesley Powell had named for Mormon archenemy Lyman Trumbull, whose Illinois supporters had murdered Joseph Smith, forcing the Mormons to flee Illinois just as they were finishing their proud temple at Nauvoo—the Trumbull who had now sent his friend and protégé Cyrus Hawley to find and persecute them.

If Hawkins was hanging out with the leaders of the Mountain Meadows Massacre and they knew anything about the fate and whereabouts of the Howlands and Dunn, Hawkins might have won their trust and learned their secrets. Yet Hawkins had another good opportunity to learn the location of the bodies. The road to Mount Trumbull followed the same route that the Howlands and Dunn would have taken.

There were two routes from St. George to Mount Trumbull, both starting from St. George and heading southeast to Fort Pearce, the stone fort the Mormons had built to guard their southern approach from Indians. From there one road headed north to a break in the Hurricane Cliffs a few miles south of the current town of Hurricane, then climbed the cliffs and went to Antelope Springs, where lumber from Mount Trumbull was stockpiled during the summer to get it safely out of the snowier areas near the mountain, and from where it was transported the rest of the way to St. George during the winter months. The other route, called the Black Rock Road, headed south from Fort Pearce and stayed below the Hurricane Cliffs until it reached a natural set of switchbacks near Diamond Butte and climbed onto the plateau above. A century later the Bureau of Land Management erected a historical marker atop the cliffs here, headlined Temple Trail and ending, "The wagons created a trail still in evidence today."

Because of Hawkins's time as a professional teamster, he could have put him to work on the wagons hauling the timber to St. George, which meant he would have been working directly for Isaac Haight.

When the Howlands and Bill Dunn emerged from Separation Canyon and looked to the north, the defining feature of the landscape would have been the Hurricane Cliffs, running north-south and directing them toward St. George. If they were not killed far out on the Shivwits Plateau, they would have followed Main Street Valley northward, or perhaps veered a bit farther east into the Hurricane Wash at the base of the cliffs, which should have offered better chances of finding springs, standing water, and game animals. Eventually they would have reached Fort Pearce. For the latter half of this distance they would have been following the route of the future Temple Trail.

In the years between 1869 and 1874 there was little reason for Mormons to follow this route, but with the temple project there was frequent traffic along it, and a far better chance that someone might spot a glint of white or metal in the brush or rocks and stumble upon three skeletons there. Such a discovery would have aroused much curiosity and speculation. Who could they be? Why three? What were they doing way out here? The only known story that would fit was the story of Powell's three missing men. If the discoverers didn't already know it, they would soon find out, as talk spread, that another of Powell's men was working among them. They would tell Hawkins, and take him to see the bodies, which he might recognize. Then, "with a party of some others," he would have buried them.

Since we have decided to take seriously Hawkins's statement about burying the Howlands and Dunn, perhaps we should also take seriously his statement that this occurred "some years afterwards." He did not say "two years" or "ten years" or "two decades," but "some years," which seems a reasonable fit for the five or six years after 1869 that he would have been working at Mount Trumbull. As far as we know, this is the only period when Hawkins would have spent any time in this area. Like much else in this scenario, this remark about "some years" is much too vague to take as proof, but at least it does fit.

Yet it is puzzling that Hawkins was so reticent about this event. He does not seem to have told any authorities about it, not even the Mormon authorities in St. George, or told Powell or other crewmembers, or tried to seek out the Howland or Dunn families. It was only shortly before he died that he finally mentioned it, and then with no details. Did Hawkins have something to hide? If he had found the skeletons pierced by arrows, in a location frequented by Indians, then it would have fit into the accepted story, and there was no need to keep quiet about the details. But what if there was evidence or talk that the killing had been done by Mormons? Hawkins was now a Mormon, with new friends, a good Mormon marriage and a child, and a new community that competed against any loyalties he still felt for Powell's crew. Yet Hawkins was still a new convert whose loyalties were far less proven than those of the church veterans all around him, many of whom had helped build the temple at Nauvoo. He was working daily with the leaders of the Mountain Meadows

Massacre, nationally portrayed as bloodthirsty maniacs, who were extremely nervous about being betrayed. Even worse, and ironically, he was working at Mount Trumbull, which Powell had named for Lyman Trumbull, whose supporters had murdered Joseph Smith and who had sent William Hawkins down the river and who had now sent his friend and former law partner Cyrus Hawley to find the Mountain Meadows Massacre killers and extinguish Mormon independence. Hawkins would have felt uncomfortable. Was he going to blow the whistle and bring federal marshals to dig up the skeletons and interrogate his new friends, to bring arrests and national scorn? Hawkins would spend the rest of his life in Mormon communities; he would never be free to betray them, except perhaps near his death, and then only with a hint.

Hawkins's Panguitch Valley ranch must not have worked out, for by 1879 he had moved to Grass Valley about twenty miles north of Circleville. Here his third child, John Nelson Hawkins, was born in 1879. The previous summer Hawkins had joined a group that was part of John Wesley Powell's continuing survey of the West. Hawkins's duties are not clear, but in January 1879, from Kingston Circle, Piute County, he wrote to Powell: "We had a good time this sumer with your Party at least I call it a good time as I find rambling in the mountain there is all wais a good time as I have spent the greater Part of my life in the mountains." Hawkins was expressing hope that Powell would hire him again for another summer's work, but he was also miffed that he had not been paid more than others in the group: "I have Ben with you longer than Eny of the other Boys.... I think I art to have mor."[9] Yet Powell had no further use for Hawkins. In the memoir he wrote for Robert Stanton in 1907, Hawkins complained that Powell had never paid him what he had promised for the river expedition.[10]

Hawkins and his family didn't get to stay in Grass Valley for long. During these years the Mormons were setting up new colonies in Arizona, and in 1881 Hawkins was sent to southern Arizona to help found a new community that would be called Eden, on the Gila River northwest of Thatcher in Graham County. It was hardly an Eden: The first settlers sometimes had only one can of beans per day to sustain hard labor in the heat. Yet here Hawkins became a community leader and here he remained for nearly four decades, until his death in 1919. He seems to have retained his Powell expedition spirit, for when Eden was suffering from an epidemic and the Gila River was flooding and no one else dared to try to cross, Hawkins swam across it to get medicine.

As Eden and other Arizona Mormon communities were being developed, Mormons were wrestling with the question of polygamy. Mormon leaders had long desired statehood for Utah, but this would never happen as long as the Mormons were practicing polygamy, which was also, in the peak of the Victorian era, by far the largest barrier to winning new converts. The church would not officially disavow polygamy until 1890 (allowing Utah to become a state in 1896), but already in the 1880s it was backing away from it, which greatly annoyed Mormons who had embraced polygamy as both a religious creed and as their essential lifestyle. Diehard polygamists gravitated to Arizona, out of the reach of Utah authorities, and soon they gravitated to Mexico, out of the reach of all American authorities. Hawkins was never a polygamist; he did have three wives, but in succession, after being widowed each time. Yet some of his neighbors would ignore the church directive against polygamy. Being the Mormon colony closest to the polygamist colonies across the border with Mexico, Graham County became a conduit for polygamists heading to or from Mexico. Graham County and Mexico also became hiding places for leaders of the Mountain Meadows Massacre, who were still on the run—Isaac Haight had a $1,100 price on his head. Massacre participants known to be in Mexico included William C. Stewart, who had worked at the lumber mill at Mount Trumbull, and Isaac Haight, who was living in Casas Grandes in 1885. Haight had a nephew in Thatcher in Graham County and visited him there during that year, if not earlier, and early in 1886 Haight settled in Graham County, feeling it was close enough to the Mexican border that he could make a quick getaway. Haight would die in Thatcher that September, a dozen miles from the home of William Hawkins, and even in death he remained secretive, being buried under his nephew's basement for twenty-seven years, when he was moved to the Thatcher cemetery.

In April 1886 Haight wrote to his son Caleb:

> Everything continues quiet in this part of the country. There was a deputy to Safford last week.... Past Layton was here yesterday, to meeting said if I was in danger, he thot they could run me off to a place of safety in about 3 days. That was all the time he wanted to cross the line to [Mexico]. I feel quite safe here yet, but only time will tell. I should be over the line to be perfectly safe, but my trust is in the Lord, as there is no trust in men."[11]

Two months previously Haight had written his daughter that he felt reasonably safe because "there are a great many in this part of Graham County that came from Utah, the Ransoms and Dodges, James Pace from Harmone, St. George, and other places. I have heard of none but all says were my friends."[12]

In 1882 Hawkins announced that he was seeking election as sheriff of Graham County. This was the first election since Graham County had been established the previous year. Territorial governor John C. Frémont had appointed George H. Stevens, who was postmaster in the town of Safford, as acting county sheriff. In the November 1882 election Stevens was running as a Democrat, which by party enrollment would give him an advantage over the Republican nominee. Hawkins was running as a Republican. The election also inevitably became a contest between Mormons and non-Mormons, and here, too, Hawkins was at a disadvantage. A primary election was set for September 5, though this would only select delegates to county conventions, which would select the nominees. If anyone needed any reminders that Graham County was still the Wild West, the local newspaper carried a story on September 9 that Ike Clanton, having survived the shootout at the OK Corral the previous year, had arrived in the county to try to start a business. And before long Graham County would be the hideout of the most wanted killer of Mountain Meadows, Isaac Haight.

Isaac Haight and William Hawkins were on different trajectories in the Mormon world. Haight had converted to the church in 1838, a decade before Hawkins was born, and had gone through many of the church's early tribulations; he had been a temple guard in Nauvoo when Joseph Smith was killed. In southern Utah he had become one of the most important civic, church, and military leaders. At Mount Trumbull, even in disgrace and hiding, he was still widely recognized, and inspired respect and fear. At Mount Trumbull, Hawkins was a nobody, his presence not worth recording. He was a recent convert, probably incapable of reciting much LDS scripture, dependent on the church for his job, housing, friends, and marriage. If he had worked as a teamster hauling lumber from Mount Trumbull, he might have been dependent directly on Isaac Haight. If he had learned the secret that the Mormons had killed the Howland brothers and Bill Dunn, he was powerless to do anything about it, except to secretly bury their remains.

But now, in the fall of 1882, when Isaac Haight had been a fugitive, frightened by shadows, for a quarter of a century, Hawkins stood to become the law in Graham County: the gateway to the Mormon colonies in Mexico, the refuge of unrepentant polygamists, and the hiding place of leaders of the Mountain Meadows Massacre. Now if Isaac Haight encountered Sheriff Hawkins on the street, Hawkins would recognize him instantly, and both men would recognize that Hawkins now had the power to bring Haight to justice for Mountain Meadows, and that Hawkins held a long grudge over the murder of the Howlands and Bill Dunn.

What could Isaac Haight or anyone else do to make sure that Hawkins kept his mouth shut?

When Hawkins arrived in Arizona in early 1881 he became a distant neighbor to his old friend Andy Hall, with whom he had shared a boat and many trials on the river. Hall was living in Florence, about a hundred miles away, and working for Wells Fargo as a messenger and freighter between Casa Grande and Globe, which was even closer to Hawkins. In the decade Hawkins had lived in Utah, it wasn't likely that he and Hall had seen one another. But now they would have had a chance to get together and talk about old times and old companions, although we don't know for a fact that they did.

In the introduction to my inquiry about the Howlands and Dunn I warned that we were going to be building scenarios, some grounded in facts but others based mainly on circumstantial evidence, circumstances that might get piled up one atop another until they threatened to become a house of cards. This chapter has built up layers that add up to a finale that seems sufficiently possible to warrant presenting. But, I would like to note, we are about to overload the house of cards and end up in terrain where only conspiracy nuts could be happy.

If Hawkins and Hall did get together, it's likely they would have talked about their old river companions. If ever Hawkins was going to tell anyone about burying the Howlands and Dunn, this was the time and the person. And Hawkins might have told Hall that the Mormons were the killers. When Hall went home to Florence or traveled around the area, he could have repeated this story to a few friends, or even to strangers in saloons. A story like that tends to get around. Hall's talk might have gotten back to the Mormons in Graham County, the Mormons who had already started the process of handing William Hawkins the power of enforcing the law over themselves.

On August 20, 1882, two weeks before the primary election that would nominate candidates and eleven weeks before Hawkins might get elected sheriff, and in the same week that newspapers around the West carried stories that John Wesley Powell was heading back to Arizona for further geological studies of the Grand Canyon, Andy Hall waited atop Pioneer Pass, ten miles west of Globe, as the Wells Fargo wagon arrived with its freight, which this time included $5,000 in gold, the payroll for a mine beyond Globe. Pioneer Pass was the end of the stage road, and from there into Globe there was only a pack trail. Hall and his coworker Frank Porter transferred the cargo onto the mules of their pack train and headed down the pass toward Globe. In about four miles the trail crossed a gully, beside which sat a huge boulder. As they passed it, rifle fire rang out, striking the mule carrying the gold, and wounding

Andy Hall in the thigh. The other mules panicked and raced ahead half a mile. When Hall got the team under control he sent Porter ahead with them to get help. Hall, though bleeding, headed back to look for the robbers. Hall found them, but one of the robbers got behind him and shot him in the back, then emptied his pistol into Hall, leaving eight or nine bullets in him. Nine bullets were far more than was necessary to disable or kill a man. It was more like a Mafia-style execution.

What was the name of the man who executed Andy Hall?

Curtis Hawley.

Yes, Curtis Hawley belonged to the same old New England Hawley family that had participated in the Mountain Meadows Massacre, that had founded Pine Valley, where William Hawkins would live and the timber business in which he would work, and that had provided a law partner whom Senator Lyman Trumbull, hater of Mormons and sponsor of the Powell expedition, had sent to Utah to track down the leaders of the Mountain Meadows Massacre, break the authority of Mormon courts and sheriffs, and grind the Mormons under his federal boot, and who had foolishly started this process with a case in which three non-Mormon men had been sentenced to be shot.

Curtis Hawley was caught and taken to Globe, where a few facts about him soon emerged. He was from Utah. He was in the lumber business. Unlike most robbers he was not destitute, for he quickly wrote a will leaving his wife thousands of dollars in property. Curtis Hawley didn't have much chance to say anything else, for four days after he executed Andy Hall, a mob dragged him from the jail and lynched him from a giant sycamore tree.

That same day, August 24, 1882, Tucson's *Arizona Daily Star* reported that "Hawley, the ringleader, took charge of it. He is presumed to be an old offender and one of those engaged in the Mountain Meadows massacre."

But here the newspaper was mistaken. It seems to have confused Curtis Hawley with the Hawley brothers who were involved—one way or another—in the massacre. In 1857, the year of the massacre, Curtis Hawley was only seventeen years old and had not yet moved to Utah. But the Tucson newspaper was right that Curtis Hawley had a bad reputation. A few days later, on August 30, the *Deseret News* printed the following: "It is reported all over town that one of the men lynched was a former citizen of this city—C. B. Hawley. There are two facts that point to this probability…[which are] the character of the Hawley who used to live here, which was notoriously bad, and the fact of his having gone to the Arizona country." Part of his bad reputation was that in moving to Arizona he had abandoned his wife and three children in Utah, forcing his wife to go to work as a clerk to support their children.

Curtis Hawley's connection with John, William, and George Hawley lay far back in the Hawley family tree, in the late 1600s, in the third generation of Hawleys in America, with Joseph Hawley's grandchildren, one of whom, Ephraim, gave rise to Utah's Hawley brothers, and another of whom, Samuel Jr., gave rise to Curtis Hawley and (Judge) Cyrus Hawley. The lines of Curtis and Cyrus branched in the next generation, with two sons of Samuel Jr., much more than a century before the three branches of the family mingled again in Utah.

Curtis Hawley was born in Ohio in 1840, where his father had settled by the 1820s, probably part of the tide of New Englanders who heard the call of better farm lands in the West. But Curtis's father died when he was about five years old, the family land was lost, and by age ten Curtis was living with his married sister in Indiana. We don't know why Curtis moved to Utah by 1867, the year his name first surfaces in public records: the 1867 Salt Lake City Directory lists him as "proprietor of sawmill, and lumber dealer." Curtis could have been hearing, yet again, the call of the West. Utah was growing and held plenty of opportunities for a young man trying to start his own business and life. Curtis Hawley's sawmill was in Provo Canyon, and by the 1880 census he had moved to the nearby town of Provo. When Curtis moved to Arizona, he worked supplying timber to a mining company. It is curious that Curtis got into the same business as the Hawleys of Pine Valley. We don't know of any connection. Lumber was a profitable business in the rapidly developing West, especially in more-arid regions, like Utah, where the timber supply was limited and hard to get. Even if Curtis had never heard of the Pine Valley Hawleys before he settled in Utah, even if it was entirely a coincidence that Curtis went into "the family business," the two Hawleys would have soon heard about one another, through lumber customers asking if they were related, or assuming they were. Curtis would have heard dark rumors that his distant relatives were involved in the Mountain Meadows Massacre, and perhaps he was aware of assumptions that he himself had been there.

It does not appear that Curtis Hawley went to Utah because he was a Mormon. When he married Hannah Beatie in May 1869 it was not within the church, but a year later he and Hannah had their marriage sealed at the Salt Lake City LDS Temple, which means he had become a church member. This could have been for the sake of Hannah, who seems to have been born in an LDS family. However, two acquaintances later testified that Curtis was not a Mormon. This question came up in 1922, when the Phoenix *Arizona Republican* published a fortieth anniversary account of the Globe killings and lynching, and stated that Curtis Hawley was a Mormon. This claim annoyed S. W.

Lillywhite of Mesa, Arizona, formerly of Utah, who wrote to LDS president
T. N. Taylor, sending him the article. He complained that church opponents
were always trying to pin bad deeds on Mormons, and asked if it was true
that Curtis Hawley was Mormon. In response, someone in the church must
have gone to considerable trouble to hunt up former acquaintances of Curtis
Hawley. Mrs. Hannah Davis said, "The Hawley family lived as our neighbor
in my husband's house. I worked for them and visited with them quite a bit.
Mr. Hawley took no part in any religious activities and was not considered a
Mormon." Joel A. Johnson was reported to have "stated that he had worked
for Curtis B. Hawley two years running a saw mill for him in the North Fork
of Provo Canyon, and was well acquainted with him. When asked in regard to
Hawley's religion, Mr. Johnson said: 'He was not a Mormon; he didn't believe
in any religion at all; he was really an infidel.'" In another statement Johnson
said that Hawley "didn't believe in God, man, or the Devil." It appears it was
also Johnson who reported that Hawley had been "an accessory after the fact"
in the theft of a cow and served time in the Utah State Penitentiary.[13] Since
Curtis's marriage record indicates he did join the church, at least we can say
that his acquaintances refused to consider him a genuine Mormon.

More testimony about Curtis Hawley's bad character was given by the *Salt
Lake City Tribune,* the non-Mormon newspaper, on August 26, 1882:

> C.B. Hawley, one of the murderers, was well known in this city, where
> he resided for several years, and at one time was the owner of consid-
> erable property here. He was for a time engaged in operating a saw
> mill in the Cottonwood canyons. Being interested in some coal mine
> claims at Coalville, he got into trouble some three or four years ago,
> and a sensation was created by him and the contending parties en-
> gaging in shooting. At one time he was looked upon by acquaintances
> as a good sort of man, but wild speculation and drink seemed to take
> him down.

Curtis Hawley was living in Salt Lake City when Judge Cyrus Hawley
showed up there in the summer of 1869 and began hunting for Hawleys and
anyone else who had taken part in the Mountain Meadows Massacre, and
began making life uncomfortable for all Mormons. Like the Hawleys of Pine
Valley, Curtis Hawley must have felt especially uncomfortable. People perhaps
asked him if he was related to Judge Hawley, and treated him with suspicion.
Salt Lake City was a modest-sized town then, with about 10,000 people, and
Curtis and Cyrus lived near one another, so their trails probably crossed.

We have now found an unlikely constellation of events. In 1882 the combined population of Arizona and Utah was more than 125,000. What are the odds that among all these people, the one person who stepped forward and executed the boatmate of William Hawkins bore the same name as the perpetrators and the prosecutor of the Mountain Meadows Massacre, and that this happened at the moment Hawkins might be on the verge of gaining the power to apprehend massacre leaders?

When I first noticed this constellation of events, I thought it could not be a coincidence. It had to mean something, apparently something ominous. So I investigated this possibility thoroughly, from every angle I could imagine and find. I even attended the seventy-eighth annual Hawley Society reunion in Kansas City in 2008. But I am not in their group photo, because I was the one taking the photo. We were meeting just down the road from Independence, Missouri, the world headquarters of the Reorganized Church—now renamed the Community of Christ—that John and George Hawley had left Utah to join, and the featured speaker that year was a church historian (and Hawley in-law) talking about Pierce Hawley, the father of John, George, and William Hawley. The Reorganized Church had never been shy about digging up and throwing dirt at Brigham Young and his misguided Utah followers. But neither here nor in the rest of my research could I make a case about Curtis Hawley that added up into anything convincing. Indeed, the closer I looked, the more the case melted away.

In order for this case to be plausible, in order for Curtis Hawley to have a motive for taking such a strong action connected with the Mountain Meadows Massacre, he would have needed to have a strong connection with it. But it's hard to come up with such a connection.

First of all, Curtis Hawley wasn't close to having any personal involvement with the massacre, so he had no personal stake in it.

As far as we know, Curtis Hawley never had any personal connection with the Hawley brothers who could have taken part in the massacre. Their family connection lay nearly two hundred years in the past, which does not usually create strong bonds. Only a few years after Curtis arrived in Utah, John and George Hawley left. They lived in opposite ends of the state and were not very likely to meet one another, although they probably heard about one another. Furthermore, the Hawley brothers denied being involved in the massacre and claimed they had opposed it and denounced it; by 1870 they had denounced Brigham Young and the Utah church, so even in 1870 they had no further motive for trying to hide the church's crimes or criminals. After a dozen more years, John and George were far removed from these events and the people of southern Utah.

Given Curtis Hawley's poor standing as a Mormon, it is unlikely he would have cared about their unfinished business or done them any favors, and it is unlikely they would have trusted him with any secrets or important missions.

While it is likely that Curtis Hawley was highly aware of Judge Cyrus Hawley while they were both in Salt Lake City, Judge Hawley had been gone from Utah for many years by 1882, and it is not obvious how their awkward connection might have led to the Hall killing.

In 1882 Isaac Haight had not yet taken up residence down the road from William Hawkins, so his presence there was not yet a possible motive—although it is true that the Mormon towns of Graham County were the conduit for polygamists hiding out in Mexico.

One of the largest problems with this case is that Hawkins never stood much chance of getting elected sheriff, due to the large voter registration disadvantages faced by a Republican and a Mormon. Another disadvantage was that the county newspaper was strongly supporting his opponent, George Stevens.

On October 7, 1882, the *Graham County News* announced the results of the Republican county convention, at which Hawkins served on the platform committee and defeated Jonathan Foster for the nomination for sheriff. That same issue showed that Hawkins's opponent was no slouch at public relations: "Hon. G H. Stevens caused a building owned by him in San Jose, in which was a saloon, to be vacated and placed at the disposal of the School Trustees, for a school house."

A week later, on October 14, the *News* pronounced,

> Mr. Hawkins is presented for Sheriff. He is a good citizen and being a Mormon is naturally a man who would uphold the law; but it is not known that he possesses the necessary requisites, either in education or energy to give satisfaction to the public. Certainly there is no comparison between him and G. H. Stevens, a man whom we all know, who has been satisfactorily tried as Sheriff, who knows the haunts and habits of every scoundrel in the county, who has the nerve and sagacity to hunt out, arrest and bring them to justice; and who from his experience and education is qualified for any office within the gift of the people.

Two weeks later, on October 28, the *News* dismissed Hawkins again: "The Republicans have no enthusiasm for their ticket, and there is no heart in one-half of that party to support it…. The Democratic ticket of Graham is mainly composed of men who have been in office since the organization of the county. Against these the Republicans have placed an untried class of men." On November 4, with the election only days away, the *News* ran several mini-plugs for Stevens: "Vote for G. H. Stevens, the most useful and capable man that ever lived in this county. Seek not for the public good in ignorance and incapacity." And, "Take no chances. Try no uncertain experiments. The safety and prosperity of Graham County depends on the election of the Democratic ticket."

Considering how "ignorant and incapable" he was, Hawkins did well to win 206 votes against Stevens's 363 votes, or 36 percent of the total. The count by precinct mapped out where the Mormons lived. Hawkins carried one precinct 43 to 0, another 18 to 1. But he lost other precincts 2 to 79 and 23 to 166. Of course, Hawkins's solid support among Mormons also indicates that they weren't worried about him taking power over them.

Two weeks later, on November 18, the *News* reported, "Hawkins is taking his medicine with good grace. He says he is partial to crow—always did like the meat pretty well."

The most important argument against this case is that Andy Hall's killing appeared to be simply a botched robbery attempt. Hawley was one of three conspirators, and they all gave confessions about planning the robbery, which was not supposed to involve any killings. But events got out of their control. The other two conspirators, Lafayette Grime and his brother Cicero, had no incentive to kill Andy Hall except the $5,000 they stood to gain. In his written confession Hawley mentioned that one of the Grime brothers had been involved in another stage robbery in Northern California.

In conclusion, it's easy to see Hall's killing as part of a robbery, while it's quite circuitous and tenuous to see it as a method of intimidating William Hawkins into silence. The psychology required to motivate Curtis Hawley is also tenuous. The only way to salvage this theory is to suppose that someone who knew William Hawkins when he was at Mount Trumbull, and who knew that Hawkins knew about the killings of the Howlands and Dunn, was in southeastern Arizona in 1882 and was getting nervous about Hawkins being elected sheriff, and that this person also knew Curtis Hawley and his namesake connection with the Mountain Meadows Massacre Hawleys and thus hired Curtis to kill Andy Hall. This is a big detour to take when a much easier explanation is available.

As unlikely as this constellation of events might be, coincidences do happen, and they happen much more often than conspiracy theories might indicate Yet if the scenario developed in this chapter has fizzled out along the way, this does not diminish its beginning, and the possibility that William Hawkins did bury the bones of his friends and knew what had happened to them.

NOTES

1. William Wallace Bass, *Adventures in the Canyons of the Colorado by Two of its Earliest Explorers, James White and W. W. Hawkins* (Grand Canyon, AZ: Self-published, 1920), 29.

2. Mary Esther S. Putnam, *Descendants of Pine Valley Pioneers* (self-published, 1980), 6.

3. Bess Snow and Elizabeth S. Beckstrom, *O' Ye Mountains High: The Story of Pine Valley* (St. George, UT: Heritage Press, 1980), 47.

4. Hazel Bradshaw, ed., *Under Dixie Sun* (Panguitch, UT: Garfield County News, 1950).

5. LDS Records, and Hawkins Family Records.

6. Hawkins to John Wesley Powell, December 28, 1873, Hawkins File, Marston Collection.

7. James William Nixon, *The Autobiography of James William Nixon* (Washington, DC, 1937).

8. Ibid., 8.

9. Billy Hawkins to Powell, January 24, 1879, Hawkins File, Marston Collection.

10. Included in Stanton's never-published book. Manuscript in New York Public Library. Included in condensed version of *Colorado River Controversies*.

11. Isaac Haight to son Caleb, April 12, 1886, Box 34, folder 53, Collection of Caroline Parry Wooley, Special Collections, Sherratt Library, Southern Utah University, Cedar City, UT (hereafter Wooley Collection).

12. Haight to daughter, February 21, 1886, Wooley Collection.

13. Statements on Curtis B. Hawley, Special Collections, Harold B. Lee Library, Brigham Young University, Provo, UT, mss. 66.

·36·

Conclusion?

H AS MY EXPLORATION finally solved the Howland–Dunn mystery? No. Part VI of this book has remapped the Howland–Dunn story, introducing new documents, new facts, new circumstances, and new scenarios. It has questioned, diminished, or entirely closed off some old claims, assumptions, and theories, yet opened up several new possibilities. It has given both the Southern Paiutes and the Mormons clearer motives for wanting to kill Powell's men. Yet in some respects my exploration has only further complicated the mystery, introducing too many new circumstances and not enough new facts to sort the circumstances into clearer shape. It certainly stops well short of proof.

If we were to apply Occam's razor, the scientific rule which says that using a simple theory that works is preferable to weaving far more complicated theories, then we should stop with the theory that the Shivwits killed the Howlands and Dunn simply for being white men trespassing on their land. We don't even need the Mormons' version, that the Shivwits acted in retaliation for a crime against the Shivwits, or Joseph Johnson's version, that they acted to commit robbery. It was motive enough that the Howlands and Dunn were simply there, crossing Paiute lands, hunting on Paiute lands, in an era when the Paiutes were being pushed toward extinction.

If we skip over the Paiutes and pursue the possibility that the Mormons killed the Howlands and Dunn, things get far more complicated. We have to suppose that somewhere along the way the three men ran into the wrong Mormons, who made a less-than-inevitable connection between Powell's men and their political situation, their own threat of extinction, and decided that Powell's men were a convenient outlet for their anxieties. Psychologically, this scenario might be plausible, but as far as evidence goes, it remains not just tentative but also tenuous. The evidence for a Mormon cover-up seems more solid and incriminating, yet exactly what they were covering up remains an open question. When it comes to naming names or places, on either the Paiute or Mormon side, we are left with little more than rumors or guesswork. In the end, the killings remain a mystery. We can't even rule out the possibility that they weren't killings at all, but some sort of accident as the men tried to find their way up the unknown and steep passages of Separation Canyon, though it is hard to imagine a fall or other accident that would claim all three of them. The mystery will be solved only when we find the bodies of the Howlands and Dunn, which are still hidden somewhere in a vast desert haystack.

Yet this exploration has reshaped the mystery in significant ways, opening up new possibilities and new lines of inquiry. Perhaps future researchers will come across documents that will fit into some of my scenarios and carry them farther, one way or another.

In the end it might be appropriate, even poetic, to leave the disappearance of the Howlands and Dunn as a mystery. Before John Wesley Powell started down the river, the Grand Canyon region was the last great mystery on the American map. Powell referred to it with the enduring phrase, capitalized, "the Great Unknown." After a century and a half in which humans and their technologies have swarmed all over the Grand Canyon, mapping it, measuring it, photographing it, regulating it, fencing it, damming it, and putting a price on it, humans might imagine that they know it thoroughly. Yet ultimately, philosophically, the Grand Canyon remains "the Great Unknown." By holding onto three of Powell's men, and by teasing us with a less abstract mystery, the type of mystery that keeps novel readers and movie goers riveted, the canyon reminds us that it still holds deep mystery.

Afterword

Ten Who Bored

THE WEST CALLED OUT. The mythic romance and promise of the West called out with a whistle and a roar and a powerful westward motion that flavored his dreams of both night and day. A boy named Walt Disney grew up on the main line of the Santa Fe Railway, in Marceline, Missouri, in the era when trains were the embodiment of human ingenuity, power, and adventure. Walt was a dreamy kid, spending hours lying under the backyard giant cottonwood tree he called his "dreaming tree" and imagining stories about his barnyard animals or about himself having adventures. So when a train shot by, rushing westward, full of vague, dreamy silhouettes behind the curtains, he imagined all the famous places those people would see and the adventures they would have: Los Angeles, with its magical ocean beaches, palm trees, and movies; mountains and deserts; cowboys and Indians; the Grand Canyon. Disney was born in 1901, the year the Santa Fe Railway started passenger service to the Grand Canyon, its number one attraction, and the railway placed Grand Canyon posters and brochures in its stations all along its line, including the Marceline station. Sometimes when the train stopped, Walt watched neighbors returning from Western trips, and he heard their tales.

The Santa Fe Railway had founded Marceline in 1888 and remained central to the town's economy and identity. Walt's uncle worked for the Santa Fe, and when Walt was sixteen, he worked for the Santa Fe, too. Wearing a spiffy blue uniform with shiny gold buttons, he rode trains to sell newspapers, snacks, cold drinks, and souvenirs to passengers. He was based out of the new Union Station in Kansas City, the largest train station in America. All its restaurants and shops were run by the Fred Harvey Company, whose national headquarters was upstairs, including the office where architect Mary Colter drew up her plans for new buildings, including those to be built at the Grand Canyon.

Disney caught the railroad bug and remained obsessed with trains for the rest of his life. In his huge backyard in Los Angeles he built a rideable mini-train, and when he built Disneyland he circled it with a steam train with a locomotive named the "E. P. Ripley," for the man who during Walt's youth headed the Santa Fe Railway and built its tracks to the Grand Canyon; the Disneyland train ran through its own Grand Canyon. Disneyland also included an imitation Harvey House restaurant. Walt remained enthralled with the heroic saga of Western pioneering.

In the mid-1950s Disney launched not just Disneyland but also a weekly TV show, and both would feature the American frontier. For his first TV hero Disney selected Davy Crockett, who became a national craze, inspiring millions of kids to wear coonskin caps and sing Davy's hit ballad. Yet there was something a bit unusual about Disney's Crockett. Instead of the usual brash tough-guy heroes of Western movies, Disney selected as his Davy an unknown young actor, Fess Parker, because he was soft-spoken and courteous. And in one episode in which Crockett was serving in the U.S. Congress he denounced President Jackson for his mistreatment of Indians; this was not the only time Disney expressed sympathy for Native Americans at a time when most Hollywood movies were still sending in the cavalry to wipe them out.

Thrilled with the success of Davy Crockett, Disney looked for his next hero. He sent Fess Parker west again in "Westward Ho, the Wagons," and the next year he tried Johnny Tremain, boy hero of the American Revolution. Neither hero came close to the popularity of Davy Crockett, perhaps because both were fictional characters, so Disney decided to try another genuine frontier hero. He chose John Wesley Powell. Disney sent Norman Forster, the cowriter and director of *Davy Crockett: King of the Wild Frontier,* on a river trip through the Grand Canyon to scout out filming possibilities.

Walt Disney probably realized he was breaking some of the rules of Western movies and heroism, for instead of giving top billing to his Powell actor, John Beal, he gave it to Brian Keith, who played Bill Dunn. Keith would go on to become one of Disney's leading stars, but this was his Disney debut, so he didn't get top billing because of studio seniority or name recognition. He probably got it because in many ways the Dunn character was a better fit than Powell for a typical Western hero. Dunn was a buckskin-wearing, rattlesnake-twirling, hard-fighting, hard-drinking mountain man. Never before had Hollywood offered a one-armed "cripple" as a Western hero, and Powell was also a nerd, a professor looking for fossils, not gold, and he didn't fight any Indians or bears, only rapids. Disney didn't even acknowledge Powell in the title, calling the movie *Ten Who Dared,* an ensemble credit also unusual in a Western.

Disney filled the cast with capable actors, some of them well-known. For George Bradley he cast Ben Johnson, who had already appeared in five John

Wayne movies. For Walter Powell he chose James Drury, who would soon begin a decade of starring in TVs "The Virginian." Seneca Howland was played by Stan Jones, the songwriter of "Ghostriders in the Sky" and other hits, who wrote and sang songs for the Powell movie. Other cast members were familiar faces, if not famous names. John Beal, the Powell character, was one of the less recognizable faces, his film career being mainly in the 1930s.

Disney seemed to be trying to do justice to Powell's story, for as a consultant he hired river historian Dock Marston, but of course Disney added his own touches, the most blatant of which was Andy Hall smuggling aboard his boat a cute little dog. Walter Powell orders Andy to shoot his dog—an echo of Disney's recent movie *Old Yeller*—until John Wesley Powell has a heart and relents.

The basic story is intact: ten men start down the Great Unknown in four boats, run rapids, wreck one boat, go hungry, have doubts and conflicts, and in the end three men walk off the expedition. Many details are quite accurate, such as Andy Hall being a youngster with a Scottish accent, Walter Powell being a moody former prisoner of war, and the crew smuggling a keg of liquor aboard and rescuing it from the wreck of the *No Name*. Disney added additional, unauthentic conflict and drama by adding a Confederate veteran to fight with the Union veterans, and an alcoholic Billy Hawkins to fight over a bottle—much to the annoyance of Hawkins's descendants. There are plenty of genuine river and canyon scenes, including running rapids, with river veterans like Buzz Belknap standing in for the actors, who only got to row and buck and get splashed on Hollywood sets in front of screens showing river scenes.

We don't know why Disney chose Powell and not someone else from the pantheon of Western heroes, many of whom were far better known and celebrated. Disney grew up near Hannibal, Missouri, so perhaps he had caught Mark Twain's love of rivers—Disney had started Mickey Mouse's career with a steamboat, and had built a Disneyland steamboat and Tom Sawyer's Island. Perhaps Disney felt the old magic lure of the Grand Canyon. Or perhaps Disney's famous sentimentality—for which intellectuals often scorned him—deserves a bit more credit, exhibited in compassion for a disabled man: Disney's first movie, *Snow White,* had taken a big risk, dismaying Walt's own wife, by breaking the long habit of portraying dwarfs as evil or buffoons and instead making them kindly, industrious, and brave.

Disney's main motive for selecting Powell was probably the largest historical event that occurred in the five years between his Crockett and Powell movies. In October 1957 the Soviet Union launched Sputnik, which shattered America's long-held confidence in its superiority in science and technology.

After some soul-searching, Americans made a strong commitment to enhancing science education. John F. Kennedy got elected president in 1960 with images of "the New Frontier," in which America's pioneering spirit would apply itself to space exploration and to science and technology in general. Disney premiered his own science-minded John in theaters on November 1, 1960, only days before Kennedy got elected. John Wesley Powell was Disney's version of old frontier spirit serving the cause of science.

Disney had been way ahead of other Americans. He had always loved not just America's pioneer past but also its glorious technological future, another of the main themes of Disneyland and his TV show. In 1955 he began offering shows about the coming American conquest of space. He was also finding great popularity with a series of nature documentaries. Occasionally his Powell movie sounded like a nature documentary, with Powell looking at the scenery and admiring the powers of erosion. In the pantheon of Western heroes, Powell was the only one who was driven mainly by scientific curiosity.

One of the movie's dominant themes is the tension between Powell the scientist and the crew of frontiersmen. Near the start Powell is trying to find their location by using a sextant, while Bill Dunn, nearly illiterate, is studying his almanac on astrology. They'll have several exchanges about the merits of astronomy versus astrology. As Powell continues stopping to study geology and collect fossils, his crew complains about the delays (as did the real crew), and accuses Powell of secretly finding gold or silver, and Powell lectures them about how scientific knowledge is its own sort of gold. For sport, Bill Dunn teases rattlesnakes, and Powell warns him he is foolish, and of course Dunn gets bitten and learns his lesson. In the end Dunn refuses to accept Powell's astronomical readings that say they are nearly at the end of the canyon, and Dunn leads the Howlands overland, where, we learn at the end of the movie, they are killed by Indians. Bill Dunn is the most Crockett-like character in the movie, and Disney is telling us that the frontier virtues that might have worked for Crockett aren't good enough in the age of science.

The New Frontier might have worked for John F. Kennedy, but it was a flop for Walt Disney. Movie critics branded *Ten Who Dared* a huge bore, and some were downright hostile to it. Later, Leonard Maltin graded it a "Bomb," because "action is sparse." Audiences agreed.

The Grand Canyon boring? Movie critics do tend to be city slickers who have little appreciation for nature, and in 1960 very few Americans had any experience of whitewater adventure. But the outright hostility toward *Ten Who Dared* suggests there were deeper cultural undercurrents at work. After making Davy Crockett a national icon, Walt Disney had committed the sin of dissing Crockett-like frontiersmen in favor of a science nerd. In the heyday of Western movies and TV shows, Disney had made an anti-Western.

Walt Disney usually had a good feel for American history, which is why he was so successful, but he had slipped up in not noticing that Powell had long ago been rejected from the ranks of Western icons. Disney could have checked the titles of four popular 1950s series of books about American history and biography aimed at young readers. Their heroes included Davy Crockett, Daniel Boone, Buffalo Bill, Lewis and Clark, Kit Carson, George Custer, Wyatt Earp, and Wild Bill Hickok, and included stories about the Oregon Trail and Pony Express. Even Geronimo got a biography. In hundreds of titles, John Wesley Powell was nowhere to be found.

The public and critical rejection of *Ten Who Dared* only recapitulated the rejection of Powell that had happened nearly a century before. In a way, Powell had been rejected even before his river expedition. While other Western explorations were federally organized and funded, the U.S. Congress saw little point in exploring a river that was unnavigable and lands that were uncultivatable and largely uninhabitable. Exploration was supposed to serve the interest of national expansion and prosperity, but the Southwest was a worthless desert and Powell only an egghead looking for fossils. Powell's river heroism did impress the country, for he fitted the American image of explorer heroes. Powell was well aware of that image and was eager to live up to it, and he doctored his book to make himself look better. The Powell expedition helped further enhance the heroic image of river explorers, an image Teddy Roosevelt would pursue half a century later by descending South America's River of Doubt, a trip that nearly killed him. Powell turned his hero status into a Washington career, but then he violated the contract of American heroism. During the Wild West era when Americans were more preoccupied than ever with expansion and national wealth and power, Powell opposed Manifest Destiny in the name of science. After his exposure to the aridity of the West, Powell tried to warn the nation that the settlement practices that had worked in the wetter East or Midwest were doomed to fail in the West. Americans didn't want to hear this; Powell made powerful enemies and wrecked his own career. National myths were far stronger than science. Powell retained some of his status as a heroic explorer, but it was more personal heroism than national heroism, for unlike other explorers Powell added no new territory, military victories, or economic resources to the nation.

American identity and values are powerful and do not change quickly. Exactly a century after Powell went down the Colorado River, American astronauts landed on the moon. They became big heroes, for a moment, heroes

Powell in his later years. Photo courtesy of Grand Canyon
National Park Museum Collection.

who instilled national pride. But after a few landings, the astronauts were doing
nothing new, nothing but collecting rocks, and the American people got bored
and Congress eliminated funding for further landings.

Yet we can wonder if Disney's Powell would have been better received if
it had been released a decade later, when America's pantheon of heroes was
changing dramatically. The Western genre that had dominated TV in 1960 was
almost all gone, and then one of the most popular TV characters was a Vulcan
science officer. George Custer and Kit Carson were being evicted from the
pantheon for their brutalities against Native Americans, and people couldn't
remember why Wyatt Earp and Wild Bill Hickok had gotten in there. John
Wayne and even Davy Crockett now seemed highly unreliable role models for
American identity and foreign policy. Traditional domestic ladies like Betsy
Ross and Dolley Madison were being muscled aside by Susan B. Anthony and
Harriet Tubman, and Tubman had joined George Washington Carver, who
was deemed the only black person safe enough to be an American hero. Being

able to win a fistfight was no longer obligatory for male heroes, and Franklin Roosevelt's leg braces and wheelchair weren't embarrassments, but marks of character. The astronauts might be valued mainly for national pride, but they were, after all, New Frontier heroes with graduate degrees.

Today hardly anyone watches *Ten Who Dared*. The critics still declare it to be a huge bore.

Yet Walt Disney's selection of a disabled, science-loving, nature-loving, Indian-friendly, abolitionist and environmentalist as a Disney hero might have meant that Disney did, after all, have his finger on the pulse of history, for Americans were on the verge of a national soul-searching that would redefine national mythology and values substantially. Within ten years, the long American mission of conquering nature for the sake of national expansion and wealth was no longer accepted as the whole story or a healthy story. While other Western heroes would fail or fade, Powell would only gain respect. Today people still admire Powell for his personal daring, but also for the respect for nature that motivated both his river trip and his later environmental efforts. For all his personal vanity, Powell offered a humility before nature that was almost impossible to find among other American heroes in 1960. His survival and growth as an American icon is a symptom of a healthier society. John Wesley Powell's place as a hero has stood the test of time and no doubt will be alive and strong a century from now.

Bibliography

MANUSCRIPT COLLECTIONS

Abraham Lincoln Presidential Library, Springfield, IL
    Shelby Cullom Papers
    Lyman Trumbull Papers

Brigham Young University, Harold B. Lee Library, Provo, UT
    James G. Bleak Collection
    Curtis Hawley file
    James Leithead Papers
    John Pulsipher Diary

Church of Jesus Christ of Latter-day Saints,
Church History Library, Salt Lake City, UT
    James G. Bleak Papers
    Robert Gardner Diaries
    Seth Johnson Papers
    Nauvoo Legion, Iron Military District Records
    Erastus Snow Papers
    John Steele Reminiscences and Journals
    Brigham Young Office Files

Colorado Historical Society, Denver, CO
    Jim Baker Papers
    William Byers Papers
    Thomas Dawson Papers
    William Palmer Papers
    Henry Teller Papers

Community of Christ Archives, Independence, MO
    John Hawley Papers

Denver Public Library, Denver, CO
    Jim Baker Papers
    William Byers Collection

Dixie State University Library, St. George, UT
    Oral and Pioneer History Collection

Huntington Library, San Marino, CA`
    Juanita Brooks Collection
    Otis "Dock" Marston Collection

Illinois College, Jacksonville, IL
    College History Archives

Illinois Wesleyan University, Ames Library, Bloomington, IL
    John Wesley Powell Collection

Iowa State University, Parks Library, Ames, IA
    Charles Parry Papers

Kansas State Historical Society, Topeka, KS
    Fort Dodge Records
    Lewis Keplinger Papers

Library of Congress, Washington, DC
    Collection of Mormon Diaries

McLean County Museum of History, Bloomington, IL
    Edward J. Lewis Diaries
    Daily Pantagraph Reports on Powell Expedition

National Archives, Washington, DC
    Civil War Military Records
    U.S. Geological Survey, Letters Sent and Received

Northern Arizona University, Cline Library, Flagstaff, AZ
    Marty Anderson Collection

Pipe Spring National Monument, Fredonia, AZ
    Oral and Pioneer History Collection

Southern Utah University, Gerald R. Sherratt Library, Cedar City, UT
    William R. Palmer Collection
    Caroline Parry Woolley Collection
    Dilworth Woolley Collection

State Historical Society of Iowa, Des Moines, IA
    Robert Lucas Papers

St. George Public Library, St. George, UT
    Oral and Pioneer History Collection

University of Arizona Library, Tucson, AZ
    Frederick Dellenbaugh Collection

University of Kansas, Spencer Research Library, Lawrence, KS
  Donald Worster Collection

University of Utah, J. Willard Marriott Library, Salt Lake City, UT
  Joseph E. Johnson Papers

University of Wyoming, American Heritage Center, Laramie, WY
  Arthur Powell Davis Papers

Utah State Historical Society, Salt Lake City, UT
  William Culp Darrah Collection

BOOKS

Adams, Eilean. *Hell or High Water: James White's Disputed Passage through Grand Canyon, 1867.* Logan: Utah State University Press, 2001.

Adler, Douglas D., ed. *Honoring Juanita Brooks: A Compilation of 30 Annual Presentations from the Juanita Brooks Lecture Series, Dixie State University.* St. George, UT: Dixie State University, 2014.

Allen, Everett S. *Children of the Light: The Rise and Fall of New Bedford Whaling and the Death of the Arctic Fleet.* Boston: Little, Brown, 1973.

Allen, James B., and Glen M. Leonard. *The Story of the Latter-day Saints.* Salt Lake City, UT: Deseret Book Company, 1976.

Anderson, George. *Kansas West: An Epic of Western Railroading.* San Marino, KS: Golden West Books, 1963.

Anderson, Karl Ricks. *Joseph Smith's Kirtland: Eyewitness Accounts.* Salt Lake City, UT: Deseret Book Company, 1996.

Bagley, Will. *Blood of the Prophets: Brigham Young and the Massacre at Mountain Meadows.* Norman: University of Oklahoma Press, 2002.

Baker, Leighton L. *Jim Baker: The Redheaded Shoshoni.* Tavares, FL: Golden Lifestyles Books, 1993.

Bancroft, Caroline. *Gulch of Gold: A History of Central City, Colorado.* Boulder, CO: Johnson Books, 2003.

Baskin, Robert N. *Reminiscences of Early Utah.* Salt Lake City, UT: Signature Books, 2006. Originally published 1914, unknown publisher.

Bass, William Wallace. *Adventures in the Canyons of the Colorado by Two of Its Earliest Explorers, James White and W. W. Hawkins.* Grand Canyon, AZ: Self-published, 1920.

Bell, John. *The Confederate Seadog: John Taylor Wood in War and Exile.* Jefferson, NC: McFarland Books, 2002.

Berton, Pierre. *Niagara: A History of the Falls.* Albany, NY: SUNY Press, 1992.

Bierman, John. *Dark Safari: The Life Behind the Legend of Henry Morton Stanley.* New York: Alfred Knopf, 1990.

Bigler, David L., and Will Bagley. *Innocent Blood: Essential Narratives of the Mountain Meadows Massacre.* Norman: University of Oklahoma Press, 2008.

———. *The Mormon Rebellion: America's First Civil War, 1857–1858.* Norman: University of Oklahoma Press, 2011.

Bitton, Davis. *George Q. Cannon: A Biography.* Salt Lake City, UT: Deseret Books, 1999.

Booker, Helen Hawley, ed. *The Life of John Pierce Hawley.* Self-published, no date available.

Bradshaw, Hazel. *Under Dixie Sun: A History of Washington County by Those Who Loved Their Forefathers.* Panguitch, UT: Garfield County News, 1950.

Brooks, Juanita. *The Mountain Meadows Massacre.* Norman: University of Oklahoma Press, 1962.

Brown, Daniel James. *The Indifferent Stars Above: The Harrowing Saga of a Donner Party Bride.* New York: William Morrow, 2009.

Brown, Robert L. *Central City and Gilpin County: Then and Now.* Caldwell, ID: Caxton Printers, 1994.

Buresh, Lumir F. *October 25th and the Battle of Mine Creek.* Kansas City, MO: Lowell Press, 1997.

Burton, Gabrielle. *Searching for Tamsen Donner.* Lincoln: University of Nebraska Press, 2009.

Butler, Susan. *East to the Dawn: The Life of Amelia Earhart.* Reading, MA: Da Capo Press, 1999.

Canfield, Gae Whitney. *Sarah Winnemucca of the Northern Plains.* Norman: University of Oklahoma Press, 1988.

Chittenden, Hiram Martin. *History of the American Fur Trade of the Far West.* Palo Alto, CA: Stanford University Press, 1954.

Coffin, Howard. *Nine Months to Gettysburg: Stannard's Vermonters and the Repulse of Pickett's Charge.* Woodstock, VT: Countryman Press, 1997.

Colvin, Verna Rae. *The Garden and How It Grew: Eden 1881–1981.* Eden, AZ: Self-published, n.d.

Compton, Todd M. *Jacob Hamblin: Explorer and Indian Missionary.* Salt Lake City: University of Utah Press, 2013.

Cook, Robert J. *Civil War Senator: William Pitt Fessenden and the Fight to Save the American Republic.* Baton Rouge: Louisiana State University Press, 2011.

Coyner, David H. *The Lost Trappers.* Edited by David J. Weber. Albuquerque: University of New Mexico Press, 1970. Originally published 1847.

Cullom, Shelby M. *50 Years of Public Service.* Chicago: A. C. McClurg, 1911.

Daniel, Larry J. *Shiloh: The Battle That Changed the Civil War.* New York: Simon and Schuster, 1997.

Darrah, William Culp, ed. "The Exploration of the Colorado River in 1869." *Utah Historical Quarterly* 15 Utah State Historical Society, Salt Lake City, 1947.

———. *Powell of the Colorado.* Princeton, NJ: Princeton University Press, 1951.

Dellenbaugh, Frederick S. *A Canyon Voyage: The Narrative of the Second Powell Expedition.* Tucson: University of Arizona Press, 1988. Originally published 1908.

———. *The Romance of the Colorado River.* New York: G. P. Putnam's Sons, 1902.

Dolnick, Edward. *Down the Great Unknown: John Wesley Powell's 1869 Journey of Discovery and Tragedy Through the Grand Canyon.* New York: HarperCollins, 2001.

Donald, David Herbert. *Charles Sumner.* Cambridge, MA: Da Capo Press, 1996.

Dorsett, Lyle W. *The Queen City: A History of Denver.* Boulder, CO: Pruett, 1977.

Dubinsky, Karen. *The Second Greatest Disappointment: Honeymooning and Tourism at Niagara Falls.* New Brunswick, NJ: Rutgers University Press, 1999.

Dupree, A. Hunter. *Asa Gray.* Cambridge, MA: Harvard University Press, 1959.

Elkins, Roger Robin. *George Q. Cannon and the California Mormon Newspaper Wars of 1856–1857.* Spokane, WA: Arthur H. Clark, 2002.

Ellis, Elmer. *Henry Moore Teller: Defender of the West.* Caldwell, ID: Caxton, 1941.

Evans, Beatrice Cannon. *Cannon Family Historical Treasury.* Salt Lake City, UT: George Cannon Family Association, 1967.

Farmer, Jared. *On Zion's Mount: Mormons, Indians, and the American Landscape.* Cambridge, MA: Harvard University Press, 2008.

Ferris, Warren. *Life in the Rocky Mountains: A Diary of Wanderings on the Sources of the Rivers Missouri, Columbia, and Colorado, 1830–1835.* Denver: Old West Publishing, 1893.

Firmage, Edwin Brown, and Richard Collin Mangrum. *Zion in the Courts: A Legal History of the Church of Jesus Christ of Latter-day Saints, 1830–1900.* Urbana: University of Illinois Press, 1988.

Fowler, Don D. *Cleaving an Unknown World: The Powell Expeditions and the Scientific Exploration of the Colorado Plateau.* Salt Lake City: University of Utah Press, 2012.

Gasebier, Dennis. *Camp El Dorado, Arizona Territory: Soldiers, Steamboats, and Miners on the Upper Colorado River.* Tempe, AZ: Arizona Historical Foundation, 1970.

Ghiglieri, Michael P. *First Through Grand Canyon: The Secret Journals and Letters of the 1869 Crew Who Explored the Green and Colorado Rivers.* Second, revised edition. Flagstaff, AZ: Puma Press, 2010.

Goetzmann, William H. *Exploration and Empire: The Explorer and the Scientist in the Winning of the American West.* New York: W. W. Norton, 1966.

Graves, John Card. *Genealogy of the Graves Family in America.* Buffalo, NY: Baker, Jones, and Co., 1896.

Gregory, Herbert E., William Culp Darrah, and Charles Kelly, editors. *The Exploration of the Colorado River and the High Plateaus of Utah by the Second Powell Expedition of 1871–1872.* Salt Lake City: University of Utah Press, 2009.

Groom, Winston. *Shiloh 1862.* Washington, DC: National Geographic, 2012.

Hafen, Lyman. *Far from Cactus Flat: The 20th Century Story of a Harsh Land, a Proud Family, and a Lost Son.* St. George, UT: Arizona Strip Interpretative Association, 2006.

Hafner, Arabell Lee. *100 Years on the Muddy.* Springdale, UT: Art City Publishing, 1967.

Hall, Marvin S., C. Keith Rooker, and Larry T. Wimmer. *The Kirtland Economy Revisited: A Market Critique of Sectarian Economics.* Provo, UT: Brigham Young University Press, 1977.

Hammond, John J. *Crisis in Mormon Kirtland: A Temple and an Illegal Bank.* Lexington, KY: John J. Hammond, 2013.

Hicken, Victor. *Illinois in the Civil War.* Urbana: University of Illinois Press, 1991.

Ives, Joseph C. *Report Upon the Colorado River of the West, Explored in 1857 and 1858 by Lieutenant Joseph C. Ives.* Washington, DC: Government Printing Office, 1861.

Jeal, Tim. *Stanley: The Impossible Life of Africa's Greatest Explorer.* New Haven, CT: Yale University Press, 2007.

Johnson, Rufus David. *Trail to Sundown, Cassadaga to Caca Grande, 1817–1882: The Story of a Pioneer.* Joseph Ellis Johnson Family Committee, no location available, 1961.

Kennedy, W. J. D., ed. *On the Plains with Custer and Hancock: The Journal of Isaac Coates, Army Surgeon.* Boulder, CO: Johnson Books, 1997.

Kenney, Scott G., ed. *Wilford Woodruff's Journal, 1833–1898.* 9 Vols. Midvale, UT: Signature Books, 1983–85.

Krakauer, Jon. *Under the Banner of Heaven: A Story of Violent Faith.* New York: Doubleday, 2003.

Krug, Mark M. *Lyman Trumbull: Conservative Radical.* New York: A. S. Barnes, 1965.

Larsen, Wesley P., and Lois Meyers. *Tales from Toquerville and Other Southern Utah Towns.* Self-published, 1986.

Larson, Andrew Karl. *Erastus Snow: The Life of a Missionary and Pioneer for the Early Mormon Church.* Salt Lake City: University of Utah Press, 1971.

———. *I Was Called to Dixie—The Virgin River Basin: Unique Experiences in Mormon Pioneering.* St. George, UT: Dixie College Foundation, 1983.

———. *The Red Hills of November: A Pioneer Biography of Utah's Cotton Town.* Salt Lake City, UT: Deseret News Press, 1957.

Lavender, David. *Colorado River Country.* Albuquerque: University of New Mexico Press, 1982.

———. *River Runners of the Grand Canyon.* Grand Canyon, AZ: Grand Canyon Natural History Association, 1985.

Lingenfelter, Richard E. *First Through the Grand Canyon.* Los Angeles: Glen Dawson, 1958.

Lovell, Mary S. *The Sound of Wings: The Life of Amelia Earhart.* New York: St. Martin's Press, 1989.

MacKinnon, William P. *At Sword's Point, Part 1: A Documentary History of the Utah War to 1858.* Norman: University of Oklahoma Press, 2008.

Malach, Roman. *Adventurer John Moss: Gold Discovery in Mohave County.* Kingman, AZ: Mohave County Board of Supervisors, 1977.

Martineau, LaVan. *Southern Paiutes: Legends, Lore, Language, and Lineage.* Las Vegas: KC Publications, 1992.

Mason, Patrick Q. *The Mormon Menace: Violence and Anti-Mormonism in the Postbellum South.* Oxford, UK: Oxford University Press, 2011.

Maxwell, John Gary. *Gettysburg to Great Salt Lake: George R. Maxwell, Civil War Hero and Federal Marshal among the Mormons.* Norman: University of Oklahoma Press, 2010.

———. *Robert Newton Baskin and the Making of Modern Utah.* Norman: University of Oklahoma Press, 2013.

McBee, Mary Richardson. *A Deep Map of Western Grand Canyon and Upper Lake Mead Country.* Tama, IA: Old Lands, 2014.

McDonough, James Lee. *Shiloh: In Hell Before Night.* Knoxville: University of Tennessee Press, 1977.

McGreevy, Patrick V. *Imagining Niagara: The Meaning and Making of Niagara Falls.* Amherst: University of Massachusetts Press, 1994.

McKay, Ernest. *Henry Wilson, Practical Radical: A Portrait of a Politician.* Port Washington, NY: Kennikat Press, 1971.

Meadows, Paul. *John Wesley Powell: Frontiersman of Science.* Lincoln: University of Nebraska Studies, 1952.

Mortensen, A. R. *Utah's Dixie: The Cotton Mission.* Salt Lake City: Utah State Historical Society, 1961.

Mulderink, Earl F. III. *New Bedford's Civil War.* New York: Fordham University Press, 2012.

Mumey, Nolie. *The Life of Jim Baker, 1818–1898, Trapper, Scout, Guide, and Indian Fighter.* Denver: World Press, 1931.

Neilson, James W. *Shelby M. Cullom: Prairie State Republican.* Urbana: University of Illinois Press, 1962.

Nixon, James William. *The Autobiography of James William Nixon.* Library of Congress Manuscript, Collection of Mormon Diaries, Washington, DC, 1937.

Olivia, Leo E. *Fort Dodge: Sentry of the Western Plains.* Topeka: Kansas State Historical Society, 1998.

Paher, Stanley, ed. *Callville: Head of Navigation.* Las Vegas: Nevada Publications, 1983.

Parish, John C. *Robert Lucas.* Iowa City: State Historical Society of Iowa, 1907.

Parkin, Max H. *Conflict at Kirtland: A Study in the Nature and Causes of External and Internal Conflict of the Mormons in Ohio Between 1830 and 1838.* Salt Lake City, UT: Self-published, 1966.

Perkins, Robert L. *The First Hundred Years: An Informal History of Denver and the Rocky Mountain News.* Denver: Denver Publishing, 1959.

Peterson, John Alton. *Utah's Black Hawk War.* Salt Lake City: University of Utah Press, 1998.

Pierson, Francis J. *Summit of Destiny: Taming the Pike's Peaks Country, 1858–1918.* Denver: Charlotte Square Press, 2008.

Pike, Zebulon. *The Journals of Zebulon Montgomery Pike.* Edited by Donald Jackson. Norman: University of Oklahoma Press, 1966.

Powell, John Wesley. *The Arid Lands.* Edited by Wallace Stegner. Lincoln: University of Nebraska Press, 2004. Originally published 1878, Government Printing Office, Washington, DC, 1878.

———. *The Cañons of the Colorado.* Golden, CO: Outbooks, 1981.

———. *The Exploration of the Colorado River and Its Canyons.* New York: Viking Penguin, 1987. Originally published as *Canyons of the Colorado.* Meadville, PA: Flood and Vincent, 1895.

Putnam, Mary Ester S. *Descendants of Pine Valley Pioneers.* St. George, UT: Self-published, 1980.

Quinn, Michael. *The Mormon Hierarchy: Extensions of Power.* Salt Lake City, UT: Signature Books, 1997.

Reeve, W. Paul. *Making Space on the Western Frontier: Mormons, Miners, and Southern Paiutes.* Urbana: University of Illinois Press, 2006.

Roberts, B. H. *A Comprehensive History of the Church of Jesus Christ of Latter-day Saints.* Provo, UT: Brigham Young University Press, 1965.

Roske, Ralph J. *His Own Counsel: The Life and Times of Lyman Trumbull.* Reno: University of Nevada Press, 1979.

Sage, Leland. *A History of Iowa.* Ames: Iowa State University Press, 1974.

Sage, Rufus B. *Scenes in the Rocky Mountains.* Philadelphia: Carey and Hart, 1846.

Schafer, Leo. *Law and Disorder in Pioche: Crime and Punishment in Lincoln County During the 1800s.* Pioche, NV: Book Connection, 2009.

Scott, John. *Story of the 32nd Iowa Infantry Regiment.* Nevada, IA: Self-published, 1896.

Shelley, Mary. *Lodore.* Peterborough, Ont.: Broadview Literary Texts, 1997. Originally published 1835.

Shingleton, Royce Gordon. *John Taylor Wood: Sea Ghost of the Confederacy.* Athens: University of Georgia Press, 1979.

Simmons, Virginia McConnell. *Drifting West: The Calamities of James White and Charles Baker.* Boulder: University Press of Colorado, 2007.

Slack, Charles. *Hetty: The Genius and Madness of America's First Female Tycoon.* New York: Ecco, 2004.

Smith, Joseph Jr. *History of the Church of Jesus Christ of Latter-day Saints.* Salt Lake City, UT: Deseret Books, 1930.

Smith, Timothy B. *Rethinking Shiloh: Myth and Memory.* Knoxville: University of Tennessee Press, 2013.

———. *Shiloh: Conquer or Perish.* Lawrence: University Press of Kansas, 2014.

———. *The Untold Story of Shiloh: The Battle and the Battlefield.* Knoxville: University of Tennessee Press, 2006.

Snow, Bess, and Elizabeth S. Beckstrom. *O' Ye Mountains High: The Story of Pine Valley.* St. George, UT: Heritage Press, 1980.

Southey, Robert. *Poems of Robert Southey.* London: Oxford University Press, 1909.

Stanley, F. *E. V. Sumner: Major-General, United States Army, 1797–1863.* Borger, TX: Jim Hess Printers, 1969.

Stanton, Robert Brewster. *Colorado River Controversies.* New York: Dodd, Mead & Company, 1932. Reprint, Boulder City, NV: Westwater Books, 1982.

Stegner, Wallace. *Beyond the Hundredth Meridian: John Wesley Powell and the Second Opening of the West.* Boston: Houghton Mifflin Company, 1954.

Stewart, David O. *Impeached: The Trial of President Andrew Johnson and the Fight for Lincoln's Legacy.* New York: Simon and Schuster, 2009.

Stewart, George R. *Ordeal by Hunger: The Story of the Donner Party.* Boston: Houghton Mifflin, 1960.

———. *Pickett's Charge: A Microhistory of the Final Attack at Gettysburg, July 3, 1863.* Boston: Houghton Mifflin, 1959.

Strate, David K. *Sentinel to the Cimarron: The Frontier Experience of Fort Dodge, Kansas.* Dodge City, KS: Cultural Heritage and Arts Center, 1970.

Sykes, Godfrey. *A Westerly Trend.* Tucson: Arizona Pioneers Historical Society, 1944.

Taylor, Anne-Marie. *Young Charles Sumner and the Legacy of the Enlightenment, 1811–1851.* Amherst: University of Massachusetts Press, 2001.

Thomas, Marcia L. *John Wesley Powell: An Annotated Bibliography.* Westport, CT: Praeger, 2004.

Trefousse, H. L. *Benjamin Franklin Wade: Radical Republican from Ohio.* New York: Twayne, 1963.

Walczynski, Mark. *Massacre 1769: The Search for the Origin of the Legend of Starved Rock.* St. Louis, MO: Center for French Colonial Studies, 2013.

———. *Starved Rock State Park: The First 100 Years.* Denver: Outskirts Press, 2011.

Walker, Charles Lowell. *The Diary of Charles Lowell Walker,* Volume 1. Edited by Karl Larson and Katherine Miles Larson. Logan: Utah State University Press, 1980.

Walker, Robert W., Richard E. Turley Jr., and Glen M. Leonard. *Massacre at Mountain Meadows.* New York: Oxford University Press, 2008.

Wallace, Isabel. *Life and Letters of General W. H. L. Wallace.* Carbondale: Southern Illinois University Press, 2000.

Ward, Eric, ed. *Army Life in Virginia: The Civil War Letters of George G. Benedict.* Mechanicsburg, PA: Stackpole Books, 2002.

Watson, Elmo Scott. *The Professor Goes West: Illinois Wesleyan University Reports of Major John Wesley Powell's Explorations, 1867–1874.* Bloomington: Illinois Wesleyan University Press, 1954.

Watts, Steven. *The Magic Kingdom: Walt Disney and the American Way of Life.* Boston: Houghton Mifflin, 1997.

Weber, William A. *King of Colorado Botany: Charles Christopher Parry, 1823–1890.* Niwot: University Press of Colorado, 1997.

Wert, Jeffry D. *Gettysburg: Day Three.* New York: Simon and Schuster, 2001.

West, Elliot. *Contested Plains: Indians, Goldseekers, and the Rush to Colorado.* Lawrence: University Press of Kansas, 1998.

Winters, Kathleen C. *Amelia Earhart: The Turbulent Life of an American Icon.* New York: Palgrave Macmillan, 2010.

Woody, Clara T., and Milton Schwartz. *Globe, Arizona: Early Times in a Little World of Copper and Cattle.* Tucson: Arizona Historical Society, 1997.

Wordsworth, William. *The Poems,* Vol. 1. London: Penguin Books, 1977. Originally published 1793.

Worster, Donald. *A River Running West: The Life of John Wesley Powell.* New York: Oxford University Press, 2001.

Yorgason, Blaine M., Richard A. Schmutz, and Douglas D. Adler. *All That Was Promised: The St. George Temple and the Unfolding of the Restoration.* Salt Lake City, UT: Deseret Books, 2013.

Zanjani, Sally. *Sarah Winnemucca.* Lincoln: University of Nebraska Press, 2004.

ARTICLES

Barrows, Eliza J. "Howland Brothers Join the John Wesley Powell Expedition to Explore the Colorado River that Flows Through the Grand Canyon—April 1869." *Howland Quarterly,* July 1986.

Barry, Louise, "The Ranch at Cimarron Crossing." *Kansas Historical Quarterly* 39 (Autumn 1973): 345–66.

Brooks, Juanita. "Old Toab." *The Utah Magazine* (April 1946): 20–47.

Canby, William M., and J. N. Rose. "George Vasey: A Biographical Sketch." *Botanical Gazette* (1893): 170–78.

Cullom, Shelby M. "Enforcement of Laws in Utah." Speech delivered in the U.S. House of Representatives, February 17, 1870. Washington, DC: F. & J. Rives & Geo A. Bailey, 1870.

Dawson, Thomas F. "The Grand Canyon: An Article Giving the Credit of First Traversing the Grand Canyon of the Colorado to James White, A Colorado Gold Prospector, who it is Claimed, Made the Voyage Two Years Previous to the Expedition Under the Direction of Maj. J. W. Powell in 1869." Washington, DC: Government Printing Office, 1917.

Ivins, Anthony W. "Traveling over Forgotten Trails: A Mystery of the Grand Canyon Solved." *Improvement Era* 27, no. 11 (September 1924): 1017–25.

Knipmeyer, James. "The 1864 Explorations of Octavius Dacatur Gass and Co." *The Ol' Pioneer* (Fall 2007).

Larsen, Wesley P. "The Letter: Or Were the Powell Men Really Killed by Indians?" *Canyon Legacy* (Spring 1993): 12–18.

Lyons, Paul C., and Elsie Darrah Morey. "A Tribute to an American Paleobotanist: William Culp Darrah (1909–1989)." *Comptes Rendus* 2 (1993).

McKenzie, Daniel. "Discoveries in the Pacific." Howland Quarterly (June 2015).

Penn, Chris. "Frontiersman Andy Hall Served Major Powell and Wells Fargo." *Wild West* (August 2009).

Riggs, John L. "William H. Hardy of the Upper Colorado." *Journal of Arizona History* 6, no. 4 (Winter 1965): 177–87.

Stegner, Wallace. "Jack Sumner and John Wesley Powell." *Colorado Magazine* 26 (1949).

Welch, Vince. "Frank's Early Exit and Long Goodbye." *Boatman's Quarterly Review* 17-3 (Fall 2004): 14–17.

UNPUBLISHED MANUSCRIPTS

Bleak, James G. Annals of the Southern Utah Mission. Typescript in Special Collections, Dixie State University, St. George, UT.

Hawley, John Pierce. Autobiography of John Pierce Hawley. Community of Christ Archives, 1885, Independence, MO.

Lago, Nils Henderson. "The Utah Expedition, 1857–1858." Master's thesis, University of Oklahoma, Norman, 1939.

Morris, Lindsey Gardner. "John Wesley Powell: Scientist and Educator." Master's thesis, Illinois State University, Normal, 1947.

Ott, James A. A Sketch of the Life of Seth Johnson. Church of Jesus Christ of Latter-day Saints Archives, Salt Lake City, UT.

Pulsipher, John. Diary of John Pulsipher. Special Collections, Harold B. Lee Library, Brigham Young University, Provo, UT.

Quartaroli, Richard. "Boys Left Us." Paper presented at Arizona History Convention, Pinetop, AZ, 2001.

Steinbacher-Kemp, William F. "The Illinois Natural History Society: 1858–1871." Master's thesis for Illinois State University, Normal, 2000.

Woolley, Edwin G. *Extracts from the Biography of Edwin G. Woolley*. Special Collections, St. George Public Library, St. George, UT.

ORAL HISTORIES

Esplin, Spencer (Spence). "Ranching on the Arizona Strip." Interviewed by unnamed interviewer, January 22, 1997. Dixie Pioneers and Story Tellers Oral History Collection. Dixie State University, St. George, UT, #97-006A.

Fotheringham, Marilyn. Public talk at the Institute of Continued Learning at Dixie College, St. George, Washington County, Utah. Found in Dixie Pioneers and Story Tellers Oral History Collection, Special Collections, Dixie State University, St. George, UT, 98-003.

Guererro, James (Jimmy). Interviewed by Wallace Mathis. Grand Canyon–Parashant National Monument Oral History Collection. Special Collections, Dixie State University, St. George, UT, #13-008 AB.

Huntsman, Orson Welcome. "Diary of Orson Welcome Huntsman." Collection of Mormon Diaries [1935–38], Library of Congress, Washington, DC, reel 4, item 5, vol. 1, 1–2.

Mathis, Gordon Wallace. Interviewed by Delmar D. Gott, May 1, 1975. Delmar D.
Gott Oral History Collection, Dixie State University, St. George, UT, #75-007.
Seegmiller, George, and Maudie Miles. Interviewed by Delmar D. Gott, May 6, 1975.
Delmar D. Gott Oral History Collection. Dixie State University, St. George, UT.
#75-008.
Stratton, Oliver L. (Ivy), and Jennie Higgins Stratton. Interviewed by Delmar D.
Gott, January 14, 1975. Delmar D. Gott Oral History Collection. Dixie State
University, St. George, UT. #75-001.

Acknowledgments

This book is the result of twenty years of ongoing research, and numerous people have helped me out along the way. A special thanks goes to Judy LeFevre for her support.

Most crucial are the librarians and archivists who guard our historical treasures and guide people through them. Richard Quartaroli at Cline Library Special Collections at Northern Arizona University knows Powell and river history exceptionally well and is always ready to share his insights; he reviewed this manuscript and caught some mistakes and made some valuable suggestions. Roy Webb at Marriott Library Special Collections at the University of Utah is another river history expert who reviewed this manuscript with sharp eyes. Of course, any remaining mistakes are my own responsibility. Other skilled archivists are Kim Besom, Mike Quinn, and Colleen Hyde at the Museum Collection and Betty Upchurch at the park library at Grand Canyon National Park; Marcia Thomas and Anke Voss-Hubbard at the Ames Library at Illinois Wesleyan University; Bill Frank, Peter Blodgett, and Robert Ritchie at the Huntington Library; Barbara Dey, Debra Neiswonger, and Jean Garralda at the Colorado State Historical Society; Brent Wagner and Janice Prater at the Denver Public Library; Preston Hawks and Patricia Hamilton at the McLean County Museum of History; E. Sheryl Schnirring at the Illinois State Historical Library; Becky S. Jordan at Iowa State University Parks Library; Jane Kelsey at the Kansas State Historical Society; and the reference librarians at the Flagstaff Public Library.

This book is also much richer for all the contributions from the Colorado River history and guides community, including Earle Spamer, Brad Dimock, Michael Ghiglieri, Karen Greig, Drifter Smith, Art Christiansen, Tom Myers, Larry Stevens, Tom Martin, Hazel Clark, Stewart Aitchison, Linda Jalbert, Wayne and Helen Ranney, Mike Anderson, Scott Thybony, Mary Williams, Keith and Nancy Green, John Alley, Al Holland, Donald Worster, Jim Babbitt, Jerry Snow, Bill Bishop, Patrick Conley, Dave Wegner, Kim Crumbo,

John O'Brien, Vince Welch, Dan and Diane Cassidy, Tom Bean, Susan Lamb, Don Fowler, Shane Murphy, Dove Menkes, Greg Woodall, Roger Clark, Dave Mortenson, James Aton, James Knipmeyer, Gus Scott, Richard and Sherry Mangum, and Terra Waters, and all the members of Clio, a river history group.

The families of the crewmembers have contributed much important new material and context to the history of the Powell expedition. First of all is Ray Sumner, whose own enthusiastic quest for his family story was a source of inspiration to me, as well as a source of new information. From the Howland family: Gail Adams, Kenneth H. Barrows, Kenneth Graves, Judith Elfring, Judith L. Howland, and Kenneth Howland Molloy. From the Hawkins family: Glenna Hawkins, Emert Hawkins, Scott Carrall, John Cochran, Jeannie Hawkins Wood, and Nolan Reed. From the Dunn family: Scott G. Wolff, Jeanne Couch, David P. Dunn, Doug Lynn, and Wilander Dunn Ruby. From the Hall family: John Verbout and Dorothy Bremer-Hall. From Lyle Durley of the 1868 Colorado trip: Walter Durley Boyle.

Several talented researchers unearthed important materials and made important connections, especially Jean Craig, Kathy Marine, Suz Pubal, and Alice Kingsbury.

At Pipe Springs National Monument, National Park Service ranger Autumn Gillard verified the cover photo as being Paiute chief Chuarumpeak, also known as Tau-gu.

For help in securing photographs, a double thanks goes to Judy LeFevre, Ray Sumner, Kenneth Barrows, Mike Quinn, Michael Ghiglieri, and Brad Limoge.

Many historians, authors, archivists, and historical societies have taken the trouble to pursue my questions and come up with information, too many to name them all: Stacy D. Allen, Karl Anderson, Sharon Avery, William Bach, Ranson Baker, Joan Barney, Barbara Bernauer, John Bradbury, Christine Bradley, Ralph Bradley Jr., Carol Brooks, Dennis Buck, Christine Chandler, Robert J. Chandler, Sharon Clausen, Howard Coffin, Verna Rae Colvin, Bill Creech, David E. Dunn, Bob Ervin, Jan Gerber, Ardian Gill, Charles H. Glatfelter, Alan Graham, J. Peter Gratiot, Hazel Harrington, Glen Harris, Trudy Hawley, John Heiser, Jack Henkels, Shayla Hilt, Bob Holcombe, Robert F. Huber, C. Mitch Ison, Arlene Jenkins, Leigh Ann Jero, Neil Jordan, Joe Kelley, Bob Knecht, Deanna LaBonge, Lisa Lloyd, Kandy Maharas, Bruce Michelson, Olga Montgomery, Eric Moody, Mary Francis Morrow, Frank Nickell, Allen Nossaman, Fred Pendleton, Chris Penn, Christine Pommer, James J. Prochaska, Chris Reid, Thomas Reider, Doris Reinke, Dolores Riggs, Bob Rowe, Cecil

Sanderson, Peg Schall, Janet Seegmiller, Jane Seilaff, Ruby Shirk, Tim Smith, Mary Skoglund, Charles M. Spearman, Mark Stalker, Bill Steinbacher-Kemp, Ginger Strand, Jason D. Stratman, Robert Tatem, Dorothy Thayer, Dorothy Van Cleef, Joan and Gerald Vogel, Mark Walczynski, Charles B. Wallace, David H. Wallace, Amy L. Waters, William Weber, Virginia Whitney, Aaron Wilson, R. Michael Wilson, Terrence Winschel, and Martha E. Wright.

Zack Zdinak, whose talents are usually devoted to wildlife illustrations, drew the map for this book, and Alison Hope was the highly capable copy-editor. A special thanks goes to Justin Race and the whole crew at the University of Nevada Press.

About the Author

DON LAGO, one of the most respected historians of the Grand Canyon, is the author of *Grand Canyon: A History of a Natural Wonder and National Park* (University of Nevada Press, 2015) and a book of new research into canyon history, *Canyon of Dreams: Stories from Grand Canyon History* (University of Utah Press, 2014). He has spent thirty years exploring the Grand Canyon, kayaking it six times and conducting National Park Service research into rafting on the Colorado River. He has spent more than twenty years researching formerly unknown aspects of the Powell expedition. He is also well known for his literary nature and astronomy writing, which has won awards and been collected into two books, including *Where the Sky Touched the Earth* (University of Nevada Press, 2017). He is also the author of *On the Viking Trail: Travels in Scandinavian America* (University of Iowa Press, 2004). He lives in a cabin in the pine forests in Flagstaff, Arizona.

Index

Page numbers in *italics* refer to illustrations

Dunn, William H.: background of, xvi, 127–28, 129; in Civil War, 126–36; Civil War letter of, 132, *133*; and Comanches, 126, 127, 134, 136; in Disney movie, 364, 366; family of, xi; in father's will, *135*, 136; Hawkins on, 126, 127; and Hot Sulphur Springs, 138–39; in inscription, 281–82; leaves expedition, xi, 81, 159, 178; letter of, from expedition, 138–40; and plaque at Separation Canyon, 274, *275*; and Powell, 126, 127, 134; and Powell Memorial, xii, 69, *70*, 81, 274; and Sumner, 70, 126, 127, 128, 178; in Sumner letter, 198. *See also* Howlands and Dunn fate

Earhart, Amelia, 121–25
Eaton, A. E., 219, 221, 228
Edmunds, George, 225–28
El Dorado Canyon (NV), 22, 26, 44
Emma Dean (boat), 265, 266
Engelmann, George, 48, 54, 55
Esplin, Spencer, 284
Exploration of the Colorado River and its Canyons (Powell), 146, 252–53

Farrell, Ned, 75, 139
Fell, Jesse, 71, 222
Ferris, Warren, 16–17
Fessenden, William Pitt, 229–30
Fort Bridger, xvi, 116, 197
Fort Dodge, 27–35, 38, 43, 50–51, 66
Fort Lyon (CO), 32, 51, 54
Fort Mohave: Bradley and Hawkins stop at, 342; and Dunn, 138; and Hall letter, 159; and Mellon, 267; and Powell order, 259; and Wheeler, 268–69
Fort Pearce, 296, 317, 334, 348, 349
Fort Sumner, 188
Frémont, John C., xv, 6, 38, 49, 192, 352
Fryer, Richard, 293–97
fur trappers, 6, 14–17, 30, 36–39. *See also* Ashley, William; Baker, Jim; Smith, Jedediah

Gardner, Robert, 347
Garfield, James, 63, 208, 222, 224
Garman, Samuel, 75
Gass, Octavius, 258
Gettysburg (battle), 82–88

Ghiglieri, Michael, xiv, xvii, 127
Gibbons, Andrew S., 258–59, 278
Goldwater family, 265–66
Goodman, Frank, xiv, xvi, xvii, 198
Grand Canyon, *4*, 236, *274*; and Disney, 363–69; and Dunn letter, 132; geology of, 218–19; in IMAX movie, 235–36, 238; and lover's leap stories, 242; navigability of, 13, 261; and Powell, ix, 13, 209, 223, 252,53, 353; Powell emerges from, 141, 214, 257, 261; rapids in, xvii, 5, 235, 237; and Santa Fe Railway, 363–64; and White controversy, xii, 19–66. *See also* Colorado River; Powell expedition
Grand Canyon National Park: and Berthoud letter, 63; and Hall letter, 159, 160; and Powell Memorial, xii, 57–58, 69, *70*, 274
Grandin, E. B., 22, 25, 26, 42
Grand River, 7, 9, 10, 141, 263
Grand Wash Cliffs, 21, 25, 257
Grant, Ulysses S.: and *Alabama* case, 98; and Cyrus Hawley, 304, 313; and Johnson impeachment, 218, 219–21, 228; and Latter-day Saints, 300, 304–5; and Powell funds, 217–30; as presidential candidate, 224, 229; at Shiloh, 203, 204, 207, 208, 210–11; and C. C. Wilson, 308, 313
Graves, Elizabeth, 112–19
Graves, Elvira, 72–73, 112
Graves, Franklin Ward, 112–19
Graves, Linus, 71–73, 213
Graves, Thomas, 73
Graves, Walter, 73, 331
Gray, Asa, 46, 47
Green River, *139*; and Ashley, 7; and Jim Baker, 39; and Colorado River, 7; in Coyner book, 15; and Dunn letter, 138; geography of, 141; and Hall, 164; and Hawkins, 148, 342, 343; map of, xviii; navigability of, 8; and *No Name*, 94; and Powell, ix, xv, 9, 14, 77, 141; and Jack Sumner, 190–91, 195; and Union Pacific Railroad, 9, 141
Guererro, Jimmy, 283, 284, 286

Haight, Isaac C.: in Graham County, AZ, 351, 359; and Hawkins, 348–50, 352–53, 358; in Mexico, 351; at Mt. Trumbull, 347–48; and Powell, 334